Anonymous

Souvenir of Loretto Centenary

1899

Anonymous

Souvenir of Loretto Centenary
1899

ISBN/EAN: 9783744653091

Printed in Europe, USA, Canada, Australia, Japan

Cover: Foto ©ninafisch / pixelio.de

More available books at **www.hansebooks.com**

1799
1899

SOUVENIR OF LORETTO CENTENARY

OCTOBER
10
1899

CRESSON, PA.:
SWOPE BROS., PRINTERS.

PREFACE.

THE following work is simply what its title indicates,—a Souvenir of the Centenary of this parish, the oldest in Western Pennsylvania. It makes no pretence to originality, but is merely a compilation of papers, facts, names and dates, which show forth the progress made during the century just closed, and furnish valuable and interesting data for the future historian of the church in this diocese. Even as a compilation it is far from perfect, for its matter was collected and arranged during the hours that could be spared from a busy pastoral life; and many items, well worthy of being recorded, have been passed without notice, and others, herein noted, have been inadequately treated. Such as it is, however, it is offered to the public in the hope that whatever measure of success it may meet with may stimulate other pastors to diligently gather, and to preserve in permanent and easily accessible form, the records of their respective parishes, and to collect the fragments of parochial history, lest they be forever lost. Such work will be appreciated in future years.

The compiler desires to express here his lasting gratitude to the contributors of various papers included in this Souvenir; to Mr. John J. McCormick, of Wilmore, and to the Pittsburg Catholic, for valuable historical and biographical notes; and to Rev. Regis Canevin, Rector of St. Paul's Cathedral, Pittsburg, and Rev. Brother Angelus, Superior of the

Franciscan Brothers. Loretto, for timely and appreciated assistance on the occasion of the celebration of our Centenary.

FERDINAND KITTELL.

St. Michael's Church, Loretto, Pa.
   December 1, 1899.

NOTE.—On page 76 it is stated that "the whole population of the parish......numbers 1234 souls." A more careful revision of the returns of the Census taken on August 15th, brings the total number up to 1326.

The "Memoranda of Rev. M. W. Gibson," page 79, were written in his old age from memory, which failed him when he stated that he was appointed pastor of Worcester, Mass., in 1843. It was not until the spring of the following year that he left Loretto, for his baptisms and marriages are recorded in his own handwriting all through the year 1843, down to February 21, 1844.

CONTENTS.

PART FIRST.

SKETCH OF THE LIFE OF FATHER GALLITZIN . 1
LOCAL HISTORICAL NOTES
  First Settlement on the Alleghenies . . . 27
  Inscription on Tombstone of Capt. Michael McGuire 31
  Captain Richard McGuire 31
  Other Pioneers 32
  Father Gallitzin 33
  Father Gallitzin at Wilmore . . . 38
  The Wilmore Family 39
  Extracts from Father Gallitzin's Letters . 40
  His Chief Persecutor Retracts . . 43
  He is a Total Abstainer 45
  He Endeavors to have Loretto made an Episcopal See 48
  His Opinion of Mendicant Friars, and His Defence
    of Father McGirr 49
  He is Empowered by Act of Assembly to Resume
    His Family Surname 53
  Captain McGuire's Company 53
  Father Gallitzin's Life in Peril . . 54
  His Death and Funeral . . . 57
  His Monument . . . 59
  Mission at Loretto, 1851 60
  Visit of Monsignor Bedini, the Papal Nunzio . 62
  Dedication of the Brick Church . . . 64
  Collapse of Church Floor 66
  Pastors and Assistants since 1840 . . . 66
  Index of Parish Records, 1800–1896 . . . 69
  The Borough of Loretto 71
  Act Incorporating the Borough . . . 72
  Supplement to the above 75
  Loretto Notes 76
  Memoranda of Rev. M. W. Gibson . . 79
  Dates in Local History 88

PART SECOND.

MATRIMONIAL AND BAPTISMAL RECORDS OF FATHER GALLITZIN	93
REGISTER OF DEATHS, 1793–1899	165
OLD INSCRIPTIONS ON HEADSTONES IN LORETTO CEMETERY	201
TWO INTERESTING DOCUMENTS, 1794–1795	206
PASCHAL COMMUNIONS, 1810	207
PASCHAL CONFESSIONS, 1811	210
CONFIRMATION, 1811	216
NOTES ON FATHER GALLITZIN	219
COPY OF AN OLD DEED, 1806	231
CURIOUS NOTICES	232
FATHER GALLITZIN'S APPEAL FOR ASSISTANCE, 1827	232
HIS ACCOUNT WITH JOSEPH ITEL, POSTMASTER	234
THE MURDER OF BETSY HOLDER	235
CHURCH REGISTER FROM 1841	236
OFFICIATING PRIESTS, 1799–1899	237
MARRIAGES AND BAPTISMS, 1799–1899	241
MINUTES OF CHURCH MANAGERS, 1844–47	242
LIST OF SUBSCRIBERS TO THE MONUMENT, 1847	243
BUILDING COMMITTEE OF BRICK CHURCH, 1847	245
SUBSCRIPTION TO BRICK CHURCH, 1847	246
SUBSCRIPTION FOR COMPLETION OF CHURCH, 1853	249
EXPENSES OF BRICK CHURCH, 1849–54	250
ITEMS FROM CHURCH ACCOUNT BOOKS, 1848–69	252
EXPENSES OF CHURCH WELL	254
COLLECTION FOR CHURCH WELL	255
MEMORANDUM OF R. SCANLAN, CONTRACTOR	255
CARROLLTOWN AND VICINITY	257
THE FRANCISCAN BROTHERS IN LORETTO	259
THE SISTERS OF MERCY IN LORETTO	266
REMINISCENCES OF FATHER LEMKE	270

PART THIRD.

Census of St. Michael's Parish, Loretto, August 15, 1899. Names of the Parishioners	291
The Centenary, October 10, 1899	309
Erection of the Statue	316
Arrival of Monsignor Martinelli	317
The Ceremonies of the Day	320
First Holy Communion and Confirmation	321
Pontifical High Mass. Sermon by Very Rev. Father Bush, V. G.	323
The Unveiling of the Statue	329
Letters of Regret	330
Address of Rev. Ferdinand Kittell	335
Letter of Mr. and Mrs. C. M. Schwab Donating New Church	337
Address of Mr. C. M. Schwab	337
Address of Archbishop Ireland	339
Address of Governor Stone	352
The Papal Benediction	354
Notes on the Centenary	355
Biographical Sketches	
Rev. M. W. Gibson	78
Rev. Andrew P. Gibbs	81
Rev. H. P. Gallagher	82
Rev. William Pollard	83
Rev. Michael J. Mitchell	85
Rev. Pollard McC. Morgan	86
Rev. H. Seymour Bowen	87
Most Rev. Mgr. Martinelli, Apostolic Delegate	358
Rt. Rev. R. Phelan, D. D.	359
Rt. Rev. A. A. Curtis, D. D.	363
Charles M. Schwab	363
Very Rev. E. A. Bush, V. G.	368
Rev. Martin Ryan	369
Rev. Ferdinand Kittell	369
Rev. William Kittell	371
Rev. R. C. Christy	372

Rev. Henry McHugh	374
Rev. Thomas McEnrue	375
Rev. Hildebert P. Connery	376
Rev. C. O. Rosensteel	377
Rev. Thomas W. Rosensteel	379
Rev. John C. McAteer	380
Rev. Francis C. Noel	381
Rev. George W. Kaylor	382
Rev. Francis Hertzog	383
Brother Lawrence O'Donnell, O. S. F.	384
Adam Rudolph	385
Joseph Null	386
Mrs. Cooper,—Mrs. McConnell	388
Mrs. Susan Gallagher	389
Thomas Wills	390
Arthur Comerford	390
Mrs. Veronica Freidhoff	391
Mrs. John Elder	396
Philip Dever	392
Augustine Hott	392
FATHER GALLITZIN'S WILL	393
THE STORM FAMILY RECORD	395
THE NEW CHURCH	397
MEMBERSHIP OF BRANCH III. C. M. B. A.	400
MEMBERSHIP OF LORETTO COUNCIL, Y. M. I.	403
CHURCH OFFICERS	405

ILLUSTRATIONS.

The Statue Unveiled	1
Rev. D. A. Gallitzin	16
Julia Morgan Harding	26
Rev. P. H. Lemke	32
Rev. M. W. Gibson	48
The Tomb of Father Gallitzin	59
Rev. H. P. Gallagher	64
St. Michael's Church, 1899	65
Rev. Jos. A. Gallagher	80
William A. McGuire	81
Rev. William Pollard	96
Rev. T. S. Reynolds	112
Rev. M. J. Mitchell	128
Very Rev. E. A. Bush, V. G.	144
Rev. M. Ryan	160
Rev. Ferdinand Kittell	176
Father Gallitzin's NOTICE	192
St. Michael's Pastoral Residence	208
Father Gallitzin's APPEAL	220
Subscriptions to Appeal	221
Recommendation of Charles Carroll of Carrollton	223
The Dever Homestead	224
Summer Residence of C. M. Schwab	224
Father Gallitzin's Account with Joseph Itel	228
After Mass	240
The Oldest House in Loretto	240
The Loretto Jail	256
St. Francis' College	259
The Children's Home. Front View	266
The Children's Home. Side View	269
The Village of Munster	272
Rear View of Church Buildings	272
First Meeting of Father Lemke and Father Gallitzin	278
The Parrish Homestead	279

Group of Church Workers	288
Hon. James J. Thomas	289
Loretto Road Station	304
The Old Church, Chapel and Pastoral Residence	308
Chapel and Residence, 1899	313
O. E. Wilkinson	314
The Main Street of Loretto	315
Arrival of the Base of the Statue	316
View at Midday, October 10	319
Interior of St. Michael's Church	320
The Procession from Immergrün	328
The Statue Veiled	329
Gift of the New Church	336
Archbishop Ireland	338
Archbishop Ireland Delivering His Address	344
Governor Stone	352
Monsignor Martinelli, the Apostolic Delegate	358
Bishop Phelan	360
Bishop Curtis	362
C. M. Schwab	364
St. Paul's Cathedral Choir	368
Rev. William Kittell	372
Rev. R. C. Christy	373
The Old Loretto Postoffice	373
Rev. Henry McHugh	374
Rev. Thomas McEnrue	376
Rev. H. P. Connery	377
Rev. C. O. Rosensteel	378
Rev. T. W. Rosensteel	380
Rev. J. C. McAteer	381
Rev. F. C. Noel	382
Rev. Geo. W. Kaylor	383
Rev. Francis Hertzog	384
Brother Lawrence O'Donnell	385
Adam Rudolph and Joseph Null	386
Mrs. Cooper and Mrs. McConnell	388
Mrs. Susan Gallagher	389
Thomas Wills	390

Arthur Comerford 391
Mrs. Veronica Freidhoff . . 391
Philip Dever 392
Augustine Hott 393
The Altar Boys 401
The Choir 402
The Church Committee 404
The New Church.

PAROCHIAL HALL. THE STATUE UNVEILED. CHURCH.

SOUVENIR OF
Loretto Centenary.

PART FIRST.

SKETCH OF THE LIFE OF REV. DEMETRIUS AUGUSTINE GALLITZIN, PRINCE, PRIEST, AND PIONEER MISSIONARY OF THE ALLEGHENIES.

(CONTRIBUTED BY JULIA MORGAN HARDING.)

SINCE the twelfth of October, 1492, when Columbus planted the cross for the first time on the shores of a new world, many strong souls have found there a life work, have endured torture and privation, and have lost their lives in their self-imposed efforts to convert the Aborigines and to administer the rites of the Church to the hardy pioneers who had first opened a way through the American wilderness. To Francis Parkman we are indebted for a brilliant narrative of the experiences of the Jesuits in Canada and the lake region, and of the short-lived Catholic colonies on the southern Atlantic coast. The noble Las Casas, the splendid figure of Marquette, the many times martyred Jogues, are themes well calculated to arouse the most eloquent of American historians; but their strange environment has perhaps added somewhat to the remarkable interest and reverence with which we approach the story of their adventures, their sufferings and alas! their failures.

The record of such work for religion does not, however, end with the last "Relation" of the Jesuit Fathers, and from their day to the present time it has been carried forward with quite as much self-sacrifice, and quite as much burning zeal, as that of the pioneer priests of New France. The workers have been for the most part unknown to the world in general, but here and there in the annals of both Church and State are preserved instances of heroic devotion and deeds of consecrated labor which shine forth through the gathering mist of years, and, like "yon little candle," still shed their beams upon a naughty world.

Directly in the line of this succession stands the figure of a missionary priest in a backwoods settlement in Pennsylvania, whose quiet life was one of persistent accomplishment in the face of serious and trying obstacles, and of unfaltering devotion to an humble work for which he relinquished a princely inheritance and a brilliant career and separated himself forever from home and kindred.

When Demetrius Augustine Gallitzin was born at The Hague on December 22, 1770, he was welcomed as the heir to a Russian family whose pedigree was longer and nobler than that of the imperial Romanoffs: a family which had produced great generals, great statesmen, and at least one martyr in the cause of religion, and which had always held positions of importance at the Russian Court. The father of Demetrius was Prince Dmitri Alexeivich Gallitzin, at one time in high favor with the Empress Catherine, and the friend of Diderot, Voltaire, and D'Alembert, with whom he was intimate during a long residence in Paris, as Russian Ambassador. In 1768 he married the Countess Amalia von Schmettau, a sister of the Prussian Field-Marshal von Schmettau, a soldier of great celebrity in his day, and shortly afterwards went to The

Hague, where he lived many years and represented the Russian Government. It was a period when society in the capitals of Europe had reached an unprecedented pitch of splendor and extravagance, and the Princess Amalia was plunged into a life of excitement in one of the most brilliant courts. She is described as beautiful, gracious and eager for knowledge, intellectual in her tastes, of a most enthusiastic temperament and a strong character. Though in her heart she longed for a higher life her buoyant spirits led her into the gay world, where she was so much admired that she was called "The Star of Holland."

But the brilliant and beautiful princess soon grew weary of an empty round of pleasure, and her long concealed desire to abandon it and to devote herself to her own education and that of her two children was so strengthened and encouraged by Diderot, that she finally obtained her husband's consent to her withdrawal to a simple but charmingly situated residence between The Hague and Scheveningen, which she named "Nithuys," (not at home) where for some years she led an almost ideal life. The children were trained in accordance with plans which for that day were unusually scientific, and though severe, were calculated to develop in them firmness, decision and healthy constitutions. Her own studies were incessant and carried her into the regions of the most advanced philosophies of the age. In her retirement she was sought by her husband's distinguished friends, and around her was a little circle which represented all that was best and brightest in Holland.

But the lonely tranquil years at Nithuys came to an end when, after mature consideration and the consent of the prince, she removed to Muenster, at that time at the height of its fame as a University town, in order to give her son every educational advantage the world could offer. In the quaint old city many happy years were passed and agreeable as well as more sincere friendships were formed.

The story of the influences which worked a great change in the princess' character and led her into the Roman Catholic Church is of peculiar interest, but must only be touched lightly in this brief sketch of her son, who, when he was seventeen years of age, was confirmed in the Catholic Church, and took the name of Augustine to please his mother, who was an intense admirer of the great Bishop of Hippona, and whose own devotion and maternal love were strikingly similar to those of Monica.

The young Prince had been well prepared for the part he was to play in the great world, from which, as the heir to a princely name and fortune and the nephew of a great general, he had much to expect. His education, as far as book learning was concerned, was unusually broad for the times, and in all manly sports, especially in that of horsemanship, he easily excelled. He was rather tall and slight, his air was high-bred and reticent, his figure lithe, his eyes dark and brilliant. His mother's training had developed in him a shyness and restraint, and, in spite of her absorbing devotion, he was not at ease or even frank in her presence. Possibly this may be explained by a certain dreamy and sensitive note in his nature which she failed to understand, and by a timid reserve which grew out of the childish awe which her imperious and forceful character had early inspired.

The time arrived when the future of the young Prince Demetrius should be determined; but the unsettled state of Europe made all plans uncertain and any decision difficult to form. It had long been his father's intention to place him in the way of a military career, and in his twenty-first year the appointment of aide-de-camp to the Austrian General von Lillien was secured for him. He was about to take his command when the order was issued that no foreigners should hold commissions in either the Austrian or Prussian army, and there seemed to be no other military career opened to him save in Russia. While considering the advisability of sending the young Prince to that country, General von Schmettau suggested that it might be of great advantage to remove him from Europe for a period, for the terrible uncertainty and the threatened collapse of old existing institutions made a successful career most doubtful; and moreover might exert a deteriorating influence on a character which his nearest friends persisted in thinking was still unformed.

The elder Prince, while at The Hague, had formed a friendship and had conceived a profound admiration for John Adams who had there represented the United States. The prince was a broad-minded man, deeply interested in the American experiment, and when the theme was broached that Demetrius should travel for two years in the New World he at once expressed approval, feeling, as he said, that in the existing revolutionary state of Europe his son would be nowhere under such calm and well ordered influence as that of his friend, John Adams, and the President, George Washington, for whom he entertained a great respect. The plan was discussed from every point of view, though Demetrius himself seems not to have been especially consulted; and the final arrangement placed the young man under the care of a traveling companion, a young priest, Rev. Felix Brosius, who was about entering on a missionary career in the United States. His father instructed him carefully in all that he knew of American affairs, and his mother procured for him from the Prince-Bishop of Hildesheim a letter of introduction to Bishop Carroll of Baltimore, a brother of the Signer, who she trusted would keep him firm in his religion, and would have over him a fatherly care. It was the decision of the prince and the general that Demetrius should lay aside his princely title and estate, and should travel in America under the unpretentious name of Mr. Schmet, an abbreviation of von Schmettau. This was in accordance with the custom of the times and relieved him from the expense of a retinue and the inconvenience of constantly living in a state befitting his rank; and, more than all, would, in the opinion of his mother, prevent his being spoiled by adulation. At the last moment it was with sudden, swift-coming regret and sad premonitions that this Spartan Monica accompanied her son to the pier from which he was to sail. He, too, was overwhelmed with direful presentiments. His timid, long controlled nature could scarcely endure the impending relaxation of the stern, though well intentioned, rule under which he had hitherto lived; he was afraid of the sea, of the strange lands and people, of everything, and most of all, of himself. He implored his mother to let him stay; and when his eyes quailed under her flashing gaze and indignant accusation of cowardice he was so overcome with varied emotions that he lost his balance and fell backward into the ocean. Being an expert swimmer he was soon rescued and having thus, as it were, emerged from a sea of doubt, indifference and inexperience, he entered upon a new life and into a new world.

On the twenty-eighth day of October, 1792, Prince Demetrius Augustine Gallitzin arrived in Baltimore, the most important town in the first Catholic colony in the United States, and the headquarters of the Catholic Church in America. Accompanied by his friend Brosius, he presented his letter to Bishop Carroll, whose kindness and cordial welcome made the young Russian feel instantly at home.

The stately, aristocratic ecclesiastic, whose life was given to the work of organizing the Church in the United States, found that it was out of the question to allow Prince Demetrius to accompany Brosius to his mission, and equally impossible to permit the latter to travel, as the princess had expected, with her son. So for some time Demetrius remained in Baltimore, showing no inclination to make use of the letters of introduction to prominent families in other cities with which Bishop Carroll had provided him. There was plenty of time, he said. For the first time in his life he was his own guide, free from the dominion of the strong minds of his mother and her advisors, and from the keenly critical observation in whose focus he had always lived. The fierce light of love and ambition which beat upon him had blinded the eyes of those who most cared for him, and had only refracted the manifestation of his true character, making his very strength appear weakness.

This sudden relaxation left him open and sensitive to new impressions, and new thoughts came crowding into his mind. The freedom and the peace of the New World life, its simplicity and quiet, were mediums through which his soul looked out and saw a new purpose, a different career from that to which his family had destined him. All at once his way was illuminated, and he could no longer remain in doubt of the fact that his duty and his desire were one. He says himself of his decision to give up his travels and to adopt the priestly vocation, that he was led to it because, the unexpected and incredible progress of the Jacobins; the subversion of social order and religion, and the dreadful convulsions in all the countries of Europe on one side, compared with the tranquil, peaceable and happy situation of the United States, together with some consideration on the vanity of wordly grandeur and preferment, caused him to renounce his schemes of pride and ambition and to embrace the clerical profession for the benefit of the American mission.

Bishop Carroll was unfeignedly embarrassed by Demetrius' resolve to abandon the life planned out for him by his parents, and to renounce his high position and estate in Russia, where an exalted military appointment awaited him and where the almost royal rank of his family opened to him honors, favors, and distinctions; and it was known to all concerned in the matter that by the law of the Empire Demetrius would be disinherited the moment he entered the priesthood. The Bishop wrote to the princess, telling her of her son's unalterable resolve, and at twenty years of age Demetrius Gallitzin, born to a life of ease and wealth, entered the Sulpician Seminary in Baltimore, and chose a life of toil, privation and self-denial for his own. As soon as the strange news reached his friends in Europe echoes of the storm of disappointment and reproach began to assail him, and letter after letter arrived begging him to reconsider what his family felt to be a rash and ill-considered step which he would soon regret having taken. To his mother to whom Prince Demetrius had ever seemed strangely lacking in force and character, and who had no confidence in his consistency of spirit, came the fear that her son was unconsciously deceiving himself, that he had no true vocation, that he would be incompetent and ever unworthy to fill so great an office; she dreaded the effect of the news upon his father who she knew would be bitterly disappointed and even unreasonably angry;

and it was many months before his own letters and those of his superior and the Bishop convinced her of the profound strength of his convictions and of his purpose, whereupon she rejoiced over his perseverance and was assured that his vocation was real.

To the prince his father, to General von Schmettau his uncle, courtiers and men of the great world, Demetrius' choice seemed unaccountable and hateful; for in it they saw forever buried the splendor of the family and their ambition for its further distinction at the imperial court. It took some time for the progress of events to change Prince Gallitzin's outlook and his opinion of court life and court favors and to enable him to see the wisdom of a step which forever removed his son from the ingratitude and uncertainties of a worldly life at a court, where religion and high principles counted for naught.

While stormy, reproachful, beseeching letters were passing back and forth over the Atlantic, in those days a much wider ocean than in these, Demetrius' life in the Seminary was beautiful and strenuous in his effort to overcome his faults and weaknesses, and it is of interest to read that Bishop Carroll insisted upon his giving much time to the study of American geography, history and forms of government. He joined the society of St. Sulpice, evidenced great piety and sanctity and many signs of steadiness of purpose; and was finally ordained a priest on one of the spring Ember Days, March 18, 1795, a little less than three years from the time of his leaving Europe.

Thus was fulfilled the desire expressed by the young Prince when in his seventeenth year he was confirmed in the Catholic Church and declared his wish to become a priest. At that time his father was indignant and his mother distrustful; and in the story of his life nothing seems more remarkable than the complete misunderstanding as to his fundamental character which existed in the mind of the Princess Amalia, that brilliant and devoted parent, and her consequent attitude toward him. To her he was thoughtless, volatile, cowardly, light of purpose and yet obstinate as only people so limited can be. The knowledge of his true nature, his tremendous will, his nervous energy, his unswerving intensity of purpose, came to her at last as a complete surprise and through sorrowful experience.

Demetrius Augustine Gallitzin, Prince of the Russian Empire, known to his own world friends as a handsome, accomplished nobleman, a child of fortune, was, as the Rev. Mr. Schmet, or Smith, "the first born of the Catholic Church in America—hers from the first page in his theology to the moment he arose from the consecrating hands of the Bishop;" for although he was the second priest ordained by Bishop Carroll, yet he was the FIRST in this country to have conferred upon him all the orders up to the sacred priesthood; the Rev. Stephen Badin, the first to be ordained priest having received the Deaconate in France. In order to restore his physical strength, weakened by his mortifications, penances and sedentary life at the seminary, Father Smith, as he was then generally called, was sent to a mission on the Susquehanna called Port Tobacco, a part of the Conewago mission, but to the great anxiety of the Bishop he showed absolute indifference to the trying changes of the American climate, his naturally impetuous temperament leading him in his zeal for a saintly life, to take great risks. There was a short period of residence at Port Tobacco, followed by another at Conewago, near Gettysburg, and then he returned to Baltimore, where he remained until some time in the year 1796, when he again took up the work that Bishop Carroll had planned for him, and traveling to and fro throughout the great frontier district of the Conewago mission he ministered to the Catholics scattered through the forest from Cumberland, Md., to Huntingdon and the heart of the Alleghenies in Pennsylvania.

His first journey to the mountain region destined to hold for him his life work, was taken in response to an urgent call which came to him at Conewago the summer after his ordination. A rough Indian trail led him through a primeval forest to a settlement high up on the Allegheny mountains, the furthest outpost of civilization, where he fulfilled his mission, said mass in the largest of the rough log huts, and impressed by the beauty and magnificence of the scenery, as well as inspired by a desire to help the struggling settlers, he purchased a tract of land for himself.

The story of Prince Gallitzin's early experiences, the severe schooling which taught him more mildness than his imperious impatient nature had ever known, is both edifying and interesting, but lack of space forbids entering upon it in detail, anymore than to say that the wise and good head of the church in Baltimore found it necessary to admonish the strenuous young priest to be less prodigal of authority, milder in demeanor, gentler in his methods.

At last, and most unexpectedly, he was called to his work. The little community which he had visited during his stay at Conewago was sometimes known as McGuire's Settlement, and later was called Clearfield. In response to a request from the settlers, who had not forgotten his first ministrations, and in accordance with his own earnest desire, Bishop Carroll assigned him to an arduous post, a field as yet untilled and unbroken.

In July, 1799, Father Gallitzin arrived upon the scene of his life work, full of zeal and inspiration, such as can alone animate the hearts of those who feel that their one desire in life is to save souls. His high hopes, fiery energy, and self-effacement recall the similar devotion of the Jesuit martyrs of Canada and the Northwest. His ambition was to found a church in the wilderness, a community free from worldliness, forever apart from the vexing questions which were shaking society to its foundations, from which, in time, should flow a reviving, kindling influence, a spirit of true Catholicism which would leaven the spiritual and national life of the United States.

It was a glorious though a rugged country where he chose to plant the ensign of his Church, and to sow the seed of a perfect spiritual life in which his community should grow and thrive. The gracious curves and sinuous lines of the grand old Alleghenies were softened then, even more than now, by the variegated forests which covered the land with dense foliage. In every little valley and dale were clear streams and crystal springs; the atmosphere was unpassingly pure and elastic; and the broad outlook on every side was in perfect harmony with the vast religious purpose which had taken possession of his great missionary soul. He entered upon the work with a joyous, buoyant enthusiasm, which, though sadly tried, was never entirely exhausted, and upheld him to the last through trials and disappointments which seem to find no parallel except in the lives of the Catholic priests and pioneers in New France.

A log hut was built on the hillside, one-half mile from the chief McGuire farm, in which the heir to a Russian principality lived contentedly. With eager helpfulness his people set to work. Under his direction and at his expense, the first church on the Alleghenies was built of logs hewn from the primeval forest which surrounded it on every side. Great preparations were made for its solemn dedication to St. Michael; the women of the parish made many candles, and through the snow drifts the men dragged laurel boughs and hemlock with which to hide the rough walls. From far and near the worshipers gathered, including hunters and trappers, in the motley crowd that filled the mountain sanctuary.

It was on Christmas Eve, the last Christmas Eve of the last century, December 24th, 1799, that Father Gallitzin celebrated the mass, and placed the only house of God from the Susquehanna to the Mississippi under the protection of St. Michael.

And what manner of man was this, who, forsaking parents and country, wealth and distinction, had built an altar in the forests of the Alleghenies? Tall and stately, his bearing was decidedly soldierly, his figure slender, his complexion clear, his eyes dark and flashing. His head was rather long, his nose aquiline, and though his features were regular and eminently aristocratic in mould, they were not devoid of force and character. Trained to every form of exercise as befitted a nobleman's son, destined to military service, he was above all things a superb horseman. His education had left no field of intellectual activity untouched, and, to a knowledge of history, philosophy, and the languages, he added some acquaintance with science. His voice was charming in conversation, though terrible in its force when he spoke in displeasure, and its exultant richness of timbre when intoning the service of his Church was such that those who heard him could not express themselves in terms unmoved by its thrilling effect.

His own story of the first impressive service, his great hope of building up a prosperous Catholic community, his profound joy in his self-abnegating work, was written to Bishop Carroll, on the ninth of February, 1800, and is told in direct and simple language. His life in Europe was as the memory "of old, forgotten, far-off things, or battles long ago;" and with heart and soul he threw himself into the "familiar matters of to-day." He lived simply and even rudely in a log cabin, slept upon the floor with a book for a pillow, ate coarse food, wore coarse clothing, was untiring in his manual labor for his people, unrelenting in his austerities. It was a solitary life with no intellectual companionship: long tramps on foot over Indian trails, long journeys on horseback to isolated settlements to minister to the sick and dying; hours of fasting and prayer in a church that was never warmed by a fire; but it was lived in cheerfulness and brightened by buoyant hope. For him the light shown clearly and from one place.

In 1802 Prince Gallitzin became an American citizen, his naturalization papers having been granted to him by the court of Huntingdon county under the name of Augustine Smith, by which he was still generally known; and shortly after occurred the first of a series of unfortunate incidents and perplexing problems connected with his family relations and financial affairs, and resulting in serious inconvenience and not a little sorrow. The prince, his father, who had never been entirely reconciled to his son's career, and who had been very anxious to see him once more, died suddenly in Brunswick, Saxony, in March, 1803, without leaving a will. His mother implored him to return to Europe, in letters whose pleadings and tenderness it must have required iron strength of soul and purpose to resist. Not only did the

Princess Amalia long to see her son once more, but the administration of her husband's estates was complicated by Russian law and his death in Saxony, and still further hampered by Demetrius' American citizenship, ordination to the priesthood, and absence from his old home. His friends and the friends of his family in Russia and Germany added their entreaties and warnings to those of the princess; Bishop Carroll not only gave his sanction and permission, but urged him to make the journey in order to save his inheritance, but Father Gallitzin could not see his way clear to thus suddenly desert his post, even for a fortune to be applied to the furtherance of the divine work to which he was giving his life.

He went to Baltimore to convince the Bishop that it was impossible for him to return to Europe even for a short time, stating as his reason that he had been the cause of many Catholic families having settled in the mountains, that the parish was poor and struggling and needed his constant care, and there was no one to whom he could surrender his post even for a time, as priests were few and the number of Catholic settlers in Pennsylvania and Maryland was constantly increasing.

Of all the sacrifices that the Russian Prince made during a life of unceasing abnegation, none so rent his heart as this voluntary surrender of the last hope of seeing his mother. Doing the best that he possibly could in the circumstances, Prince Gallitzin appointed as his agents, Baron von Furstenberg, prime minister of the Elector of Cologne; Count Frederic Leopold von Stolberg, and Count Clement Augustine von Merveldt, and they, together with the princess, in their efforts to secure his inheritance entered into an expensive and practically fruitless litigation which lasted many years.

In 1808 the news was sent to him that in consequence of having adopted the Catholic faith and clerical profession he was excluded from any share in his father's estate, and that (his mother having died in the meantime) his sister was sole heiress. This decision of the Russian Senate and Council of State was sanctioned by the Emperor and was therefore irrevocable.

The Princess Marianne, or Mimi, as she was called, could not give away her property, but she wrote her brother that she would faithfully divide the income with him, and led him to believe that it was her dearest wish to do so; but her promises were not kept. He received a few small remittances, and some years later the princess put an end to all hope of future financial assistance by her marriage, late in life, to Prince de Salm, a profligate spendthrift, who soon squandered her large fortune.

The complications resulting from Prince Gallitzin's failure to receive even a modest portion of his inheritance led to serious results, and cast a deep shadow of misunderstanding over many of the best years of his life, making it impossible for him to carry out many of his cherished plans and causing some of his best friends and parishioners to lose confidence in his ability and motives. This, together with a stupid tale which grew from the failure of the simple mountain folk to comprehend the reason for his having changed his name, brought upon him troubles which may well be called persecutions.

The remittances which were sent to Father Gallitzin by his mother, and such fragmentary amounts from his rightful inheritance as were sent to him at long intervals by his sister, all told perhaps reaches the sum of $170,000, certainly not less than $150,000. This money was all spent upon his mission and for his people in clearing and buying land, building houses and churches, and relieving the frequent and pressing immediate necessities of a poor and struggling community. Prince Gallitzin was robbed and cheated by those in Europe who should have been faithful to his interests, and his agents, all of them men illustrious and noble, seem to have been credulous and even criminally negligent in carrying out their charge.

Of all the incidents in this distressing phase of his history nothing seems more unnecessarily unfortunate than the disappearance of a large sum of money obtained from the sale of a valuable collection of Grecian and Roman antiquities, which the princess had bequeathed to her confessor, the Rev. Dr. Overberg, to be sold for charitable or educational purposes. The King of Holland bought the collection for $20,000 with the clear understanding that the money should be sent to his old friend Prince Demetrius, for use in his mission in the United States. But the proceeds fell into the hands of Prince De Salm, who sent Father Gallitzin less than half, retaining the rest for his own use.

In the meantime, the Russian Prince and Priest was making the history of a portion of the great state of Pennsylvania. The town that he laid out, partly on his own land, he named Loretto, in honor of the celebrated Italian shrine. In 1804, preliminary steps were taken to form a new county out of Huntingdon and Somerset, and three tiny settlements, one of which has entirely disappeared, not one stone being left on another, disputed the honor of being chosen for the county town. The superior claims of Loretto were urged by Father Gallitzin over those of the more flourishing Ebensburg and the ambitious Beulah.

The new county was named Cambria by the Welsh who had settled it in large numbers, and the Welsh community of Ebensburg obtained the coveted distinction, thus leaving Loretto to develop on purely spiritual lines and Beulah to a fate which was soon to overtake it. It cannot be denied that Prince Gallitzin's ways with his congregation were to a certain extent those of a Russian autocrat, though tempered with spirituality, animated by purity of thought and purpose, and inspired by the highest and loftiest ambition a human soul could have. It was hardly to be expected that a delicately organized, high-born, splendidly educated, intensely refined and sensitive aristocrat could live exactly on the same plane as that of the backwoods people among whom he chose and wished to cast his lot.

His very sacrifice which to us seems so noble was to them beyond comprehension, and aroused the suspicion ever latent in small and vulgar minds. His rigid rules and stern administration of moral law chafed the rougher element; his uncompromising attitude to the evil doer aroused antagonism, and his insistence on simplicity and seriousness did not always find compliance. He was the temporal as well as spiritual head of his flock; a slight knowledge of medicine combined with good common sense in such matters enabled him to prescribe and care for the sick when doctors were hard to find or impossible to get, and in the worldly interests of his congregation he made frequent long journeys to Greensburg and Lancaster.

He was judge and magistrate, as well as lawyer, physician and priest; he settled family quarrels as well as legal disputes, and imposed penalties and punishments. The habit of command was strong in him and allied with a slightly credulous disposition and an arbitrary manner was the cause of many of the petty annoyances and persecutions that embittered his life during the first decade of this century and sadly interfered with the ideal of perfection for which in his community he had so earnestly prayed.

In those days the fire of youth and a Russian temperament still influenced his ways, his opinions, his decisions; and though no labor was too humble, no service too arduous, and no call unanswered, there swept over the community a wave of dissatisfaction and even hatred which for a time threatened to destroy its existence. The erection of a new county, and the rapid settlement consequent on the opening up of new districts, brought politics into the factional disturbances at Loretto, and in this as in certain other instances, Prince Gallitzin, who very naturally was a staunch Federalist, was not in sympathy with the rougher element which in this part of the state constituted the Democratic-Republican party. Those who led the rebellious element, a very noisy calumnious and vicious but fortunately small part of the congregation, took their complaints to Bishop Carroll, from whom they received no encouragement and a decided reprimand. Father Gallitzin was seriously disturbed by the controversies and quarrels which for a time raged about him. His letters to the Bishop show how very unhappy he was that he should be so misunderstood and slandered, in many cases by men under great personal obligation to him, and such words of advice, confidence and encouragement as the Bishop wrote him were gratefully received.

REV. DEMETRIUS A. GALLITZIN.   PASTOR 1799–1840.

In the midst of these troubles and perplexities, in the autumn of 1806, a messenger from Baltimore brought to the little log house on the mountain the news that the Princess Amalia, Fürstin von Gallitzin, born Gräfin von Schmettau was dead. The letters which passed between the Prince, Bishop Carroll, Count von Stolberg, Dr. Overberg and the Princess Mimi are most edifying and beautiful reading. Even at this distance of time one keenly sympathizes with the profound sorrow of the self-exiled son who was most in touch with his mother during the years of separation, and who had perhaps never given up the hope of seeing her again. Princess Amalia has been the subject of memorial sketches in many languages. She was a woman of great energy and keen intellect. Her tastes were æsthetic, yet she was able to think clearly and logically, and her mastery of speculative philosophy placed her in an intellectual atmosphere far above most women of her time. A tremendous inner impulse impelled her toward self-cultivation, the highest and purest ambition stimulated her to seek perfection both for herself and her children, and a strict moral standard built upon moral principle and a true philosophy, kept her from yielding to the temptations of worldliness and vanity to which her exalted station, her talents, her beauty, and her charming personality rendered her susceptible.

One more bitter experience imposed by those of his own household followed close upon his domestic bereavement, and for a time Father Gallitzin's influence was again weakened and his soul tired by defamations and forged letters. It seems almost incredible that the self-denying and beautiful spirit, whose personality at this distance of one hundred years is still felt as a benediction wherever his name is known, should have suffered such distress and torment at the hands of those for whom he was giving his life; and it is horrible to relate that at the critical point of the battle that raged so fiercely around him, personal violence was attempted, and that but for the stout heart and strong arm of one John Weakland, Father Gallitzin would have met the fate of Becket. But the civil courts and the head of the Catholic Church in

America upheld his authority and rendered legal decisions in his favor; some of his tormentors repented, publicly retracted their accusations, and apoligized for their behavior, and the long, wearisome contest was over.

The trials which accompanied it were mean ones, the details were petty and loathesome, and the solitary man who endured them and met his enemies point by point, though rejoicing in his victory and happy in the returning and radiant confidence of his people, was sadly broken in health and spirit when that chapter of his life was closed. Financial obligations, it is true, continued to harass him for many years, but his stern integrity, severely simple rule of life, and beneficent, loving spirit enabled him to dominate his entire jurisdiction, the leader and the father of his people. In his own name Prince Gallitzin had contracted for large tracts of land for the use of the Church and for homes for the congregation. He built a fine grist mill and enlarged the church building, but his remittances failed to come regularly and were diminished in amount after the Princess Amalia died, and he soon found his temporal affairs in confusion. This embarrasment forced him into a wider acquaintance with lawyers, magistrates and business men throughout the state than he would otherwise have had, and many of the friends so made have borne testimony to his logical arguments, his flashes of wit, and rare charm in conversation. His letters written in those days tell of his aims and his projects, his needs and experiments. They contain allusions to the political affairs of the nation and the county, and to his failing health.

In a letter to Archbishop Carroll, who had been elevated to the Archbishopric of Baltimore in April, 1808, written in September of that year, Father Gallitzin says, in reference to his desire for an assistant: "It is my wish to confine myself within the limits of Cambria County, which alone would be more than sufficient to occupy two clergymen. My best time is past; I am upon the brink of thirty-nine, and besides its being contrary to the weakness of my constitution to ride about much and live upon every kind of diet, I find I could render more essential services to the mission by being more at home and carrying on a more regular correspondence with some able friends in Europe, of which I have received some very broad hints." In addition to his appeal for an assistant priest, Father Gallitzin also implored financial aid, both from his sister, who had utterly failed in her promises and her duty, and from the Archbishop, who could not help him because he was himself in debt, and the Church still in the depths of poverty. Though his debts were of a kind which at the present time would be called Church debts and would have to be met by the congregation, he assumed them as his own, and the burden was all the more distressing since, had he received his rightful inheritance, he would have been able to pay them many times over.

An additional torment was the fact that many of those for whom he had incurred debts had come to Loretto in consequence of inducements he had held out, and some among them were so ungrateful for past and present favors and kindnesses that they complained loudly.

His own life was one of extreme frugality, and his self-denials, combined with the distress consequent upon his financial troubles, almost wrecked his health, which had never been robust, and led him to the brink of utter despair.

But relief came at last in the shape of a long delayed remittance from Europe and money furnished both from known and unknown sources.

At the close of the year 1809 the embarrassment of the confusion of names was also cleared away by an act passed by the General Assembly of Pennsylvania, which authorized him to establish his name, Demetrius Augustine Gallitzin, and to enjoy the same benefits and privileges to which he became entitled by naturalization under the name of Augustine Smith.

From this painful story of debt, disappointment and broken health it is a pleasure to turn to the lighter picture of Prince Gallitzin in his personal relations with his flock; for the priest who was stern in rebuke and terrible in anger, whose keen eye never failed to detect the slightest wrong doing, who hated meanness, irreverence and duplicity, was the warmest of friends, the most approachable of pastors, the most sympathetic of advisors. Even the little children of his parish brought to him their joys and sorrows, and he settled their disputes as wisely and firmly, and with the same affectionate interest that he displayed in the affairs of their parents. His dislike of finery and ostentation found pregnant expression, as did also his hatred of intemperance; and the establishment of a whiskey distillery near Loretto was a sore trial.

He entered into the amusements of his people with great zest, and the story is told that at harvest time he provided dinners for the laborers on the Church land, and toward evening would take his violin out into the fields and play for their entertainment while they brought the harvest home in rough wains drawn by horses decorated with vines and wreaths.

He was most fastidious about the sanctuary and all things used for the service of the altar, and gave to them his personal care. Vestments and altar cloths were folded and put away without crease or wrinkle, and every article had its place. The materials were of the finest, and almost everything he used was made and sent to him by his mother and friends in Europe, and a handsome painting, "The Adoration of the Magi," received from the same source, still hangs over the chapel altar at Loretto.

He was fond of books and gathered together quite an imposing library for those days, and his thorough education, together with a fine command of his mental resources, rendered him formidable in argument and a controversialist of no mean ability.

It was as a controversial writer that he earned such fame that his pamphlets have been translated into many languages and are still in circulation. Much of his eloquence in such lines was drawn forth in answer to attacks on the Catholic Church made by Protestants ignorant of its doctrines and prejudiced by religious and political feeling. But it was the age of violence in print, and the intolerance of those who assailed the Prince and his Church, expressed in unmeasured terms, was, contrary to the example set, met with extreme moderation in language but with masterly force lightened with touches of quiet sarcasm.

The controversary between Father Gallitzin and the Protestant ministers of the neighboring towns resulted in the reception of many converts at the church in Loretto, and a most curious advertisement in the Cambria County Gazette in 1825 announces that, "A certain number of Protestants, having manifested a great desire of becoming members of the Roman Catholic Church, I hereby acquaint the said Protestants and the public in general that I have appointed the second Sunday after Easter (17th April) for admitting them into the Church, according to the rites and ceremonies of the Roman ritual." The notice is signed: Demetrius Augustine Gallitzin, Parish Priest.

While the founder of Loretto and his people were busy solving their own problems great events were happening across the water and important changes taking place nearer at hand. Archbishop Carroll had died and the passing of that wise and benign prelate was a source of profound sorrow to the missionary priest, whose friend he had ever been. Some idea of the remoteness of Loretto and its inaccessible situation in the heart of the mountains may be gained from the fact that the difficulties of the journey deterred the Archbishop from visiting that parish even after he had gone so far on his way as to reach Chambersburg.

One of Prince Gallitzin's earliest and best loved playmates during his life at Nithuys was Prince Frederick William, son of King William V, and the friendship formed in those delightful days in Holland continued until Prince Demetrius started on the long journey from which he never returned. When the two young men parted Demetrius gave unto the keeping of his royal friend a watch, rings and several trinkets which he especially valued and did not care to risk losing in his travels through a wild and unknown country. Since that day kingdoms had risen and fallen in Europe, and little Holland had its share of vicissitudes: but after the downfall of Napoleon the Congress of Vienna called Prince

Frederick William from his exile in England and placed him on the thrones of Holland and Belgium as William I, King of the Netherlands and Duke of Luxemburg.

As soon as he came to his own he gave orders to his minister in America to seek for his old friend of whom he knew nothing more definite than that he lived in Pennsylvania; and great must have been his surprise when in the person of a poor, care-worn, enfeebled priest was discovered the highborn, handsome, accomplished Russian Prince.

The King of the Netherlands offered him assistance, but did not succeed in persuading him to accept anything save the sum of $2,000—which he said was a just due and but a slight return for the jewels left in his care so many years before, and which there unfortunately appeared to be no chance of ever giving back to their owner. The money was accompanied by a renewal of their boyish vows of friendship, and kind and affectionate words passed between the King on his throne and the humble priest in his rude log hut. Shortly afterward the same royal personage bought the collection of antiques to which reference has previously been made.

It was in 1828 that the lowest ebb in Father Gallitzin's financial affairs was reached, for in that year his property and his little cabin were advertised for sale by the sheriff of Cambria County. But from this last sacrifice he was saved by liberal subscriptions from the Catholics in Cambria County and the generosity of the Russian Ambassador, who, as Father Gallitzin relates, lighted a cigar with the bond for $5,000, which was his sole security for a loan to that amount.

The occasion referred to was that of a formal dinner given in Washington by the Ambassador of the Czar, to which Henry Clay and other notable people were invited that they might meet the Prince.

It was not often, and always on urgent business, that Father Gallitzin left his mountain home. A few journeys to Washington, Baltimore and Philadelphia were all that brought him into touch with the great world east of the hills. But long and toilsome were his travels through the forests on horseback or in a rude sled, when he visited the poor and isolated families who looked to him alone for comfort, encouragement and the last offices of the Church. For this no distance was too great, no fatigue too onerous, no danger too menacing, no call unanswered.

Had Father Gallitzin carried out any of his sometimes much talked of plans for returning to Europe to recover his property he would undoubtedly have received high ecclesiastical honors, and such offers of preferment were not withheld from him by the Church of America. He persistently discouraged them, however, and was steadfast in his refusal to accept the Bishoprics offered him.

In a letter written to Archbishop Marechal, in October, 1823, after interesting reference to his own private affairs, he speaks eloquently of the need of a diocese in Western Pennsylvania, but not with any idea of having the same bestowed upon himself. However, he could not entirely avoid the responsibilities which the growing Church developed, and in 1827 he was formally appointed Vicar-General, and he entered upon a work for which his previous experience and habit of acting as both judge and mediator had thoroughly prepared him. The unsettled state of the Church in Pennsylvania during this primitive period of its history made the office of Vicar-General a difficult one to fill. But much discretionary power was left in his hands, and the heads of the diocese in Philadelphia, by their frequent expressions of confidence and approval, showed that they looked up with reverence and esteem to the frail but still princely forest missionary.

Bishop Egan had visited Loretto in 1811, and in the autumn of 1830 the coadjutor of the diocese, Bishop Kenrick, administered confirmation to no less than five hundred people gathered from near and far and assembled in St. Michael's Church. It is recorded that he was amazed at the piety and prosperity of the little village, and profoundly impressed by the stateliness, simplicity and radiant sanctity of the priest who had been buried in the wilderness for thirty years.

New missions were now springing up around Loretto and in the country lying between Cambria County and Greensburg, and the priests assigned to them received not only a kindly welcome from the pioneer at St. Michael's, but many good words of advice and encouragement; and more than one has left an account of his first impressions of the high-bred gentleman whose keen eyes beamed with benevolence, whose manner was at once haughty and gracious, and whose quick intelligence seemed fitted for a far wider field of activity.

As years passed by, with increasing age, a broader field of responsibility and multiplied duties, came also bodily infirmities, and it grew more and more difficult for the fast aging priest at Loretto to continue unassisted the work for which he alone laid a thorough foundation. Small congregations had grown up at Ebensburg, Johnstown, Indiana, Wilmore, Hart's Sleeping Place, and Carrolltown; and these were placed in charge of the Rev. James Bradley, thus relieving Father Gallitzin from the fatigue of constantly journeying on rough roads to officiate at outlying missions. But after two years, during which he was of great use to Father Gallitzin, Father Bradley was sent to Newry, Blair County, and in response to a request from both pastor and people, Bishop Kenrick sent to the mountains a German priest who has fortunately left us a most interesting and graphic portrait of Prince Gallitzin in his reclining years.

The Rev. P. H. Lemke was a Prussian and a convert. Before leaving Europe he had read a biography of Princess Amalia, and as soon as he came to America he inquired the whereabouts of her son. The Bishop, who had just received Prince Gallitzin's request for an assistant, found that Father Lemke was not only willing but even anxious to be appointed to that position, and therefore as soon as arrangements could be made he was sent to Loretto, having been warned beforehand that great care and discretion should be observed in his conduct and manner of approaching his superior. This was a necessary bit of advice, for long years of solitude, intellectual isolation and absolute authority had accentuated and intensified every peculiarity in the venerable priest's character, and his growing eccentricities made him a rather difficult person with whom to live and work.

In his "Leben und Wirken," Father Lemke describes his first meeting with the subject of his biography. It was in September of the year 1834, when guided by Thomas Collins, a young lad, the son of the inn keeper at Munster, Father Lemke started through the woods on horseback on his way to Loretto. He alludes to the glorious weather, the forest, the birds, the squirrels and the merry chatter of his young companion; and then he tells us that he saw in the depths of the woods, coming toward him, a sled drawn by two stout horses, in which reclined a venerable man in worn peasant's clothing and reading a book.

"Are you the pastor of Loretto?"

"Yes, I am he." "Prince Gallitzin?" "At your service;" and then laughing, "I am that exalted person."

It happened he was on his way to say mass in a farmer's house. The two spent the day together. Father Lemke learned something of what his own work was to be, and in the quiet house at Loretto they talked together about the great changes which in the forty-two years since Prince Gallitzin had left Germany had occurred there and all over Europe. The singular old nobleman, as Father Lemke calls him, stationed his new assistant at Ebensburg, and from there he attended to a district some forty or fifty miles in extent. They lived together in harmony, the Prince recognizing Father Lemke's energy and spirit, and rejoicing in his vigorous manner of prosecuting his work.

Father Lemke founded the village of Carrolltown near the old mission of St. Joseph's, and was much disappointed that the Prince would not allow him to name it Gallitzin. Thus relieved of responsibility and confident that his assistants were conscientiously prosecuting the work which he had founded and still directed, the venerable man of God entered upon the evening of his life.

Harmony reigned where once had raged factional quarrels; the wild mountain sides and forest-tangled valleys were smiling gardens and fertile fields; his debts were almost entirely paid, and at home and abroad he was adored by a people who looked to him as to a father, a priest, and a king.

Though fragile in appearance, and evidently nearing his end Father Gallitzin was never absent from his post on Sundays. His voice was still strong, clear, and beautifully modulated, his glance keen, his interest in affairs of Church and State as lively and decided as in his earlier days of warfare. It was not until the bitterly cold winter of 1839-40, that it became evident to those who anxiously watched their beloved pastor that he would be with them but a short time longer, though almost to the last moment his daily round of duties was faithfully performed, at what cost to himself none but himself could know.

On Easter morning his last words to his congregation were said, a short exhortation on the Resurrection, ending with the words spoken on the cross. When it became known that Father Gallitzin was seriously ill his people from all parts of the county gathered together at Loretto, and the dying Prince bade each a serene and hopeful farewell, insisting that no one, not even the most humble, should be excluded from his presence. He lingered until the sixth of May, and not until the early evening hours did he find rest at last, and complete the sacrifice begun forty-five years before, when he joyfully renounced power, riches, and the promised gifts of smiling fortune for poverty, obscurity and a life of sanctified toil. As the angels of God said of Jacob, we may say of Demetrius Augustine Gallitzin: "As a Prince hast thou power with God and with men, and hast prevailed."

JULIA MORGAN HARDING.

LOCAL HISTORICAL NOTES.

BY WILLIAM A. M'GUIRE.

NOTE.—The following is merely a compilation of facts and events that have a bearing on the life of Rev. D. A. Gallitzin and on the development of the territory which was the theatre of his sanctified labors. The compilation is made from Miss Brownson's Life of Rev. D. A. Gallitzin; from histories of Pennsylvania and Cambria County; from the files of the Pittsburg Catholic and local papers, and from the recollections of aged citizens. No originality whatever is claimed for the work.

1788—1799.

FIRST SETTLEMENT ON THE ALLEGHENIES.

With the first permanent settlement in Cambria County begins the history of Catholicity on the Allegheny mountains. About one hundred and eleven years ago, and sixteen years before the county was organized, the standard of Christian civilization was first erected on these heights. Previous to the year 1788 the tract of land now included within its limits was an unbroken wilderness. The frontier of the inhabited parts of Pennsylvania was east of the Allegheny mountains. The "Frankstown Settlement," a few miles below where Hollidaysburg now stands, was the most western opening in the wilderness. Through the forests of the western slope of the mountains still prowled a remnant of the savage tribes, and wild animals had not yet learned to fear the conditions of civilization.

But about this time began the era of territorial development. In the year 1788 Captain Michael McGuire, a hero of the Revolutionary War, brought his family from Maryland to a spot quite near the present town of Loretto, and there planted the first permanent settlement within the limits of what is now Cambria County. A large portion of the tract on which he settled is even yet owned and occupied by his descendants. As a captain in the War of Independence he served with honor and distinction on the "Maryland Line," and not many years after the end of the war he undertook to carry out the design that he must have formed many years previously. For being a noted trapper and hunter, he was accustomed, even before the revolutionary struggle broke out, to start at intervals from his home in Taneytown, Md., and to make expeditions far into the interior of Pennsylvania. On one of these trips, about the year 1768, he crossed the summit of the Alleghenies and established his hunting camp near the present village of Chest Springs, on land now owned by Mr. Robert Sisk; as is to be seen on an old draft of the country made as far back as 1793, which shows the exact location of "Captain McGuire's Camp." It is practically beyond all dispute, notwithstanding assertions to the contrary, that the captain was, as Robert L. Johnston, the historian of early Cambria, wrote, "the first white man who settled within the present bounds of Cambria County." Records, deeds, papers, etc., in the possession of his many descendants are more than sufficient to verify this statement.

From Taneytown, Md., the extreme limit of travel had hitherto been Conewago. The distance from this place to the spot chosen by Captain McGuire for his new abode was about 130 miles. In those days of frontier life such a journey could not be other than dangerous and daring. Through wild, unbroken forests, on horseback, with no beaten path to guide them, and through brushwood so thick that a passage had to be cut as they slowly advanced, did the captain and his family travel to what is now Cambria County. The exact spot chosen by him for a settlement was the valley just below the present town of Loretto to the east. In a short time a few log cabins were built, and these served for shelter and protection until more permanent structures could be erected. This land is now part of the tract owned by the Franciscan Brothers. Some scarcely distinguishable marks of excavations for the foundations of the log cabins, and a few old apple trees, the most of which were uprooted during the terrible wind storm of May 16th, of the current year (1899), were for a long period the only visible signs to designate this historic spot. But it was verily here that the strong arms of the stalwart captain and his brave sons laid the foundations of "McGuire's Settlement," and of the prosperous community that arose and flourished from such humble beginnings. In 1790 Luke McGuire, eldest son of the captain, took up his residence on the farm now owned and cultivated by his grandson, George Luke McGuire, about one-half mile east of Loretto, on the road leading to the town of Gallitzin. This point was not far from the original cabin, and is distinguished as being the location of the oldest house now standing in Cambria County. Completed in 1794 it was first occupied by Luke McGuire and his newly wedded wife, Margaret O'Hara, and in it they reared a family of eleven children. Standing more than one hundred years this house still defies the fierce storms of the Alleghenies, is still well preserved, and has ever since its construction served as a domicile for the family and descendants of Luke McGuire, son of Captain Michael. Some years later, Richard, a younger son of the captain, also located and built in the same vicinity.

From 1758 until 1768 the line of Indian reservation followed the line between the present counties of Somerset and Bedford, Cambria and Blair, to the corner of Center, Blair and Cambria, from which point it passed eastward and joined the Susquehanna. In 1768 the purchase was extended to a line following from the western boundary of Pennsylvania up the Ohio and Allegheny rivers to Kittanning; thence eastward by a line to Canoe Place (afterwards called Cherry Tree, and lately Grant), from which spot, now marked by a beautiful monument, the line followed the west branch of the Susquehanna, thence in a northeasterly direction into Bradford County, joining the Pennsylvania-New York boundary where the north branch enters the state from New York. Cambria County was included in this purchase. Until after this treaty with the Indians no land was patented within these lines. When the land office was opened Captain Mc-

Guire was among those who "took up" land on which he subsequently planted the "McGuire Settlement." His first, and for several years his only neighbors, were the settlers at Blair's Mills, more than twelve miles away, with a dense, unbroken forest between.

Captain Michael lost no time in providing for the future spiritual needs of his family and of his settlement. Being a devout Catholic his first and greatest desire seemed to be that of firmly establishing the Church in the new location. He had taken up a large tract of land, 400 acres of which he made over to Bishop Carroll (brother of Charles Carroll, of Carrollton, the last survivor of the signers of the Declaration of Independence) for the establishment of religion and the maintenance of resident clergy. On this land now stands the brick church of St. Michael and pastoral residence; the monument of Father Gallitzin, his chapel and stone house which served as the pastoral residence until 1874; St. Francis' College, and The Children's Home, formerly St. Aloysius' Academy. On the same tract also stood the old log church (the first building dedicated to the worship of God between Lancaster, Pa., and St. Louis), erected in 1799, enlarged to double its capacity in 1808, and in 1817 replaced by a frame building 40x80 feet, which was used as the parish church until 1854: also the log house of Father Gallitzin, replaced in 1832 by St. Mary's Chapel and the old log barn. In 1891 the chapel was taken down and rebuilt of the same material, thus making it practically the same as before; but the barn and the frame church, entirely dilapidated by the ravages of time and the weather, were razed to the ground. The area of the church was enclosed and laid out in burial lots, the sanctuary part, where the first altar on the Alleghenies stood, being reserved for the interment of the resident clergy.

About the year 1790, after Bishop Carroll had taken possession of the new See of Baltimore, the first erected in the United States, an effort was made to provide for the spiritual needs of "McGuire's Settlement." At least once, and probably twice, Father Brosius, who had accompanied the young Gallitzin to this country, visited the place, and upon one occasion set apart a portion of the land donated and consecrated it for a cemetery. Faithful and persevering during the half decade of pioneer mountain life, too brief a period in which to see even the commencement of the realization of his hopes, Captain Michael McGuire was all too soon called to his eternal reward. He died November 17, 1793, in the 76th year of his age, and was the first to be interred in the ground which he had donated for the purpose of a cemetery. After 111 years the fullness of his ambitious designs is fully realized. The little settlement that he founded on these rugged heights has grown into a populous and prosperous community, and his progeny has multiplied and filled the land. Many of his descendants of the sixth generation, as well as of the fifth and fourth, are living to-day. For many years his grave was marked by a large brown slab of mountain sandstone, on which a brief epitaph was sculptured; but later on this was replaced by a neat marble tombstone which bears this inscription:

> HERE LIE THE MORTAL REMAINS
> OF
> CAPTAIN MICHAEL M'GUIRE,
> DEPARTED THIS LIFE NOV. 17, 1793.
>
> He manifested his zeal for the glory of God and the salvation of souls by bestowing this land for the benefit of the resident clergy.
>
> MAY HE REST IN PEACE. AMEN.
>
> Erected by A. J. McGuire, of Baltimore, and R. Scanlan, of Loretto, 1856.

CAPTAIN RICHARD M'GUIRE.

Richard, son of Captain Michael McGuire of Revolutionary fame, was born in Frederick County, Md., December 12th, 1771. He came with his father to what is now Allegheny Township, Cambria County, in 1788, and on May 15,

1800 was united in marriage to Eleanor, daughter of John and Ann Byrne. In the Baptismal Register of St. Michael's Church are recorded the births of ten children from this union, the last being born on January 1, 1822. When the estate of Captain Michael was divided after his death in 1793 among his children, Richard fixed his residence on land now owned by Mr. Joseph D. Hertzog, a short distance south of the location of the original settlement. A spring marks the site and there are still a few old apple trees standing near. The barn stood above the old "Glass Lane," a township highway, which formerly connected the road from Loretto to Gallitzin with the old road from Loretto to Munster. Both the latter road and the "lane" have been vacated for several years. The last architectural landmark of early origin on the land of Captain Richard was an old log barn, long used by the tramping fraternity as a convenient place of refuge, and familiarly and generally known as "The Tramps' Hotel." This was swept off its foundation and completely destroyed by the terrific storm of May 16, this year (1899).

Richard McGuire commanded a company in the war of 1812. While his patriotism was thus evinced, he was ever remarkable as a devout Catholic, and exemplified in his life how intimately the love of country may be connected with the love of God. He had seen the beginnings of the Church in Cambria County, had taken an active part in its difficulties and struggles and he lived to see its triumph. He died peacefully January 13, 1855, in the 84th year of his age.

OTHER PIONEERS.

The settlement founded by Captain Michael McGuire attracted other pioneers to the Alleghenies, and he was soon followed by William Dodson, Richard Nagle, Cornelius Maguire, Richard Ashcroft, Michael Rager, James Alcorn and John Sturm. Still following these were John Trux, John Douglas, John Byrne, William Meloy and many others whose names, together with the names of their descendants, are preserved in the Registers of St. Michael's Parish, Loretto. Mr. John Sturm, or Storm, built the first grist mill in Cambria

REV. PETER H. LEMKE.   PASTOR 1840-44.

County, where Dawson's (Sybert's) mill now stands. The rapid improvements of this part of the county are due to the efforts of these early pioneers, who struggled against obstacles of which in our day we can form but a slight idea. The word "road" is a dignified term for the path by which they held intercourse with the settlements across the mountain to the east. A rough Indian path led from the present site of Loretto and intersected the "Frankstown Road" about two miles west of the Summit. Exposed to the inclemency of an Allegheny winter—for against the rigor of such a winter their hastily constructed and poorly furnished cabins afforded but slight protection—their sufferings were almost beyond human endurance. Yet with unyielding firmness, characteristic of the pioneer race of frontiersmen, those hardy men wrested from the grasp of nature and preserved the inheritance which we now enjoy.

Of their adventures with the savage beasts and still more savage Indians then infesting the neighborhood, many anecdotes, as narrated by the older citizens of Allegheny Township, are handed down to the present generation. The Indians were not slow to seize upon every opportunity of aggression which presented itself to their blood-thirsty minds, and consequently not only property but even life itself was held by the inhabitants in a very uncertain tenure. The truth of the Alcorn story is vouched for by the most reliable citizens of this neighborhood. In the vicinity of the spot where Loretto now stands James Alcorn had built a hut and made a clearing a short distance away. One day his wife went out to this patch and did not return. Although search was immediately made no trace leading to her discovery could be found. To this day the manner of her disappearance remains a mystery, though it is generally supposed that she was borne away by the savages.

FATHER GALLITZIN.

In the summer of 1796, Mrs. John Burgoon, a Protestant, living near "McGuire's Settlement," was taken seriously ill, and begged so hard and repeatedly to see a Catholic priest that

Mrs. Luke McGuire and a companion undertook the long and dangerous journey to Conewago, near the Maryland border, 130 miles, to find one who would be able and willing to visit her. The message coming to Father Gallitzin he hastened to join the good Samaritans and to carry the consolations of religion to the stranger in the wilderness. Mrs. McGuire fretted very much at the many delays necessarily incidental to the journey, fearing lest the woman would die before they could reach her, but she was made confident by the priest's assurance that if Mrs. Burgoon were as anxious as they said she was to see a priest, God would not permit her to die until her desire was fulfilled. His words were so far made good that she recovered her health, and after being instructed she was received into the Church and until her death, many years afterwards, lived a truly Catholic life.

The coming of Father Gallitzin on this occasion was hailed with joy by the few families scattered in that unbroken country to which only at long intervals a priest had ever penetrated. He said mass in the new log house of Luke McGuire, which stands a firm monument of the celebration to this day, and administered baptism to a number of children, and even one or two old persons: exhorted them all to faith, prayer, courage and perseverance and before he started to return he had resolved to invest in land with the liberal pecuniary allowance from his mother, and to establish a church on the Alleghenies.

Returning, he remained in Baltimore until some time in 1796, when he took charge of the Conewago mission, from which central point he visited Taneytown, Pipe Creek, Hagerstown and Cumberland, in Maryland, not far from the Pennsylvania border; Chambersburg, Path and Shade Valleys, Huntingdon, and even the Allegheny mountains, in Pennsylvania. The Maryland congregations were principally English speaking people, which gave him a better fluency in the English language. In the neighborhood of Chambersburg great ignorance prevailed, which, as usually happens, was accompanied by prejudice, bigotry and persecution.

Deliverance from this mission came to him at last. The scattered settlers on the mountains amounting to ten or twelve families, forming what was generally known as "McGuire's Settlement," sometimes called Clearfield, where he had visited the sick woman, to which place he had since made several journeys, sent a petition to Bishop Carroll, begging for a priest to reside among them, trusting that with the aid of some land previously given to Bishop Carroll by Captain McGuire for church property, and such tithes as they could give him, the priest might be able to provide for his physical subsistence, while he cared for their spiritual needs. Several petitions were forwarded, a couple of which were sent through him on his return from occasional visits to the settlement, entreating that, if conformable to his own wishes, he might be the pastor chosen for them. He finally made this request his own, and it was cordially granted.

Following is the reply:

Rt. Rev. Bishop Carroll to Rev. D. A. Gallitzin:

WASHINGTON CITY, March 1, 1799.

Rev. and Dear Sir:

I fear you have been disappointed in not receiving an earlier answer to your letter which covered a list of subscribers in Clearfield, Frankstown and Sinking Valley. I had come hither on business immediately before the arrival of yours at Baltimore. Your request is granted. I readily consent to your proposal to take charge of the congregations detailed in yours and hope that you will have a house built on the land granted by Mr. McGuire and already settled or cleared, or if more convenient on your own, if you intend to keep it. . . . .

My intention was, before I received yours, to advise you of the notice lately given by Mr. Egan, that he would return to Ireland in the spring or summer. I meant to have offered you with your present congregations that of Emmitsburg and the mountain (now Mt. St. Mary's) united in one.

JOHN, BSP., Baltimore.

Thus sanctioned by his Bishop, called by the people, and urged on by a voice higher than all, the young priest lost no time in making preparations, but packed up his few possessions, mounted his horse, and turned his face northwestward "over the hills and far away" to found a Catholic community on the lasting basis of virtue and true religious simplicity.

In the latter part of the summer of 1799 Father Gallitzin reached his mission. About a dozen families were found already settled in the neighborhood, and these, with a few families that had just come from Maryland and Conewago, formed his immediate parish; but all the Catholics who could not be conveniently reached from Conewago were under his charge and jurisdiction. At McGuire's Settlement he commenced to put things in order, thankful enough that as yet the field was untouched. Settling on the donated land he at once divided his own, which had cost him about four dollars an acre, into lots which he sold to the newcomers for a mere trifle on most easy terms. It was seen before long and gratefully acknowledged that with this frail young priest a new and invigorating spirit had been infused not only into the settlement, which was at comparative ease, but into all the Catholic pioneer families within a circuit of sixty miles at least.

When Father Gallitzin arrived to take up his permanent abode he lived for some months in the houses of the settlers until his own log cabin, 14x16 feet, could be built on the site selected by him, about a half mile from the chief McGuire farm. His first care, however, was for the erection of a church which he commenced soon after his arrival, and completed on Christmas eve following. This was the first, and for a time the only, House of God between Lancaster, Pa., and St. Louis. Great preparations had been made for the midnight Christmas mass, the first that was offered up in the humble building. The snow lay waist-deep around the edifice and the stars shone bright and cold above it, as on that other December night over the scarcely humbler stable at Bethlehem. The men had been instructed to bring in branches of the beautiful evergreen trees which grew thick upon the mountain and at their very doors. The women set the candles they had made for the occasion amid the dark green foliage which covered the rude walls; and just at midnight, when the people who had gathered from long distances through the wilderness of snow were hushed in rapt expectation, Father Gallitzin ascended the altar and commenced the mass. Never did the *Gloria in Excelsis* come more joyously and exultingly from his heart or lips than when he now, for the first time, opened and gave to the Incarnate Lord a refuge in the wilderness, a home on the Alleghenies.

Shortly after the holidays, being anxious to provide for the poor settlers who were flocking to the settlement, he went to Conewago to procure seed and implements for the spring planting. From there, on February 9th, 1800, he wrote as follows to Bishop Carroll: ". . . . Our church which was only begun in harvest got finished fit for service the night before Christmas. It is about 44 feet long by 25, built of white pine logs, with a very good shingle roof. I kept service in it at Christmas for the first time, to the very great satisfaction of the whole congregation, who seemed very much moved at a sight which they never beheld before. There is also a house built for me, 16 feet by 14, besides a little kitchen and a stable. I have now, thanks be to God, a little home of my own for the first time since I came to this country, and God grant that I may be able to keep it. . . . . The congregation consists at present of about forty families, but there is no end to the Catholics in all the settlements round about me; what will become of them all, if we do not receive a new supply of priests, I do not know: I try as much as I can to persuade them to settle around me." This was written in 1800, yet for more than twenty years afterwards he was obliged to administer, unassisted, to the spiritual wants of the constantly increasing population.

In his history of the Pittsburg diocese, Rev. A. A. Lambing, LL. D., who in 1869 was stationed at St. Francis College, and assisted the pastor of St. Michael's, Rev. Michael J. Mitchell, says: "The Loretto colony appears to have had as yet but one common center, although it was increasing in numbers and widening in extent, for the persecutions of which the pastor had been the victim, served to make him better known and attracted more settlers from the east. The log church was now filled to excess, and in 1808 he enlarged and otherwise improved it, at his own expense, for it may be stated here, once for all, that he never received any salary or income from the people, but paid out of his own resources the expenses of the church as well as the maintenance of his own household. In fact, it was his extreme antipathy to the pew-rent system that induced him to apply to the Bishop for permission to leave Taneytown and come to the mountain, where he could mould the affairs of the Church after his own views. The colony began to branch out and lay the foundations of other congregations that have a separate history of themselves—Ebensburg, Carrolltown, St. Augustine, Wilmore, Summit, etc. In September, 1808, Father Gallitzin wrote to the Bishop, asking for a priest to take part of his territory, and leave him to labor for the Catholics of Cambria County alone, and to manage the temporalities of Loretto; but owing to the scarcity of priests, that prelate was unable to comply with the request. The temporalities gave him no little anxiety. His just expectation of receiving aid from Europe was constantly doomed to partial, often to total, disappointment, so that for almost thirty years, his mind had but meagre repose."

FATHER GALLITZIN AT JEFFERSON (WILMORE).

After Father Gallitzin had settled at Loretto and began his visits to the outlying communities which extended over the greater portion of the Pittsburg diocese, he found located near the confluence of the Little Conemaugh and the North Branch near the present town of Wilmore, a family whose name is now appropriately commemorated in the name of the village for which these people did so much. Godfrey Wilmore, the father of the family, was a negro, but, intellectually and morally, was far above the average of his race. His wife was a white woman, of Irish nationality, a "redemptioner." Both lived in Harford County, Md.; and the husband being energetic, worked enough extra outside of his servitude to buy his freedom. He then saved money and bought the time of servitude of his wife, whose maiden name was Mary Higgins, married her, and about 1792 moved to a place about a mile south of Wilmore, known to early settlers as the "Jimmy Rhey Place," and from thence to the place above noted. Wilmore was a Baptist, while his wife was a Catholic. When Dr. Gallitzin first visited them he and Wilmore had sincere conversations about religion, the result of which was the latter's conversion to the faith of his wife, and he was ever after a most exemplary member of the Church, and in his house Father Gallitzin sometimes stopped and said mass when on his visitations to that and the more southern sections of the county.

The children of this union were: Bernard, the founder of the town which now bears his name; James, who for many years lived on a farm about two miles north of Wilmore; John, who lived near the town; Mary, wife of James Young, and Elizabeth, who died November 11, 1832. Bernard Wilmore was, by trade, a bookbinder, and also taught school, as did his father, who died April 2, 1815, in his 64th year. He was a cripple and was never married. His father, in his lifetime, had built a saw mill on the Little Conemaugh below Wilmore, which was subsequently washed away, and he then located about 800 yards east of the present Pennsylvania Railroad depot. Near this place Sylvester Welch's corps of engineers, running the lines for the Allegheny Portage Railroad, in 1829, founded a little village which they marked on their map "Guinea," an appellation which the Irish laborers who built the road adopted until the matter was made a subject of complaint to Dr. Gallitzin, who from the altar denounced this insult to a family for whom he had the greatest respect. It is said that he almost anathematized any person who would call the town by the opprobrious name and declared that it should be called Jefferson, the name it bore until 1859, when the town was incorporated into a borough under the name of Wilmore. The first postoffice established in Jefferson, in August, 1832, received the name of Wilmore. Thomas J. Power, Esq., was its first postmaster.

It was the sixth postoffice in the county. (Summit was the seventh)

Bernard Wilmore, in his will, bequeathed to Father Gallitzin a parcel of land in the center of the town for the purpose of erecting thereon a Catholic Church. This land was afterwards sold by the executors of Father Gallitzin's estate to 'Squire Miller and Mr. George Settlemeyer, and on a portion of the latter conveyance the Evangelical Lutheran Church now stands. We have heard many testify that it was under an apple tree in the meadow of Bernard Wilmore and Young that Father Gallitzin used to say mass when the old Portage road was being graded, no building then there, being large enough to accommodate the Irish Catholic laborers.

EXTRACTS FROM FATHER GALLITZIN'S LETTTERS.

TO BISHOP CARROLL.

July 15, 1800.

The congregation is considerably increased since the time I moved hither; and I feel the greatest satisfaction in seeing the most unequivocal signs of the sincerest repentance and conversion in some of the most inveterate sinners. The church which I got built last August is very often almost full, and will have to be enlarged in a couple of years. I live at my own cabin ever since Christmas last, though in a very poor style yet, as your lordship may expect. The moving to a country where I had to begin in the woods, the furnishing myself with everything necessary for housekeeping, when I had nothing of the kind, the great improvements I have made in order to put the place in such a state as to afford a maintenance for a priest, ... have exhausted my finances. . . . . It is very likely that I shall see your lordship in Baltimore next October, when I send my wagon down.

TO THE SAME.

CLEARFIELD SETTLEMENT, February 5, 1801.

I am happy to see that your lordship has altered the resolution of removing me from here, which removal would be attended with the destruction of this new establishment. Catholics are gathering in from all quarters upon the promise that I made not to forsake them, in as far as I had it in my power to make such a promise. The plantation will hardly be able in two years to maintain a priest, unless there is yearly as much money spent in the improving of it as the congregation's salary amounts to. (Note by Miss Brownson: This means the salary which the congregation would be able to give. Father Gallitzin never received any salary, either from the Bishop or from any of his congregations) Between clearing of land, building and purchasing all the necessary furniture of the church, the house and the place, I have sunk in about sixteen months almost £400, though I could not accuse myself of a great many useless expenses.

TO THE SAME.

February 4, 1805.

I am now in Aughwick Settlement, about seventy miles from home, traveling in a sleigh, or rather sled, from one valley into another, until I go through all the different congregations under my jurisdiction. The winter is so severe, the snow so deep, that a great portion of the congregation, particularly poor people not sufficiently provided with clothing, could not attend. Out of several hundred communicants that never miss their Easter or Christmas communion, I had only about sixty of these last holidays. I hope, if your lordship will assist me, that the church property here shall, in a few years, exceed any other church property in this State.

TO THE SAME.

May 11, 1807.

I am on the point of starting for Greensburg; whilst my horse is eating his feed, I cannot forbear giving myself the satisfaction of writing a few lines to your lordship. I feel very curious to know what is going on at Greensburg; I doubt very foul and dirty work. However, I shall know better to-morrow evening. . . . The greatest satisfaction to me is that I am completely innocent in all those cases in which I am accused, as far as I have been informed of the accusations. Another satisfaction is that not one person in the whole congregation, except a handful of the vilest blackguards, believes any of the accusations. No, my very Protestant neighbors have shown as much indignation at the base, malicious, and foul steps that are taking, as some of the most zealous Catholics; they have offered their signatures to the within instrument which the trustees and congregation thought fit to send to your lordship. I thanked them very kindly for their offers, but I did not think proper to insert their names, wishing to confine myself to my own congregation. . . . Another satisfaction is the increase of the Church amidst these persecutions; three of my Protestant neighbors have come forward since Easter and solemnly abjured heresy and made profession of Catholic faith, and there are more coming.

TO THE SAME.

May 11, 1807.

—— and —— and some more, being partly through my fault, disappointed of getting the offices of the county, are from disappointed ambition raised to the highest pitch of anger; and some of them have declared, if they get no satisfaction from your lordship, they will try the civil law, and if that won't do, they will try something else.

P. S.—I shall be back from Greensburg in about two weeks; if I find certain charges to be true I shall hardly leave Westmoreland County before I enter suits against —— and ——. Such men are not afraid of spiritual punishments, and, therefore, ought to be handled more roughly.

TO THE SAME.

LORETTO, June 20, 1807.

Since I came home I found my enemies here in the utmost consternation. We now enjoy perfect peace and quietness; not a loud word is to be heard; all their plots (they find) are defeated and turned against themselves; every one tries to clear himself and blames his neighbor for leading him astray. Some have sold their places and are gone: others are in the way of selling; and in a short time, thanks be to God's mercies, our settlement will get rid of the most corrupted set of villains that ever disgraced the Church; who were endeavoring to engross into their own hands all the most important offices of our new county, from which calamity, however, my persevering endeavors have fortunately delivered our poor country. This it was that drew the whole weight of their anger and revenge upon my head, and caused one of the blackest conspiracies to be instituted against me which human malice, assisted by the power of hell, could devise. God be praised, the storm has subsided, peace is restoring fast, and all the county offices will, in a short time, be filled with the most respectable characters of the settlement; the ecclesiastical and civil authorities will then go hand in hand and mutually assist each other in promoting the public welfare and happiness. Amen.

TO THE SAME.

LORETTO, July 27, 1807.

It is with the greatest pleasure I comply with Mr. ——'s request of sending your lordship the enclosed act of retraction, which was also, at his request, read in church last Sunday week.

—— 'S RETRACTION.

July 18, 1807.

My Dear and Rev'd Sir:

The horror which I feel in the heinous crimes committed against your innocent character and the faults of my unsuspected heart, demand of me to humble myself before you and the congregation. First, I sincerely ask your pardon and pardon from the congregation in general: of my lord, the Bishop of Baltimore, I ask pardon, and of an injured and offended God I implore forgiveness and pardon. I am sincerely sorry from my heart for the many scandals I have committed by keeping bad company, and suffering myself to be deluded in believing the most abominable lies against your innocence, and in joining in plots against your reverence, and being made the messenger of so many contaminated lies to my lord, the Bishop of Baltimore.

I also feel sorry for breaking the laws of the Church by leaving you, my immediate pastor, to go to be married out of your parish. I do sincerely acknowledge the gratitude I received from Almighty God in opening my eyes and discovering the falsity of those infamous accusations alleged against your reverence. Though unworthy of the least favor from you, from man, or from an injured God, I do solemnly declare, in the presence of the congregation, future obedience and submission, with a determination of shunning all evil company, particularly those who have so basely betrayed me; and, if required, I am willing to elucidate both their wicked proceedings and their names before the congregation. As to temporal punishment, I will, with cheerfulness, submit to your reverence. I am willing to submit my bare back to flagellation publicly, in the church, by your trustees, for I consider no punishment too good to be inflicted on me, the most unworthy of sinners.

N. B.—With my permission you may publish this. I am sorry it is out of my power to come to church. I am called upon to go to Somerset: on my return I will humbly submit to the chastisements herein mentioned.

TO THE SAME.

LORETTO, September, 1807.

I have been wonderfully low this great while, and begin seriously to apprehend that my days will not be very long. I can better feel than describe the gloomy and melancholy state of my mind, especially since the death of my mother; the remembrance of former times, her tender affection to me, her last dying expressions concerning me, my own solitary situation in the wilds of Allegheny, my sufferings and persecution here, all seem to conspire to overwhelm me with sorrow and melancholy. Oh, my dear Lord! For God's sake send me a companion; a priest to help and assist me, for my heart is ready to break. If you have one that does not even know one word of English, only for my comfort and consolation, a good, virtuous clergyman, a friend to help me to bear the burden.

Your lordship has heard how much I have had to suffer from a restless set of unprincipled ruffians. You know that I have sued the ringleaders of the conspiracy against me. God knows my intention was not to hurt them ; no, I wish to return good for evil. My intention was only to frighten them; to compel them to do justice to my character and to retract those abominable charges of which they know in their conscience I am entirely clear. . . .

I beg for a few words of a speedy answer to be sent (via Greensburg) to the postoffice at Beulah, near Loretto, Cambria County.

TO THE SAME.

LORETTO, December 3, 1807.

I am so exceedingly fatigued after walking since last Monday about fifty miles through rocks and mire after sick people (having lost my riding horse) that I am obliged to confine myself to a very few words. . . . . From what little experience I have it appears to me that total abstinence from spirituous liquors is the only sure way of breaking up a habit of that kind; and *as I never keep any kind of liquor, nor drink anything but water or milk,* I think if he seriously means to leave off the practice of drinking he will have a fine chance of curing himself effectively by living with me.

TO THE SAME.

LORETTO, September 23, 1808.

It is my wish to confine myself within the limits of Cambria County, which alone would be more than sufficient to occupy two clergymen. My best time is past; I am upon the brink of thirty-nine.

I beg of your lordship to tell the clergyman whom you shall pitch upon that he may depend upon a handsome maintenance without being beholden to the congregation for one cent. I wish him to be convinced of the necessity of harmonizing with me in all matters; two clergymen well united, perfectly disinterested, and guided by the sole motive of promoting the glory of God and salvation of souls, may do a great deal in this part of the country. I have now on hand several Protestants and Presbyterians who show a great desire to embrace the Catholic faith.

An experience of several years teaches me that faithful domestics are very seldom to be found. After changing several times I got one whom (on account of her skill, age and experience, and especially her assiduity in frequenting the sacraments of the Church) I thought I might safely depend upon. After keeping her almost five years I had to turn her off, finding her guilty of dissipating my substance to the benefit of her friends and relations.

I am very much afraid of the issue of the next election. (Note.—Father Gallitzin, like Bishop Carroll, was a strong Federalist in his political views.) Our Irishmen are ready to go mad for Snyder, and Charles Kenny, Esq., of West Chester, by his artful and virulent publications in the "Aurora" and in Dickson's Lancaster paper, keeps them up in a state of enthusiasm for Snyder and against sound, genuine principles. Under the signature of Tyrconnell he made an attack upon my political character and principles in order to prevent his countrymen of Cambria and Huntingdon Counties from listening to me. I yesterday sent my reply to be published in "Hamilton's Federal Gazette," of Lancaster.

TO THE SAME.

LORETTO, November 22, 1808.

Whilst I thank Almighty God for your lordship's promotion (to be Archbishop of Baltimore), which adds so much to the lustre and dignity of the American Church, I sincerely lament and regret my own fate in being no longer under the immediate jurisdiction of your lordship, whose paternal affection, prudence and authority have so often afforded most powerful protection against the poisonous shafts of slander and persecution, surrounded as I am by a set of the most corrupted class of Irish, who are as void of religion as they are of honor, and know of no kind of happiness but that of intemperance. . . . . I have still reason to thank God for the increase and propagation of religion in this part of the world; the greater part of my congregation, and even a good many of the Irish, frequent the sacraments and are of edifying principles and conduct. Some Protestants open their eyes; last month I took a whole numerous family of them into the Church; and I dare venture to assert that numbers would follow their example were it not for the bad and scandalous example of our own members. . . . . After spending enormous sums in converting a most frightful forest into a fine plantation, I have met with serious losses by being obliged to depend, in my absence, upon unfaithful domestics. Besides that, I find that the absence of the pastor, even for one Sunday, from the flock, gives a great chance to the wolf to tear the sheep. Instances of the kind have been so frequent here that I never absent myself from home without the greatest uneasiness and anxiety of mind, being almost certain to hear bad news on my return.

TO THE SAME.

PHILADELPHIA, November 29, 1809.

I feel very grateful for the interest which your lordship seems to take in my truly distressful situation. I arrived in the city on the eleventh day of this month, very much fatigued and very much distressed in mind, not knowing how to extricate myself or where to apply for assistance; as I was sensible that I had not that kind of security to offer which would induce even the wealthiest to lend money. I applied to many; all pitied me and lamented my case, but nobody thought himself safe in assisting me. Mr. A. promised help and (without assigning any reason) recalled his promise. Left with only a couple of dollars in my pocket, the remainder of what I had borrowed for traveling expenses, I was thrown into a state of despondency. The shock was so great, the anguish of mind such that I fainted upon Mr. Carrell's floor.

TO ARCHBISHOP MARÉCHAL.

LORETTO, Cambria County, October 28, 1823.

I hope that you have received the letter which I had the honor to write to you in the spring, in which I detailed my reasons for refusing the Bishopric of Detroit. As Your Grace did not reply to it, I took your silence as proof of your approbation. Indeed, if you knew the mission of Loretto you would agree with me that it is one of the most important in the United States, and that it would ruin it and ruin me to remove me from this mission. When I established myself here in 1799 the entire county of Cambria was but an immense forest and almost impenetrable. By force of labor and expense (expenses which already reach to more than forty thousand dollars), I have succeeded, with the help of God, in forming an establishment wholly Catholic, extending over an immense extent of country, which is being rapidly augmented by the annual accession of families who come here from Germany, Switzerland, Ireland, and from different parts of America. Now, to form my establishment, I have been to great expense in establishing the various trades which are the most necessary, so that I have part of my funds in tanneries, etc., etc., and it is impossible to draw them suddenly without ruining many families.

Several years ago I formed a plan for the good of religion, for the success of which I desire to employ all the means at my disposal when the remainder of my debts are paid. It is to form a diocese for the western part of Pennsylvania. What a consolation for me if I might, before I die, see this plan carried out, and Loretto made an Episcopal See, where the Bishop, by means of the lands attached to the bishopric, which are very fertile, would be independent, and where, with very little expense, could be erected college, seminary and all that is required for an Episcopal establishment.

Permit me to add that no Bishop has ever penetrated to the distant missions of Western Pennsylvania. Archbishop Carroll was on his way in 1802, but frightened by the horrible description they gave him at Chambersburg of the mountains, the roads, etc., he retraced his steps. Bishop Egan penetrated as far as Pittsburg and the neighboring congregations, but went no further. Bishop Conwell has not done so much. There are, then, many missions which have never seen a Bishop, and never will, at least not until a Bishop is

REV. MATTHEW W. GIBSON. ASSISTANT 1841-44.

established on the mountains, and one willing to fulfill the duties of his charge, even at his own expense, without waiting for other recompense than that which comes from above. I hope that my experience of more than twenty years on these missions will be a guarantee to you that I speak with knowledge of the subject, and that I am animated with the sincere desire of advancing God's work.

TO REV. FATHER HEYDEN.

LORETTO, December 3, 1827.

I really did not know him (Bishop Conwell, of Philadelphia), he was so close to me. After getting his blessing he took me away to the Archbishop's, and told me on the road that he had nominated me as coadjutor, and had written or was going to write to Rome on the subject. I told him I hoped not. The Archbishop and the Bishop seem to be united in their desire to see me appointed.

TO THE SAME.

December 13, 1828.

From all mendicant friars, Oh, Lord! deliver us. I have always revered the holy institutions of St. Francis, whether Capuchins or Franciscans, but an observation of many years has convinced me that if you take a member of these sacred institutions out of his monastery and put him on a mission, you take the fish out of the water and put him on dry land to perish. This I believe admits of very few exceptions. Freed from their vow of poverty they become most raving mad for money.

TO VERY REV. WM. MATTHEWS.

December 13, 1828.

I just now read a letter which your reverence wrote to Rev. Mr. McGirr, in which you state that you have appointed Very Rev. Mr. Maguire to take cognizance of and to pronounce upon the subject of certain accusations against the said Rev. Mr. McGirr. This is tantamount to a suspension.

If Bishop Carroll, that almost perfect man, had proceeded in the same manner in my case in 1807, there can be no doubt that I should have been suspended: the accusations against me were more grievous than those against Mr. McGirr, and also supported by an old clergyman; the messenger selected was E. J. ——, Esq., prothonotary of our county. Bishop Carroll, having read the deposition and certificate. turned about and said: "Sir, I am very sorry for one thing." "What is that, my Lord?" "Why, to find your name on this infamous paper. And now, sir, clear yourself immediately from my presence; go home and give satisfaction to your pastor."

This I have from Mr. J—— himself, whose testimony in such a case cannot be suspected, and who accordingly came on the following Sunday to the church, and at the foot of the altar, before the whole congregation, acknowledged and deplored his guilt in calumniating me; which example was followed by several more of them. Thus ended my business, and thus, I contend, ought Rev. Mr. McGirr's business to end.

It is shocking to both Catholics and Protestants (and you must know, Very Reverend Sir, that Rev. Mr. McGirr, a gray-haired gentleman, is much respected by all the respectable characters of both parties), it is shocking then, I say, to hear that impious Free Mason, Mr. K——, who is no Catholic (no matter what signs of Catholicity he may have exhibited at Washington), to hear him relate with how much respect he was received by you; to see him made, by your reverence, the bearer of your letter to Mr. McGirr, and to hear him exult in his victory.

. . . . Would you be willing, after the lapse of so many years, even to listen to such stuff, or to permit the character and livelihood of a clergyman to have to depend on such untimely testimony? When our worthy Bishop appointed me Vicar-General over the districts of the Rev. Messrs. McGirr, O'Neill, Heyden and O'Reilly, he particularly recommended me to be like a father to them.

I had reason to suppose that my age, my thirty-three years' residence on this mountain, and my thorough acquaintance with persons and circumstances, would give my recommendation some weight. Alas! I find myself mistaken; and while on the one hand an impious man, breathing spite and revenge, brags of your respectful attention, I have to acknowledge that no attention whatever is paid to my letter.

TO BISHOP KENRICK, COADJUTOR OF PHILADELPHIA.

LORETTO, May 22, 1830.

Whenever it is made manifest to me that you are my Bishop I shall cheerfully acquiesce and sincerely thank Divine Providence, which, in its kindness has relieved me from all apprehension of ever becoming Bishop of Philadelphia. Both the late Archbishop (a very particular friend of mine) and our own present Bishop (Conwell) spoke to me in Baltimore, November, 1827, and begged of me to suffer my name to be mentioned at Rome for the coadjutorship of Philadelphia. I at first opposed it, and if I finally concluded to remain neutral, it was merely with the view of availing myself of the chance I might derive from such a nomination, to obtain from Rome a division of this immense diocese, and to have this place, which is the center of a large Catholic settlement, raised to the dignity of an Episcopal See, for I always dreaded the idea of being Bishop of Philadelphia.

. . . . I have stood by him (Bishop Conwell), and the most of his clergy have stood by him. We considered him as an injured and persecuted man; it was not enough that he was spat upon and dirt thrown at him in the streets of Philadelphia, which he bore with the utmost meekness. I have spent thirty-five years in this mission, and I can safely declare that during the seven or eight years of Dr. Conwell's administration religion has made more rapid strides than it had during the twenty-six or twenty-seven preceding years.

. . . . At any rate, giving confirmation now would be premature. I wish to have at least the month (of June) to prepare my immense congregation for so great a blessing, of which as many as one hundred will partake, and which cannot be reiterated. For this extensive congregation, the members of which have almost exclusively to earn their living by hard labor, the very best time for confirmation would be after harvest, say at the end of September or the beginning of October. In the eastern part of the diocese, where the congregations are chiefly confined to towns, any time will do.

TO REV. FATHER HEYDEN.

LORETTO, August 27, 1831.

I met the Bishop (Kenrick) in Ebensburg; he arrived on the 18th, at 2 o'clock, and left next day at 7, without being able to promise positively to return the same way. Whilst at Ebensburg he received four letters from Philadelphia, which seemed to agitate his mind considerably. From what I can learn it is not the trustees alone that give him trouble. . . . . Poor Bishop! Had he known whilst in Kentucky all that was before him he would have paused awhile before he consented to accept of the mitre. Oh, my friend! How much reason I have to thank God.

TO THE SAME.

LORETTO, January 24, 1838.

In consequence of your promise to render me any office of friendship in your power, I beg of you, my dear friend, to reject as a temptation the wish to see me appointed to an Episcopal See. Could I even deceive myself so far as to suppose (which God forbid) that I really possess the necessary qualifications, my age (I am, since December 22nd, in my 68th year) and my inability to travel are insuperable objections to the discharge of Episcopal functions. The only object of my ambition is to give the finishing stroke to my undertaking in this flourishing Catholic establishment, by building a large and permanent church as soon as a favorable change of times will justify so costly an undertaking. This being accomplished, I shall then (if I live to see it accomplished) consider it my duty to resign my trust into my Bishop's hands, to enable him to transfer it into better hands.

PETITION.

To the Honorable the Senate and House of Representatives of the Commonwealth of Pennsylvania, in General Assembly met:

The petition of your very humble servant respectfully sheweth:

That your humble petitioner, Demetrius Augustine, Prince of Gallitzin, having come to the United States about seventeen years ago, solely with the intention of improving himself by traveling, and having, in obedience to the dictates of his parents, adopted the name of Augustine Smith, as they conceived that his name or title would or might expose him when traveling through this or other parts of the world to very considerable and useless expense. Your humble petitioner, having afterwards abandoned the idea of returning to his own country, and having, under his adopted name, Augustine Smith, by naturalization, become a citizen of the United States; finding, moreover, that his real name is known to a great many, which obliges him to make use of it on many occasions, and fearing that inconveniences, or, at least, trouble and uneasiness might arise to himself or others after him, with regard to the holding of real property or conveying of the same, etc., he, therefore, prays that your honorable body may enact a law to establish his name, Demetrius Augustine Gallitzin, so that he may, under that name, enjoy the same benefits and privileges to which he became entitled, by naturalization, under the name of Augustine Smith; and your humble petitioner, as in duty bound, will ever pray, etc.

DEMETRIUS AUGUSTINE (SMITH) GALLITZIN.
December 5, 1809.

This was referred, on the 16th, to a committee composed of Mr. McSherry, Mr. Bethel and Mr. Weiss, and an act was passed in compliance with the requests contained in it.

CAPTAIN M'GUIRE'S COMPANY.

In the late summer of 1814 word reached the remote districts of Pennsylvania that the British troops were advancing on Washington; the President (Madison) appointed a day of fasting and prayer; enlistments were made in haste, and the citizen soldiers hurried to the defence of the National Capital, arriving rather late in the day, however, for the English had already leisurely entered Washington, burnt, pillaged, and as leisurely left it.

Among those who hastened to the country's defence on this occasion was Richard, son of Captain Michael McGuire, who raised a company of volunteers, in which he was ably assisted by Father Gallitzin, whose soldier nature had long outstripped his Federal politics. Nothing could be more touching than the departure of this little band from Loretto. After mass, at which each member received Communion, they were drawn up in front of the church, their banner blessed with the greatest solemnity, a parting blessing given with an exhortation to courage, to faithful devotion to God and their country, fresh from the heart of the soldier priest who bade farewell to each as to a beloved son.

Sometime afterwards two members of Captain Richard's company returned home without permission, and on the following Sunday morning held forth to the usual crowd around the church, telling of their marvelous adventures by field and flood, and making themselves the heroes of the hour, in spite of the shadow of uncertainty concerning the propriety of their unexpected reappearance. They enjoyed the wonder, the attention of their audience until Father Gallitzin appearing at the door of his cabin, the usual hush of respect and expectancy took place, while they watched him coming brightly, cheerily and stately as ever along the path to the church. Then it was that one of the travelers, concealing all embarrassment under an appearance of heartiness, went forward with outstretched hand to receive the expected "welcome home." But Father Gallitzin's slender hand kept its place clasped behind his back, and the dark eyes raised to the face before him expressed surprise but no welcome. "I never shake hands with one who deserts his post," he said quietly, and passed on. The rebuke was so pointed that the deserters, from self-constituted heroes, became objects of pity and commiseration.

HIS LIFE IN PERIL.

It was during this time of real persecution (1806-07) that his enemies, their ranks recruited by two or three, worse even than themselves, wild "border ruffians," who, attracted by the mischief gathering there, had drifted to the frontiers of his parish to be on hand, ready for any wickedness that could be devised, forced their way, armed with clubs, into the church to tear him, as they had threatened, from the altar if he made the first attempt to say mass. It was a terrible day, and a really awful hush fell upon the people as with ringing step, and head erect, and keen, searching gaze, he passed up the aisle and on to the little stand where the vestments were laid out. All knew what was intended; all more than half expected to see him murdered before their very eyes, while they looked on as if in a spell; for although his friends were many and strong they were cowed, as the orderly and quiet majority too often is, by the swearing, swaggering few.

Being vested he came out before the altar and said: "I now proceed to offer up the Holy Sacrifice of the mass. Let no one dare to profane this church, or insult the Christ here present by one word or movement. And I tell you this," advancing one step more and speaking in a voice of consecrated power, "and I tell you this, if any man raises hand or foot to take me from the altar, or to interrupt my words this day, another day shall come when he will call for me and I will not be there." Mass went on without interruption, and never again did anyone dare to repeat the attempt to prevent it.

His words were never forgotten, and of those who then or later publicly defied him, *not one received the last consolations of religion;* although in one case, at least, that of a man suddenly injured, almost superhuman efforts were made by the priest sent for to reach him while life remained. But it was not to be: no human effort of religious zeal or Christian charity was permitted to over-ride the decree of the Almighty.

One more effort had to be made by his enemies to get him out of the way. The appeal to Bishop Carroll had failed so ignominiously that any satisfaction from the ecclesiastical authorities was out of the question; and recourse to the civil law was no less hopeless, for they were already under its ban. There was but one means left, brute force, and to that they now resorted.

Father Gallitzin's house and church were then in a completely isolated site, far out of reach of ready assistance. A party, therefore, thought well to call upon him in his lonely residence, and to demand accession to their wishes, with no idea of limiting themselves to mere words if he refused. After opposing and defying them, and scorning to enter into any thought of compromise with them, he in an almost exhausted condition succeeded in reaching the church, to die at the altar should they dare to attack him in the house of God. No one knows what might have happened if the noise of the tumult had not attracted the attention of one John Weakland, who happened to be passing near, and brought him upon the scene. John was truly a remarkable character. He was the tallest and stoutest man within a radius of one hundred miles. It was mere amusement for him to capture a wolf with his bare hands, or to overpower the fiercest denizen of the forest armed only with a branch torn from the nearest tree. Withal he was inclined to peace, but roused by the peril of his beloved pastor, whom he had accompanied from Maryland to the mountains, he snatched up a fence rail, and his sudden appearance in the church caused the sacrilegious rioters to quickly disperse.

THE END.

The severe mountain winter of 1839–40 was still lingering in excessive cold, and the roads were fast assuming their spring form of snow, mud and melting ice, when Lent with its multiplied duties and the increasing sick calls of the unhealthy season, came to exhaust Father Gallitzin's failing strength. The trouble resulting from a fall from his horse, when, returning from a sick call one night, years before, and which had prevented his ever riding again, now assumed a very serious form, always painful, and at times excruciatingly so. He went through all the services of Holy Week, and heard confessions for half a day at a time, at what cost can never be told. Early Easter morning he was in the confessional again, but was so exhausted by ten o'clock that he could only say a low mass, and give a short exhortation on the Resurrection, which he ended with the words spoken on the cross: *It is consummated.* They were his last to his congregation. He then sought his bed, from which he arose only to a life of eternal glory.

The news of his fatal illness spread rapidly and his faithful flock was filled with consternation. The nearest priests, Father Lemke from St. Joseph's, Father Bradley from Newry, and Father Heyden from Bedford, were hastily summoned, and were with him at the end. "My will," he said, "is made. I trust as far as that is concerned I can depart in peace, that no one will lose anything through me, that there may even be something over. Now, I wish first of all to receive the last Sacraments, and then do with me as you will." As soon as midnight had passed Father Lemke said mass in the sick room, all the household being present, and gave him Holy Communion.

So he lay there resting until the evening of the 6th of May, between six and seven o'clock. When the hour came for the laborers to go home from their work, they saw that he was going also. Father Heyden read the prayers for the dying, the room door was opened, the crowd in the house and adjoining chapel prayed with tears and sobs. In a few minutes, without any perceptible sign, all was over; the heavens were open, all their joy-bells were ringing a welcome peal; he had gone home to his own country.

The funeral was set for Saturday, May 9th. By that time, notwithstanding the bad roads and the fact that no invitations or public announcement were given, the entire population for fifty miles around had gathered in Loretto. It was but a few steps from the chapel to the church, and the only direction in regard to the funeral which Father Gallitzin himself had given, was that he might be laid between the two, where he had passed a thousand times from his house to the altar, and where his children gone before would be around him. But as so many contended for the honor of bearing him to the church, and then to his last resting place, it was decided that the procession should pass through the village and back to the church. Although the route extended nearly a mile, and the pall-bearers were exchanged every few minutes, many had not been able to enjoy the coveted distinction by the time the procession reached the church. The mass was sung by Father Heyden, assisted by Fathers McGirr, Lemke and Rattigan. Father Heyden preached a funeral sermon in English from the text: *The just shall live in everlasting remembrance;* and Father Lemke made some remarks in German, taking as his text: *Of whom the world was not worthy: wandering in deserts, in mountains, and in dens, and in caves of the earth.* The people were forced from the coffin and the lid closed. It was placed in one of zinc, and amid heartrending wails lowered into the earth, midway between the church and the chapel.

In his will Father Gallitzin directed that his debts and funeral expenses should be paid as soon after his decease as possible. He left the farm upon which St. Michael's Church was built, and the lands belonging to it, to the Bishop of Philadelphia, or to his successors who might be appointed to the Western Diocese of Pennsylvania, and his successors, in trust forever for the support and use of the Roman Catholic clergy duly appointed to officiate at St. Michael's Church; also to the same a square of six lots in the town of Loretto, upon which to erect a new church. The remainder of his estate was to be appropriated for the relief of poor widows and orphans; for masses for the faithful departed; to aid in the erection of a Catholic Church in Loretto upon the lots mentioned, and for legacies to several persons who had been brought up in his house.

The little furniture his house contained was eagerly bought by his parishioners, who cherish with pride and affection, and transmit as a sacred inheritance to their children, the least thing that had once been his.

It seems strange to us at this late day that his last wishes in some respects were so utterly disregarded. It was his desire that his mortal remains should be interred in the midst of those of his flock who had gone before him, but seven years after his demise they were lifted and moved to a considerable distance from the spot from which he had hoped to be summoned to judgment. The six lots that he had set aside for the location of the new church in the borough of Loretto were otherwise disposed of, and the church eventually built in the township. Of the hundreds of acres bequeathed for the resident clergy, not two score yet remain to serve the original purpose. Of his bequest "to aid in the erection of a Catholic Church in Loretto upon the lots mentioned" there is an account in the church books of only $192.36.

THE TOMB.

In pursuance of the plan to beautify the tomb of the illustrious pioneer missionary of the Alleghenies, Rev. Ferdinand Kittell, the present pastor of the Loretto congregation, thought well to commence with the coffin which held his venerated remains. It was known that the coffin was in an advanced state of decay, for even the zinc casing had rusted

THE TOMB OF FATHER GALLITZIN.   ERECTED 1847.

away, and there was reason to fear lest in a short time the frail tenement would collapse; in which event the mortal remains of the sainted Gallitzin would fall to the ground beneath. Accordingly, having procured a metallic air-tight casket, the Reverend pastor fixed on Monday, July 20, 1891, as the date for the solemn transfer of the remains. They were carried with appropriate religious ceremonies from the vault, where they had rested for more than forty years, into the sanctuary of the church. When the zinc casing was removed it was found that the lid and sides of the coffin were almost entirely decayed. Nearly all the bones had crumbled into dust, but the skull was found to be almost perfect. The wooden chalice which had been placed in his hands still preserved its form, but would not bear much handling. A piece of the lining of the chasuble, the ribbons that bound it around the body and the soles of the shoes were found to be still intact. All the rest was a mass of human dust commingled with the decayed wood and lining of the coffin. And this was all that remained of one who might have been among the first in the government of an empire, if God had not called him to be the Apostle of the Alleghenies.

The bottom of the coffin, being in a reasonably good state of preservation, was tenderly lifted, and with its precious freight carefully deposited in the new casket, which was then borne back to the vault.

The following persons assisted at the solemn ceremony: The pastor, Rev. Ferdinand Kittell; Rev. J. C. Bigham, of New Brighton; Rev. P. May, of Mt. Pleasant; Rev. M. M. Sheedy, of Pittsburg; Messrs. Adam Rudolph, W. A. B. Little, Philip J. Sanders, members of the Church Committee; Sebastian Fry, undertaker; Messrs. Eugene and Bernard W. Litzinger; and Augustine Conrad, sexton.

Every summer since then the vault has been a place of pilgrimage. But it is to be regretted that relic-hunters, abusing the privilege of access to the vault, have defaced the casket by unscrewing and deliberately carrying away the silver-plated knobs that ornamented it.

MISSION AT LORETTO, 1851.

During the pastorate of Rev. Hugh P. Gallagher, the first Mission in the Diocese of Pittsburg was given in the old frame church at Loretto in the year 1851. One of the most interesting periods of the Catholic Church in Cambria County was the time of this Mission, which commenced on Low Sunday and closed on the third Sunday after Easter. The priests who conducted the Mission were Rev. Fathers Alexander, Hecker, Walworth and Hewitt, all converts to the Catholic faith. This flourishing and important Catholic settlement, in which so much zeal was manifested, and such noble sacrifices made by the illustrious Father Gallitzin, was thus singularly favored in having such a rare opportunity of reviving the spirit of religion. Here were witnessed scenes of such edification and spiritual fruit as must have vividly recalled to mind the fervor of primitive times, and those halcyon days of the Church when the multitude of believers had but one heart and one soul.

From early dawn until far into the shades of night Father Alexander occupied the confessional, and, making himself the servant of all, he dispensed comfort and peace to his many penitents. With the other Rev. Fathers assisting, many an inveterate prodigal, and many a seemingly lost one, were gathered in and reconciled. The instructive and practical part of piety fell principally to the lot of Father Hecker, and ably, day after day and night after night, did he discharge his task. On the evening of the last day of the Mission the ceremony of the planting of the Cross took place to perpetuate the remembrance of the happy event. The Cross was fifty feet in height, and was decorated with evergreens from top to bottom. A grand procession, consisting of some thousands of both sexes, followed by the Franciscan Brothers, religious societies, acolytes, local clergy, pastors of neighboring congregations and the Missionary fathers, was formed at the church. The Cross was borne by sixty hardy men of the congregation, and escorted by the Cambria Volunteers, who had signalized themselves by their valor in the Mexican War, and who now, by their presence and admirable discipline, contributed to the splendor of religion. For about three-quarters of a mile the great cortege was spread, and it ceased not to maintain the most perfect order and discipline while marching to the place appointed, which was in front of the new brick church, then in course of erection, and of the monument erected but a few years previously to the memory of the venerable Gallitzin. The pulpit used during the Mission had been carried by the multitude to the same spot, and ascending it Father Walworth addressed the vast attentive crowd. More than three thousand people responded with sobs and tears to the spirit stirring appeal of the Rev. Father: and after the sermon the Papal Benediction was imparted to the prostrate multitude. When the Cross had been blessed the joyful and happy people planted it in its destined place, amid volleys from the soldiers; and the crowd gradually dispersed, each one seeming to say to his neighbor: "It is good for us to be here."

It is here worthy of remark that among the many articles placed in the corner stone of St. Paul's Cathedral, Pittsburg, laid on Sunday, June 15, 1851, by the Rt. Rev. Michael O'Connor, D. D., the then Bishop, was a copy of the latest issue of The Pittsburg Catholic, which contained a complete account of the great Mission described above.

MONSIGNOR BEDINI, THE NUNZIO TO BRAZIL, IN CAMBRIA COUNTY.

On the evening of Tuesday, December 6, 1853, Monsignor Bedini arrived in Hollidaysburg from the east. Rt. Rev. Bishop Michael O'Connor met him there and accompanied him in his tour through the diocese. The Nunzio spoke in Italian, and his words were interpreted as expressing much gratification at the reception given him, and great delight at finding such a truly Catholic spirit everywhere in this country.

On the next day, after solemn exercises in St. Mary's Church, Hollidaysburg, and an eloquent sermon by Rev. E. A. Garland, the Nunzio was conducted in a large procession to Newry, where ceremonies similar to those in Hollidaysburg took place, and a sermon was preached by Bishop O'Connor.

About six o'clock the same evening the Nunzio, with his cortege, arrived at the Summit. There the church was beautifully decorated in a style that evinced the correct taste and Catholic feeling of the congregation. But the next day, Thursday, Feast of the Immaculate Conception of the Blessed Virgin, was the "Great Day" on the mountain; a day which is yet remembered by old parishioners as one of immense joy and special benediction. From an early hour multitudes came pouring in from all directions. The spacious church at the Summit was crowded to its utmost capacity, and thousands were compelled to remain outside. The Irish laborers on the Pennsylvania Central and Portage Railroads had turned out in great numbers, and with their green sashes and military bearing elicited the admiration of all. Bishop O'Connor preached an eloquent and forcible sermon on the perpetuity of the Church, and how it depended upon the unity and supremacy of the Holy See of Rome.

Under the direction of Captain William Ivory, as chief marshal, assisted by P. Clarke, A. Kelly, J. Collins and others as aids, a long and imposing procession moved along the pike westward towards Munster. In no part of the United States was Monsignor Bedini greeted with a more cordial welcome than that which he received in this truly Catholic locality. This immense crowd, of all ages and classes, principally from Loretto and Summit congregations, but largely represented by the Loop (St. Augustine), Chest Springs, Carrolltown and other neighboring towns and adjacent country, and swelled into unusual dimensions by a large force of laborers on the railroad, assembled to welcome to their mountain home the distinguished prelate who came to represent the Vicar of Christ. The procession, marching by way of Munster and what is now Kaylor, was met at the upper end of Loretto by a strong body of horsemen from the Loop.

At Loretto the reception to the Nunzio was as imposing as it was unmistakably Catholic. A large body of the congregation, with music resounding and banners flying, met him on the hill at the north end of town, while about fifty of the Germans, nearly all of venerable age, with Philip Hertzog in the lead, rendered the "Grosser Gott" in magnificent style. The procession divided near the church to allow the

Nunzio and his cortege to pass through. The address prepared in the name of the Catholics of Cambria was here delivered by Mr. Thos. Collins, the gentleman who represented the county in the Legislature of the State. Very Rev. Father Heyden preached the sermon. The Loretto demonstration in honor of the representative of our Holy Father was most imposing and is talked of to this day.

On the following morning the Nunzio visited Ebensburg, and in the afternoon the clergy of the mountain district accompanied him to Jefferson (now Wilmore), where he took the train for Pittsburg. During his entire trip through Cambria County, though it was made in the usually rough month of December, the weather was most beautiful.

DEDICATION OF THE BRICK CHURCH.

The ceremonies took place on the Feast of the Epiphany, January 6, 1854, the Rt. Rev. Dr. Neuman, Bishop of Philadelphia, officiating on the occasion. After the dedication a Solemn Pontifical Mass was celebrated by Bishop Neuman, assisted by Revs. H. P. Gallagher, M. Corbett and J. O'Farrell. The pastors of the churches in Altoona, Hollidaysburg, Carrolltown, Summit and Johnstown were present in the sanctuary and assisted in the ceremonies. Dr. Moriarity, of Philadelphia, who had been announced to preach the dedication sermon, was prevented by serious indisposition from fulfilling his engagement. His place was filled by Rev. Thomas McCullagh, and Rev. Utho Huber, O. S. B., preached in German.

The two former parish churches, log and frame, had borne the name of St. Michael, under whose protection the parish had been placed by its holy founder, Father Gallitzin, in 1799; and it was strange that the new parish church should have been placed under a different invocation, that of St. Mary. Soon after he assumed charge of the parish in 1870 the Rev. Father Bush very properly restored the rightful title.

REV. HUGH P. GALLAGHER. PASTOR 1844-52.

ST. MICHAEL'S CHURCH, LORETTO, PA., AND TOMB OF FATHER GALLITZIN. 1899.

SINKING OF THE CHURCH FLOOR.

When the present brick church was built (1850-53), an excavated basement was considered unnecessary. It was before the days of hot air, steam or hot water apparatus, and the churches, when heated at all, were heated by stoves set in the aisles or against the side walls. Hence in building the present Church of St. Michael, the joists supporting the floor rested but a short distance above the ground, and as little or no provision was made by the architect for ventilation, they were soon affected by the dry rot which gradually consumed them. It was only a question of time when the floor was bound to collapse; and so it happened during high mass on Sunday, May 13, 1866. A regular panic took possession of the people who filled the church. Many were trampled nearly to death in the excited crowd rushing for the front and sacristy doors. Some even broke out the window glass to make their escape more quickly. Believing that the entire church was collapsing, Rev. Father Reynolds, the pastor, who was celebrating mass, hastily left the altar; but learning the nature of the catastrophe, and knowing its cause, he immediately returned and quickly restored order. Those who had fled to the outside now returned and mass was continued. Had the people reflected for an instant they might have known that nothing serious could have occurred; for on the north side, at any rate, where the panic was greatest, the floor could not have sunk more than a few inches before resting on solid ground.

To add to the confusion, just as mass was ended a most violent wind and rain storm burst forth with remarkable fury; and many, whose nerves were already excited by the experience just gone through, imagined that the church was about to fall. At both masses on this day a collection was taken up for Rev. Pollard McCormick Morgan, the assistant priest of the parish, who, on the following morning, was to start on a trip to Europe.

PASTORS AND ASSISTANTS SINCE 1840.

After the death of Father Gallitzin, on May 6, 1840, Rev. Thomas Heyden was appointed pastor of St. Michael's; but not wishing to be separated from his congregation at Bedford to which he was much attached, he declined the appointment. He afterwards regretted this step, for by that means Father Gallitzin's letters and papers, which were of the greatest literary and historical, as well as personal, value, were suffered to become scattered and lost. Father Peter Henry Lemke was then appointed, and he continued as pastor until September, 1844, residing principally at Carrolltown, and giving the pastoral residence at Loretto over to the assistants for the time being. His assistants were Rev. Matthew William Gibson, Andrew P. Gibbs and Thomas B. O'Flaherty.

Rev. Hugh Patrick Gallagher became pastor September 27, 1844, and remained until 1852. During his pastorate the first foundation of the Franciscan Brothers in the United States was established at Loretto; a branch House of the Sisters of Mercy, whose first foundation in the United States had been established a few years previously in Pittsburg, was started here with very humble beginnings; the monument of Father Gallitzin was erected; the pew-rent system of supporting the church and pastor introduced; and the new brick church commenced and carried nearly to completion. The corner stone was laid in 1851, in which year also the great Mission was held.

In the congregation at this time, according to Bishop O'Connor's notes, there were 2,500 souls. Although three prosperous congregations have since been organized from the territory then included in the Loretto parish, the population of the latter on August 15th, this year, was 1234. Father Hugh Gallagher's assistants were his brother, familiarly known as "Father Joe," and Rev. N. Haeres.

Rev. Joseph A. Gallagher succeeded to the pastorate in 1852. He completed the new church the following year, and had it dedicated on January 6, 1854. Owing to its hasty construction, and to the further fact that the soft brick were placed in the back wall, the tower, soon after it was completed, fell in on the roof of the church and caused considerable damage. It was rebuilt, but only to within about twenty feet of its original height. It was topped with a spire, which in after years on account of the weakness of the tower, was taken down. The architect was Haden Smith, whose plans were revised by Joseph Null, the foreman of construction. The contractor was Richard Scanlan. The cost of the building was $13,024.10. Father Joseph Gallagher had the honor of entertaining the Nunzio, Monsignor Bedini, during his visit to Loretto in December, 1853. He was assisted by Father Albinus Magno, C. P., one of the little band of Passionist Fathers, who, a short time previously, had established in Pitttburg their first foundation in the United States, and by the Benedictine Fathers of Carrolltown, who regularly for many years afterwards attended to the wants of the Germans of the Loretto parish.

In 1855 Rev. Wm. Pollard became pastor. He added the upper half story to the stone pastoral residence. He was assisted by Revs. John Ford and Francis J. O'Shea.

In November, 1859, Rev. Terence S. Reynolds succeeded to the pastorate. He was assisted by Revs. John Ford, F. J. O'Shea, Pollard McC. Morgan, Edward A. Bush, Andrew J. Brown and Henry McHugh. In the summer of 1868 he was succeeded by

Rev. Michael J. Mitchell, who was assisted by Revs. H. McHugh, Andrew A. Lambing and H. Seymour Bowen.

In the early part of 1870 Rev. Edward A. Bush assumed charge of the parish, and wisely ruled it for full twenty years. From 1854, when the old frame church was abandoned and the new brick one was ready for occupation, the pastors suffered no slight inconvenience in being obliged in all kinds of weather to traverse so frequently the long distance between the pastoral residence and the church. At any rate the former, which eighty years ago was considered a respectable domicile, did not meet the requirements of modern ideas of comfort and convenience; and having more than served its purpose as a residence for the pastors of Loretto, it was fully time to erect a new one. This Father Bush did in 1874, completing the building in 1879. It stands close to the church, and for size, comfort, convenience and furniture, compares favorably with pastoral residences in large city parishes.

Father Bush also made many improvements in and around the church. He had the interior frescoed, steam heating apparatus put in the church, and hot water in the house; the roof of the church was covered with tin, and the cemetery enlarged. His assistants were Revs. H. S. Bowen, Daniel Devlin and Michael F. Foley.

April 18, 1890, Rev. Martin Ryan became pastor, and remained in that capacity until March 8, 1891.

On April 1, 1891, Rev. Ferdinand Kittell, the present pastor, assumed charge of the parish. During his pastorate the old frame church and log barn of Father Gallitzin, being far beyond the possibility of repair, were razed to the ground; the chapel erected in 1832 was rebuilt of practically the same material; the old pastoral residence was repaired, and is again used as a domicile; a tower was built for the church bell, which for many years had rested on trestles on the ground; the Gallitzin monument was repaired, the massive blocks of stone being removed and re-set; the remains of Father Gallitzin were transferred from the original, much decayed coffin to a metallic casket; the front of the church lot was graded and sodded; horse sheds were put up; a two-story frame Parochial Hall, 40x80 feet, was erected at a cost of over $5,000; the space between the pastoral residence and the church built up and occupied; the frame part of the pastoral residence raised to a level with the brick front, etc. For these repairs and improvements, and for current expenses, there has been collected and expended up to September 1st, this year, 1899, the sum of $40,500, and the congregation is practically free from debt.

Father Kittell found the records of Father Gallitzin, from 1800 to a few days before his death in 1840, written on loose sheets and kept in a box. He arranged the sheets in chronological order, and had them bound, together with the records of Father Lemke, in two volumes. He then copied the subsequent entries down to January 1, 1896, and had them also bound. These bound volumes he took with him to Rome in the spring of 1896, and during three months of the summer season which he spent in the ancient monastry of Galloro, on the Alban hills, six miles from the Eternal City, he made up his "*Index of Parish Records, Loretto, Pa. 1800-1896.*" This Index comprises an alphabetical list of 1301 marriages, giving names and surnames of husband and wife, with date of marriage and name of officiating priest in each instance; an alphabetical list of the maiden names and surnames of the married women (1850), which could be found in the records, set opposite the names of their husbands; and finally, an alphabetical list of all those (6949) baptized during the ninety-six years. These are arranged in family groups under the names of the parents, and in each instance are given the number of the entry, the name of the child, the date of birth, and the name of the priest who administered baptism. The labor in making up this Index was herculean, but the result is of the utmost importance; and it is doubtful if any other parish in the country has such a complete and convenient set of baptismal and matrimonial records. The number of families represented in this Index is 2143. The following table will be of interest, as showing the number of some families bearing the same surname, and the number of children baptized in them:

Family Surname.	No. of Families.	No. of Children Baptized.	Family Surname.	No. of Families.	No. of Children Baptized.
Adams	12	57	Litzinger	19	69
Bradley	25	93	McConnell	20	52
Brown	11	28	McCoy	13	61
Burgoon	11	40	McDermitt	12	44
Burke	10	36	McGough	15	66
Byrne	13	57	McGuire	25	114
Christy	12	34	McMullen	17	55
Conrad	13	55	Miller	11	30
Coons (Kuhns)	12	71	Myers	23	94
Dimond	10	43	Nagle	16	56
Dougherty	22	57	Noel	23	98
Eckenrode	23	107	O'Neill	10	33
Flick	10	49	Parrish	12	61
Glass	20	94	Skelly, O'Skally	12	41
Hertzog	10	39	Smith	14	21

Family Surname.	No. of Families.	No. of Children Baptized.	Family Surname.	No. of Families.	No. of Children Baptized.
Hoover (Huber)	11	34	Stevens	11	49
Kane, Kean, Cain.	12	28	Storm	12	64
Kaylor	12	71	Sweeney	10	20
Kelly	10	24	Weakland	14	55
Little	10	63	Will	20	83

During the nine months absence of Father Kittell in Rome in 1896, the parish was in charge of Rev. Patrick J. Hawe.

THE BOROUGH OF LORETTO.

This town was so named by Father Gallitzin after the famous Loreto on the Adriatic coast, Italy. A plan of the town is on file in Vol. I, page 503, Recorder's office, Ebensburg, Pa. It is a neat village, containing three rows of lots, divided by two principal streets, sixty feet wide, running fifty-three degrees east of north. St. Mary's street is at present the main thoroughfare, and it runs parallel to the lower street, St. Joseph's, which was the original highway. Three cross streets, each sixty feet wide, intersect the two named streets at right angles within the plot of the borough. The central row of lots between St. Mary's and St. Joseph's streets contains forty-eight lots, each one hundred and sixty feet in depth. The exterior rows contain the same number of lots, forty-eight, but these are two hundred feet in depth. The first cross street, as one goes north through the town, is named St. John's street, the second, which leads on to St. Francis' College, St. Peter's, and the third, St. Paul's. Half way between the cross streets there is an alley; and an alley also at the rear of each of the exterior rows of lots. The lots are numbered from North to South in each row. Thus the town is divided into twelve squares, of twelve lots each.

The above is according to an old drawing entitled: "A plan of the town of Loretto, in the County of Cambria, and State of Pennsylvania, laid out by the Reverend Demetrius Gallitzin," and is certified to as follows:

"Be it remembered that on the tenth day of May, in the year of our Lord one thousand eight hundred and sixteen, before me, the subscriber, one of the Justices of the Peace in and for said County of Cambria, personally appeared the Rev. D. A. Gallitzin, and acknowledged the within plan of the town of Loretto to be his act and deed, for the end the same may be recorded as such according to law. In testimony whereof I have hereunto set my hand and seal, the day and year aforesaid.

[SEAL] LUKE McGUIRE.

Though laid out in 1816, the town was not incorporated as a borough until 1845.

ACT OF INCORPORATION.
No. 93.

An Act to Incorporate the Village of Loretto, in Cambria County, into a Borough.

SECTION 1. Be it enacted by the Senate and House of Representatives of the Commonwealth of Pennsylvania in General Assembly met, and it is hereby enacted by the authority of the same, That the village of Loretto, in the County of Cambria, shall be and the same is hereby erected into a borough, which shall be called the Borough of Loretto, and shall be bounded and limited as follows, viz: Beginning at a point on the Philipsburg road, six perches north of the widow Walter's house; thence east to a point which includes the church and parsonage of St. Michael's; thence south to a point from which the line running west will include the town lots laying south of St. Mary's street; thence west to a point opposite to the place of beginning; thence north to the place of beginning.

SECTION 2. That the inhabitants of the said borough entitled to vote for members of the general assembly, having resided within the bounds of said borough at least six months immediately preceding the election, shall have power, on the Friday preceding the third Saturday in March next, to meet at the public school house, and on the same day annually thereafter at the place aforesaid, and shall then and there, between the hours of one and six in the afternoon of said day, elect by ballot, one respectable citizen residing therein, who shall be styled the burgess, and five citizens of said borough to be a town council, and shall elect also as aforesaid one citizen as high constable: but previous to said election the citizens qualified as aforesaid shall choose one citizen to act as judge, and two citizens to act as inspectors, one of whom shall act as clerk of said election: and the election to be conducted throughout according to the general election laws of this commonwealth, and the officers of the same shall be subject to the same penalties for malpractice, as by the said election laws are imposed; the said judge and inspectors, before they enter upon the duties of their respective offices, shall take the same oaths or affirmations before any justice of the peace of the same county, as are prescribed by the laws of this commonwealth, and after the election shall be closed shall declare the persons having the greatest number of votes to be duly elected, and the certificates required by the general election laws shall be duly made out and signed by them, and filed amongst the records of said borough.

SECTION 3. That from and after the first day of April next, the burgess and town council, and their successors in office, shall be one body politic and corporate, by the name and style of the "Burgess and Town Council of the Borough of Loretto," and shall have perpetual succession, and shall be capable in law to sue and be sued, plead and be impleaded, in any court of law of this commonwealth in all manner of actions whatsoever, and to have and use a common seal.

SECTION 4. That if any person, duly elected to the office as burgess, member of town council, or high constable as aforesaid, shall refuse or neglect to take upon himself the duties of said office, he shall forfeit and pay for the use of said borough the sum of ten dollars, to be collected in like manner as sums of like amount are now recoverable by law.

SECTION 5. That all officers of said borough, before entering upon the duties of their respective offices, shall take and subscribe before any judge or justice of the peace of said county, to "support the Constitution of the United States, and of the State of Pennsylvania, and to perform the duties of his office with fidelity," and the certificate of the same shall be filed among the records of said corporation.

SECTION 6. That the said burgess and town council shall meet on the first Monday after their election, in each year, and appoint a clerk of said borough, whose duty it shall be to take charge of all the papers, records and common seal of said borough, and be responsible for the same; and shall keep a fair record of all proceedings, resolutions, by-laws and ordinances of said council; and the said burgess and town council shall have power to make, erect, alter, revise, repeal or amend all by-laws, rules, regulations and ordinances as shall be determined by a majority of them, necessary to promote the peace, good order, benefit and advantage of said borough, and particularly providing for the regulations, improving, repairing and keeping in order the streets and alleys. They shall have power to assess and apportion such taxes as shall be determined by a majority of them, and also to appoint a street supervisor, treasurer and such other officers as may be deemed necessary, from time to time: Provided, That in the assessment of taxes, such tax shall not exceed one-half of the tax assessed for county purposes, on the citizens of said borough.

SECTION 7. That the burgess is hereby empowered to issue his precept to the high constable as often as occasion may require, commanding him forthwith to collect all taxes so assessed, and the same to pay over to the treasurer.

SECTION 8. That the treasurer, street supervisor, and high constable, shall, before entering upon the duties of their respective offices, enter into bonds with sufficient sureties, to be approved by the burgess, conditioned for the faithful performance of their duties.

SECTION 9. That the high constable of the said borough, shall, on giving surety and being qualified in the court of quarter sessions of the county, have and exercise all the powers appertaining to the offices of township constable.

FINDLEY PATTERSON,
Speaker of the House of Representatives.
WILLIAM P. WILCOX.
Speaker of the Senate.

Approved—The eighth day of March, one thousand eight hundred and forty-five. FRS. R. SHUNK.

No. 141.

A Supplement to an Act, Entitled "An Act Erecting the Village of Loretto, in the County of Cambria, into a Borough.

SECTION 1. Be it enacted by the Senate and House of Representatives of the Commonwealth of Pennsylvania in General Assembly met, and it is hereby enacted by authority of the same, That the said borough of Loretto shall hereafter be bounded and described as follows: Beginning at a post on the Church farm; thence north thirty-one and one-half degrees, west one hundred and twenty-nine perches; thence north fifty-eight and one-half degrees, east twenty and one-half perches; thence north thirty-one and one-half degrees, west forty-nine perches; thence south eighty-eight and one-half degrees, east thirteen perches; thence north ten perches; thence east seventy-five perches; thence south twenty-three degrees, east one hundred and fifty-one perches; thence north eighty-eight and one-half degrees, west nineteen and one-half perches; thence south fifty-eight and one-half degrees, west sixty-four and one-half perches, to the beginning.

SECTION 2. That so much of the act to which this is a supplement which is hereby altered or supplied, be and the same is hereby repealed. FINDLEY PATTERSON,
Speaker of the House of Representatives.
DANIEL L. SHERWOOD,
Speaker of the Senate.

Approved—The twenty-fourth day of March, one thousand eight hundred and forty-six. FRS. R. SHUNK.

LORETTO NOTES.

In 1830 Loretto contained a population of only seventy-one people; on the 15th of August of the current year, the resident population numbered 209 souls, all Catholics. The number of houses is fifty-nine, of which six are untenanted. There are six stores for general merchandise and one for furniture; one livery stable, one undertaking establishment, one barber shop, two blacksmith shops; and several carpenters and painters, but no butcher or shoemaker within the limits of the town. Within the limits of the parish outside the town there are three stores, as many saw-mills, one grist-mill, and some shoemakers, blacksmiths and other tradesmen, the rest of the people living on farms. The whole population of the parish, which covers an area of about seventy square miles of rough mountain territory, numbers 1234 souls, of whom all, with very few exceptions, are Catholics.

Loretto is situated on a ridge, just six miles from Gallitzin to the east, Ashville to the northeast, Chest Springs to the north, and Ebensburg to the west; five miles from Cresson to the south, and eight miles from Wilmore to the southwest. It is an ideal place of residence, there being no public works in or near the town, and enjoys exceptional advantages. A public hack runs twice a day to and from Cresson, on the main line of the Pennsylvania Central railroad, and on each round trip takes and brings the mail. Just one mile west of the town is Loretto Road station on the Cambria and Clearfield Division of the Pennsylvania railroad.

One of the wonders of the district is "the big pine tree" in the yet unbroken forest, two miles out of town, near the road to Cresson. It has four prongs, which, starting from the trunk, reach to a great height. Its age cannot be calculated.

Three miles east of Loretto, on the road to Gallitzin, stands Sybert's, formerly Dawson's, grist-mill, which is on the site of the old John Sturm mill, the first in the county. Early in the century Father Gallitzin built a grist-mill a short distance below his residence and its ruins were visible until quite recently.

One mile east of Loretto is the site of the once famous "Loretto Springs." At this place there are several springs of excellent water; and sometime prior to 1830, a mill-race had been dug, diverging from the left bank of the creek about half a mile above, and crossing the road now leading to Gallitzin no less than four times, and supplying water to a neat dam which furnished the power for a saw-will a short distance below. The farm on which the mill was erected belonged to Henry J. McGuire, who constructed the race and built the mill and operated it for many years. It was later sold to Mr. Forrester, and still later operated by Mr. Samuel Stoy, and then sold to Mr. William Hurd.

The "Loretto Springs" hotel was famous in its day as a summer resort. The buildings were erected about the year 1857, and were capable of accommodating about 150 guests. The proprietor was Mr. Francis Gibbons. The annual retreat for the diocesan clergy was held here for some years, the last being held in 1872. The place was then sold to Mr. Robert Burdine, and on the third day of May, following, while preparations were being made for the usual influx of city guests, fire broke out and consumed the entire establishment.

The old "Plank Road" between Loretto and Cresson was built and managed by a private company, and supported and kept in repair until abandoned as an unprofitable speculation, by the revenue from a toll-gate located at McManamy's "Half-way House."

For some years the Franciscan Brothers taught the Loretto public school for boys, and the Sisters of Mercy the school for girls. When the new school house was built the Sisters had charge of both boys and girls until 1891, since which time it has been conducted by the following lay-teachers: Mr. Andrew J. Sanker, 1891-93; Prof. R. H. Biter, with Misses Lizzie Sweeney and Tillie Bradley, 1893-96; Prof. J. S. Foley, with Miss Mary Cramer, 1896-97; Prof. A. P. Weakland, with Misses Mary Cramer and Loretto Sargeant, 1897-99; and for the present term (1899-1900), Mr. W. J. Little and Miss Sargeant are employed as teachers.

One of the earliest enterprises of any kind for Loretto was a foundry for the manufacture of all kinds of castings useful in that age and locality. It was erected in the years of 1849-50 by Peter J. Little, a son of Barnabas Little, one of the earliest pioneers of Allegheny Township. Peter J. Little moved from Bedford County and occupied the house formerly owned by Lewis Storm, the first undertaker of Loretto. Mr. Storm was one of the assistants at the last mass said by Rev. D. A. Gallitzin, and was the undertaker who had charge of the mortal remains after his death, May 6, 1840. Shortly after this he was succeeded by Mr. Sebastian Fry, who carried on the undertaking business until the year 1890, when he made it over to Mr. James Biter, who continues to ably conduct it.

The Loretto Hattery, at which were made felt hats of fine quality, worn by almost all the residents, was an enterprise of the town for many years prior to and after the death of Dr. Gallitzin. This business was owned and managed by Mr. John Riffle, who died in 1852, and of whom John, James and George were sons. His establishment was on the corner of St. John's and St. Joseph's streets, on lot No. 37, just opposite the present home of Mrs. Margaret McElheny.

OBITUARY NOTICES.

REV. MATTHEW WILLIAM GIBSON.

Father Matthew William Gibson was born in Hexham, England, in 1817, and received his primary education at Ushaw College in the County of Durham, after which he was sent by Cardinal Wiseman to the Propaganda in Rome, where he remained eight years. In 1832 he came to the United States and was ordained priest in Philadelphia in 1841, by Bishop Kenrick. His first charge was at Loretto, Cambria County, where he acted as assistant to Rev. Lemke, the successor of Father Gallitzin, remained there until he was appointed pastor of St. Bartholomew's Church, Wilmore, in 1842, where he remained for several years. His name is found in the Baptismal and Matrimonial Registers of St. Michael's, Loretto, until 1844. He was next appointed pastor of St. John's Church, Worcester, Mass., and had charge of three other congregations in that vicinity, where he remained eight years and then went to Racine, Wis., where he continued his ministrations during the War of the Rebellion. After the war he returned to England and was appointed by the Bishop of "Hexham and New Castle," pastor of Monkwearmouth, in Sunderland, where he built a large stone church. After some years he was appointed Chaplain of Callaly Castle, Northumberland, where he remained about four years. Returning to this country he took charge of the congregation at Beverly, N. J.

In the latter end of March, 1888, he went to Ebensburg, Cambria County, Pa., where he intended to live the remainder of his days, his health having become much impaired. He had been a great traveler, having crossed the ocean seventeen times, and had traveled through Ireland, Scotland, Prussia, Belgium, Switzerland and France.

Father Gibson was a highly educated man and spent an active and busy live in ministering to the spiritual wants of the various congregations in this country and in England committed to his charge. He was a sincere and zealous priest and was loved and respected by all who knew him.

He died at the residence of his niece, Mrs. J. A. Shoemaker, in Ebensburg, Pa., June 9, 1888, in the 72nd year of his age.

MEMORANDA OF REV. M. W. GIBSON.

(Copied from a paper in his own hand writing).

I am the priest who said the first mass in Fitchburg, Mass. I was appointed pastor of Worcester in 1843. Previous to my going to Fitchburg Father Strain, from Waltham, had attended a few sick calls.

I attended a sick call at Mr. Manam's woolen mill, where a few Catholics were employed, and in a week or so afterwards said the first mass in Fitchburg. That was in 1843, and from that time I was recognized as pastor of Fitchburg, in fact, of nearly the whole county. I have no notes or records whatever to refer to, but I remember it well. I was always on the move, officiating in all the towns in Worcester County.

Mr. Cahill, an Irish contractor, when he completed his contract on railroad from Fitchburg to West, gave me the shanties of his men, which I took down and built a small church with them on the spot where the house stood which I afterwards built a short distance south of the present Church of St. Bernard. It was a long, narrow building, capable of holding 100 people. It got the name of "The Cathedral Shanty." When I blessed foundations of it, Fathers Reardon, my assistant then, and Williams and O'Brien assisted. O'Brien preached on the occasion from a chair with the American flag over his head on a Liberty pole. We tried to make a great memorable day of it, but I cannot give the dates: it was in the year 1844.

When the church was up we opened it with a solemn high mass. A few months after there were two windows in the sanctuary, one on each side of the altar, with turkey red curtains and a borrowed carpet. The church held all the Catholics of Fitchburg and surrounding country. This shanty church was used until the new church of St. Bernard's had a foundation up, which we covered and used as a church and school. I afterwards got a grave yard on the other side of the river.

I was born in Hexham, Northumberland, England, May, 1817, and educated in Propaganda, Rome.

I was ordained by Bishop Kenrick, in St. John's Cathedral, Philadelphia, Pa., August, 1841. First mission, Loretto; succeeded Rev. Dr. Gallitzin. In 1843 went to Worcester, Mass.

Built St. John's Church, Worcester; also St. Ann's Church, Worcester: St. George's, Saxonville: St. Polycarp's, Leicester; St. Bernard's, Fitchburg; St. Luke's, West Boyls-

REV. JOSEPH A. GALLAGHER.   PASTOR 1852-55.

ton: St. Louis', Webster: St. Bridget's, Millbury; St. Martin's, Templeton.

Bought St. Leo's Church, Leominster, from Protestants.

Founded the congregations of Southbridge, Spencer, Holden, Leicester, Gardner, Barre, Uxbridge, Grafton, Whittinsville, Holliston, Framingham, Hopkinton, Winchenden, N. H.

In Wisconsin built St. Charles', Cassville; St. Patrick's, Racine: St. Lawrence O'Toole's, Mt. Hope; St. Clement's, Lancaster.

Built Church of SS. Joseph, Patrick and Cuthbert, in Coonforth, County Durham, England. Built the Presbytery of Coonforth, England, and of Beverly, N. J.

WILLIAM A. M'GUIRE.

REV. ANDREW P. GIBBS.

Father Gibbs was a native of Queens County, Ireland, where he was born in 1815. He entered on his studies for the sacred ministry in St. Charles Borromeo's Seminary, Philadelphia, and on the conclusion of his theological course was ordained priest on the 20th of September, 1840, by Bishop F. P. Kenrick, of Philadelphia. For at least forty-five years prior to his death he was on the Missions of Western Pennsylvania. From some time in 1844 until 1846 he was an assistant at St. Michael's, Loretto, during the pastorate of Father Lemke. In 1846 he became the first pastor of the Summit. For thirty-one years just prior to his death, which occurred July 19, 1885, he was pastor of St. Mary's congregation, Lawrenceville, Pittsburg, which he organized in 1854. Since that time four congregations, two English and two

German, have been organized out of the original territory of his parish.

No one worked with more earnest zeal in the Lord's vineyard than did Father Gibbs. Wherever he labored during the forty-five years of his ministry the good fruits are visible to this day. But the greatest monument which he leaves behind to perpetuate and endear his name to a grateful people is St. Mary's Church, with its convent, school buildings and pastoral residence, and the ample grounds around them. At his death he was the oldest officiating priest in the diocese. He died Sunday morning, between the hours of 2 and 3 o'clock, at his residence on Forty-sixth street, Pittsburg, in the 70th year of his age, after an illness of only a few days.

His mortal remains were consigned to their last resting place in St. Mary's cemetery.

REV. HUGH PATRICK GALLAGHER.

Father Gallagher was born in Killygordon, County Donegal, Ireland, on Easter Sunday, in the year 1815. Having been elevated to the holy ministry, he labored in the mission of the Diocese of Pittsburg for about eight years while the diocese was yet in its infancy. His last field was that of Loretto, where he became pastor September 27, 1844, and remained until 1852, breaking the bread of life and directing the spiritual affairs of that part of the Lord's vineyard up to his departure for California in the latter part of the year. Among people of all creeds and classes, and wherever he was known, he was highly esteemed, and all who had the pleasure of his personal acquaintance loved "Father Hugh" for the purity of his life, the edification of his example, the charity of his heart, and above all, the zeal with which he devoted his life to the spread of the true faith and the enduring glory of God. He was truly a priest of God.

In word and work, with prudence and perseverence, his whole energy was devoted to the propagation of the faith and the founding of institutions which would give Catholic instruction to the youth, save the fallen sinner from further iniquity and shelter the orphan from the rude blasts of the heartless world.

Having been in California for twenty-nine years after severing his connection with St. Michael's, Loretto, Father Hugh Gallagher resigned his pastorate of St. Joseph's Church, San Francisco, and on advice of his physician, started on a journey to eastern States and Ireland to recruit his health. Returning he finished his course on earth and died in St. Mary's Hospital, San Francisco, on Friday morning, March 10, 1882, in the 67th year of his age.

It is to be regretted that no biographical notes of his esteemed brother, Rev. Jos. A. Gallagher, who succeeded him in the pastorate of St. Michael's Church, Loretto, are at present to be found.

REV. WILLIAM POLLARD.

Father Pollard was born in the "Isle of Saints," having first breathed the air of the County Kilkenny. He anxiously looked forward to the goal of his ambition, the sacred priesthood; and with this end in view he labored to adorn his mind and to cultivate his heart. America appeared to him as the place in which God had destined him to work for His honor and glory. Though with no prospect before him but one of hard work and much suffering, he affiliated himself to the Pittsburg Diocese, under its then Bishop, Rt. Rev. Michael O'Connor, by whom he was raised to the priesthood in May, 1850.

His first mission as a priest was a most uninviting one. He was sent to administer to the wants of the Catholics living along the Pennsylvania Railroad which was then being constructed near Greensburg and vicinity. After a successful period of two or three years in this locality he was selected by Bishop O'Connor to accompany him to the newly created See of Erie, Pa. The Bishop knew the merits and capabilities of Father Pollard, and his appreciation of the same was amply shown in his desire to appoint this youthful priest to the rectorship of the new Cathedral in Erie.

However, "Man proposes but God disposes," and Bishop O'Connor was re-appointed to Pittsburg. Father Pollard returned also, and was sent to the parish of the sainted

Prince Gallitzin, Loretto, Pa., where he remained four years, when he was called, by his superiors, to a vaster field of labor in the South Side, Pittsburg. He then became Rector of St. John the Evangelist's Church, which position he held for about twenty-five years.

Father Pollard's first experience in this part of God's Holy vineyard was certainly novel and not very encouraging. He was obliged to sleep in a rented room, so pervious as to admit the falling rain. His ardor, however, was not dampened at all by this cooling reception, for he went to work as soon as convenience and means allowed to better his habitation as well as to procure everything needful for his growing congregation.

How well he worked and with what success he met are grandly exemplified in the property belonging to St. John's, Fifteenth street, South Side, which he left three years before his death to accept the pastorate of St. Mary's, 46th St., Pittsburg. A spacious and well furnished church, a large and commodious pastoral residence, a school and a convent, both amply large to accommodate the children of the parish and the good Sisters in charge; a dwelling for the janitor, besides some vacant ground adjoining these buildings. All these are monuments to the zeal and faith of the people he guided so long and so successfully.

It was not long after his acceptance of St. Mary's that declining health warned him to be ready for the Master's call. Twice stricken with paralysis, he was conscious of his approaching dissolution.

On Sunday, September 16, 1888, having no symptoms of unusual weakness, he prepared to celebrate the Holy Sacrifice of the mass. He had gone on with the mass as far as the Offertory, when he was admonished by his own feelings to summon assistance. This was readily extended, and with another paralytic stroke, he was carried from the altar to the chamber from which he never afterwards came alive. He was unconscious for some time, but rallied sufficiently to receive all the last Sacraments, not excepting Holy Viaticum.

Surrounded by the good Sisters of Mercy, and by his two faithful assistants, Fathers Foley and Brennan, he went to God at 8.30 a. m., on the same Sunday mentioned above. (September 16.)

REV. M. J. MITCHELL.

Michael Joseph Mitchell was born in County Longford, Ireland, in March, 1820. After pursuing his studies in his native land he came to this country about the year 1838, and enterd the Seminary of St. Charles Borromeo, Philadelphia, where he completed his course in theology. Attaching himself to the newly erected Diocese of Pittsburg, where he was ordained by Bishop O'Connor on the 3d of March, 1844, being the second priest ordained by that illustrious prelate, he was appointed to the little congregation of Butler, where he remained until May, 1847, when he was transferred to Freeport. Finding the church at that place too small, he undertook the erection of a new edifice which was completed at the close of 1851. But before the completion of the church he was transferred to Murrensville, where he remained until April 1854; soon after which he was placed in charge of the church at Wilmore. At the close of the following year we find him pastor at Ebensburg, where he remained till the end of 1864, with the exception of the time from December, 1856, to September, 1857, when he had charge of St. John's Church, South Side, Pittsburg, during the absence of the pastor—Rev. T. S. Reynolds—who accompanied Bishop O'Connor on his trip to Europe and the Holy Land. During part of the time he was in charge of the church at Ebensburg he lodged with the Franciscan Brothers at St. Francis' College, Loretto, of whom he was then Ecclesiastical Superior. Early in the winter of 1863 he was appointed pastor of the newly formed congregation of New Brighton. Having remained till the spring of 1865, ill health rendered it necessary for him to retire for a time from the active duties of the ministry, and he does not appear to have resumed their exercise before February, 1866. He was then appointed pastor of St. Andrew's Church, Allegheny. In the summer of 1868, he was placed in charge of St. Michael's Church, Loretto, where he continued until February 24, 1870, when failing health obliged him to retire to the Mercy Hospital, where for a time his life was despaired of. During his brief stay at Loretto he baptized thirty-nine persons and married nine couples. At length in September, 1871, he took charge of St. Michael's Church, Pittsburg, but he was forced after three months again to return to the hospital. Here he remained, exercising the duties of chaplain, with little interruption, till the fall of 1879, when he became pastor of St. Thomas' Church, Braddock. A permanent decline in his health, however, forced him to resign and return to the hospital only a few months prior to his death. In the decrees of Providence it seems that he was never more to leave the hospital, from which he was called to his final rest after having exercised the duties of the sacred ministry for almost thirty-eight years—for the most part in thinly settled districts which tried men's bodies no less than their souls.

He died Wednesday, January 11, 1882, at 10 o'clock a. m., at Mercy Hospital, Pittsburg, and his mortal remains were interred in St. Mary's cemetery.

Father Mitchell was a man of vast and varied experience, a ripe scholar, and was gifted with a remarkable talent for organization. He was charitable to the poor, gentle with the erring, but where the honor of God or the interests of the Church were concerned, he knew no compromise. His perfect command of language, which for precision, elegance and incisiveness well compares with that of Junius, supplied him with a weapon which it was dangerous to call into play.

REV. P. M'C. MORGAN.

Rev. Pollard McCormick Morgan was a convert to the Catholic faith from the Presbyterian Church, for the ministry of which he was, at the time of his conversion, a student in the Western Theological Seminary, Allegheny City. After embracing the Catholic faith he entered St. Michael's Seminary for the purpose of preparing himself for the priesthood. He was ordained in the year 1862. He remained at the seminary for some time as Professor of Rhetoric and Theology, which position he filled with credit to himself and to the satisfaction of his ecclesiastical superiors. From the latter part of 1864 to May 14, 1866, Father Morgan officiated as assistant at St. Michael's, Loretto, baptizing during that time, twenty-eight persons. On May 14, 1866, he left Loretto for London, England, and in the latter part of the following year he returned to Pittsburg. During the remainder of his too short career he labored incessantly for the good of souls and after an illness of over twelve months, died on Sunday morning, April 14, 1872, in Pittsburg, in the 38th year of his age, having been born in 1834. Rev. H. Denny preached his panegyric at the funeral obsequies, after which he was buried in St. Mary's cemetery.

THE REV. H. S. BOWEN.

Horace Seymour Bowen was born in Pittsburg, June 22, 1822. His parents were among the most respectable and influential people of the city. They were in religious belief Protestants. The Reverend Father went to school at a very early age, at Mt. St. Mary's College, Emmitsburg, Md. He developed a wonderful talent for music, applied himself most assiduously to its cultivation, and in his prime, both as a layman and a priest, he was a celebrated performer and a most successful instructor.

He remained at the Mountain College until about the year 1841, but before his departure thence to engage in the busy world, he saw the light of God's Holy Faith, and always honest and sincere he followed it. He was received into the Catholic Church and evinced great piety and fervor. After leaving college he gave his attention to music. Whilst practicing the duties of his religion faithfully, he supported himself by instructing others in the chosen branch.

For many years during the pastorate of the present Bishop of Erie, Rt. Rev. Tobias Mullen, he was in charge of the organ and choir of St. Peter's Church, Allegheny, Pa.

God, however, designed him for greater things, and called him to the sacred ministry. Well versed in the Latin and Greek languages as well as the ordinary sciences of a collegiate course, he began the study of theology. He was ordained a priest in the year 1868.

As a priest he was most devoted and zealous. For seventeen years, while living and teaching music at St. Francis' College, he was chaplain to the Sisters of Mercy, Loretto, Pa. Although he had a considerable distance to walk every morning to the Convent chapel, and at a time when he was broken down in health and declining in years, still in the most inclement weather he was at his post. He left the scene of his labors only when he was carried to the Mercy Hospital, emaciated and fast sinking into the grave.

Fortified by the Sacraments, with the kind attention of his beloved sister, Mother Neri of the Order of Mercy, he breathed his last in peace. Owing to the time in which he died there was no mass over his remains on the day of his funeral, Good Friday, April 8, 1887.

On the afternoon of this day his remains were taken to St. Paul's Cathedral. There were present in the sanctuary some twenty or thirty priests to do honor to the beloved deceased.

Bishop Phelan was also there. The vespers of the Dead were chanted by the assembled clergymen and then the Bishop pronounced the absolution. Rev. Father Neason, a particularly dear friend of Father Bowen, delivered a touching eulogy. The Rt. Rev. Bishop and many priests accompanied the remains to St. Mary's cemetery, where the interment took place.

DATES IN LOCAL HISTORY.

1788. Captain Michael McGuire made the first settlement in what is now Cambria County, Pa.
1791. Joseph Jahns (Yahns) settled at Johnstown.
1793. November 17, Captain Michael McGuire died. He was the first to be buried in the cemetery at Loretto.

1795. March 18, Rev. Demetrius A. Gallitzin ordained to the priesthood by Bishop John Carroll, in Baltimore. He had sailed from Rotterdam, August 18, 1792, and reached Baltimore on October 28th following.
1799. August, Father Gallitzin came to McGuire's Settlement and built the first church between Lancaster, Pa., and St. Louis.
1804. March 26, Cambria County was organized.
1810. First census of Cambria County taken.
1811. Bishop Egan, of Philadelphia, administered confirmation in the log church at Loretto.
1819. John Weakland settled at Hart's Sleeping Place.
1826. Canal begun at Allegheny river.
1830. December 10, canal finished to Johnstown.
1831. April, work of construction begun on Old Portage railroad.
1832. August, postoffices established at Jefferson (Wilmore) and at Summit.
1833. May 12, the old cherry tree, the boundary mark at Canoe Place, washed out of root.
1833. November 20, first train passed over the Old Portage railroad.
1834. Boats first transferred from canal to cars on Old Portage railroad.
1835. Second track completed on the Old Portage railroad.
1840. Work commenced on Lake Conemaugh. Completed 1853.
1847. Monument of Father Gallitzin erected. Franciscan Brothers came to Loretto.
1848. Sisters of Mercy came to Loretto. Congregation at St. Augustine detached from Loretto. August 27, corner stone of Franciscan Monastery laid.
1850. December 25, St. Benedict's Church, Carrolltown, dedicated.
1851. Corner stone of new church at Loretto laid. First Mission in the diocese held at Loretto, opening on Low Sunday. June 8, corner stone of the new St. Paul's Cathedral, Pittsburg, laid. June 20, St. Aloysius Church, Summit, dedicated.

1852. January 14, Johnstown's second Catholic Church, frame, 40x60 feet, dedicated.
1853. December 9. Papal Nunzio, Monsignor Bedini, at Loretto.
1854. January 6, St. Michael's new brick church at Loretto dedicated.
1855. The new Portage railroad completed. December 8, church at New Germany dedicated.
1857. The Pennsylvania Railroad Company purchased the line of public improvements, the old and new Portage railroads, canal, etc. July 4, grand celebration at Loretto.
1859. First church built at Chest Springs.
1860. March 20, above named church dedicated.
1863. June 4, heavy frost. August 27, frost.
1864. September 11, new church at New Germany dedicated.
1865. June 4, oil tapped at Jerome Dawson's by William Tyne for Collins & Co., at 340 feet.
1867. January 17, blockade of roads commenced. High winds and snow for twelve days in succession.
1867. January 27, Sunday. Not more than sixty persons at church; not one sled or sleigh on the ground. All during May very wet and cold. Oats, corn and potatoes could not be planted.
1868. December 8, a very stormy day. Roads blocked, and not more than seventy persons at church.
1875. From July 2 to August 6 rain about every other day. Bad harvest. Much wheat, rye and grass damaged. October 3, jubilee commenced and ended on the 10th. Was well attended.
1879. August 26, first lots in new part of cemetery sold to the following persons: A. J. Christy, M. F. McDonald, W. J. Buck, J. Gibbons, F. D. Saupp and William Glass. September 8, Jacob Gibbons' monument completed. The first in the new part of the cemetery: in 1885 removed to Milton, Pa.
1882. May 25, dedication of new Court House at Ebensburg.

1884. January 14, first telegram sent over the Loretto wire.
1886. December 9, big fire at St. Francis' College.
1889. May 31, Johnstown flood. December 7, Rt. Rev. Bishop Tuigg died in Altoona.
1890. April 6, Easter Sunday. Rev. E. A. Bush, for twenty years pastor of Loretto, delivered his farewell sermon. On the Wednesday following he assumed charge of St. John's Church, Altoona. On the 18th of the same month Rev. Martin Ryan left St. Augustine and became pastor of Loretto.
1891. March 14, Rev. M. Ryan left Loretto to take charge of St. Patrick's Church, Gallitzin. No ceremonies during Holy Week.
1891. April 1, Rev. Ferdinand Kittell was installed as pastor of Loretto.

PART SECOND.

BY REV. FERDINAND KITTELL, PASTOR.

MATRIMONIAL AND BAPTISMAL RECORDS

—OF—

REV. D. A. GALLITZIN.

NOTE.—Father Gallitzin in making entries of baptisms, was not accustomed to express the maiden surname of the mother. Hence such surnames, when not found in the Matrimonial Register, have been in some instances supplied from other sources, but in too many cases they are unfortunately wanting. The dates after the names of the children, all of whom were baptized by him, denote the year of birth of the first and of the last. All the marriages recorded by Father Gallitzin are here noted. But it is certain that he performed many baptisms and marriages which he failed to record, for the reason that, administering these sacraments while traveling among his scattered flock, he would frequently, as he himself stated, lose the memoranda which he intended, on returning home, to copy into the Registers.

ADAMS John and Ann ——.
 John, Robert, William, Susan, Louisa Ann. (1800-17.)
ADAMS William and Eve Sanker.
 Jacob, John, James, Mary Magdalen, Thomas, William, Joseph, Juliana. (1807-25.)
ADAMS Ignatius and Honoria Burgoon. Married June 18, 1815.
 Veronica Ann, Matthew, Winifred, Barnabas, Ignatius, Thomas Samuel. (1816-27.)
ADAMS Thomas and Rachel McGuire.
 Mary Ann, Thomas, Julia Ann, Rachel. (1821-33.)

ADAMS Richard and Margaret McConnell. Married September 18, 1821.
    John, Elizabeth, Peter, Jacob, Richard, Francis, Demetrius Silas. (1822-34.)

ADAMS Joseph and Maria Inlow. Married December 30, 1823.
    Thomas, Elizabeth, Joseph, Ann Magdalen, Jane, Mary Magdalen, Anastasia. (1824-37.)

ADAMS Peter and Mary Gallagher. Married January 8, 1833.
    Richard, Joseph, Elizabeth. (1834-36.)

ADELSBERGER Michael and Elizabeth Hughes.
    Mary, Thomas, Ann Mary, Mary Rebecca, Ann Elizabeth, Catharine. (1824-37.)

AKELS Samuel and Jane ——.
    Elizabeth. (1806.)

ANDERSON Andrew and Patience ——.
    Rhoda, John. (1794-96.)

ANDERSON John and Emily Burgoon. Married January 10, 1815.

ARNELL Joseph and Mary ——.
    William. (1808.)

ASHCROFT Richard and Mary ——.
    Ellen. (1821.)

BAILIFF John and Eve ——.
    Elizabeth, Mary, Martha Jane. (1805-13.)

BAKER John and Mary ——.
    Ann, Thomas, John. (1809-13.)

BAKER William and Christina Helfreit.
    Mary Ann, Christina. (1835-38.)

BAKER John and Catharine Fox. Married August 25, 1835.

BARNHART John and Frances ——.
    Elizabeth, John. (1837-38.)

BARNICLE Thaddeus and Sarah ——.
    Mary Ann, Bridget, Catherine. (1802-08.)

BARNICLE William and Susan ——.
    William Michael, Sarah, Bartholomew, Mary. (1815-24.)

BARNICLE William and Mary Ann ——.
  William. (1828.)
BARNICLE Michael and Margaret ——.
  John, Ambrose Aug., Michael. (1827-30.)
BARNICLE Philip and Margaret Gillespie. Married September 2, 1834.
BARTLETT Charles and Elizabeth ——.
  Sarah. (1826.)
BAUMGARDNER John and Mary ——.
  Sarah Jane, Edward. (1835-37.)
BEAMER John and Abigail Coleman. Married August 17, 1817.
  Henry, Mathias, John, William, Solomon, Samuel. (1820-31.)
BEAMER John and Elizabeth O'Hara. Married November 8, 1831.
  Thomas, Catherine, Daniel. (1832-36.)
BEARER Casper and Catharine Huber. Married January 11, 1825.
  Casper Joseph, Catharine, Henry, John. (1826-31.)
BEARER Melchoir and Theresa Huber. Married January 11, 1825.
  Casper Nicholas, William, Mary Ann, Rebecca, Joseph Paul. (1826-33.)
BEBER Christian and Mary Magdalen ——.
  Adam, William, Juliana, Henry, Margaret, Demetrius Aug. (1816-31.)
BECHER John and Elizabeth ——.
  Mary Catherine, Mary Elizabeth. (1808-11.)
BECHER Nicholas and Christina Coons.
  Samuel John, Henry Aug., William Jos., Apollonia, Mary Ann, Linus Nicholas, Matilda. (1827-39.)
BECHT Philip and Mary ——.
  Elizabeth. (1807.)
BEHE Anthony and Mary Noel. Married September 14, 1813.
  Mary, Elizabeth, Veronica. (1814-21.)

BEHE Conrad and Elizabeth Noel. Married October 26, 1817.
    John, Thomas, Ellen, Susan, Joseph, Henry, William, Jos. Conrad, Nicholas. (1820-38.)
BEHE Mathias and Catherine Kaylor. Married March 26, 1818.
    James, Elias, Elizabeth Ann, John, Mary Ann, Joseph, Henry, Mary Magdalen, Francis Elias, Luke. (1819-38.)
BEHRINGER George and Margaret ———.
    Eliza Jane, John. (1830-33.)
BEIGLEY Henry and Cynthia ———.
    John. (1798.)
BEIGLEY John and Mary Walsh.
    William, Mary Ann, Thomas, John. (1822-31.)
BELFORD William and Mary Rush. Married August 27, 1822.
    George, Jacob, James, William, John, Thomas, Margaret, Ann. (1823-39.)
BENDEN John and Mary ———.
    Thomas, Margaret. (1807-20.)
BENDEN Robert and Mary Caroline Trexler. Married August 21, 1838.
    Mary Elizabeth. (1839.)
BENDER Emerick and Mary Magdalen ———.
    Mary Ann, Jacob, Lydia Apollonia, Joseph, Margaret Ann, Catherine Ann, Henry, John. (1810-28.)
BENDER Henry and Mary Ann Myers. Married February 17, 1828.
    James Augustine, Mary Ellen. (1828-32.)
BERTRAM John and Martina Heit. Married January 29, 1839.
BIGLIN James and Ann Early.
    Margaret, Eugene, James, Mary Ann. (1832-38.)
BITNER Louis and Ann Mary ———.
    William. (1837.)
BLAIR Obediah and Mary ———.
    John. (1825.)
BLAKE Henry and Elizabeth ———.
    George. (1816.)
BLONDIN Edward and Ann ———.
    Rosanna. (1838.)

REV. WILLIAM POLLARD.   PASTOR 1855-59.

BOLAN Michael and Margaret ——.
   Ann, Thomas. (1835-37.)
BOLAN Landelin and Elizabeth Beber. Married October 21, 1834.
   Christian. (1836.)
BOLEY Sebastian and Agatha ——.
   Henry, Peter Paul. (1835-39.)
BOONE Joseph and Priscilla ——.
   Ellen, Thomas. (1819-21.)
BOONE Henry and Catherine Fels. Married May 27, 1823.
   Mary Jane, William Francis, Eliza Amanda. (1824-28.)
BORTMAN Peter and Mary Ann Hertzog.
   Elizabeth Ann, Joseph. (1837-39.)
Bow John and Mary ——.
   Mary. (1832.)
BOYLE Henry and Elizabeth ——.
   Catherine, John, Mary Ann, Andrew. (1806-13.)
BOYLE John and Margaret ——.
   Joseph, James, Hugh, Sarah, Mary, William, Ann. (1812-24.)
BOYLE Edward and Ellen ——.
   Margaret. (1821.)
BOYLE Eugene and Bridget ——.
   Sarah Ann. (1832.)
BRADDOCK Michael and Sarah ——.
   Margaret, James. (1816-17.)
BRADDOCK John and Ann ——.
   Simon Peter, Mary Ann, Catherine, Emily. (1811-17.)
BRADDOCK John and Elizabeth Malone (Storm.) Married May 25, 1826.
   Mary Ellen, Ann Elizabeth, Michael John, Leo Joseph, Henry James, Susan Margaret. (1827-37.)
BRADLEY Manasses and Frances ——.
   John, Susan. (1799-1801.)
BRADLEY Charles and Mary ——.
   Joseph. (1800.) The first baptism recorded by Father Gallitzin.

BRADLEY James and Ellen ——.
   Patrick, John, Charles, Joseph, Michael. (1814-27.)
BRADLEY Patrick and Mary ——.
   Cornelius, James, Elizabeth. (1817-21.)
BRADLEY William and Rosanna McMonigle.
   William, Ellen, Francis, Sarah Jane. (1823-39.)
BRADLEY Edward and Sarah Neason. Married October 14, 1824.
   Mary, Charles, Martha. (1825-29.)
BRADLEY Charles and Catherine McGuire. Married February 17, 1828.
   John Chrys., Mary, Richard, Anselm, Mark, Sylvester. (1829-37.)
BRADLEY John and Mary ——.
   James, Mary. (1836-38.)
BRADLEY Charles and Jane Bradley.
   Susan. (1837.)
BRADLEY John and Catherine Bradley. Married December 9, 1838.
BRADLEY Dennis and Mary McCoy. Married January 12, 1840.
BRADY Terence and Ellen ——.
   Ellen, Rosanna. (1820-23.)
BRADY Hugh and Catharine ——.
   Margaret. (1833.)
BRADY Charles and Margaret Skelly. Married November 22, 1835.
   Susan. (1836.)
BRANIOWISKY Thomas and Catharine Huber.
   Mary. (1822.)
BRANNIFF Michael and Margaret ——.
   Ambrose, Philip, Barnabas, Michael. (1809-14.)
BRANNIFF John and Elizabeth ——.
   Ann, John, William. (1814-19.)
BRANNIFF Philip and Catharine ——.
   Mary Ann, Michael. (1836-37.)
BRANT Joseph and Dorothy ——.
   Mary Ann, Catharine, Augustine. (1809-13.)

BRANT Augustine and Mary Noel.
    Daniel Demetrius. (1840.)
BRAWLEY Dennis and Catharine ——.
    Margaret, Dennis, Catherine, John, Elizabeth. (1805-17.)
BRAWLEY David and Mary Ann Burgoon. Married November 24, 1828.
BRAWLEY Michael and Mary Magdalen Burgoon. Married January 15, 1839.
BRIDGE George and Jane Bailey.
    Mary. (1834.)
BROOKBANK John and Ann ——.
    Matilda Ann. (1815.)
BROOKBANK William and Sarah ——.
    John, Emily Ann, Mary Ann, Eliza Jane. (1823-1832.)
BROOKBANK Thomas and Mary Brady. Married October 18, 1831.
    Mary Ellen, Margaret Ann, Edward, Alice Matilda. (1832-43.)
BROWN Phanuel and Elizabeth ——.
    John. (1802.)
BROWN John and Susan ——.
    Michael, John, Sarah, James, Thomas, Henry. (1797-1817.)
BROWN Daniel and Apollonia ——.
    Henry, Sarah Ann, Margaret, William Daniel, Helen. (1821-35.)
BROWN Michael and Catharine Platt. Married November 5, 1817.
    Mary Ann Matilda. (1823.)
BROWN Michael and Cecilia Waters. Married September 20, 1825.
    John, Martha Jane. (1826-29.)
BROWN Moses and Mary Gallagher. Married November 10, 1829.
    James, Susan Catherine, John. (1830-35.)
BROWN Thomas and Margaret Roberts. Married September 3, 1833.

Susan Ann, Sarah Jane, John. (1834-39.)
BROWN Henry and Mary ———.
Mary. (1836.)
BROWN John and Lavina Sharp. Married May 16, 1839.
BRUCE John and Mary ———.
George. (1809.)
BRUCE George and Juliana McKinney. Married May 26, 1833.
John C. (1834.)
BRUCE George and Amelia McManamy. Married October 8, 1837.
James Alexander. (1838.)
BUCHANAN John and Mary ———.
William. (1823.)
BUCK Joseph and Elizabeth Eckenrode.
John, Christian, Sarah Ann, William, Jacob, Jerome, Mary Ann. (1823-38.)
BUCK Christian and Mary Young. Married September 2, 1827.
Joseph, Jacob, William. (1828-32.)
BUCK Henry and Agnes Ann Byrne. Married November 17, 1829.
Thomas, Daniel, Sarah Ann, Susan. (1832-38.)
BUCK Joseph and Rebecca ———.
Clothilde. (1835.)
BURGOON Robert and Catharine ———.
Leo, Catherine, Mary Ann, Joseph, Elizabeth, Sarah Ann, Susan, Bridget. (1801-21.)
BURGOON Barnabas and Mary ———.
George, Jacob. (1803-05.)
BURGOON Joseph and Mary Ann ———.
Juliana, Margaret, Susan, Joseph, John Baptist, John Chrysostom, Mary Ann, Jacob. (1807-27.)
BURGOON John and Mary Ann ———.
Susan, Jacob, Margaret Ann. (1809-15.)
BURGOON Levi and Ann Lilly. Married June 6, 1813.
Charity. (1817.)

BURGOON Richard and Ann Delozier. Married May 16, 1814.
 Ann, Jacob. (1815-16.)
BURGOON John and Rhoda Anderson. Married January 10, 1815.
 Andrew. (1816.)
BURGOON Jacob and Mary Burkle. Married December 26, 1815.
BURGOON Benedict and Catherine Weaver. Married November 14, 1824.
 Michael, William, Margaret Ann, Susan, Joseph. (1826-35.)
BURGOON Jacob and Elizabeth Weaver.
 Mary Clothilde, Luke. (1837-39.)
BURKE Patrick and Apollonia ———.
 Thomas, Theresa, Prudence, Susan, Catherine. (1810-23.)
BURKE John and Esther McGough.
 Ellen, Augustine Edward, Elizabeth, James, Patience, Juliana, John, William, Mary Bridget, Silas, Cecilia Esther, Rachel Ann. (1812-33.)
BURKE Nicholas and Margaret Woodburn. Married January 19, 1813.
 Elizabeth. (1814.)
BURKE Edward and Catherine Noel. Married May 14, 1822.
 Susan Prudence, Nicholas Augustine, William James, Catherine. (1823-28.)
BURKE Edward and Ellen Keefers.
 Mary Jane. (1839.)
BURKE William and Alice ———.
 Mary. (1834.)
BURKE James and Veronica McGuire.
 James. (1837.)
BURKE James and Elizabeth Catherine McKinzie. Married October 21, 1838.
BURLEY William and Catharine ———.
 Simon and Alexander. (1829.)
BUTLER Richard and Ann Dodson. Married April 29, 1817.
 Andrew, Sarah Ann. (1818-26.)

BYRNE Thomas and Sarah ———.
> Barnabas, Catherine, Michael, Demetrius Aug., Agnes, Henry, James, Margaret, Elizabeth, Thomas, John Chrysostom, Francis, Mary Ann. (1802-26.)

BYRNE John and Mary Ann Bender. Married June 11, 1811.
> James, Thomas, Mary Ann Elizabeth, Henry, Agnes Ann. (1813-24.)

BYRNE Patrick and Sarah Creswell. Married August 11, 1819.
> Timothy. (1820.)

BYRNE Barnabas and Mary Driskel. Married October 11, 1825.
> Mary Magdalen, Sarah Jane, Juliana, Anastasia, Silas Augustine, Michael, Charles Thomas, Agnes Elizabeth, Margaret Catherine. (1826-38.)

BYRNE Michael and Susan Walters. Married October 9, 1827.
> Mary Ann, Elizabeth Margaret, Sarah Jane, Thomas Augustine, Susan. (1829-38.)

BYRNE Augustine and Mary Ann Driskel. Married May 6, 1828.
> Michael, Alice, Thomas, Mary, Margaret, Sarah Ann, Jane Matilda. (1829-39.)

BYRNE George and Margaret Flowers.
> Jacob. (1832.)

BYRNE Joseph and Ann ———.
> John, Rosanna. (1833-35.)

BYRNE Edward and Susan O'Neill. Married August 3, 1834.
> Thomas, John. (1835-36.)

CALLAN Owen and Ann Martha Coates.
> James. (1819.)

CALLAN James and Martha O'Keefe. Married February 13, 1820.
> Ellen. (1821.)

CAMPBELL Patrick and Ann Connery.
> James, Henry, Sarah, Michael, Philip N., Mary Ann, Bridget, Jane. (1802-20.)

CAMPBELL John and Catharine ———.
   John. (1805.)
CAMPBELL John and Susan Myers. Married June 4, 1826.
   Henry, Catharine. (1827-29.)
CAMPBELL Philip N. and Judith Maher. Married October 1, 1839.
CANNUM William and Mary ———.
   Theresa. (1802.)
CANTWELL James and Susan ———.
   Mary, Thomas, James. (1812-17.)
CARL John and Emily Short. Married July 17, 1827.
   Andrew Simon, Martha Ann, Mary Elizabeth, Thomas, Emily Susan. (1831-39.)
CARL Louis and Ellen Krise. Married September 17, 1833.
   Mary Ellen, Margaret, Henry Andrew. (1834-38.)
CARL Caspar and Mary Ann Adams. Married January 22, 1839.
CARLAND John and Mary Ann Lilly. Married October 7, 1821.
   Henry, Charity, William, Mary Ann. (1822-32.)
CARNEY John and Susan Weakland.
   Ann, Sarah, Bartholomew, John, Catherine, Michael. (1818-30.)
CARR Eugene and Sarah ———.
   Rosanna. (1832.)
CARROLL Richard and Mary Ann ———.
   Charlotte Ann. (———.)
CARROLL Thomas and Mary Ann Brown. Married June 25, 1839.
CASELLY Joseph and Susan Skelly. Married April 26, 1836.
CASSIDY James and Sarah ———.
   Robert. (1775.)
CASSIDY James and Elizabeth ———.
   Mary Mechthilde. (1810.)
CASSIDY Francis and Ann ———.
   Juliana Jane. (1815.)
CASSIDY James and Margaret McHugh. Married October 23, 1818.
   Mary, Alice, William, John, Matthew, Margaret, James, Michael. (1820-34.)

CASSIDY John and Thersa ——.
    Mathias, Robert, Michael. (1831-34.)
CASSIDY Lawrence and Mary McManamy.
    Lawrence, Grace. (1835-37.)
CHERRY Nicholas and Elizabeth Burgoon. Married June 9, 1803.
    (The first marriage recorded by Father Gallitzin.)
    John, James. (1804-08.)
CHERRY James and Honoria ——.
    Catherine. (1811.)
CHERRY John and Eva Lukehart. Married March 14, 1819.
CHERRY Anthony and Susan Contner. Married April 29, 1824.
CHRISTY Archibald and Mary ——.
    Augustine Ambrose, Amelia Theresa, Joseph Thomas, Sylvester Luke, Juliana Jane. (1808-19.)
CHRISTY Francis and Susan McConnell.
    Elias, Agnes, Louisa, John, Josiah, Sarah, Augustine, Henry, Archibald Francis. (1819-38.)
CHRISTY Martin and Mary ——.
    Elizabeth. (1826.)
CHRISTY Peter and Catherine Shirley. Married November 23, 1828.
    Richard Callixtus, Samuel, Eliza Jane, Andrew James, (1829-37.)
CHRISTY Augustine and Mary ——.
    William. (1833.)
CHURCHILL Jesse and Hannah ——.
    Matthew Egidius. (1791.)
CLARKE Lawrence and Elizabeth Campbell. Married October 6, 1822.
    Margaret Ann, Mary. (1823-25.)
CLARKE Hugh and Mary ——.
    Isabella. (1833.)
CLARKE William and Jane Rafferty. Married February 24, 1837.
COCHRAN Thomas and Alice Kennedy. Married November 11, 1832.

COLEMAN Bartholomew and Rachel ——.
    Thomas, William. (1794-95.)
COLEMAN Thomas and Mary ——.
    Ann Rachel. (1819.)
COLLINS Robert and Ann ——.
    Ellen. (1804.)
COLLINS Peter and Sarah Meloy (Friel.) Married May 18, 1820.
    Philip, James, Thomas, Mary, John, John. (1821-36.)
COMERFORD Edward and Mary ——.
    Elizabeth, John. (1836-38.)
COMPASS Francis and Christina ——.
    Caroline. (1823.)
CONFER John and Margaret Palmer.
    John Alexander. (1817.)
CONNERY Patrick and Susan ——.
    Elizabeth. (1801).
CONNERY George and Catherine ——.
    James. (1806.)
CONNERY Patrick and Judith McMullen.
    Patrick. (1809.)
CONNERY John and Mary ——.
    William, Mary Ann, Eliza Jane, Margaret, John. (1812-30.)
CONNERY Patrick and Margaret McCloskey. Married June 20, 1819.
    Ann, Michael, Margaret, Mary Ellen, Sarah, John, James, Theresa, Eliza Jane. (1820-40.)
CONRAD John and Catherine Adelsberger. Married June 4, 1827.
    Francis, Stephen, Juliana. (1828-31.)
CONRAD James and Susan Coons. Married October 21, 1834.
    Francis Jerome, John Hilary, Juliana Elizabeth, Thomas Anthony. (1835-40.)
CONRAD Joseph and Lucy Griffin. Married November 18, 1834.
CONRAD Peter and Margaret Coons. Married May 1, 1836.
    Ambrose, Elias. (1837-39.)

CONRAD Joseph and Ann Walters.   Married September 18, 1836.
   Cecilia. (1838.)
CONRAD John and Ellen McAteer.   Married October 11, 1836.
   Demetrius Augustine. (1838.)
CONRAD David and Esther McKinzie.   Married November 11, 1838.
CONWAY Samuel and Patience ——.
   Ann. (1800.)
CONWAY Charles and Elizabeth McIntire.   Married October 17, 1830.
   Peter, James, Mary Ann. (1831-34.)
CONWAY Patrick and Margaret Benden.
   Mary. (1839.)
COOK Richard and Ann McCoy.   Married June 23, 1830.
COOK Henry and Ellen ——.
   Anthony. (1831.)
COONS John and Christina Wolf.
   Apollonia, Mary Ann, Susan, Joseph, Margaret, Sarah Ann. (1808-19.)
COONS John and Hannah Howell.   Married February 2, 1829.
   William Joseph, John Henry, Mary Ann, Joseph Ambrose, Susan, Christina Catherine. (1829-40.)
COOPER Henry and Mary ——.
   Elizabeth, Joseph, Mary. (1803-07.)
COOPER Philip and Sarah ——.
   Augustine, Stephen, Mary. (1806-11.)
COOPER Leonard and Juliana Elder.   Married October 19, 1824.
   Henry Joseph, Elias, Michael, Elias, Mary Ellen. (1825-32.)
COOPER Francis and Mary McGough.   Married February 19, 1828.
   Philip, Susan, Joseph, Mary, Elizabeth, Michael. (1830-40.)
COOPER Raphael and Sarah Kane.   Married February 4, 1834.
   Margaret Lucinda, John. (1836-38.)

COOPER Joseph and Catherine Walters. Married April 28, 1835.
    Mary, Rebecca Jane, Susan. (1836-39.)
COPP Daniel and Isabella Anderley. Married August 23, 1836.
CORCORAN Luke and Ann ———.
    Luke. (1831.)
CORNYN Charles and Susan ———.
    Ann. (1818.)
CORNYN Philip and Sarah Troxell.
    John. (1828.)
COSTELLO James and Elizabeth ———.
    Henry, David, Mary Ann. (1804-07.)
COSTELLO Henry and Susan ———.
    John. (1823.)
COSTELLO David and Ann McKinzie. Married April 19, 1830.
    Mary Jane. (1834.)
COTTERMAN Samuel and Juliana ———.
    Mary Priscilla. (1832.)
COULTER Alexander and Mary Ann Nagle. Married April 28, 1829.
    John. (1833.)
CRAMER Joseph and Regina Eberly. Married October 3, 1837.
    Francis Joseph. (1838.)
CRAVER Louis and Magdalen Hogue. Married August 25, 1834.
    Demetrius Augustine. (1837.)
CRAYTON (Cretin) Joseph and Ann ———.
    James, Elizabeth, Josue, Joseph, Mary, Martha. (1822-35.)
CRILLEY Peter and Elizabeth Kenny.
    Peter. (———.)
CRISTE John and Sarah O'Hara. Married June 14, 1808.
    Daniel, Robert Aloysius, Joseph, Margaret Rachel, John, Susan, Mary Elizabeth, Francis, Margaret Rachel, Thomas, Sarah Ann, David, Augustine, James. (1809-39.)

CRISTE Joseph and Theresa Noel. Married November 26, 1833.
CRISTE Robert and Mary Dougherty. Married November 10, 1835.
    Peter, Joseph, John. (1836-38.)
CROSBY Thomas and Ann ——.
    David. (1797.)
CROTZER Christopher and Mary Fels. Married March 3, 1829.
CRUM Reuben and Catherine ——.
    Ann, Elizabeth, Thomas, Peter, Catherine. (1809-17.)
CRUM Elias and Ann Walsh. Married May 5, 1835.
    Susan. (1836.)
CUMMISKEY John and Bridget ——.
    Mary, Joseph, John, Bridget, Cecilia, Francis. (1808-24.)
CUNNINGHAM Michael and Mary ——.
    Mary, Joseph, John. (1821-26.)
CUNNINGHAM James and Temperance Weakland. Married June 26, 1838.
CURRAN Bartholomew and Martha Smith.
    Mary Ann (——.)
CURRAN Hugh and Sarah Weakland. Married February 23, 1813.
    John, Catherine, Ann, Hugh, Francis, James, Michael, Thomas. (1814-26.)
CURRAN John and Bridget Carney. Married September 11, 1821.
    James Edward, Mary Jane, Alice, Elizabeth, John, Eliza Matilda. (1822-43.)
CUSHING Martin and Mary Brady. Married September 17, 1832.
DAILY Edward and Mary ——.
    Martha, Joanna, Bridget, Mary Ellen, Margaret, John. (1820-29.)
DAILY Edward and Ellen Gahagan.
    Margaret Ann. (1839.)
DAILY Bartholomew and Margaret Gibbons.
    Catherine, Mary Isabella, William James. (1830-38.)

DAILY Patrick and Ann Johnston. Married July 6, 1837.
DAILY Joseph and Unity McCoy.
    Bridget. (1837.)
DAVIS David and Elizabeth ——.
    Mary Ann, James Augustine, William, Ellen. (1815-22.)
DAVIS Michael and Mary ——.
    Mary, Eugene, Ann, Susan, Sarah. (1818-26.)
DAVIS William and Mary Ann ——.
    John, Catherine Amanda. (1831-32.)
DEAR John and Alice Jane Shirley. Married November 24, 1829.
DECKER John and Elizabeth ——.
    Sarah, Nicholas. (1806-07.)
DELANY William and Mary McCabe.
    Daniel, William, George. (1834-40.)
DELOZIER Daniel and Providence ——.
    John, Susan, William, Daniel, Jesse, Francis, Ann, Henry, Terence, Emily. (1805-28.)
DELOZIER John and Catherine Eckenrode. Married February 17, 1833.
    John. (1838.)
DELOZIER Jesse and Margaret Nagle. Married September 10, 1833.
    William. (1834.)
DEMPSEY Patrick and Elizabeth ——.
    Esther, Sarah Ann, James. (1807-11.)
DEMPSEY John and Ann Branniff. Married October 12, 1834.
DEVER Cornelius and Margaret Noon.
    William, Philip, James, Cornelius, Margaret, Dennis, Charles, John. (1817-34.)
DEVER Neal and Catherine Campbell. Married February 15, 1820.
    William B., Catherine. (1821-24.)
DEARMITT. (See McDermitt.)
DICKERHOOF Ferdinand and Catherine ——.
    Elizabeth. (1804.)
DICKERHOOF John and Jane ——.
    Mary. (1814.)

DIEBOLD Peter and Catherine Sherry. Married April 21, 1835.
: John. (1836.)

DIELICH George and Catherine Gerret. Married April 20, 1835.

DILLON Charles and Catherine Brawley. Married August 10, 1830.

DILLON Samuel and Susan Noel.
: Mary Ann. (1833.)

DIMOND Michael and Sarah ——.
: Joseph, Daniel, Mary, John, Michael, Elizabeth, James, Sarah Ann. (1805-21.)

DIMOND Philip and Sarah ——.
: James, Margaret, Mary, Susan, Daniel, William Augustine. (1807-17.)

DIMOND Daniel and Mary ——.
: Mary Margaret, John Chrysostom, James Gregory, Dominic, Anastasia, Daniel Augustine, Vincent Michael, Dennis Boniface. (1807-28.)

DIMOND John and Elizabeth Dempsey. Married June 21, 1818.
: Patrick, Daniel Augustine, William, John Michael. (1819-27.)

DIMOND Caspar and Mary Kearns. Married November 22, 1825.
: John, Elizabeth, Mary Ann, Sarah Ann, Susan, Charles. (1826-38.)

DIVINNEY Cornelius and Ann ——.
: William. (1808.)

DODSON Richard and Eleanor Grove. Married January 9, 1816.

DODSON William and Elizabeth Short. Married July 23, 1816.
: Ann Eliza, Catherine. (1823-26.)

DODSON Andrew and Ann Mageehan. Married February 15, 1820.
: Sarah, Martha, Joseph, William, Mary Ellen. (1820-30.)

DONECKER Joseph and Mary ——.
: Joseph, Agnes, Mary. (1800-07.)

DONOUGHE Paul and Mary ——.
> Cornelius, Lydia Ann, Mary Honoria, Elizabeth. (1815-22.)

DONOUGHE John and Ann ——.
> David Augustine, Catherine Ann. (Twins, 1830.)

DONOUGHE John and Mary Neason.
> Elizabeth. (1831.)

DONOUGHE John and Apollonia Coons. Married November 22, 1831.
> Joseph Andrew, John Zephyrinus, James Patrick, Mary Elizabeth. (1832-37.)

DONOUGHE Patrick and Mary Reilly.
> Margaret, Thomas. (1833-35.)

DOPP John H. and Ann Riffle. Married August 4, 1835.

DORN Michael and Rosina Hertzog. Married December —, 1835.

DOUGHERTY Edward and Margaret ——.
> Ann, Margaret Barbara. (1806-07.)

DOUGHERTY Patrick and Mary ——.
> Dennis, Edward. (1807-15.)

DOUGHERTY George and Elizabeth ——.
> Andrew. (1809.)

DOUGHERTY Peter and Catherine Dowlan.
> Sarah, Mary, John, Margaret, Felix, Ann, Daniel, Catherine. (1809-30.)

DOUGHERTY John and Elizabeth Little. Married January 7, 1812.
> George, Mary Ann, Margaret Ann, Mary Ann. (1812-17.)

DOUGHERTY Michael and Frances ——.
> John. (1818.)

DOUGHERTY John and Mary Brookbank. Married September 25, 1821.
> Edward, James, Edward, Patrick. (1822-33.)

DOUGHERTY Charles and Unity ——.
> Charles. (1824.)

DOUGHERTY Dennis and Margaret ——.
> James, Margaret Ann, Hugh. (1826-32.)

DOUGHERTY John and Elizabeth McDermitt. Married November 11, 1828.
　Mary Catherine. (1829.)
DOUGHERTY Patrick and Ann Bradley. Married January 19, 1830.
DOUGHERTY Cornelius and Mary Magdalen Nagle. Married May 13, 1834.
　Michael James. (1835.)
DOUGLAS John and Sarah ——.
　Ann, William, John, Augustine, Thaddeus, Silverius, Louis. (1816-29.)
DOUGLAS Jonathan and Monica Delozier.
　James, Ann Jane, Mary, John, Ellen, Margaret. (1818-28.)
DOWNEY Dennis and Elizabeth ——.
　Dennis, Mary, Sophia. (1823-28.)
DOWNEY James and Bridget Ann ——.
　Sarah, John, Bridget Ann. (1825-33.)
DOWNEY Daniel and Alice Carney. Married January 21, 1827.
　Catherine, Henry, James, Ann, Mary, Daniel, Michael. (1827-40.)
DOYLE James and Ann ——.
　James, John, Joseph, Thomas. (1833-39.)
DRISKEL Charles and Ann ——.
　Mary, Michael. (1805-07.)
DRISKEL James and Mary Ann Barnicle. Married May 16, 1822.
　Mary Ellen, Charles, Michael John, Elias. (1823-35.)
DRISKEL Michael and Matilda Kaylor. Married April 12, 1836.
　Catherine, John. (1837-38.)
DUMM George and Sarah Eckenrode. Married September 20, 1835.
　Magdalen. (1838.)
DURBIN Thomas B. and Mary McGuire.
　Michael, Joseph, Richard, Augustine, Margaret, Sarah. (1800-13.)

REV. TERENCE S. REYNOLDS.   PASTOR 1859-68.

DURBIN **Stephen** and **Elizabeth** McConnell. Married **May 17,** 1818.
  Augustine, Sarah, Basil, Mary Ann, Rachel, **William,** William Augustine, Stephen Andrew, Ellen Elizabeth, Matilda. (1819-39.)

DURBIN Thomas and **Sarah** McConnell. Married April 11, 1826.
  Mary Ann, Thomas, **Francis, Jesse,** John, Catherine, Luke. (1828-39.)

DURBIN Augustine and **Catherine Fels (Scanlan.)** Married May 24, 1838.

ECKENRODE Peter and Mary ———.
  Susan. (1824.)

ECKENRODE Jacob and Mary Wangler. Married June 1, 1824.
  John Chrysostom, Mary Magdalen, Ezechias. (1831-37.)

ECKENRODE Jacob and Martha ———.
  Sarah. (1831.)

ECKENRODE **Benjamin** and **Catherine** Miller Married November 1, 1827.
  Jacob, Mary Ann, Joseph, Francis, **Charles,** William, **Silas.** (1828-37.)

ECKENRODE Peter and Christiana **Fox.** Married October 12, 1830.
  Peter Augustine, **Sarah Ann, Mary Ellen, Lucinda.** (1831-38.)

ECKENRODE John and Barbara Illig. **Married** July 21, 1833.
  John Chrysostom, **Sarah Ann.** (1834-35.)

ECKENRODE Joseph and Sarah **Dumm.** Married August 16, 1836.
  Mary Ann, Thomas. (1837-39.)

ECKENRODE **Peter** and **Ann** Miller. Married **June 10, 1828.**

ECKENRODE **John** and **Rebecca** Lyons. **Married November 14, 1830.**

ECKENRODE **Jacob** and **Mary Beber. Married February 15,** 1831.

ECKENRODE Jacob and Notburga Stevens. Married May 29, **1834.**

EGER Joseph and Crescentia Stehle. Married September 12, 1839.
EIGENNUS **Mathias** and Mary Ann ——.
    Gertrude, Anthony. (1825-27.)
ELDER James and Catherine ——.
    John, Henry, Juliana, Margaret. (1802-10.)
ELDER Walter and Priscilla Elder.
    Juliana, Thomas, Sophia, James, Joseph, Richard, William, Mary Ann, Rebecca. (1805-20.)
ELDER John and Mary Ann Myers. Married November 28, 1822.
    Ann Lucretia, Alexis, Priscilla, Sophia. (1824-33.)
ELDER Charles and Mary Cooper. Married July 1, 1830.
    Henry, Augustine, Thomas, Joseph. (1831-37.)
ELDER James and Margaret ——.
    Alexius. (1831.)
ELDER George and Jane Douglas. Married June 5, 1832.
ELDER James and Ann O'Connell. Married January 13, 1835.
    William. (1838.)
ELDER Richard and Margaret Myers. Married April 9, 1839.
ELLIOTT James and Mary ——.
    Isaac, Mary Ann, Susan, Eliza, Sarah. (1824-31.)
ELLIOTT Benjamin and Susan ——.
    Elizabeth. (——).
ERHART Mathias and Margaret Herman. Married August 12, 1838.
    Magdalen. (1839.)
ESMENARD John Baptist and Zelia Marie Bergerac. Married August 12, 1816.
EVERHART Landelin and Mary Magdalen ——.
    Magdalen, Philippina, Sophia. (1833-37.)
FAGAN Peter and Bridget Logan.
    Margaret, Elizabeth, Esther, Hugh, Simon Richard, Felix, Julia Ann, Anastasia, Susan. (1801-19.)

FAGAN James and Catharine Stocker. Married September 13, 1831.
   Joseph. (1832.)
FAGAN Simon Richard and Catherine Yost. Married August 29, 1837.
FAGELY Wendelin and Elizabeth Crow. Married September 27, 1835.
FAIRMAN John and Sarah McKinzie. Married January 22, 1833.
   Thomas. (1834.)
FALDO Martin and Mary Magdalen ——.
   John. (1833.)
FALLON Daniel and Ann Plunkett. Married April 12, 1831.
   Daniel. (1832.)
FARABAUGH Augustine and Mary Ann ——.
   Edward, Augustine. (1833-38.)
FARRELL Cornelius and Margaret ——.
   John, Thomas. (1803-07.)
FARRELL Thomas and Ann ——.
   Bernard, Cornelius, Margaret. (1819-30.)
FARRELL James and Margaret Nagle. Married July 20, 1819.
   Mary Ann, Ruth, Emily, Rachel, Andrew. (1821-28.)
FARRELLY Michael and Mary ——.
   John, Mary, James, Ellen. (1831-37.)
FARREN John and Sarah ——.
   Thomas, Ann, John, Mary (1817-24.)
FARREN Daniel and Mary ——.
   Philip, Daniel, John, Jane, Patrick. (1821-30.)
FAUCHE Solomon and Mary ——.
   Mary Ann, Margaret. (1812-15.)
FECHTER Napoleon and Bridget Hickenour. Married November 24, 1839.
   John. (1848.)
FELLMAN Francis and Elizabeth ——.
   Mary Ann. (1827.)
FELS John and Mary ——.
   Mary Theresa, Mary Margaret, John Baptist. (1808-16.)

116 SOUVENIR

FELS Jacob and Catherine Scanlan.   Married April 12, 1825.
    Mary Elizabeth, John Andrew, Mary Ellen. (1826-34.)
FENLON James and Mary ——.
    Edward. (1833.)
FIELD Felix and Sarah ——.
    John, Samuel. (1818-22.)
FIELZER Michael and Margaret ——.
    Caroline. (1834.)
FINNEGAN Bernard and Margaret Callan.
    Margaret. (1838.)
FISHER Tobias and Magdalen Lenz.   Married July 6, 1834.
FISHER Charles and Mary Ann Hertzog.   Married August 17, 1837.
FITZGIBBONS Michael and Ellen ——.
    Mary, John, Priscilla, Thomas, Charles. (1820-27.)
FITZGIBBONS Michael and Catherine Conrad.   Married September 29, 1833.
    Ellen, John. (1834-38.)
FLANIGAN Peter and Ann ——.
    Peter, Joseph, Mary, Catherine, Margaret, Ann, Susan, John. (1804-19.)
FLANIGAN Michael and Isabella McMullen.   Married November 22, 1825.
    Peter, Ann Elizabeth, James, Bridget Lucretia, Daniel, Francis. (1827-38.)
FLANIGAN Peter and Margaret Reinzel.   Married February 15, 1831.
    John. (1832.)
FLOWERS Jacob and Magdalen ——.
    Mary Magdalen. (——.)
FLOWERS Jacob and Barbara Isler   Married August 10, 1819.
    Ann Clara, Daniel, Catherine, Susan, Mary Ellen. (1820-27.)
FLOWERS John and Mary ——.
    Mary Ann, Joseph. (1832-34.)
FLUM Francis Xavier and Ann ——.
    Peter, John Peter, Mary Leah. (1824-33.)

FORMAN Daniel and Delia Brown. (Negroes.)
    Henry. (1816.)
FORRESTER Patrick and Jane Ivory. Married April 17. 1819.
FREIDHOFF Henry and Mary Ann Baker.
    Henry. (1840.) (The last one baptized by Father Gallitzin.)
FREIDHOFF Nicholas and Veronica Beiter. Married November 20, 1838.
    Magdalen. (1840.)
FRESH John and Catharine Shrum. Married April 15, 1834.
FRY John and Mary ——.
    Jacob, Rosanna. (Twins, 1828.)
FRY John and Cunegunda Fox. Married November 2, 1828.
    Rufina. (1832.)
FURY Edward and Bridget Gorey.
    Ann, James. (1835-38.)
FYAN Robert and Alice ——.
    Robert Washington. (1835.)
GALLAGHER James and Ellen Bradley. Married January 31, 1815.
GALLAGHER Hugh and Mary McCabe. Married March 31, 1818.
    James, Ann, Patrick, John. (1818-29.)
GALLAGHER Francis and Elizabeth Glass. Married February 8, 1831.
    Mary Jane, Susan, George. (1832-38.)
GARDNER Joseph and Ann ——.
    Rebecca. (1799.)
GARDNER John and Catherine Weaver.
    Mary. (1837.)
GARMO Matthew and Mary Ann ——.
    Bartholomew. (1805.)
GARRA Henry and Susan McGuire.
    Veronica. (1817.)
GARRA Peter and Margaret ——.
    Mary Ann. (1818.)
GEORGE Philip and Elizabeth ——.
    Christopher. (1799.)

GEORGE Paul and Margaret Kerrigan.   Married September 16, 1817.
   Mary Magdalen, Michael Frederick, Philip, Prudence, Cecilia Rachel, Peter Paul. (1821-35.)

GEORGE Christopher and Martha Myers.   Married April 12, 1825.
   William Michael, Elizabeth Ann, Margaret, Ann, Michael, Mary Matilda. (1826-38.)

GEORGE Philip and Margaret Branniff.   Married February 19, 1828.
   Ann, Henry, Sarah Ellen. (1828-35.)

GEORGER Stephen and Margaret Exner.   Married April 19, 1835.

GERSTEBACH John and Anna Wangler.   Married May 13, 1823.
   Mary, Catherine, Joseph, Jacob, John, Ann Elizabeth, Magdalen. (1824-32.)

GERSTENWEILER Andrew and Catherine ——.
   Mary. (1807.)

GIBBONS William and Isabella Amelia Thompson (Gardner).
   Margaret, Francis Augustine. (1810-11.)

GILFOYLE Lawrence and Juliana ——.
   Mary. (1838.)

GILLAN Roddy and Ellen ——.
   Elizabeth. (——).

GILLAN William and Mary ——.
   Mary. (1821.)

GILLAN Henry and Ann ——.
   Mary. (1829.)

GILLAN Michael and Mary Ann McCloskey.   Married February 22, 1824.
   Catherine, Ann, Dennis, Margaret. (1827-33.)

GILLESPIE Francis and Isabella ——.
   Rosanna, Patrick, Elizabeth. (1821-26.)

GILLESPIE Francis and Hannah Miller.
   Mary Elizabeth. (1827.)

GINTHER Henry and Elizabeth Mardis.
   Mary Ann. (——).

GINTHER Godfrey and Mary Ann ——.
    William, Godfrey, Joseph. (1824-29.)
GLASS George and Susan Dougherty.
    Margaret, Mary, Susan, Jacob, Elizabeth, George, John, James, Edward, William, Sarah, Augustine. (1801-22.)
GLASS John and Esther O'Hara.
    Margaret, Henry. (1805-08.)
GLASS Jacob and Rufina ——.
    Henry, Daniel, Belinda Ann, Elizabeth, Catherine Sabina. (1807-15.)
GLASS William and Ruth Gorman.
    Mary Ann. (1809.)
GLASS William and Martha Smith.
    William. (1810.)
GLASS Henry and Elizabeth ——.
    Jacob, Margaret, William, Sarah, Juliana. (1811-21.)
GLASS George and Margaret Brown.
    Andrew, William, George, Jacob, John. (1833-39.)
GLASS William and Mary Ann Miller. Married November 5, 1833.
GLASS Henry and Rebecca Burke. Married November 10, 1833.
    Mary, Ann Elizabeth. (1836-39.)
GLASS Jacob and Jane Gorman. Married January 22, 1839.
GORMAN Michael and Sarah Ann ——.
    Agnes, Charity, Dennis, Ann Dorcas. (1804-13.)
GORMAN John Baptist and Sarah ——.
    Joseph Anthony. (1820.)
GORMLY Francis and Mary ——.
    Mary Ann. (1832.)
GREEN Samuel and Sarah ——.
    John. (1791)
GREEN John and Catherine ——.
    Mary. (1824.)
GREENAWALT John and Elizabeth ——.
    John, Margaret Ann, Ann, Rose, Joseph. (1823-30.)

GREW Edward and Mary ——.
    Catherine. (1832.)
GRIFFIN John and Catherine Kelly.
    Edward, Ann. (1837-39.)
GRIMES Felix and Sarah ——.
    John. (1804.)
GRIMES Michael and Bridget ——.
    Mary. (1835.)
GROVE John and Margaret Cherry. Married October 17, 1816.
GUTWALT Landelin and Catherine ——.
    Sarah, Francis Jos., Landelin, Mary, Elizabeth, Christian. (1824-35.)
GWINN James and Catherine Cummiskey.
    James (1826.)
HASS Benedict and Mary Ann ——.
    Mary Ellen, Catherine Barbara. (Twins, 1829.)
HABERMACHER Thomas and Mary Antonia ——.
    Thomas, Peter. (1828-31.)
HABERMACHER Joseph and Ellen Rutler. Married June 9, 1833.
    Susan Catherine, Thomas. (1837-40.)
HAGAN John and Mary ——.
    Mary. (1796.)
HAGAN John and Alice Bradley. Married July 4, 1837.
HAGERTY John and Mary ——.
    William. (1832.)
HAGY Jacob and Mary ——.
    David. (1825.)
HALL William and Mary Shirley.
    Rachel. (1791.)
HALL James and Charity McGuire. Married September 9, 1827.
    Elizabeth Susan, Ann Rachel, James George Washington, Martha Susan. (1828-38.)
HALL Robert and Catherine ——.
    Sarah Ann. (1834.)

HALLER John Baptist and Valeria Stocker.   Married November 2, 1830.
HAMILTON John and Elizabeth ——.
   Mary Jane, John. (1827-30.)
HAMILTON John and Margaret ——.
   Robert. (1837.)
HANDLEY Peter and Anastasia ——.
   John. (1820.)
HANEY William and Elizabeth ——.
   Bridget, Elizabeth, Unity. (1833-38.)
HANLON —— and Sarah ——.
   Henry. (1829.)
HANLON Patrick and Bridget ——.
   Michael, Ann. (1832-33.)
HANLON James and Bridget ——.
   Edmund. (1833.)
HANLON Felix and Mary O'Connor.   Married August 22, 1833.
   Unity, Mary. (1834-36.)
HANLON Philip and Mary ——.
   William. (1838.)
HANSON John and Ann ——.
   Mary. (1812.)
HARKINS John and Ellen ——.
   Catherine. (1832.)
HAROLD Patrick and Hannah Walsh.   Married May 14, 1828.
HARRIN Thomas and Elizabeth ——.
   Daniel. (1799.)
HARRISON Francis and Sarah ——.
   John. (1834.)
HARTMAN John and Mary Magdalen ——.
   Augustine, Simon Peter. (1814-16.)
HAYS Samuel and Barbara ——.
   John, James. (1806-11.)
HAYS Thomas and Ellen Shields.
   James. (1830.)
HEITMAN Conrad and Mary Elizabeth ——.
   Elizabeth, Christina. (1835-37.)

HELSEL Henry and Elizabeth ——.
  Philip, Mary Ann, Jacob, Sarah, Susan, Henry, John Augustine. (1814-31.)
HEMLER Christian and Catherine ——.
  Elizabeth, Henry. (1806-08.)
HEMM Jacob and Barbara ——.
  Joseph Anthony, John. (1830-34.)
HENRY Joseph and Alice McNeil.
  Ann, Catherine. (1835-37.)
HERMAN John and Sarah ——.
  Sarah Ann. (1818.)
HERMAN John and Mary ——.
  Elizabeth, John, Thomas. (1820-28.)
HERMAN Robert and Jane ——.
  Margaret Jane. (1832.)
HERTZOG Stephen and Mary Ann ——.
  Catherine, Frances, John. (1823-27.)
HERTZOG Dominic and Rufina ——.
  Thomas, Theresa, Joseph Dominic. (1824-29.)
HERTZOG Lambert and Rosina ——.
  William. (1825.)
HEYNISS Meinrad and Mary Ann ——.
  Henry, Regina. (1834-36.)
HIMMEL Bruno and Ann Mary Ballweber. Married April 21, 1834.
  John. (1838.)
HINES Francis and Caroline Magdalen ——.
  Catherine, Joseph Francis. (1834-35.)
HINES Jacob and Elizabeth Sanders. Married February 25, 1838.
  Mary Matilda. (1839.)
HOAK Jacob and Ann ——.
  Catherine. (1798.)
HOFF Louis and Catherine Bolan. Married December —, 1835.
HOFFMAN John Baptist and Elizabeth Sherry. Married September 22, 1833.
  Michael, Anthony Joseph, John Baptist. (1836-39.)

HOGUE Sebastian and Magdalen ——.
    Joseph, Mary Ann, Thomas, John. (1826-32.)
HOLDER John and Elizabeth Yost. Married June 22, 1807.
    Jacob. (1808.)
HOLDER Jacob and Mary Lilly. Married May 24, 1831.
    Richard. (1835.)
HOOVER John and Elizabeth ——.
    Louis. (1813.)
HOOVER Francis and Mary Wharton.
    Martha Ann, Margaret Adeline. (1836-39.)
HOOVER Jacob and Lucy Strasler. Married May 16, 1837.
HOPKINS Patrick and Mary ——.
    Thomas. (1831.)
HOUSTON Edward and Mary Connery. Married February 28, 1835.
HOWELL Thomas and Ann ——.
    Mary, Mordecai, Jacob, Hannah, William, Susan, Thomas, Sarah, John Chrysostom, Ann Elizabeth, Thomas. (1804-29.)
HOWELL Jacob and Ann ——.
    Susan, Hannah. (1833-36.)
HOWELL Mordecai and Ann Topper. Married September 29, 1833.
    Mary Ann, Elizabeth Catherine, Thomas. (1835-37.)
HUBER Joseph and Catherine Bearer. Married January 11, 1825.
    Joseph, Mary Ann, Mary Ellen, Henry. (1825-32.)
HUBER Anthony and Margaret Hemm. Married May 27, 1832.
    Joseph Anthony, Anthony. (1833-35.)
HUBER. (See also Hoover).
HUBERT Frederick and Christina Zick. Married April 19, 1835.
HÜBSCH Adam and Frances Baker. Married June 17, 1832.
    Mary. (1833.)
HUDSON William and Ann ——.
    William. (1793.)

HUDSON William and Esther Burke. Married October 3, 1819.
    James, William Demetrius, Henry, Charlotte, John Augustine. (1822-32.)

HUGHES James and Jane ——.
    Mary. (1823.)

HUGHES John and Elizabeth ——.
    Rachel, Thomas Henry. (1825-27.)

HUGHES John and Margaret McHugh. Married September 3, 1829.
    Alice. (1830.)

HUGHES James and Eliza ——.
    Esther, James, Elizabeth. (1834-38.)

HUGHES Edward and Mary Barry.
    Elizabeth. (1837.)

INEICHER Joseph and Sarah Steiner. Married October 30, 1828.
    Sarah Ann. (1829.)

INLOW John and Elizabeth ——.
    Anastasia, James, Rosanna, Ann, John, Josiah. (1807-19.)

INLOW James and Elizabeth Litzinger. Married September 29, 1835.

ITEL John and Mary Ann Seubert.
    Sarah Ann, Francis, Mary Ann, Catherine, Margaret, Anthony, Henry, Joseph, Susan. (1823-38.)

ITEL Joseph and Catherine Eberly. Married November 17, 1830.
    John, Ann Mary, Theresa, Mary Mechthildes. (1831-37.)

IVORY Jeremiah and Sarah Ann Shirley. Married May 9, 1819.
    John Chrysostom, Mary Jane, Eliza Ellen, Rebecca. (1820-27.)

IVORY Matthew and Mary McGuire. Married June 10, 1819.
    William, Rebecca, Luke, Patrick, Henry Joseph, Mary Ellen. (1820-37.)

IVORY Patrick and Ellen Connelly. Married May 19, 1822.

IVORY John and Martha Wharton.   Married August 31, 1824.
JACKMAN William and Mary ——.
    Robert. (1790.)
JACKMAN Robert and Jane ——.
    Mary. (1813.)
JACKSON James and Mary ——.
    Ann (1790.)
JOHNSON Charles and Sybil ——. (Negroes.)
    William, Eliza. (——.)
JOHNSON John and Mary ——.
    Catherine, Mary, Charles, Ellen, James, Sarah, Ann, Elizabeth. (1818-30.)
JOHNSON Thomas and Mary ——.
    Ann Mary. (1826.)
JONES Nelson and Catherine ——.
    Mary, William. (1831-33.)
JORDAN William and Ellen ——.
    John, James, Ann. (1802-07.)
JULAY John and Agatha Shultz.   Married September 17, 1833.
    John, Jacob. (1836-38.)
KANE James and Sarah ——.
    Sarah. (1813.)
KANE James and Mary ——.
    Michael, Ellen, James, John. 1814-34.)
KANE Henry and Susan Beamer.   Married December 8, 1816.
    John, Sarah. (1817-20.)
KANE Francis and Sarah ——.
    James, Alice. (1821-23.)
KANE James and Millburg McGuire.   Married April 27, 1819.
    Margaret, Mary Ann, Henry, Elizabeth, Catherine. (1820-26.)
KANE John and Elizabeth Cooper.   Married November 4, 1828.
KAUFMAN George and Susan ——.
    Mary Elizabeth. (1831.)
KAYLOR Jacob and Catherine McConnell.   Married April 23, 1816.
    Matilda, Elizabeth, Catherine, John, James J., Mary

Ann, Peter William, Esther Caroline, Francis Augustine, Hilary Robert. (1817-38.)

KAYLOR Peter and Agnes Leavy. Married April 28, 1816.
Eliza Ann, Thomas, James, John G., Michael, Peter, Henry, Augustine, Richard, Charles, William Joseph, Agnes. (1817-39.)

KEARNS John and Margaret ——.
Philip, Catherine, William, Anastasia, Mary Ann, Michael. (1823-34.)

KEECH George and Mary ——.
John, Daniel, Michael, Augustine, Stephen George. (1797-1807.)

KEECH George and Ellen ——.
William, James Victor, Henry. (1810-26.)

KEECH John and Catherine Kuhnsman. Married August 5, 1819.
Ellen Jane. (1822.)

KEEFERS Isaac and Ellen ——.
John Baptist. (1805.)

KEEFERS John and Hannah ——.
Ellen, Louisa, Ann Margaret, Isaac, James, John Chrysostom, Catherine. (1805-23.)

KEFFER Joseph and Christina ——.
Christina, Henry, Elizabeth, Joachim, Margaret Alice. (1822-31.)

KEFFER Jacob and Catherine Gutwalt. Married October 9, 1827.
Mary, Magdalen. (1828-30.)

KELLY Charles and Mary ——.
Mary. (1819.)

KELLY Thomas and Mary McMullen. Married August 21, 1821.
Margaret, Michael, Susan, Hugh, Mary Jane, Ann. (1822-34.)

KELLY John and Elizabeth Pflaum. Married April 11, 1826.
Michael Francis. (1827.)

KELLY Daniel and Martha ——.
Barnabas, Daniel. (1835-37.)

KELLY Peter and Mary Litzinger. Married May 26, 1835.
    Michael James, Mary Elizabeth. (1836-38.)
KENNEDY Charles and Mary ——.
    Mary, James, Charles, Sarah, Dennis. Dominic, Margaret, Dennis Augustine. (1808-24.)
KENNEDY Michael and Mary ——.
    Jane Ann, John, Mary, Sarah, James, Dennis. (1811-21.)
KENNEDY Michael and Mary Ann Bender. Married February 16, 1830.
KENNEDY James and Lydia Apollonia Bender. Married April 15, 1834.
KEPPLER Jacob and Sarah ——.
    Elizabeth, Theresa Jane. (1836-38.)
KERRIGAN Peter and Elizabeth ——.
    Cecilia. (1802.)
KERRIGAN Michael and Mary Ann Matay (Matthews).
    Michael. (1824.)
KETTERER Bartholomew and Mary Ann Baker. Married June 17, 1832.
    John, Ann. (1833-36.)
KIERNAN Charles and Susan ——.
    Esther. (1816.)
KIMMONS Henry and Thecla ——.
    Elizabeth, Mary Catherine. Peter. (1808-12.)
KING Christopher and Ann ——.
    Christopher. (1790.)
KING William and Margaret ——.
    Mary. (1821.)
KIRKPATRICK James and Mary ——.
    Elizabeth, John, Margaret, Thomas, Agnes. (1821-30.)
KIRKPATRICK Thomas and Matilda Miller. Married May 9, 1822.
    Mary Ann, Catherine, James, John George. (1823-29.)
KLEIN Bernard and Mary ——.
    Barnabas. (1813.)
KLEIN Adam and Elizabeth ——.
    Catherine. (1832.)

KLEIN Philip and Christina Zimmerman.
    Caroline. (1833.)
KOCH John and Mary ——.
    Magdalen. (1833.)
KOHL John and Mary ——.
    Gregory. (1831.)
KREBS William and Catherine ——.
    Adam. (1835.)
KRISE (Greiss) George and Sarah ——.
    John. (1788.)
KRISE John and Mary ——.
    Catherine Ann, Susan, David, Mary Ann, John. (1816-24.)
KRISE Henry and Margaret ——.
    Ellen, Susan, John, Louisa Ann, Bridget Ann, William George. (1817-29.)
KRISE David and Ruth Adams. Married June 24, 1827.
    Mary Ellen, Mary Elizabeth, Henry, Peter. (1828-33.)
KRISE John and Sarah Litzinger. Married September 22, 1829.
    Elizabeth Matilda, Julia Ann, Henry George, Daniel Demetrius. (1830-38.)
KRISE George and Ann Ritz.
    Henry, Michael. (1835-37.)
KRÜCHTEN Anthony and Catherine ——.
    Barnabas, Susan. (1836-37.)
KRUG Valentine and Margaret ——.
    David, John Valentine, Peter. (1831-37.)
KRUMENACHER Joseph and Mary Ann Myers.
    Mary Magdalen. (1838.)
KUNTZ Jacob and Magdalen Rometsch.
    Anthony, John George, Michael. (1833-47.)
LAKE William and Ann McCloskey. Married August 23, 1831.
    Elizabeth, Ann Theresa, Mary Jane, John G. (1834-40.)
LAMBACH Anthony and Naomi ——.
    Anthony. (1797.)

REV. MICHAEL J. MITCHELL. PASTOR 1868-70.

LAMBACH Anthony and Sarah Todd. Married January 14, 1817.
  Naomi, John Stephen. (1819-22.)
LANTZ Jacob and Jane ———.
  Abraham. (1807.)
LANTZ Abraham and Mary Magd. Flowers. Married June 3, 1827.
  Mary Ann, Susan, Mary Magdalen, Joseph William, Stephen. (1828-38.)
LANTZY Joseph and Ursula Bitters.
  John, Mary Ann. (1827-30.)
LATCHFORD Alexander and Magdalen ———.
  Benjamin. (1807.)
LEAVY Michael and Mary Ann Little.
  Agnes Ann, Ellen Catherine, James, Bernard, Mary Magdalen, John Thomas, Susan, Henry, Michael Patrick, Francis, William Alexander, Matilda Jane. (1821-39.)
LEWIS George and Eliza Johnson. (Negroes.) Married April 2, 1826.
  Charles, Mary Ann, Rosalia, Martha, Emily, Sabina. (1827-37.)
LILLY Joseph and Charity ———.
  Luke, Theresa, Isidore. (1802-09.)
LILLY Richard and Elizabeth ———.
  Mary, Leo, Rebecca, Elizabeth. (1809-27.)
LILLY Thomas and Catharine Myers. Married September 24, 1816.
  Praxedis, Praxedis, Ann Praxedis, Lucy Ann, Celestine, Catherine, John Chrysostom. (1817-33.)
LILLY Joseph and Mary Ann ———.
  James Hyacinth, Januarius, Charity Elizabeth, Sarah Ann, Samuel. (1825-38.)
LILLY Samuel and Catherine Troxell. Married February 3, 1825.
  Thomas, Joseph, William, Isidore. (1826-39.)
LILLY Luke and Rachel Fels. Married October 17, 1826.
  Jane Elizabeth, Mary Theresa. (1828-30.)

LILLY Isidore and Margaret Ramage.
  William. (1839.)
LINDER John and Lydia ——.
  Elizabeth, Sarah Ann, James, Thomas, John. (1809-21.)
LINDER Michael and Mary Ann ——.
  John, Mary Ann. (1824-27.)
LITTLE Bernard and Mary Ann ——.
  Susan, Peter J. (1806-09.)
LITTLE John and Elizabeth Bradley. Married June 20, 1820.
  Mary Ann, Catherine, Henry, Sylvester, Elizabeth Jane, John Edward, Margaret. (1821-37.)
LITTLE George and Catherine Byrne. Married October 3, 1824.
  Lucinda Ann, Philip James, Bernard, Agnes Ann, Mary, Lucinda Ann, David Thomas, Susan, Sarah Catherine, Emily. (1825-39.)
LITZINGER Jacob and Sarah ——.
  Apollonia, James. (1804-07.)
LITZINGER Leonard and Elizabeth Miller.
  Sarah, George, Daniel, Mary, James. (1805-15.)
LITZINGER John and Apollonia Adams.
  Elizabeth. (1806.)
LITZINGER Michael and Ann Brawley. Married October 22, 1816.
  Mary Ann, Dennis Augustine, Eliza, John, William Augustine. (1821-30.)
LITZINGER Barnabas and Honoria Nagle.
  Mary Ann, John, Catherine, Ann, Michael, Margaret, Eveline Ann. (1824-37.)
LITZINGER David and Ann McManamy. Married January 12, 1832.
  Mary Jane, Demetrius Augustine, Thomas Anthony. (1835-38.)
LITZINGER Michael and Ellen Keech.
  Margaret Ellen. (1834.)
LOGAN Dennis and Catherine Gallagher. Married August 17, 1813.

LOGAN Joseph and Rachel ——.
    Joseph Ferdinand. (1831.)
LONG Henry and Mary McCalley.
    Daniel, John, Henry. (1815-19.)
LONG Andrew and Elizabeth ——.
    Mary Ann, William, Catherine, Elizabeth Sarah, Simon, Sarah. (1823-32.)
LONG John and Catherine ——.
    Mary Elizabeth. (1830.)
LONG Anthony and Mary Ann Coons. Married October 27, 1830.
    Christina, Mary Ann, Elizabeth Amanda. (1831-37.)
LONG Joseph and Barbara Schwab. Married June 30, 1833.
LONGSTRETH John and Margaret ——.
    Margaret. (1784.)
LONGSTRETH Daniel and Ann ——.
    Ellen, Mary Ann. (1803-11.)
LONGSTRETH Bartholomew and Margaret ——.
    Catherine, Philip, Margaret. (1808-11.)
LONGSTRETH Michael and Mary Dimond. Married May 8, 1827.
    Sarah Ann. Susan. (1828-30.)
LUCKETT John and Sarah ——.
    Elizabeth, Demetrius Augustine, Thomas, John, Martha Ann, James Sylvester. (1823-32.)
LUCKETT Thomas and Elizabeth McKinzie.
    Elizabeth, James Francis Xavier, Ellen, Thomas. (1828-35.)
LUTHER Conrad and Elizabeth ——.
    (Elizabeth, wife of Conrad, 1770). Ann Mary, John, William, Christian, Jacob. (1796-1806.)
LUTHER Christopher and Rebecca ——.
    John, Jacob, Eliza, Levi, Mary, Joseph, Sarah Ann, Elizabeth. (1815-32.)
LUTHER John and Mary Ann Byrne. Married May 31, 1825.
    Henry, Demetrius Augustine, Sarah Ann, Agnes Elizabeth, Lucinda Martha. (1826-32.)

LUTHER William and Mary Zern.   Married February —,
    1832.
    Rosanna. (1832.)
LYNN Patrick and —— ——.
    Michael. (——.)
MADDEN Patrick and Ann ——.
    Daniel. (1850.)
MAHER John and Bridget ——.
    Mary Ann. (1818.)
MAHONEY John and Elizabeth ——.
    James. (1815.)
MALLOY James and Susan Kelly.   Married April 8, 1834.
    Mary, Michael, Mary, John. (1835-39.)
MALONE Charles and Elizabeth ——.
    Charles. (1804.)
MALONE Daniel and Rosanna ——.
    James, Elizabeth, Chrysostom. (1807-10.)
MALONE Patrick and Mary ——.
    Mary Ann. (1815.)
MALONE Patrick and Elizabeth Storm.   Married January 17,
    1819.
    Charles Augustine. (1822.)
MALONEY James and Barbara ——.
    Mary Elizabeth, James, Josue Robert. (1825-38.)
MANSFIELD William and Elizabeth ——.
    Henry Joseph, John. (1825-29.)
MARDIS George and Susan ——.
    Elizabeth. (1791.)
MARDIS Samuel and Abigail Yost.   Married January 31, 1815.
    Joseph, William, Catherine, Jacob. (1816-26.)
MARKS John and Sarah ——.
    Elizabeth, Michael. (1800-02.)
MARKS Jacob and Theresa ——.
    Theresa, Jacob. (1808-14.)
MARRACK (Marecque) Louis and Agatha McGuire.   Married
    January 9, 1816.
    Mary Ann, John Baptist. (1816-18.)

MATTHEWS (Matay) John and Mary Ann Ulrich.
   Ann Jane, John, Patience. (1833-38.)
MAURATH Fidelis and Magdalena Goetz. Married June 8, 1834.
McAFEE Andrew and Elizabeth ———.
   John. (1802.)
McAFEE Peter and Catherine ———.
   Michael. (1809.)
McANANY Thomas and Mary ———.
   Mary. (1833.)
McANULTY Samuel and Mary Mooney. Married February 18, 1817.
   Charles Augustine, John, Isabella. (1817-20.)
McANULTY John and Elizabeth ———.
   Mary Ann, John. (1823-25.)
McATEER Patrick and Catherine ———.
   John Joseph. (1817.)
McATEER James and Mary Ann Elder. Married November 27, 1838.
   William W. (1839.)
McBRIDE James and Ellen ———.
   Ellen, Margaret, James, Barnabas. (1814-26.)
McCALEB Hugh and Margaret O'Connor. Married March 5, 1826.
McCALL Robert and Julia ———.
   William. (1805.)
McCALL William and Mary Myers. Married August 23, 1825.
   Stephen Augustine, Julia Ann, Elizabeth, Michael, Mary Magdalen, Ellen Jane. (1827-39.)
McCALLEY ——— and Ann ———.
   Mary. (1808.)
McCALLEY Henry and Jane ———.
   John Gabriel. (1821.)
McCARTHY John and Elizabeth ———.
   Mary, James, John. (1811-15.)
McCARTHY Michael and Catherine Gillan. Married May 8, 1833.

McCarthy John and Mary ——.
    Ellen, Elizabeth, Prudence Ann, Ellen. (1835-39.)
McCartney John and Elizabeth ——.
    John (the father, 1782.)   Elizabeth (the mother, 1790.)
    Hannah, Elizabeth. (1807-10.)
McCartney Margaret, 1787.   Rosanna, 1794.
McCauley John and Mary ——.
    Charles, Alexander. (1812-14.)
McCauley Daniel and Ann Kirkpatrick.   Married June 4, 1822.
    Margaret, John, Thomas. (1823-29.)
McClain Alexander and Eliza Henry.
    John. (1820.)
McCloskey Patrick and Ann ——.
    Mary, Ann, Theresa, James, John, Cornelius, Rose Ellen, Thomas, Patrick Augustine. (1804-25.)
McCloskey Dennis and Margaret ——.
    James, Mary, John, Mary. (1804-10.)
McCloskey William and Ann ——.
    Mary Ann, James, Hugh, Margaret, John, William, Peter, Patrick, Joseph, Edward, Edward David. (1805-23.)
McCloskey James and Esther O'Hara.   Married January 28, 1834.
    Rachel Ann, Mary Matilda, William Sylvester. (1835-39.)
McCloskey Hugh and Ellen Brady.   Married March 1, 1835.
McCloskey John and Susan Flynn.   Married January 8, 1839.
McConnell Henry and Margaret ——.
    Cornelius, William, Alexander. (1806-10.)
McConnell Arthur and Catherine ——.
    Augustine, Francis. (1808-10.)
McConnell John and Margaret ——.
    Cornelius. (1811.)
McConnell James and Margaret ——.
    Ann. (1811.)

McConnell Francis and Margaret ———.
>Mary Ann, Hugh, Sarah, Elizabeth, James, John William, Lydia Matilda, Catherine. (1823-37.)

McConnell John and Margaret Tierney. Married April 26, 1825.
>Sarah Ann, Margaret, Francis, John William. (1827-33.)

McConnell Barnabas and Margaret McIntosh. Married April 11, 1826.

McConnell John A. and Hannah Watt. Married May 15, 1827.
>John Arthur, David Augustine, Catherine Jane, Francis William. (1831-38.)

McConnell Thomas and Mary Ann Skelly. Married August 3, 1830.
>William, Susan. (1831-33.)

McConnell Hugh and Elizabeth Walters. Married April 28, 1835.
>Demetrius Augustine, Mary, Ann Elizabeth. (1836-39.)

McConnell Augustine and Rebecca Branniff. Married February 5, 1837.
>Mary Elizabeth. (1839.)

McCool Charles and Jane Montgomery. Married January 30, 1821.

McCormick James and Charlotte ———.
>Martha. (1810.)

McCormick Hugh and Ann ———.
>Thomas, Mary Ann, Francis, John, Catherine, Elizabeth. (1832-39.)

McCoy John and Susan ———.
>Mary, Hugh, Patrick, Ann, Catherine, John, Margaret. (1806-17.)

McCoy Alexander and Margaret ———.
>Mary Ann, James, Patrick, John, Hugh, Catherine. (1813-22.)

McCoy Hugh and Ann O'Hara.
>Mary, Ann, John Augustine. (1816-20.)

McCoy Hugh and Margaret ——.
　　John and Andrew. (Twins, 1833). Robert. (1835.)
McCoy Charles and Ann Gorman.
　　Andrew, Thomas, Catherine, Michael. (1832-38.)
McCoy Anthony and Mary McShane.
　　Catherine, Susan, Anthony, Jane. (1833-40.)
McCoy Peter and Margaret Durbin.
　　Patrick, Rachel, Susan, Mary, Alice, Mary Jane. (1832-38.)
McCreeden James and Margaret Montgomery.
　　Jane. (1820.)
McCullough John and Bridget McAllister.
　　Catherine, Mary. (1834-36.)
McCune William and Margaret Brawley. Married November 4, 1828.
McCune William and Mary Ann Dougherty. Married May —, 1836.
McCusker Dominic and Cynthia Beigley.
　　Matilda. (1822.)
McDade John and Rosanna ——.
　　Anthony, Rosanna, Dennis. (1827-32.)
McDermitt John and Mary ——.
　　James, Jane, Elizabeth. (1811-16.)
McDermitt Michael and Ellen ——.
　　Michael, Henry, John, Mary Ellen, Martha Jane, Mary Ann, Bridget Ann, Susan Matilda. (1812-26.)
McDermitt Samuel and Mary ——.
　　John, James, William, Augustine, Mary, Michael D., Catherine A., Francis. (1812-28.)
McDermitt George and Mary ——.
　　John. (1814.)
McDermitt Arthur and Jane McMullen. Married November 6, 1815.
　　Susan, Eliza, Mary, Catherine Ellen, Margaret, Sarah Jane, Ann, Alexander, Louis Charles. (1820-39.)
McDermitt James and Sarah (Susan) Meloy. Married September 24, 1816.
　　William. (1821.)

McDermitt John and Sarah Wharton. Married January 8, 1835.
:   Demetrius Augustine, William, Joseph. (1835-39.)

McDermitt James and Ann McGuire.
:   Bridget. (1839.)

McDermitt James and Lydia Ann Donoughe. Married February 11, 1840.

McDonald Owen and Eliza ——.
:   Andrew S., Mary, James Edward, Alice S., Eliza Ann, Margaret, Rose P., Eugene, Francis. (1815-29.)

McDonald Cornelius and Rachel Apollonia White.
:   Alice, Philip, Andrew, Joseph, John. (1815-24.)

McDonald Alexander and Elizabeth ——.
:   Alan Augustine. (1816.)

McElroy —— and ——.
:   William. (1808.)

McFeely Bernard and Catherine ——.
:   Mary, Susan, James. (1805-16.)

McFeely Bernard and Frances Noble.
:   Lucy Ann. (1824.)

McFeely Bernard and Mary Ellen Dawson. Married May 21, 1826.
:   Catherine, John, Ann, Mary, Sarah Ann, Patrick Joseph. (1827-38.)

McGahan Patrick and Ellen ——.
:   Sarah, Matilda, John. (1820-24.)

McGarrity Charles and Mary ——.
:   Patrick, Mary, Bridget, Charles. (1818-29.)

McGaughey Matthew and Martha Daly.
:   John. (1839.)

McGee Patrick and Jane McConnell. Married August 23, 1814.
:   Francis, Rose, Mary, Sarah Ann. (1817-25.)

McGeehan James and Apollonia ——.
:   Michael Daniel, Rachel, Joseph, John, Ann Mary, Demetrius Augustine. (1805-20.)

McGeehan Michael Dan and Mary Glass. Married July 23, 1833.

McGILL Richard and Rose ——.
    John. (1819.)

McGINNITY James and Petronilla ——.
    Margaret Ann. (1806.)

McGONIGLE Daniel and Margaret ——.
    Patrick. (1819.)

McGONIGLE Charles and Ann Dever. Married February 15, 1824.
    Jeremiah, Margaret, Ann. (1825-31.)

McGOUGH Arthur and Susan ——.
    Agnes. (1802.)

McGOUGH Arthur and Margaret Glass. Married April 21, 1812.
    John, James, Thomas, Susan, Juliana, Mary, Margaret. (1813-27.)

McGOUGH Miles and Mary ——.
    Margaret. (1803.)

McGOUGH Thomas and Sarah ——.
    Thomas, James. (1810-13.)

McGOUGH John and Sarah ——.
    Thomas, Julia Ann, Samuel, William, Joseph, Susan, Jesse, Sarah, Peter, Mary, Martha, Catherine Caroline. (1812-34.)

McGOUGH Thomas and Mary Skelly. Married June 9, 1812.
    James, Mary Ann, William Augustine, Thomas, Daniel. (1814-33.)

McGOUGH John and Elizabeth ——.
    John. (1823.)

McGOUGH James and Margaret Glass. Married November 1, 1822.
    Ellen, George Chrysostom, Susan, Charles, Ann, James Edward, Silas Augustine, Andrew Tobias. (1823-38.)

McGOUGH James and Sophia Früh.
    Esther, Mary Ann, William Augustine, Thomas, Philip. (1827-35.)

McGOUGH James and Elizabeth Dimond. Married May 11, 1834.
   Catherine Matilda, Mary Ellen. (1835-37.)
McGOVELIN Gilbert and Catherine ——.
   Luke. (1822.)
McGRANAHAN Thomas and Grace ——.
   Mary. (1820.)
McGRANAHAN James and Bridget ——.
   Mary, Patrick. (1820-24.)
McGRANN John and Catherine ——.
   James. (1834.)
McGRAW Peter and Catherine McAfee. Married June 22, 1807.
   Edward Francis, Benjamin, Mary Ellen. (1808-15.)
McGRAW John and Charity Delozier. Married April 26, 1812.
   Edward Augustine, Joseph Daniel, Peter. (1813-17.)
McGRAW William and Jane ——.
   Eliza Ann. (1813.)
McGUIRE Michael and Patience ——.
   Luke, Rachel, John. (1800-05.)
McGUIRE Michael and Sarah Byrne.
   Mary Ann. (1803.)
McGUIRE Luke and Margaret ——.
   Elizabeth, Augustine, Margaret, Anastasia, Michael L., Catherine, Monica. (1801-17.)
McGUIRE Richard and Eleanor Byrne. Married May 15, 1800.
   Mary Ann, Bridget Rachel, Agnes, Catherine, Juliana, Michael, Agnes, John, Richard, Joseph. (1801-22.)
McGUIRE Peter and Charity ——.
   Charity, Ann Patience, Catherine, Patrick. (1801-10.)
McGUIRE James L. and Catherine ——.
   John, Charles Michael, Michael, James, Catherine. (1802-12.)
McGUIRE Ross Patrick and Margaret ——.
   Theresa. (1804.)

McGuire James C. and Elizabeth ——.
   Bridget, Charles, James, Elizabeth Jane, William, John Chrysostom, Edward. (1806-19.)

McGuire Michael and Margaret ——.
   Ellen, John, Timothy, Margaret Jane. (1810-25.)

McGuire James and Deborah ——.
   Sarah Ann. (1819.)

McGuire Luke and Martha Cooper. Married August 20, 1822.
   Mary, Rebecca, Margaret, Henry, Augustine, Luke, James, Elizabeth, Mark. (1823-37.)

McGuire Henry and Mary Burke. Married February 10, 1824.

McGuire Vincent and Margaret Eckenrode. Married November 2, 1824.
   James Ross, Mary Ann. (1826-33.)

McGuire Andrew and Elizabeth Ann Gardner.
   Cornelius, Sarah Ann, Sylvester, Andrew John, Mary Elizabeth. (1827-39.)

McGuire John and Susan Storm. Married March 3, 1829.
   Mary Ann, James, John, Nicholas, Peter. (1829-37.)

McGuire Charles and Catherine Kenny. Married October 25, 1830.

McGuire Michael and Margaret Bostick. Married February 12, 1833.

McHugh John and Elsie ——.
   Catherine, James. (1806-10.)

McHugh Matthew and Mary Ann McGuire. Married August 24, 1819.
   Agnes, John, Ellen, Michael Richard, Alice, Mary Ann, Bridget Rachel, Matthew. (1820-34.)

McHugh Michael and Elizabeth McManus.
   Matthew, Henry. (1824-35.)

McIntire Peter and Elizabeth ——.
   Mary, Elizabeth. (1798-1803.)

McIntosh Archibald and Margaret Becht. Married May 14, 1820.

McKenna James and Catherine ——.
    Ann, James. (1830-32.)
McKiernan John and Delia Brown.
    Isabella. (1824.)
McKim William and Rosanna ——.
    James, Robert, Jane. (1819-22.)
McKinney Thomas and Martha (Elizabeth) ——.
    Juliana, Margaret. (1813-29.)
McKinney Philip and Juliana ——.
    William, James, Juliana. (1830-34.)
McKinzie John and Elizabeth ——.
    Elizabeth, Clara, Sarah, Lydia, Amelia Ann. (1808-24.)
McKinzie Henry and Ellen ——.
    Sylvester, Margaret Jane, John, Mary Ann, James Demetrius, William Augustine, Mary Ellen. (1823-38.)
McKinzie John and Sarah Brown. Married November 17, 1829.
McKinzie Leo and Mary Ann Glass. Married November 27, 1832.
    John Edward, Peter Joseph. (1833-36.)
McKinzie Alan and Clara ——.
    George. (1834.)
McKinzie John and Esther Hudson. Married November 25, 1838.
McLaughlin Patrick and Mary ——.
    Rosanna, Charles, Daniel. (1891-97.)
McLaughlin John and Margaret ——.
    Mary Magdalen, James, Augustine, Rosanna. (1812-21.)
McLaughlin Mark and Susan ——.
    Patrick, Patrick. (1827-29.)
McLaughlin Charles and Margaret Kane. Married May 12, 1828.
    Sarah Jane. (1829.)
McManamy Patrick and Bridget ——.
    Daniel, Amelia, Grace, Eliza. (1814-20.)
McManamy William and Mary Matilda Cassidy. Married September 20, 1829.

McMANUS Charles and Rosanna ——.
    Mary Ellen. (1834.)
McMULLEN Samuel and Susan Logan.
    Mary, Hugh, Alexander, John. (1801-08.)
McMULLEN Enos and Catherine ——.
    Lawrence, Mary Ann, Enos. (1803-15.)
McMULLEN Henry and Elizabeth O'Hara.
    Mary. (1818.)
McMULLEN James and Rebecca McDermitt. Married May 13, 1823.
    John A., Alexander, Henry, Hugh, Michael, Mary Matilda. (1824-38.)
McMULLEN Hugh and Mary Catherine Riffel.
    James, Lucy, Susan Jane. 1835-39.)
McMULLEN William and Ann ——.
    Ann Elizabeth, Samuel. (1836-37.)
McMULLEN James and Susan McDermitt. Married November 5, 1837.
    John Edwin, Charles Augustine. (1838-39.)
McMULLEN Matthew and Adeline Ann Weakland. Married November 28, 1837.
    Celestine. (1838.)
McMULLEN John and Mary Ellen McDermitt. Married February, 27, 1838.
McMULLEN Alexander and Catherine McGuire. Married June 16, 1839.
McNALLY Owen and Mary ——.
    Mary, John. (1834-36.)
McTAMMANY Timothy and Ann Cassidy.
    Peter. (1835.)
McVEY Patrick and Susan ——.
    John, Mary Ann, James, Michael, Daniel. (1808-18.)
MEANS Daniel and Elizabeth ——.
    Elizabeth. (1792.)
MELHORN Daniel and Sarah Conrad.
    Susan Matilda, Mary Ann, Cecilia Anastasia. (1835-38.)

MELLON Patrick and Mary McCloskey. Married August 24, 1813.
    Margaret, Isabella, Lucy, James. (1814-21.)
MELOY Hugh and Elizabeth Logan.
    William Andrew, Bridget. (1810-11.)
MELOY James and Margaret McMullen.
    Edward, James, Catherine, John Chrysostom, Henry. (1815-27.)
MELOY John and Sarah Gardner. Married February 10, 1815.
    William, Mary, Susan, Charles, Michael Chrysostom, Bridget, John, Fidelis, Sarah Ann, Hugh. (1816-34.)
MELOY Charles and Sarah Freel. Married May 16, 1815.
MELOY Hugh and Mary Bradley (Freel). Married November 18, 1823.
    Mary, Sarah, Margaret. (1824-30.)
MELOY John and Ann ——.
    Mary Ann. (1832.)
MELOY Michael and Ann ——.
    Mary. (1832.)
METZGER Michael and Apollonia ——.
    Joseph, Mary Ann. (1819-21.)
MILER Gregory and Bridget ——.
    Patrick, Anastasia, Bridget Ellen. (1828-34.)
MILLER Valentine and Susan ——.
    Philippina. (1785.)
MILLER John and Catherine ——.
    Mary Ann, Joseph, John George, Margaret Ann, Henry. (1808-17.)
MILLER John and Rose ——.
    Mary Ann, Anthony. (1821-23.)
MILLER Anthony and Theresa Durbin. Married April 29, 1823.
    Henry George, Mary, Augustine, Catherine Ann, Stephen. (1824-33.)
MILLER Sebastian and Theresa ——.
    Mary, Mary Theresa, Mary Magdalen, Joseph, Peter. (1827-36.)

MILLER Daniel and Mary McCalley.   Married May 26, 1835.
MILLER Joseph and Ann Ritter.   Married February 15, 1836.
MOFFIT Richard and Margaret Glass.   Married August 17, 1823.
MONAHAN Lawrence and —— ——.
   Mary, Thomas. (1817-19.)
MONAHAN Thomas and Mary ——.
   Elizabeth. (1820.)
MOONEY Abraham and Margaret ——.
   Mary. (——)
MOORE John and Rosanna ——.
   Sarah. (1808.)
MORAN Robert and Catherine ——.
   Edward (1821.)
MORELAND Thomas and Margaret Dimond   Married April 10, 1837.
MORLAN Jacob and Mary Ann Schwab.   Married September 22, 1833.
MOSER John Baptist and Mary Magdalen Illig.   Married February 3, 1834.
MULHOLLAN David and Ann ——.
   James, David. (1803-05.)
MULLEN James and Ann ——.
   Francis. (1803.)
MULLEN Michael and Elizabeth Kerrigan.   Married July 3, 1820.
   John, Hugh, Mary Jane, Robert, Alice Ann. (1820-29.)
MULLEN Edward and Margaret Fagan.   Married November 14, 1824.
   Patrick, Mary, Thomas, Elizabeth, Simon, Ann, Peter, Anastasia, Edward James. (1825-40.)
MULVIHILL Peter and Mary Higgins.   Married July 27, 1823.
   James. (1824.)
MURPHY William and Elizabeth Werner.
   Mary Elizabeth, Michael. (1808-10.)
MURPHY Michael and Catherine ——.
   Michael, Sarah Ann. (1812-13.)

VERY REV. EDWARD A. BUSH, V. G.   PASTOR 1870-90.

MURPHY Edward and Margaret ——.
    James, Catherine, Hannah, Mary, Ann, Lawrence, Theodore. (1815-35.)

MURPHY Lawrence and Margaret ——.
    Mary, Michael, Sarah Ann, John, Felix Augustine. (1825-35.)

MURPHY Michael and Mary McDade. Married February 24, 1838.
    Margaret. (1839.)

MURRAY John and Mary ——.
    James, Henry, Joseph, Daniel, John, Patrick, Mary, Jane, Sarah Ann, Catherine, Elizabeth, Lucinda. (1798-1822.)

MURRAY Daniel and Mary Todd. Married January 17, 1819.
    Mary. (1819.)

MURRAY Patrick and Jane ——.
    John. (1822.)

MURRAY Daniel and Mary Campbell. Married February 18, 1819.

MURRAY James and Elizabeth Scanlan. Married September 25, 1827.

MURRAY James and Mary McCloskey.
    Ellen. (1839.)

MURRAY Michael and Mary Glacken.
    John, Ellen, Dennis. (1834-39.)

MUSSELMAN David and Sarah ——.
    Mary Ann Magdalen, Amelia Rachel, Daniel, Margaret, Peter. (1805-16.)

MYERS Joseph and Catherine ——.
    Catherine, Lucy, Joseph. (1804-11.)

MYERS Joseph and Rebecca Gardner.
    Mary Caroline, Augustine, John, Luke. (1825-32.)

MYERS Michael and Elizabeth Hagy.
    Bernard, Elizabeth, Peter, Mary Ann, Stephen Augustine. (1807-18.)

MYERS John and Eve ——.
    James. (1807.)

MYERS John and Catherine Decker.
> Magdalen, Anthony, Bernard, Peter, Margaret, Juliana, Luke, David. (1807-27.)

MYERS John and Ann Glass. Married May 11, 1817.
> James, Susan, Matilda, Mary Magdalen, George, John, Henry, Margaret, Catherine, William, Martha Jane. (1817-39.)

MYERS John, Jr., and Catherine ——.
> George, Peter, Anthony, Mary Ann, Catherine, John Baptist, Catherine Ann, Matilda. (1820-37.)

MYERS Adam and Elizabeth Weaver. Married January 23, 1825.
> Mary Ann, Michael, Ann, Susan, Elizabeth. (1825-34.)

MYERS Peter and Mary Eve Hertzog. Married August 26, 1829.
> James. (1831.)

MYERS George and Mary ——.
> Joseph, Mary Ellen. (1833-34.)

MYERS Thomas and Magdalen ——.
> John. (1834.)

MYERS Louis and Catherine Noel. Married February 10, 1839.

MYERS Bernard and Mary Ann Nagle. Married February 11, 1840.

NAGLE Jacob and Martha ——.
> Nicholas, Mary Ann, Margaret, Mary Ann, George, Mary Magdalen, Jacob. (1806-20.)

NAGLE Jacob and Mary Magdalen ——.
> Catherine, Richard, Michael James, Sarah Ann. (1818-28.)

NAGLE John and Catherine Coons. Married February 16, 1819.
> Michael, Mary Ann, John, Jacob Zephyrinus, Thomas, Christina, Catherine, Margaret, Rhode Ann, Susan. (1820-39.)

NAGLE John and Bridget Barnicle. Married August 29, 1826.
> Sarah Ann, Nicholas, Mary. (1828-33.)

NAGLE Nicholas and Susan ———.
> Catherine Jane. (1830.)

NAGLE George and Sarah Dougherty. Married May 1, 1832.

NEASON James and Mary ———.
> Mary. (1809.)

NEFF ——— and ———.
> Jacob. (1792.)

NEFF Jacob and Elizabeth Skelly. Married June 20, 1822.
> Susan, Margaret, Elizabeth, Sarah. (1823-37.)

NEFF Daniel and Elizabeth ———.
> John, Abraham, Mary Ann, Susan. (1827-32.)

NOEL John and Mary Burke. Married July 18, 1820.
> Rebecca, Rachel Apollonia, John, Catherine. (1821-33.)

NOEL Peter and Catherine ———.
> Margaret, Jacob, Elizabeth. (1824-29.)

NOEL Blasius and Sophia Burke. Married June 4, 1826.
> William, Mary Magdalen, Jacob Blasius, Henry Patrick. (1827-36.)

NOEL Joseph and Margaret Carney. Married February 2, 1829.
> William, Nicholas, James (Jacob), Mary Ann, Catherine. (1830-39.)

NOEL Isaac and Mary Magdalen Roudebush. Married December 13, 1829.
> Margaret, Henry Blasius, Isaac Jacob, Catherine Elizabeth, Sarah, David Peter. (1830-39.)

NOEL Peter and Catherine Hoak. Married December 20, 1829.

NOEL David and Mary Ann Fauché. Married April 30, 1833.
> Mary Ellen, John Peter, Henry Michael. (1834-37.)

NOEL Simon and Mary Ann (Margaret) ———.
> Anthony James, John Henry. (1832-34.)

NOEL Joachim and Mary Ann Criste. Married May 7, 1833.

NOEL Peter and Mary Hurley. Married August 20, 1833.

NOEL Henry and Mary Ann Plunkett.
> Catherine Felicitas, Juliana Margaret, Mary Ann Cecilia, Ellen. (1834-38.)

NOEL Daniel and Veronica Burke. Married March 3, 1840. (This was the last marriage recorded by Father Gallitzin.)

NOON Dennis and Bridget O'Donnell.
Mary Ann, Dominic, Jane, James, Ellen, Margaret, Philip, Philip. (1817-34.)

NOON Philip and Ellen Luckett. Married February 19, 1822.
Martha Jane, Margaret. (1823-26.)

NOON Charles and Catherine Dever. Married October 18, 1827.
Sarah, James, Charles, James, Sarah Jane, Charles, Catherine. (1828-38.)

NOWLAN Timothy and Mary ——.
Ann, Catherine, Mary. (1817-21.)

NUPPER Anthony and Mary Ann ——.
Charles. (1826.)

O'CONNELL William and Mary Thompson.
Elizabeth, Susan, William, Thomas, Mary Ann. (1819-27.)

O'CONNELL John and Margaret Moore.
Joseph, Elizabeth Ann, Patrick, Theresa, John, Monica. (1821-34.)

O'CONNOR John and Joanna ——.
Margaret. (1805.)

O'CONNOR John and Mary ——.
Lucy Ann. (1818.)

O'CONNOR Michael and Mary ——.
Thomas and Patrick. (1831-34.)

O'DONNELL Hugh and Esther Fagan. Married January 28, 1834.
Charles. (1834.)

O'HARA Daniel and Rachel ——.
John, Henry, Esther, Thomas. (1803-08.)

O'HARA David and Elizabeth Parrish. Married October 27, 1829.
Elizabeth Jane, Josue, Anastasia, John, Charles. (1830-38.)

O'Hara Thomas and Catherine Carney. Married January 12. 1830.
    Catherine Ann, Valentine. (1835-38.)

O'Hara Henry and Ann Patience McGuire. Married July 6, 1830.
    Mary Elizabeth, Emily Caroline, Francis, Thaddeus Peter. (1831-38.)

O'Keefe William and Esther ——.
    Bridget, Edward, William, John. (1805-13.)

O'Neill Daniel and Ann McShane. Married January 16, 1825.

O'Neill Francis and Elizabeth ——.
    Daniel. (1832.)

O'Neill Francis and Bridget ——.
    Christopher. (1833.)

O'Reilly Cornelius and Margaret ——.
    Mary Ann. (1833.)

Orr James and Mary ——.
    Mary Susan. (1834.)

Paddick Horatio Benjamin and Ann Short.
    Andrew, Mary Catherine, Martha Abigail. (1832-37.)

Parrats John and Ann ——.
    Mary Ann. (1807.)

Parrish Josue and Barbara ——.
    Thomas, Elizabeth, Mary, Peter Benedict. (1804-14.)

Parrish John and Mary McKinzie. Married April 5, 1818.
    Thomas Josue, Leo Joseph, William Augustine, Henry, Joseph, Peter, James Francis. (1819-39.)

Parrish James and Ann McCann. Married August 29, 1820.
    Edward, Joseph, Mary Ann, Henry, Bernard William, Elizabeth, James. (1822-36.)

Parrish Joseph and Catherine McKinzie. Married November 1, 1822.
    Silas Demetrius, Lydia Ann, Elizabeth Ann, Joseph, Catherine Ann, Ann Mary. (1823-36.)

Parrish George and Catherine Storm. Married February 29, 1824.
Josue Demetrius, Susan Barbara, George Michael, Ann Elizabeth Mary. (1825-37.)

Parrish Thomas and Mary Storm. Married April 9, 1826.
Barbara Susan, Louisa Dorothy, Ann Mary, Francis James, Sylvester Augustine, Charlotte Caroline. (1827-38.)

Parrish John and Mary Flanigan. Married April 15, 1833.

Parrish Peter B. and Elizabeth O'Connell. Married April 11, 1837.
Matilda Martha, Mary Jane. (1838-39.)

Peters Joseph and Cecilia Metzger Married November 21, 1826.

Petticoat James and Margaret Burgoon. Married February 16, 1808.
Mary Prudence. (1813.)

Pfoff Francis Joseph and Apollonia Shremp.
Thomas, Mary Ann, Bridget Elmira. (1834-38.)

Pfoff Joseph and Elizabeth ——.
Joseph Anthony. (1836.)

Phalen John and Mary Tierney.
John, Mary, Jane. (1822-25.)

Platt Henry and Phoebe ——.
Elizabeth, Catherine, Cosmas, John. (1804-16.)

Platt John and Sarah ——.
Elizabeth, James, Michael Joseph, Mary Ann, Agnes, Ellen Ann, John Chrysostom, Margaret, Mary Matilda. (1810-26.)

Platt Joseph and Sarah ——.
Catherine, Jerome, Elizabeth, Henry. (1819-31.)

Plummer Isaac and Susan Skelly.
John, Sarah Ann, Philip. (1822-34.)

Plummer Eliseus and Catherine ——.
Mary Ann, Elizabeth, Daniel, Susan, Catherine, Patrick, James Augustine. (1823-34.)

Plunkett John and Ann ——.
John, Ann. (1827-28.)

PLUNKETT John and Jane Watt. Married June 10, 1834.
    James Augustine, Elizabeth. (1836-38.)
PORTER Patrick and Ellen ———.
    Mary, Ellen, Ann, Jane Elizabeth. (1802-11.)
POWER David and Bridget McHugh. Married September 22, 1835.
POWERS Michael and Susan Burgoon. Married May 7, 1832.
QUARTZ John Valentine and Mary Ann Myers.
    Magdalen Elizabeth. (1839.)
QUIGLEY Michael and Ellen ———.
    Michael. (1832.)
RAFFERTY Francis and Elizabeth ———.
    Mary, Bernard, Ann, Elizabeth. (1833-39.)
RAINEY James and Sarah ———.
    John. (1804.)
RAINEY William and Charity Shirley. Married April 2, 1820.
RAINEY John and Margaret Noel. Married May 25, 1826.
    Thomas. (1833.)
REBMAN Joseph and Catherine Nist. Married October 31, 1835.
RECORD Michael and Elizabeth Skelly. Married May 27, 1833.
REDD Patrick and Mary Bradley. Married January 14, 1822.
    Mary. (1825.)
REED Joseph and Jane ———.
    Mary, William, Dennis, Eliza Jane. (1820-27.)
REILLY Patrick and Judith Lynch.
    Mary. (1834.)
REINZEL Valentine and Mary ———.
    Elizabeth, Valentine, Ann, Mary, Eve, Magdalen. (1786-99.)
RHEY John and Catherine ———.
    James, Ann, Mathias, George W. (1811-19.)
RHEY James and Susan Brookbank. Married August 23, 1814.
    Ann, Elizabeth, John Sylvester, Mary, Eliza Jane, James William, Andrew. (1815-28.)

RHODES John and Juliana ——.
> Mary. (1792.)

RICHTER Joseph and Helen ——.
> Mary Catherine, William Augustine, Wilhelmina. (1834-39.)

RIFFLE Barnabas and Margaret ——.
> Josiah, Mary Ann. (1815-20.)

RIFFLE James and Catherine Connelly. Married April 8, 1817.
> John, Mary, Thomas. (1818-20.)

RIFFLE Samuel and Alice McHugh. Married October 9, 1821.
> James, Mary Magdalen, Samuel Augustine. (1822-34.)

RIFFLE Thomas and Sarah ——.
> Rachel. (1829.)

RIFFLE John and Jane ——.
> Emily, Elizabeth Ann. (1836-38.)

RIGGLE Christian and Mary Ann ——.
> Christiana, Joseph. (1838-40.)

RITTER Joseph and Ann ——.
> Mary, John, Henry, Cornelius, Peter. (1829-39.)

RITZ Henry and Mary ——.
> Ann, Joseph, Mary Elizabeth, Michael. (1815-22.)

ROBINSON Thomas and Rachel ——. (Negroes.)
> Delia. (1823.)

ROSSITER Peter and Catherine ——.
> Richard, Eliza Jane. (1811-14.)

ROUDEBUSH Christian and Elizabeth ——.
> Mary Magdalen. (1808.)

RUFNER Henry and Elizabeth ——.
> Mary, Christina. (1803-05.)

RUFNER Simon and Susan Noel. Married July 16, 1833.

RUTLER Anthony and Mary Ann Habermacher. Married October 18, 1831.
> Catherine, Mary Magdalen, Joseph, John, William. (1832-37.)

RUTSCH Michael and Mary ——.
> Veronica. (1822.)

RUTSCH Andrew and Leah ——.
  Mary Jane. (1833.)
RYAN Patrick and Mary ——.
  James, Sarah, Mary Ann, James, Henry, Catherine. (1804-27.)
RYAN James and Honoria Durbin. Married January 21, 1812.
  William, Sarah, Thomas. (1814-16.)
RYAN William and Mary Platt. Married April 27, 1813.
  Margaret, David, Elizabeth. (1814-18.)
RYAN John and Sarah ——. (Negroes.)
  William. (1823.)
RYAN William and Catherine Barnicle. Married October 1, 1826.
  Juliana, Sarah Ann. (1827-29.)
RYAN David and Catherine Ann Krise. Married November 6, 1838.
SANDERS Peter and Margaret Noel.
  Joseph, Frances Matilda. (1834-38.)
SCANLAN John and Theresa Kaylor.
  Catherine, Mary Elizabeth, Mary Theresa, Richard, John, Peter, Henry, James, Mary Ann. (1805-25.)
SCANLAN Richard and Catherine McGuire. Married November 10, 1835.
SCANLAN John and Susan Myers. Married May 29, 1838.
  John. (1839.)
SCHAUB Henry and Christina ——.
  Margaret. (1828.)
SCHNABEL John and Christina Myers. Married October 25, 1835.
SCHULER Bartholomew and Rosina ——.
  Joseph, Mary Ann, Catherine, Caspar Melchior, Rosanna, Ann, Anthony. (1821-30.)
SCHWAB Charles and Ellen Myers. Married March 2, 1835.
  Ellen Catherine, John Baptist,. (1835-39.)
SCHWARTZ Jacob and Catherine ——.
  Mary. (1825.)

SEESE John and Catherine ——.
 William Peter, Mary Ann, Rosanna, Sarah Ann, Patrick Augustine. (1818-30.)
SETTLEMIRE John and Mary Cantwell. Married May 31, 1814.
 Elizabeth, Margaret Ann, Sarah, Joseph, John, Elizabeth. (1815-25.)
SEYMOUR Nicholas and Christina ——.
 Martin, Mary. (1834-35.)
SHAFFER John and Matilda Young. Married July 11, 1834.
SHAFFER Jacob and Mary Dorothy Dodson.
 Thomas, Mary Jane. (1836-39.)
SHALLER John and Mary ——.
 Jacob, Mary Ann, Mechthildes, John, Henry. (1824-33.)
SHAMO Joseph and Hannah Gray. Married July 11, 1824.
SHANNON John and Mary Porter. Married June 5, 1817.
 Mary. (1821.)
SHARBAUGH Jacob and Mary Eliz. Bender. Married November 24, 1835.
SHARP Henry and Margaret ——.
 William, Lavina. (1808-15.)
SHARP William and Theresa Lilly. Married August 22, 1830.
 Martha, Margaret, Henry, Samuel. (1831-39.)
SHAW Robert and Ann McIntosh. Married November 2, 1824.
SHENK Mathias and Theresa Walters. Married July 23, 1838.
SHERRY Louis and Elizabeth ——.
 Jacob, George, Mary Ellen. (1800-09.)
SHERRY John and Barbara Eliz. Ott. Married February 23, 1840.
SHIELDS John and Ellen ——.
 Edward. (1826.)
SHIELDS Patrick and Anastasia McGuire. Married May 18, 1837.
SHIRLEY Richard and Sarah ——.
 Elsie Jane, John Augustine. (1808-14.)
SHOEMAKER Edward and Mary Hanson.
 Ellen, Charles, Edward, Henrietta Elizabeth, Francis Augustine. (1832-39.)

SHORB Joseph and Ann Roberts.
   Mary Ann, Henrietta. (———.)
SHORT Peter and Catherine ———.
   Susan, Ann, Emily, Catherine, Martha. (1803-13.)
SHORT John and Ann ———.
   James. (———.) John. (1808.)
SHORT Samuel and Mary ———.
   Paul George, John Augustine, Catherine Ann, Michael Paul, Samuel Augustine. (1825-35.)
SHORT William and Elizabeth ———.
   Emiline Rachel. (1829.)
SHROFF John and Catherine ———.
   Amelia. (1817.)
SHUSTER Martin and Mary Ann ———.
   John George. (1833.)
SILL William and Agnes Haid. Married October 21, 1839.
SILVERS George and Catherine ———.
   George, Rosalia. (1829-30.)
SIMMES John and Juliana Kotterman. Married August 31, 1835.
SISK Robert and Mary (Margaret) Kearns.
   Mary. (1837.)
SKELLY Michael and Mary ———.
   William, Ann Mary, Margaret. (1801-07.)
SKELLY Philip and Margaret ———.
   Michael, Ellen, Catherine, Mary Ann, Elizabeth, Ann. (1802-15.)
SKELLY Patrick and Mary ———.
   Julia. (1819.)
SKELLY Joseph and Catherine ———.
   Elizabeth. (1823.)
SKELLY Michael and Rachel ———.
   John Augustine, James, Thomas Augustine, Susan, Michael. (1823-30.)
SKELLY Philip and Elizabeth ———.
   John, Catherine, Patrick, Esther. (1824-30.)

SKELLY John and Elizabeth ———.
> Sarah Ann, Elizabeth, Daniel Augustine, Alexander Augustine. (1825-33.)

SKELLY Hugh and Emily Todd. Married October 29, 1826.
> William Augustine. (1827.)

SKELLY Daniel and Susan Noel. Married May 12, 1831.
> Margaret, Philip, William. (1834-38.)

SKELLY Hugh and Bridget Eliz. Kennedy. Married February —, 1832.
> Mary Ann. (1832.)

SKELLY Patrick and Catherine ———.
> Philip. (1836.)

SKELLY Patrick and Margaret Skelly. Married September 28. 1834.

SLAVEN William and Mary ———.
> Mary, Catherine. (1800-04.)

SMELTZER Peter and Eliz. Kämpfersach. Married October 18, 1835.
> Mary, Joseph. (1838-40.)

SMITH Henry and Juliana ———.
> Margaret. (1820.)

SMITH James and Mary ———.
> Ellen. (1831.)

STARK Reuben and Sarah ———.
> James. (1799.)

STARK James and Mary Boone. Married December 26, 1825.

STARK James D. and Sophia Elder. Married April 23, 1833.
> Priscilla. (1834.)

STEINER Henry and Sarah ———.
> Sarah (Mrs. Henry, 1782.) Otho, Mary, Lavina. Sophia, Elizabeth. (1808-21.)

STEVENS Martin and Ann Connelly. Married January 14. 1816.
> Catherine, James. (1817-18.)

STEVENS Aloysius and Notburga ———.
> Salome. (1826.) Joseph. (———.)

STEVENS John and Mary Eckenrode.   Married September 14, 1830.
  David, Jacob, Michael, Louis. (1832-38.)
STEVENS Jacob and Mary Fox.   Married June 27, 1837.
STEWART Robert and Rose Carroll.   Married September 16, 1835.
STOKES John Terence and Abigail ——.
  John.   1799.
STOLL Jacob and Margaret ——.
  Catherine. (1821.)
STOLZ Adam and Theresa ——.
  Mary Ann. (1838.)
STOLZ John and Barbara ——.
  Catherine. (1839.)
STORM John and Susan Wysong.
  James, Susan, Louis, Joseph, Michael, Henry. (1804-15.)
STORM Joachim and Mary ——.
  Sarah, James, Francis. (1806-13.)
STORM John and Rosanna McCoy.   Married April 27, 1819.
  Arthur, John Elias, Hugh, James David, Mary Ellen, Susan. (1821-29.)
STORM Peter and Ann McConnell.
  Mary Ann, Susan, Francis Augustine, Elizabeth, Sarah, Catherine, John, Ann Emily. (1824-38.)
STORM David Thomas and Mary Jane Agnew.   Married November 10, 1828.
STORM Patrick and Mary Parrish.   Married February 17, 1833.
  James, Ann Elizabeth, Lucy Ann, Francis George. (1834-39.)
STORM Michael and Margaret Brady.   Married November 17, 1835.
  James Edward, William. (1837-39.)
STORM Louis and Margaret Pfoff.   Married April 23, 1838.
  Mary Elizabeth. (1839.)
STRÄSLER Ulrich and Elizabeth ——.
  Christopher Joseph. (1819.)

STREAMER Christopher and Elizabeth ——.
  Mary, Martha. (1820-22.)
STRITTMATTER Andrew and Frances Myers.
  Mary Ann, Peter, Paul, Andrew, Frances, Demetrius Augustine, Joseph. (1822-33.)
STUMP George and Catherine ——.
  Samuel. (1820.)
STURTZ Adam and Elizabeth ——.
  Adam. (1834.)
SUTTON Andrew and Frances Davis.
  David, Bartholomew, William. (1821-29.)
SWEENY George and Mary ——.
  John. (1813.)
SWEENY George and Jane ——.
  Mary Catherine. (1832.)
SWEENY Michael and Elizabeth McKinney.
  Elizabeth Jane. (——.)
SWEENY William and Mary ——.
  James. (1829.)
SWEENY Michael and Catherine Weakland Married January 17, 1832.
TEUFEL John and Elizabeth Kern.
  Cunegunda. (1839.)
THOMAS Michael and Jane ——.
  Rosanna, Frederick, Joseph Michael. (1822-29.)
THOMAS John and Mary Ann Campbell. Married August 29, 1836.
  Unity Ann, James. (1837-38.)
THOMPSON John and Ellen ——.
  Nicholas, Edward Augustine, John, Ellen. (1813-18.)
THOMPSON Ebenezer and Catherine Short.
  David. (1838.)
TIERNEY Joseph and Sarah Dever. Married January 18, 1831.
  Judith. (1832.)
TODD David and Mary ——.
  Sarah, William, David, Mary, Emily. (1795-1809.)

TODD William and Ellen Wharton. Married June 20, 1819.
    Andrew, James, Joseph Augustine. (1820-31.)
TODD David, Jr., and Jane ——.
    Mary Ellen, Susan, Catherine Jane. (1824-27.)
TODD Andrew and Margaret Kittell. Married April 8, 1839.
TOMLINSON Jacob and Margaret Burkle.
    Sarah Jane, Ann Catherine. (1837-39.)
TOPPER George and Elizabeth ——.
    Daniel James, Andrew Joseph, Matilda, Eliza Jane. (1826-33.)
TOPPER Andrew and Mary Steiner. Married September 10, 1826.
TOPPER Jacob and Mary Howell. Married August 12, 1827.
TOWENHOUR Francis Jos. and Sophia ——.
    Joseph. (——.)
TREXLER Joseph and Elizabeth ——.
    Peter, Ann Magdalen, Mary, Joseph, Jacob, John, David. (1808-22.)
TREXLER Peter and Ann Margaret Donoughe. Married May 21, 1833.
    Mary Elizabeth, Ann Margaret. (1834-35.)
TREXLER Joseph, Jr., and Susan Krise. Married June 26, 1838.
    John Andrew, Jacob. (1838-40.)
TRIESTER John and Margaret McKinzie. Married February 8, 1831.
    Margaret Ellen. (1833.)
TROXELL Jacob and Susan ——.
    Catherine, Sarah, Abraham, William, Henry, Samuel. (1805-18.)
TROXELL Joseph and Mary ——.
    Margaret. (1806.)
TROXELL John and Susan ——.
    Mary. (1826.)
TROXELL William and Jane Wharton. Married April 16, 1839.
TRUCKS Nicholas and Ruth ——.
    Michael, Mary. (1801-04.)

ULRICH Daniel and Ann ——.
>Mary Ann. (——.)

URBAN Francis Jos. and Elizabeth Coons.
>Clement, John, Nicholas Reynold, Caspar Nicholas, Mary Josephine, Jerome Michael, Susan Christina, Ambrose, Joseph. (1821-35.)

URBAN Clement and Mary Ann Conrad. Married March 10, 1833.
>Emanuel, Peter. (1835-37.)

VOTLEY Peter and Catherine ——.
>Magdalen, Catherine. (1833-42.)

WADE George and Elizabeth ——.
>Peter, John. (1826-29.)

WAGNER Michael and Gertrude ——.
>Jacob, Mary, Susan, Michael. (1807-16.)

WAGNER Jacob and Jane Downey. Married September 20, 1825.
>Michael, John, Charity Bridget, Elizabeth, Catherine, Susan, Daniel. (1826-39.)

WAGNER Peter and Mary Eve Ritter. Married February 3, 1835.
>Mary Ann. (1835.)

WALDKIRCH Frederick and Mary Ann Stephy. Married April 20, 1835.

WALKER Jonathan and Sarah ——.
>Mary. (1821.)

WALSH John and Susan ——.
>Nicholas, Mary. (1801-03.)

WALSH David and Isabella O'Neill. Married October 2, 1823.

WALTERS Englebert and Susan Behe.
>Daniel, John, Susan, Catherine, Elizabeth, Ann, Englebert, Joseph, Augustine. (1802-20.)

WALTERS Daniel and Susan Little. Married April 2, 1826.

WALTERS John and Mary Ann Conrad. Married September 18, 1836.
>Mary Elizabeth. (1838.)

WARNER John and Mary Ann Noel. Married April 30, 1839.

REV. MARTIN RYAN. PASTOR 1890-91.

WANTZ John George and Margaret Zern. Married October 8, 1833.
   Mary Ann, Joseph, William, Jacob. (1835-39.)
WASSER Aloysius and Gertrude Rutler. Married April 4, 1826.
   Catherine, Joseph, Mary Ann, Aloysius, Peter. (1827-38.)
WATT David and Rachel ———.
   William, Ann, Jane, Margaret, Catherine, David, Mary, James, Rachel, Joseph. (1806-27.)
WATT James and Mary Ellen McDermitt. Married April 22, 1828.
   John William, James, Ann Ellen. (1829-34.)
WATT William and Elizabeth Downey.
   Mary Jane, David, Catherine, Rachel Elizabeth. (1831-38.)
WEAKLAND John and Catherine ———.
   George, Samuel, Michael. (1800-13.)
WEAKLAND William and Mary Barbara Ruffner.
   Catherine, Simon, John, Susan, William. (1804-13.)
WEAKLAND William and Airy Burgoon. Married April 23, 1816.
   Mary Temperance, Susan, Michael, Mary Ann, Barnabas, Peter, John, Margaret. (1817-33.)
WEAKLAND James and Ruth Farrell. Married April 23, 1816.
   Catherine, Adeline Ann, John, Augustine, Simon Joseph, Sylvester, Joseph Eugene, Mary, Demetrius. (1817-38.)
WEAKLAND Michael and Mary Gardner. Married November 10, 1818.
   Sarah Ann, John, Catherine, Sophonias. (1819-30.)
WEAKLAND Peter and Theresa Adams. Married April 15, 1819.
   Eliza Ann, Mary, Henry, Charles, Juliana. (1820-26.)
WEAKLAND George and Ellen McKinney. Married October 3, 1820.
   Catherine, William, Mary Ellen, James. (1821-26.)

WEAKLAND John and Margaret ——.
　　Michael, Susan, Edward. (1819-23.)
WEAKLAND John and Mary Ann Litzinger. Married May 9, 1822.
　　Mary Emily, Mary Ann, Simon Augustine. (1823-27.)
WEAKLAND Samuel and Bridget Flanigan. Married May 23, 1826.
　　Luke, Bridget. (1827-28.)
WEAKLAND Samuel and Margaret McAteer. Married May 1, 1832.
　　Anselm. (1833.)
WEAKLAND Simon and Magdalen Little. Married October 14, 1834.
WEAKLAND Michael and Ellen Harrison. Married February 10, 1835.
WEAVER Jacob and Frances Noble.
　　Jacob Levi. (1827.)
WERNER Conrad and Lutgarde ——.
　　Catherine. (——.)
WERTNER John and Rutina Hertzog. Married September 6, 1836.
　　John. (1837.)
WERTZ Jacob and Susan ——.
　　Elizabeth. (1791.)
WERTZ Francis and Mary ——.
　　Susan, Catherine, Martha, Barbara Ellen. (1822-30.)
WEST Samuel and Elizabeth Delozier. Married June 4, 1822.
　　John, Ann. (1823-26.)
WHARTON Stanislaus and Mary McConnell. Married July 6, 1813.
　　Sarah Ann, Mary, Joseph, Jane, John, William, Cecilia, Mary Ellen, Elizabeth. (1814-27.)
WILKINSON Ignatius and Agnes Keyes. Married August 31, 1837.
WILL Peter and Ann Mary ——.
　　Joseph. (1802.)

WILL John and Rachel Durbin.
   Theresa, Thomas, Emily, Susan, Elizabeth, Basil, Rachel. (1806-16.)
WILL John and Mary Horn.   Married May 11, 1817.
   Ann Margaret, Samuel, Sarah, Mary Ann, Ellen, Augustine, Agnes, Leo, John Chrysostom. (1818-39.)
WILL Michael and Ann Wharton.   Married August 3, 1817.
   Joseph, Rachel, Anthony, Jacob, Sophia, Zachary, Mary Ellen, Joseph, Jane Elizabeth, Catherine Amanda, Ann Martha. (1818-37.)
WILL Joseph and Mary Wagner.   Married November 2, 1824.
   Henry, Thomas, Susan, Michael, Ellen, Jerome. (1826-39.)
WILL Jacob and Mary Magdalen ——.
   Catherine, Lucretia, Peter. (1822-26.)
WILL Anthony and Elizabeth McDermitt.
   Jacob, Charlotte Ellen, Martha, Agnes, Mark Augustine. (1829-39.)
WILL Thomas and Magdalen Myers.   Married May 8, 1832.
   Julia Ann. (1833.)
WILL Samuel and Margaret ——.
   Alexis. (1822.)
WILL Samuel and Elizabeth Moore.   Married January 7, 1833.
   Michael, Sarah Ann, Mary Elizabeth, Veronica. (1833-39.)
WILLEBRAND John Henry and Mary Magd. Myers.   Married November 17, 1835.
WILMORE James and Catherine ——.
   Sarah Ann, John Augustine, Elizabeth Ann, Martin Augustine, Mary, Emily Jane. (1824-33.)
WILMORE John and Esther Heltzel.
   Mary Ann, William, Ellen, Lucy Ann, Francis James. (1826-38.)
WILT John and Mary Adams.   Married April 12, 1819.
   Joseph, Lucy Ann, Richard, John, Mary Elizabeth, Susan, David Andrew. (1820-35.)
WITHEROW Thomas and Sarah Brookbank.   Married March 15, 1821.

WOELFEL Cyriacus and Cath. Dorothy Lust. Married December 15, 1823.
Catherine. (1824.)
WOLF John and Margaret ——.
David. (1797.)
WOOD Patrick and Theresa McGuire. Married May 4, 1823.
WUNDERLY Matthew and Margaret Becher. Married June 27, 1826.
John Henry, Thomas Ignatius. (1827-28.)
WUNDERLY Ignatius and Theresa Werner. Married September 30, 1829.
YAHNER Valentine and Christina ——.
Paul. (1832.)
YINGLING Peter and Elizabeth ——.
George, Barbara, Peter. (1807-14.)
YOST Jacob and Elizabeth Mardis. Married April 28, 1812.
Abigail, Jacob, Margaret, Sarah Ann, Catherine Ann, Susan, Ellen Elizabeth. (1813-26.)
YOUNG David and Jane ——.
Mary. (1807.)
YOUNG Charles and Juliana ——.
Ann Lucinda. (1815.)
YOUNG Jacob and Mary Wilmore. Married June 5, 1817.
Mary Ann, John, Elizabeth Ann, Susan, Sarah Ann, James Augustine, Anastasia. (1818-32.)
YOUNG Andrew and Mary Ann ——.
Catherine, Henry, William, George. (1828-38.)
ZERBY John and Juliana McGuire. Married October —, 1832.
Ann Mary, Sarah Victoria, Sophonias. (1833-38.)
ZERN Jacob and Louisa Illig. Married March 6, 1832.
Ann, Catherine, Ann Margaret. (1833-38.)
ZIEGLER Jacob and Catherine ——.
Anthony. (1822.)
ZIMMERMAN John and Emily Weibel. Married February 17, 1833.

REGISTER OF DEATHS
—IN—
St. MICHAEL'S PARISH, LORETTO, PA.,
From November 17, 1793, to October 10, 1899.

NOTE.—The following names and dates have been gathered and arranged with great care and immense labor from many sources, but chiefly from the headstones in St. Michael's cemetery. The object was to have as complete and perfect a record as possible of the deceased members of this parish from the beginning. The Register is still far from complete as to names, and doubtless many errors will be found in the dates; but the best has been done that could be done in the circumstances. The names of deceased children under seven years of age do not appear in this list.

NAME.	Born.	Died.
ABERNETHY, Mrs. Thomas P. (Charlotte ———)	1801	Sept. 29, 1879
ADAMS, William	1764	May 17, 1842
Mrs. William (Eve Sanker)	July 3, 1782	Apr. 24, 1867
James (of William)	May 27, 1812	Mar. 23, 1901
Susan (of John)	Dec. 18, 1815	Apr. 1, 1888
Ignatius		Nov. 18, 1896
Thomas, Sr.		Aug. 20, 1871
Mrs. Thomas (Rachel McGuire)	July 21, 1801	Oct. 9, 1886
Thomas	Jan. 14, 1823	Nov. 6, 1873
Matthew M	Jan. 20, 1818	Nov. 23, 1872
Mrs. Joseph (Barbara Susan Parrish)	Mar. 5, 1827	Feb. 2, 1890
Mrs. George (Mary Catherine Farabaugh)	1856	Mar. 3, 1894
Richard		Oct. 31, 1896
Mrs. R. (Margaret McConnell)		June 21, 1864
Elizabeth	Dec. 23, 1823	Oct. 7, 1854
Peter	May 22, 1825	Apr. 24, 1881
Mrs. Peter (Mary Gallagher)		Sept. 26, 1881
ADELSBERGER, Michael	1797	Sept. 28, 1883
Mrs. Mchael (Elizabeth Hughes)		Dec. 30, 1868
ALLEN, Silas William	1809	Apr. 27, 1895
Mrs. Silas W. (Jeannette Litzinger)	Aug. 10, 1800	Nov. 9, 1807
William		1861
Mrs. William (Cecilia Dougherty)		Feb. 2, 1856

NAME.	Born.	Died.
ANAWALT, Mrs. J. W. (Ella Sweeny)	May 21, 1868	Jan. 19, 1898
ANDERSON, Mrs. Andrew (Patience ———)	1762	Jan. 8, 1834
Benjamin P.	1810	June 11, 1892
ANSMAN, ——— ———	1809	Nov. 28, 1885
Mrs. John (Elizabeth Shenk)	June 4, 1819	Mar. 12, 1888
ANSTATT, Mrs. Michael (Mary E. Lenz)	Feb. 12, 1860	June 3, 1882
ANSTED, Mrs. Anthony (Susan Itel)	Feb. 18, 1851	Jan. 7, 1873
ATKINSON, Mrs. Hannah	1800	Feb. 25, 1873
Margaret		June 27, 1879
BAGLE, Ann Mary	1802	Jan. 14, 1827
BAKER, John	Mar. 27, 1813	July 26, 1890
Mrs. John (Catharine Fox)		Sept. 11, 1858
BANNAN, Joseph	Aug. 15, 1806	Jan. 31, 1865
Mrs. Joseph (Ann Pagan)	Oct. ——, 1804	Jan. 22, 1877
William P.	Feb. 28, 1844	Jan. 25, 1882
Peter	July ——, 1846	Nov. 8, 1887
BARD, (Barth) John	July 15, 1804	Feb. 5, 1884
Mrs. John (Elizabeth ———)	Dec. 25, 1802	Apr. 11, 1876
Peter		Feb. 5, 1884
Mrs. Peter (———)		Apr. 11, 1876
BARNETT, James		Nov. 21, 1881
BEAMER, Mrs. John (Abigail Coleman)	1799	June 9, 1831
Mrs. John (Elizabeth O'Hara)	1797	Jan. 4, 1839
BECHER, Nicholas		Dec. 19, 1855
Mrs. Nicholas (Christina Coons)	Feb. 6, 1801	Dec. 19, 1855
Apollonia	Aug. 1, 1831	Dec. 19, 1855
Mary Ann	Feb. 16, 1833	Dec. 19, 1855
BECK, Charles (of Felix)	May 20, 1878	Aug. 5, 1888
BEHE, Mathias	May 4, 1790	Nov. 4, 1882
Mrs. Mathias (Catherine Kaylor)	Feb. 14, 1793	Oct. 16, 1866
Conrad	1796	June 9, 1866
Thomas	Feb. 9, 1822	July 8, 1855
Jacob	1818	Jan. 2, 1856
Mrs. Jacob (Catherine McCoy)	1815	Feb. 5, 1857
Thomas Jacob (of Elias)	Dec. 8, 1847	Oct. 23, 1876
Elias (of Mathias)	Nov. 3, 1820	Aug. ——, 1853
BEITER, Casper	Jan. 7, 1792	Feb. 12, 1870
Mrs. Casper (Mary A. Sill)	Mar. 23, 1796	Feb. 13, 1867
Mrs. Ignatius (Regina Neice)	Sept. 7, 1821	July 9, 1890
Mrs. John (Mary Marg't Sanders)	1820	Jan. 18, 1890
BENDER, John Jacob	Jan. 31, 1740	Dec. 6, 1828

NAME.	Born.	Died.
BENGELE, Florian...	1809	Aug. 27, 1800
BERTRAM, Peter...		May 8, 1877
Mrs. Philip (———)...		Aug. 9, 1884
Fidelis...		Mar. 20, 1857
BILLER, Joseph F....	Apr. 25, 1830	Feb. 11, 1888
Peter...	June 13, 1830	Mar. 9, 1883
Mrs. Joseph (Lucinda Ann Mansfield)...	May 13, 1825	Nov. 11, 1885
Mrs. Aloysius (Bridget Fechter)...	Jan. ..., 1815	Apr. 20, 1885
Anthony...	Feb. 14, 1834	May 29, 1834
Harriet...	......, 1837	Mar. 11, 1830
BISHOP, Susan (of Val.)...	Feb. 28, 1818	......, 1855
BITER, Mrs. Otho (Sarah Ann Eckenrode)...	Jan. 5, 1834	July 9, 1873
Margaret...	Dec. 1, 1830	July 26, 1834
BOES, John, Sr...		Apr. 20, 1857
BOLAN, John...		Oct. 25, 1875
BOLEY, Sebastian...	......, 1801	Aug. 14, 1892
Mrs. Sebastian (Agatha ———)...		May 1, 1885
Peter...	Jan. 10, 1830	Dec. 9, 1878
Mary (of Peter)...	Jan. 13, 1863	Nov. 2, 1878
William J. (of Peter)...	June 3, 1855	Sept. 18, 1887
Thomas Ellsworth (of Joseph)...	July 15, 1881	Dec. 5, 1894
BORTMAN, Peter...		Nov. 18, 1888
Mrs. Peter (Mary Ann Hertzog)...	......, 1809	Nov. 20, 1871
Alexius...	July 17, 1841	Sept. ..., 1842
BOWEN, Rev. H. Seymour...	June 22, 1822	Apr. 5, 1887
BRADDOCK, N...		July 3, 1815
BRADLEY, Charles...	Mar. 25, 1750	Apr. 9, 1826
Mrs. Charles (Mary ———)...	Oct. 14, 1757	May 1, 1817
William...	1778	Dec. 28, 1846
William...	1782	May 25, 1819
Martha (of William)...	......, 1826	Nov. 22, 1846
Margaret...	1781	Oct. 3, 1839
Alice...	1781	May 28, 1844
Dennis...	1782	Oct. 30, 1857
Mrs. Dennis (Mary McCoy)...	1816	Nov. 14, 1898
Patrick (of Dennis)...	Mar. 17, 1843	Feb. 10, 1892
Edward...	June 27, 1788	Feb. 4, 1820
Charles...	1790	Dec. 23, 1882
Mrs. Charles (Ellen McGlade)...	1800	Dec. 12, 1882
Sarah A...	Feb. 2, 1793	Sept. 22, 1818
Charles...	Feb. 6, 1795	Aug. 6, 1855
Mrs. Charles (Catherine McGuire)...	May 9, 1807	Nov. 25, 1877
John...	1795	July 5, 1876
Mrs. John...	1798	Feb. 1, 1875
Martha Ann...	1798	Jan. 23, 1858

NAME.	Born.	Died.
(Bradley) John	1815	Aug. 22, 1878
Charles	Aug. 20, 1821	June 25, 1894
Charles	Oct. 16, 1826	Aug. 16, 1830
Mary Ann	1828	Apr. 1, 1882
Mrs. Edward (Mary Jos. Donoughe)	Apr. 22, 1857	May 3, 1886
George	Apr. 16, 1859	Oct. 12, 1885
Mrs. James G. (Margaret Sharp)	Jan. 27, 1859	Jan. 5, 1892
Thomas		Jan. 15, 1857
Charles		Aug. 6, 1855
Mrs. Edward (Sarah Neason)	Feb. 2, 1793	Sept. 22, 1848
Mrs. Felix (Rebecca Elder)		Apr. 24, 1855
BRADY, Edward	1776	Sept. 24, 1836
Terence	1780	Feb. 24, 1847
Mrs. Terence (Ellen ——)	1787	Jan. 11, 1850
James	1816	June 19, 1852
Mrs. James (Elizabeth A. ——)	Oct. 5, 1826	May 23, 1874
Robert	Jan. 30, 1842	Nov. 16, 1873
James	Jan. 1853	June 24, 1892
BRAWLEY, Mary Ann	Feb. 14, 1808	May 19, 1830
Michael, Jr	Sept. 15, 1843	June 29, 1875
BRENT, Mrs. R. D. (——)		May 8, 1800
BROOKBANK, John	1752	Jan. 22, 1820
BROOKS, John B	May 31, 1852	July 20, 1861
BROPHY, Timothy	1826	Oct. 14, 1806
Mrs. Timothy (Catherine Kane)	Oct. 19, 1826	Feb. 24, 1881
Henry Joseph	Apr. 29, 1849	Oct. 14, 1859
James M	1857	Mar. 20, 1882
Mary Elizabeth		Nov. 2, 1887
John		Apr. 17, 1872
BROWN, John	1753	May 20, 1820
Susan	1766	Oct. 2, 1810
Ann	1778	Apr. 13, 1823
Moses	1798	Oct. 24, 1847
Mrs. Moses (Maria Gallagher)	1798	Aug. 26, 1843
James	Aug. 6, 1830	Oct. 23, 1875
Susan Catherine	June 24, 1832	May 12, 1847
Mrs. William (Mary M. Leavy)	Sept. 17, 1826	Mar. 2, 1850
BRUCE, George	Feb. 11, 1809	July 2, 1843
Mrs. George (Juliana McKinney)	May 4, 1813	Aug. 20, 1835
John C	Apr. 15, 1834	July 11, 1892
Mrs. George (Amelia McManamy)	Feb. 22, 1816	Nov. 24, 1875
BUCK, Joseph	Nov. 16, 1797	July 31, 1871
Mrs. Joseph (Elizabeth Eckenrode)	Jan. 8, 1802	May 7, 1857
Charles (of Joseph)	Dec. 22, 1839	Oct. 3, 1856
Christian (of Joseph)	Sept. 25, 1825	June 25, 1848
Jacob (of Joseph)	Jan. 18, 1832	Jan. 6, 1896

NAME.	Born.	Died.
(Buck) Jerome (of Joseph)	Feb. 23, 1834	May 25, 1867
Christian		Feb. 16, 1868
Henry	Aug. 17, 1822	Feb. 13, 1849
Mrs. Henry (Mary McKee)	1824	July 3, 1884
BURGOON, Mrs. John (Rhoda Anderson)	1790	Aug. 9, 1874
Mrs. Sebastian (Catherine Rosalia Dougherty)	Aug. 31, 1846	Mar. 14, 1887
BURKE, James, Sr.	1758	June 5, 1817
William	1789	Apr. 23, 1839
Elizabeth (of Nicholas)	Sept. 17, 1814	Mar. 3, 1876
Mrs. Edward (Susan Burgoon)	1817	May 18, 1887
Mrs. Daniel (Agnes Christy)	Nov. 22, 1820	July 7, 1883
Mary Margaret (of Daniel)	June 23, 1851	Jan. 9, 1869
John	July 31, 1787	Apr. 4, 1861
Mrs. John (Esther McGough)	Mar. 8, 1792	May 16, 1863
Ellen	Nov. 13, 1812	July 11, 1845
Edward	Jan. 18, 1811	Mar. 7, 1868
Elizabeth	Aug. 30, 1815	July 20, 1804
Patience	May 19, 1819	Nov. 3, 1847
Julia	Dec. 26, 1820	May 4, 1867
William	Jan. 22, 1825	May 20, 1867
BURNS, Mrs. Edward (Susan O'Neill)	1815	Dec. 23, 1843
Catherine		Dec. 30, 1873
BUTLER, Mrs. Richard (Ann Dodson)	1800	July 25, 1873
Martha	1813	June 6, 1839
Mrs. —— —— (Catherine Jos. Christy)	June 7, 1848	Nov. 10, 1897
BYRNE, Thomas	1770	Sept. ..., 1830
Elizabeth (of Thomas)	Nov. 30, 1816	Dec. 25, 1838
John Chrys. (of Thomas)	Oct. 5, 1820	Jan. 25, 1839
Francis (of Thomas)	Jan. 21, 1823	Nov. 25, 1897
Mary Ann (of Michael)	May 5, 1829	Aug. 30, 1898
Augustine	1807	May 18, 1867
Mrs. Aug. (Mary Ann Driskel)	1805	Jan. 17, 1890
CAIN, see KANE.		
CALLAHAN, Andrew		Jan. 17, 1874
Mrs. Andrew (Ann Magd. Trexler)		Dec. 4, 1878
CALLAN, Mrs. Owen (Ann Martha Coates)	1787	Mar. 6, 1867
William		Oct. 6, 1873
CAMPBELL, Patrick	1770	1855
Mrs. Patrick (Ann Connery)		Sept. ..., 1838
Michael	May 27, 1810	1835
Philip	Jan. 6, 1812	1885
Bridget	June 3, 1816	1853
Mrs. James (Sarah Litzinger)	1829	June 2, 1895
Mrs. Martin (Mary Eliz. Freidhoff)	1841	Dec. 31, 1877
Morgan Philip	July 22, 1873	May 15, 1897

NAME.	Born.	Died.
CANTWELL, Thomas		Dec. 29, 1816
Sarah	1769	Dec. 5, 1840
CARL, Louis		July 29, 1895
Mrs. Louis (Ellen Urse)	May 8, 1817	Sept. 24, 1838
CARNEY, Daniel	1779	May 21, 1869
Mrs. Daniel (Margaret ——)	1791	Oct. 13, 1871
John	1829	Feb. 17, 1890
Regina	May 17, 1873	Nov. 14, 1895
Daniel		Nov. 25, 1872
Susan	1836	Nov. 9, 1895
Mrs. William (Mary McKenna)	1839	Nov. 3, 1854
CARROLL, Arthur	1793	Feb. 9, 1823
John		Oct. 3, 1869
Mrs. Jas. (Susan P. Leavy)	Feb. 15, 1830	Mar. 29, 1864
CASSIDY, Henry T.	Nov. 30, 1822	Nov. 2, 1893
Mrs. Henry T. (Alice Cassidy)	June 27, 1821	Apr. 7, 1889
William H.	May 22, 1847	Feb. 7, 1890
David W.	Jan. 16, 1849	Sept. 23, 1871
Mrs. John (Jane Campbell)	July 5, 1830	Dec. 2, 1848
CHAMBERS, Joseph	1800	Nov. 11, 1889
CHRISTY, Archibald	1760	Oct. 21, 1833
Augustine Ambrose	Apr. 3, 1808	May 29, 1881
Mrs. Augustine Ambrose (Mary Mentzer)	Dec. 21, 1809	May 7, 1877
Mary	1811	Oct. 10, 1881
Francis X.	Jan. 28, 1794	Sept. 6, 1876
Mrs. Francis (Susan McConnell)	Jan. 1, 1794	Apr. 25, 1863
Elias	July 31, 1819	Jan. 5, 1830
John M. D.	Dec. 13, 1821	Jan. 3, 1895
Henry	Mar. 3, 1821	May 12, 1896
Peter	1800	July 18, 1876
Mrs. Peter (Catherine Shirley)		Oct. 6, 1881
Rev. Richard Calixtus	Oct. 14, 1829	Oct. 15, 1878
Andrew J.	Mar. 24, 1837	Aug. 3, 1890
John		Feb. 13, 1880
Josiah M.	July 28, 1827	June 19, 1882
COLLINS, Philip	1801	Sept. 10, 1823
Peter Sr.		Feb. 22, 1875
James	Oct. 5, 1822	Jan. 30, 1839
Philip	Mar. 31, 1821	Feb. 23, 1895
CONNAHAN, Mrs. Dennis (Catherine Sisk)	1839	Dec. 7, 1862
CONNERY, Ann	1763	Oct. 11, 1819
Patrick	1797	May 17, 1878
Mrs. Patrick (Margaret McCloskey)	1792	June 17, 1870
Sarah	July 31, 1828	Sept. 8, 1887
John	June 8, 1831	Dec. 14, 1895
James W.	Nov. 4, 1834	Jan. 21, 1863
Rev. Hildebert P.	Aug. 12, 1844	Mar. 2, 1896

LORETTO CENTENARY. 171

NAME.	Born.	Died.
CONRAD, John...	Aug. 10, 1778	Mar. 31, 1882
John...	 1795	Dec. 18, 1874
Mary Ann...	July 22, 1895	Oct. 6, 1878
Demetrius Aug..	Jan. 8, 1838	Oct. 29, 1867
Amanda..	June 7, 1844	Feb. 21, 1853
Mary..	Jan. ..., 1832	June 28, 1854
James...	Mar. 4, 1841	May 8, 1879
Mrs. James (Susan Coons)..........................	Aug. 13, 1812	Jan. 22, 1895
Paul..	 1811	May 2, 1865
Mrs. Paul (Mary Ann Hogue)......................	Feb. 22, 1828	Oct. 6, 1878
John **X**...	....	Dec. 14, 1882
Mrs. John X. (Ellen McAteer)....................	....	Mar. 18, 1876
Anthony J..	Jan. 3, 1830	June 8, 1893
Mrs. Aug. (Cath. Eckenrode).....................	 1839	Oct. 7, 1892
Michael Bedini (Sean).................................	July 5, 1876	Aug. 4, 1892
Mrs. Ernest (Eliza Moore)...........................	 1879	Aug. 28, 1899
CONWAY, Hugh..	 1801	July 21, 1882
Mrs. Hugh (Margaret ———)......................	 1800	Jan. 5, 1879
John..	 1807	June 7, 1858
Patrick...	 1800	Nov. 3, 1854
Peter...	 1810	Oct. 27, 1864
COONS, John, Sr...	 1763	Apr. 23, 1851
Mrs. John (Christina Wolf)........................	Nov. 16, 1776	Jun. 21, 1856
Mary...	 1819	Mar. 13, 1881
Sarah Ann..	Nov. 24, 1819	Sept. 1, 1896
John, Jr..	Nov. 25, 1805	Mar. 23, 1883
Mrs. John (Hanna Howell).........................	Feb. 11, 1810	Feb. 2, 1887
Mrs. Joseph, Sr., (Mary Ann Watt)............	Feb. 5, 1821	Mar. 13, 1881
Mrs. Joseph A. (Cath. Keppler).................	Feb. 4, 1841	Jan. 6, 1880
William...	Nov. 19, 1829	Oct. 12, 1895
Mrs. Wm. (Anastasia Burns).....................	Feb. ..., 1837	July 16, 1856
Mrs. David (Margaret Shenk)...................	 1817	Dec. 27, 1885
Mrs. Francis (Mary Echard).....................	Aug. ..., 1865	Mar. ..., 1889
Mrs. F. J. (Apolonia Donoughe)................	....	June 23, 1886
Lavina (of F. J.)..	Dec. 2, 1877	Jan. 11, 1880
Henrietta Clara (of F. J.)............................	June 12, 1889	Jan. ..., 1889
Mrs. F. J. (Eliz. J. Reilly)..........................	 1862	Jan. 7, 1892
Leo A. (of Thos. A.)...................................	July 17, 1879	June 24, 1895
COOPER, Henry..	June 10, 1790	Dec. 18, 1855
Mrs. Henry...	....	Feb. 19, 1867
Ann...	 1789	Sept. 29, 1854
Francis...	Mar. 10, 1839	 1885
Joseph..	Feb. 19, 1847	May 11, 1871
Mrs. Jos. F. (Mary Hagan)........................	 1838	Feb. 6, 1873
COX, Mrs. Joseph (Priscilla Gallagher)..........	Jan. 30, 1804	June 19, 1889
CRAMER, Joseph..	 1810	Feb. 20, 1892
Mrs. Joseph (Regina Eberly)......................	July 21, 1817	June 20, 1883
Francis Joseph..	Oct. 19, 1858	Mar. 28, 1884
Philip L..	Mar. 21, 1843	Oct. 29, 1864

NAME.	Born.	Died.
(Cramer) Joseph	Dec. 29, 1844	Oct. 24, 1882
Mary Caroline	Oct. 3, 1854	May 20, 1866
William J	Jan. 17, 1857	Jun. 23, 1888
Mary Magdalen	Mar. 10, 1851	May 21, 1866
CRAVER, Mrs. Louis (Magdalen Hogue)		June 29, 1840
CRILLEY, Patrick	1834	Aug. 4, 1896
CRISTE, John	1783	Dec. 14, 1868
Mrs. John (Sarah O'Hara)	1794	Jan. 9, 1861
Daniel	May 20, 1809	Aug. 2, 1898
Joseph	Feb. 14, 1813	Apr. 26, 1893
Mrs. Joseph (Theresa Noel)	1806	May 17, 1895
John	June 25, 1819	July 5, 1855
Mrs. John (Ann Dougherty)	May 27, 1825	Jan. 21, 1898
Thomas	June 9, 1830	Apr. 15, 1885
Joanna (of James)	Nov. 12, 1860	Oct. 1, 1880
DAILY, Mary Ann (of Joseph)	Sept. 17, 1839	Aug. 17, 1886
DAVIS, Patrick	1811	Oct. 22, 1818
DAWSON, Patrick	1760	Apr. 19, 1846
Sarah Ann (of Patrick)	Feb. ___, 1818	Sept. 14, 1852
Michael	1809	Nov. 20, 1892
Mrs. Michael (Margaret ——)	1811	Apr. 17, 1894
Jerome	Sept. 15, 1815	Oct. 3, 1869
Mrs. Jerome (Eliza Jane Conrad)	Sept. 15, 1818	Feb. 22, 1852
Mrs. Jerome (Mary Ann Kaylor)	Sept. 22, 1824	Feb. 2, 1870
DECORT, Joseph		Sept. 11, 1881
DEGEN, (Deacon) Henry		Nov. 15, 1866
DELANY, PATRICK	1795	Mar. 25, 1881
William	1797	May 12, 1857
George	1799	Nov. 25, 1881
DELOZIER, Linny	1806	Feb. 1, 1876
Delozier Mrs. Francis (Anastasia Ryan)		May 24, 1871
DENNY, Charles F	May 6, 1867	Sept. 16, 1885
DEVER, William	1784	May 21, 1834
Jane	1816	Oct. 18, 1876
Neil		May 9, 1868
William B	June 10, 1821	Sept. 9, 1875
Cornelius	1786	Jan. 14, 1861
Mrs. Cornelius (Margaret Noon)	1792	Feb. 12, 1868
William C	Oct. 2, 1817	Oct. 15, 1894
James	July 23, 1821	Feb. 10, 1897
Mrs. James (Sarah Criste)	Feb. 12, 1832	Mar. 12, 1883
Cornelius	Mar. 1, 1823	Nov. 10, 1892
Dennis	July 16, 1827	July 12, 1839
Charles	Apr. 24, 1830	Dec. 31, 1892

NAME.	Born.	Died.
DIETRICH, Michael..	Aug. ...., 1846	Mar. 15, 1881
DIGGS, Ann..	Sept. 13, 1749	Apr. 13, 1818
DILLON, John...	....	June 30, 1884
Mrs. Charles (July Tierney)...	....	Nov. 15, 1898
DIMOND, Mrs. Joseph (Cath. Burgoon)........................	Oct. 16, 1805	Nov. 27, 1893
DIXON, Curtis F...	...................., 1802	Mar. 15, 1835
DODSON, Andrew...	Jan. 23, 1757	Oct. 27, 1876
Mrs. Andrew (Ann Mageehan)..................................	...................., 1800	Jan. 29, 1853
Sarah..	Nov. 4, 1820	Feb. 21, 1838
William...	Nov. 19, 1827	Jan. 31, 1890
Richard...	Dec. 18, 1800	Sept. 24, 1845
Mrs. Richard (Eleanor Grove)...................................	May 2, 1792	Dec. 19, 1867
DONAHOE, Mrs. Thos. (Eliza J. Connery).....................	Jan. 31, 1840	Aug. 17, 1883
DONELIN, Thomas..	...................., 1759	Feb. 27, 1832
DONOUGHE, John..	...................., 1735	Mar. 17, 1805
Mrs. John...	....	Nov. 30, 1806
Robert (of John)...	...................., 1775	...................., 1815
Paul (of John)..	...................., 1780	...................., 1852
Mrs. Paul (Mary Farrell)...	...................., 1778	...................., 1860
John (of Paul)..	...................., 1807	...................., 1857
Mrs. John (Apollonia Coons).....................................	Apr. 26, 1808	June 25, 1872
Andrew (of Paul)...	...................., 1803	...................., 1853
Ann (of Paul)...	...................., 1811	...................., 1842
Cornelius (of Paul)...	Jan. 20, 1815	...................., 1862
Honor (of Paul)...	Aug. 13, 1819	...................., 1852
Patrick (of Paul)..	Mar. 15, 1813	Dec. 3, 1872
Mrs. Patrick (Eliza McDermitt)..................................	July 9, 1822	Mar. 29, 1881
Ellen (of Patrick)...	Mar. 15, 1860	Feb. 15, 1882
DOUGHERTY, Peter...	...................., 1757	Aug. 9, 1844
Mrs. Peter (Catherine Dowlan)..................................	...................., 1776	Mar. 31, 1872
John (of Peter)..	May 31, 1816	Jan. 23, 1897
Mrs. John (Susan Fagan)..	Dec. 7, 1819	Apr. 11, 1891
Peter (of John)..	May 31, 1848	June 11, 1889
Joseph (of John)...	Dec. 15, 1850	Mar. 18, 1899
Dennis...	....	Apr. 29, 1857
Mrs. Dennis (Margaret Logan)..................................	....	Jan. 23, 1860
James...	Apr. 30, 1826	...................., 1851
Mrs. James (Catherine Little)...................................	Mar. 28, 1804	Aug. 31, 1876
DOUGLAS, Mrs. Jonathan (Monica Delozier)................	...................., 1786	July 9, 1881
John..	Mar. 22, 1826	Mar. 18, 1892
DOWNEY, Mrs. (———)..	...................., 1784	Aug. 19, 1880
Daniel...	...................., 1791	June 30, 1840
DOYLE, James..	...................., 1798	July 17, 1870
Mrs. James (Ann ———)..	Dec. ...., 1804	Nov. 15, 1889

NAME.	Born.	Died.
(Doyle) Thomas	Apr. 15, 1819	Oct. 20, 1856
Ella	Mar. 10, 1861	June 24, 1890
Mrs. Felix (Ann Kelly)	1829	May 22, 1871
DRISKEL, Michael	Aug. 15, 1807	Oct. 13, 1886
Mrs. Michael (Matilda Kaylor)	Mar. 2, 1817	Dec. 6, 1850
John	Aug. 26, 1838	Apr. 7, 1864
Michael L	Nov. 2, 1842	Aug. 18, 1888
DUMM, Solomon	Apr. 18, 1815	Feb. 24, 1897
George	June 13, 1816	Mar. 23, 1898
Peter	May 20, 1818	Oct. 28, 1897
DURBIN, Thomas	Sept. 8, 1789	Sept. 4, 1868
Mrs. Stephen (Eliz. McConnell)	1793	Aug. 21, 1883
Michael		Mar. 25, 1871
Mary	Sept. 2, 1767	Dec. 17, 1835
Susan		May 6, 1889
Mary		Aug. 26, 1860
Augustine	Oct. 14, 1807	Oct. 3, 1890
Mrs. Augustine (Catherine Scanlan)	Mar. 30, 1805	Jan. 30, 1894
James	Sept. 12, 1811	Nov. 28, 1886
Stephen Andrew	May 31, 1834	Jan. 27, 1898
Mrs. John		Oct. 28, 1872
EBERLY, Francis J	1820	Aug. 12, 1876
Mrs. Francis J. (Mary Miller)	1820	Feb. 26, 1898
Mary Ellen	Mar. 15, 1844	June 24, 1863
EBIG, Mrs. Francis (Ellen S. Eckenrode)	May 15, 1867	Oct. 4, 1893
ECKENRODE, John	1782	1844
Mrs. John (Catherine ——)		1853
Peter	1780	Nov. 28, 1858
George	Mar. 6, 1803	May 23, 1887
Mrs. Geo. (Ann ——)	May 13, 1813	Feb. 4, 1899
Joseph Ambrose	Mar. 10, 1844	June 14, 1888
William (of Jos. W.)	Aug. 10, 1852	Dec. 16, 1889
Peter	Nov. 1799	Jan. 12, 1870
Mrs. Peter (Christiana Fox)	1813	Mar. 24, 1897
Christopher	1803	Feb. 3, 1878
Martin Jesse	1813	Oct. 31, 1873
Rebecca	Jan. 26, 1813	Sept. 17, 1831
Anna	Oct. 30, 1820	Feb. 15, 1829
Peter	1851	Mar. 21, 1893
Mrs. Peter (Rutina Fry)	Mar. 28, 1832	May 1, 1864
Emily M	Oct. 20, 1860	Apr. 26, 1872
James	1823	June 9, 1895
William	Apr. 7, 1852	Dec. 16, 1889
Mrs. William (Ann Margaret Tomlinson)	Nov. 8, 1860	Feb. 28, 1888
Michael D	Nov. 21, 1853	July 31, 1895
Romanus	1857	Apr. 26, 1872
Mrs. Joseph (Rosanna Fry)	Apr. 30, 1828	Mar. 8, 1899
George (of Joseph and Rosanna)	Jan. 29, 1859	Feb. 28, 1892

NAME.	Born.	Died.
(Eckenrode) Mary Ann (of Joseph and Sarah)	May 17, 1837	Jan. 1, 1890
Elizabeth Jane (of Joseph and Sarah)	Mar. 15, 1844	Aug. 17, 1861
Mrs. Jerome B. (Catherine Flick)	July 11, 1847	May 18, 1885
Mary A. (of Daniel)	Sept. 16, 1852	May 2, 1869
Mrs. Charles C. (Ann Mary Litzinger)	1855	Aug. 16, 1897
Mrs. Albinus (Agnes Tomlinson)	Apr. 7, 1856	Oct. 11, 1891
Mrs. James (Margaret Douglas)	1863	Feb. 27, 1888
Mrs. Harry (May Cath. Eckenrode)	May 5, 1864	May 8, 1892
Maria Amanda	1854	May 4, 1870
ELDER, Walter	1771	Feb. 23, 1842
Mrs. Walter (Priscilla Elder)	1779	Apr. 17, 1852
Richard	Feb. 6, 1815	May 5, 1893
Mrs. Richard (Margaret Moyer)		Oct. 19, 1863
Ellen		Jan. 7, 1824
Thomas		Nov. 18, 1839
Charles		Mar. 27, 1841
George	Aug. 23, 1794	Sept. 29, 1875
John	Aug. 11, 1802	Aug. 30, 1879
Mrs. John (Mary Myers)	1800	Feb. 12, 1885
Alexis	Apr. 1, 1826	Apr. 23, 1839
Priscilla	Mar. 1, 1828	Jan. 7, 1831
John Duane	Mar. 30, 1836	Aug. 22, 1874
Sophia (Mrs. Jacob Luther)	Dec. 23, 1833	Jan. 29, 1887
EVERLY, Amanda	July 3, 1878	Oct. 4, 1894
FAGAN, Peter	1773	Apr. 18, 1846
Mrs. Peter (Bridget Logan)		Nov. 17, 1865
John	May 5, 1798	May 5, 1836
James		Feb. 11, 1879
Eliza	Aug. 15, 1806	Dec. 13, 1892
Jane	1799	Feb. 11, 1891
Esther	Jan. 13, 1809	Nov. 14, 1894
Hugh	May 22, 1811	Nov. 22, 1895
Simon Richard	June 2, 1813	Jan. 24, 1897
Felix	Jan. 7, 1816	Mar. 10, 1838
Julia Ann	Nov. 1, 1817	Oct. 23, 1895
Jeremiah	1821	Aug. 14, 1874
Mrs. James (Cath. Stoeker)	1811	May 4, 1835
FARABAUGH, Michael	1807	Apr. 5, 1856
George	1840	Aug. 5, 1853
Mrs. Mathias (Elizabeth Noel)	Apr. 11, 1842	Apr. 26, 1884
FARRELL, Charles	1813	Apr. 12, 1860
FARREN, Daniel	1782	Jan. 31, 1867
Mrs. Daniel (Mary ——)	1791	Nov. 25, 1851
Philip	Feb. 22, 1821	Mar. 28, 1895
Daniel	July 15, 1823	Mar. 12, 1887
Jane	May 29, 1828	June 6, 1857
Dennis	1817	Jan. 6, 1887
Mrs. Dennis (Mary Ellen Connery)	Dec. 18, 1825	Oct. 11, 1895

NAME.	Born.	Died.
(Farren) John	Feb. 3, 1826	May 11, 1897
Peter	Apr. 7, 1873	Dec. 5, 1887
Patrick	............, ...	Jan. 24, 1800
Mrs. Patrick (Ann Noon)	............, ...	Jan. 20, 1838
Edward	............, 1820	Jan. 4, 1884
James	............, ...	Aug. 26, 1874
FECHTER, Sebastian	............, 1817	May 17, 1893
Mrs. Sebastian (Martina Hald)	............, 1821	July 10, 1892
FELTZ, John B.	............, 1773	Dec. 28, 1858
Mrs. John B. (Mary ——)	............, 1772	Jan. 3, 1859
Jacob	July 16, 1799	Mar 7, 1836
FENLON, Peter	............, 1808	June 28, 1823
FISHER, George	............, 1794	Nov. 2, 1880
Mrs. George (Genevieve Bertram)	............, 1813	Jan. 3, 1880
Mrs. Simon (Catherine Zanger)	............, 1823	Mar. 3, 1895
Charles	Mar. 22, 1854	Oct. 21, 1880
FITZGIBBONS, Eleanor	............, 1801	Jan. 6, 1827
Mrs. Michael	............, ...	Sept. 4, 1867
Mary	Mar. 16, 1820	Dec. 12, 1897
FLANAGAN, Peter	............, 1759	Mar. 15, 1861
Mrs. Peter (Ann Reinzel)	............, 1773	May 8, 1854
Michael	............, 1793	May 4, 1879
Mrs. Michael (Isabel McMullen)	Aug. 5, 1805	Mar. 25, 1854
Ann Elizabeth	June 13, 1829	Oct. 20, 1838
John C	July 2, 1819	Sept. 22, 1846
FLICK, Peter	Feb. 15, 1789	Feb. 11, 1874
Mrs. Peter (Ann Mary Sier)	Oct. 12, 1788	May 5, 1853
George	Dec. 19, 1824	May 9, 1899
Charles (of George)	June 20, 1849	Nov. 1, 1863
Mrs. Martin (Mary Ann Myers)	May 7, 1826	June 13, 1897
Thomas (of Martin)	Aug. 3, 1865	Dec. 15, 1887
Mrs. Peter (Elizabeth J. Gardner)	Apr. 30, 1829	Mar. 10, 1873
Joseph Henry (of Peter)	Nov. 9, 1854	Dec. 3, 1863
Mrs. Jerome (Ann Cath. Shenk)	Aug. 18, 1853	Jan. 31, 1880
Helena Margaret (of Charles)	Mar. 29, 1855	Mar. 31, 1873
Rosalia Catherine (of Charles)	Sept. 4, 1859	Mar. 31, 1873
William (of Charles)	July 1, 1857	Sept. 16, 1887
Mary Helena (of Philip)	Jan. 11, 1875	Oct. 9, 1893
FLINN, Mrs. Peter (Mary M. Belter)	May ..., 1851	............, 1882
FOLEY, Rev. Michael F.	............, ...	May 15, 1895
FORD, Rev. John	............, ...	Oct. 1, 1888
FREEL, Cornelius	............, 1764	Dec. 20, 1829
Mrs. Cornelius (Margaret ——)	............, 1764	July 17, 1852

REV. FERDINAND KITTELL. PASTOR 1891-99.

NAME.	Born.	Died.
FREIDHOFF, John..	.............., 1796	Aug. 9, 1858
Mrs. John (Mary A. ———)....................	Mar. 24, 1802	Apr. 10, 1885
Joseph..	Feb. 20, 1808	Apr. 2, 1876
Nicholas..	.............., 1813	Dec. 23, 1881
Veronica (Sister **Stephen**)........................	Dec. 10, 1843	Nov. 14, 1867
Ellen (Sister **Regis**)....................................	Apr. 11, 1848	June 23, 1873
Susan (Sister **Gertrude**)............................	Mar. 1, 1850	Nov. 7, 1877
Caroline (Sister **Walburga**)......................	Jan. 23, 1853	.............., 1877
Henry...	.............., 1845	Mar. 16, 1890
Mrs. Henry (**Christina Conrad**)...............	June 30, 1842	Dec. 27, 1893
Mary C...	Nov. 9, 1876	Oct. 3, 1897
Mrs. Nicholas R. (**Alice C. Kaylor**).........	Oct. 3, 1861	Mar. 8, 1890
FRY, John..	Mar. 14, 1787	Jan. 3, 1857
Mrs. John (**Cunegunda Fox**).....................	Apr. 11, 1791	Mar. 29, 1870
Sebastian...	Jan. 20, 1821	Dec. 28, 1895
Mrs. Sebastian (**Catherine Downey**)........	.............., 1815	Oct. 10, 1855
Mrs. Sebastian (**Mary Ann Little**).............	Apr. 22, 1821	May 8, 1894
FURY, Edward..	.............., ...	Dec. 22, 1853
Mrs. Edward (**Bridget Gorey**)...................	.............., ...	Sept. 17, 1855
Ann..	Feb. 27, 1835	Mar. 24, 1892
John...	.............., ...	Jan. 9, 1864
James...	Mar. 8, 1838	Aug. 6, 1879
Mrs. James (**Bridget Brawley**)...................	.............., ...	July 3, 1876
John Edward (**of James**)............................	July 28, 1870	Sept. 17, 1891
GALLAGHER, James..	July 10, 1761	Apr. 5, 1837
Mary...	Feb. 27, 1763	Jan. 18, 1843
Bridget...	.............., 1782	Dec. 19, 1852
Joseph..	.............., 1790	Feb. 2, 1826
Sarah..	.............., 1798	June 5, 1881
Thomas...	Sept. 30, 1800	Feb. 4, 1865
Mrs. Thomas (**Susan Glass**).......................	Dec. 24, 1804	July 8, 1898
Francis...	May 6, 1802	Sept. 20, 1843
Thomas...	.............., ...	Nov. 14, 1869
Mrs. Thomas (———).............................	.............., ...	June 5, 1881
Hugh...	.............., ...	July 7, 1873
Martha (**of Hugh**).......................................	June 25, 1853	Aug. 14, 1891
Daniel..	.............., ...	Nov. 7, 1891
Mrs. Daniel (**Mary Ann Scanlan**).............	Aug. 15, 1825	July 3, 1890
Henry John (**of Daniel**).............................	July 9, 1853	Oct. 21, 1896
Joseph (**of Daniel**).....................................	Mar. 20, 1858	.............., 1864
Mrs. James (**Elizabeth Fox**)......................	Apr. 1, 1825	Jan. 6, 1870
Rev. Hugh P..	.............., 1815	Mar. 10, 1882
Rev. Joseph A...	.............., ...	Apr. 5, 1887
GALLITZIN, Rev. Demetrius A..........................	Dec. 22, 1770	May 6, 1840
GARDNER, Mrs. John (**Cath. Weaver**)............	.............., 1817	Mar. 23, 1877
GIBBONS, William..	.............., 1774	Mar. 2, 1840
Mrs. Wm. (**Isabella A. Thompson**)...........	.............., 1771	Feb. 28, 1848

NAME	Born.	Died.
GIBBS, Rev. Andrew P.	1815	July 19, 1885
GIBSON, Rev. Matthew W.	May 1817	June 9, 1898
GIZZI, Mrs. Vito		Oct. 13, 1891
GLASS, Jacob	July 25, 1711	Jan. 18, 1821
George	Apr. 1, 1770	Nov. 9, 1847
Mrs. George (Susan Dougherty)	Jan. 14, 1781	May 10, 1863
Jacob (of George)	Sept. 14, 1806	Feb. 17, 1885
Augusta C. (of Jacob and Jane)	May 19, 1852	July 2, 1878
Gorman P. (of Jacob and Jane)	Sept. 11, 1861	Sept. 17, 1886
John J. (of George)	Feb. 13, 1812	Apr. 24, 1872
Mrs. John J. (Eliza J. Trotter)	Oct. 22, 1816	Nov. 19, 1859
Margaret (of John J.)	Oct. 13, 1843	Sept. 20, 1875
Richard (of John J.)	July 25, 1852	Aug. 8, 1870
Edward (of George)	May 14, 1816	Apr. 26, 1874
Mrs. Edward (Margaret Kane)	Jan. 22, 1822	Dec. 24, 1854
William (of George)	Feb. 14, 1818	Oct. 5, 1896
Mrs. William (Sarah McMullen)		Jan. 29, 1877
Augustine (of George)	Feb. 15, 1822	Mar. 3, 1877
Mrs. Augustine (Alice McHugh)	Dec. 5, 1827	Nov. 16, 1859
John	1771	July 28, 1859
Henry (of John and Esther)	Jan. 2, 1808	Nov. 2, 1887
Mrs. Henry (Rebecca Burke)	1807	Mar. 24, 1891
Thomas Heyden (of Jacob and Elizabeth)	Apr. 13, 1849	Dec. 25, 1896
Leonard (of Robert)	Jan. 21, 1888	July 31, 1899
GLASSER, Mrs. Francis (Sarah Ann Itel)	Apr. 24, 1823	Dec. 16, 1877
GOODERHAM, Mrs. Wm. T. (Mary Ann Nagle)	Aug. 15, 1833	July 26, 1894
GORMAN, James, Sr.	1820	Apr. 11, 1886
GRIFFIN, Mrs. Catherine	1802	Sept. 19, 1893
Hugh	1812	Sept. 3, 1885
Mrs. Hugh (Ann McGrath)	1817	Jan. 15, 1891
Mary (of Hugh)	Sept. 29, 1840	Oct. 3, 1885
John	1805	Mar. 14, 1871
Mrs. John (Catherine Kelly)	1802	Sept. 19, 1890
GROVE, James	1799	Oct. 27, 1854
Mrs. Jas. (Juliana Adams)	Feb. 11, 1797	Feb. 17, 1885
GWINN, Mary	1796	Aug. 23, 1886
William, M. D.	1803	Aug. 25, 1870
Caroline	1813	Jan. 30, 1863
HAGAN, John	1804	Apr. 23, 1893
Mrs. John (Bridget Grimes)	1802	Apr. 19, 1887
HAID, Sylvester	Feb. 28, 1779	Mar. 3, 1859
Francis X	1821	Sept. 8, 1890
Mrs. F. X. (Leocadia Lentz)	1832	Feb. 13, 1892
Mary T	June 30, 1858	June 26, 1873

NAME	Born	Died
HALL, James...	..............., 1773	July 21, 1867
Mrs. James (Charity McGuire)..............................	..............., 1801	Feb. 9, 1881
Rachel Ann...	Mar. 6, 1832	Mar. 13, 1855
James...	July 4, 1835	Jan. 8, 1850
Martha..	Apr. 5, 1838	Jan. 2, 1850
Peter...	Feb. 1, 1845	Apr. 5, 1893
Lorenzo J (of George)..	Nov. 21, 1869	May 27, 1893
HAMMAN, Michael J...	May 19, 1874	Jan. 30, 1892
HANLON, Felix..	..............., 1805	May 4, 1852
Mrs. Felix (Mary O'Connor)..................................	..............., 1801	Sept. 2, 1885
HASSON, Mary..	..............., 1769	Mar. 23, 1834
Michael..	..............., ...	Oct. 10, 1866
HATCH, Mrs. Charles E. (Prudence E. Kerrigan).....	Apr. 30, 1856	Feb. 15, 1889
Edward A...	Aug. 13, 1875	Nov. 2, 1892
HEGY, Samuel..	..............., 1807	Aug. 27, 1829
HEM, Jacob...	Oct. 11, 1816	Feb. 8, 1832
HERTZOG, Mrs. Philip Sr. (Sarah ——)..................	..............., 1809	Jan. 24, 1874
Mrs. Philip (Mary Ann ——)..................................	..............., 1799	May 6, 1847
Philip Jr...	..............., ...	Apr. 26, 1878
Mrs. Philip (Cath. Helker)......................................	..............., ...	Jan. 3, 1879
Dominic...	..............., ...	Nov. 9, 1867
Mrs. Dominic (Rufina ——)...................................	..............., ...	June 18, 1861
Mrs. Thomas (——)...	..............., ...	Sept. 30, 1863
Charles (of John P.)..	Oct. 4, 1874	Jan. 14, 1893
HOFFMAN, John B...	..............., 1810	Apr. 25, 1881
Mrs. John B. (Elizabeth Sherry)..........................	..............., 1815	Jan. 14, 1891
Mary C...	June 10, 1834	June ..., 1848
John B., Jr...	Jan. 1, 1839	Apr. 18, 1863
Mathias W...	Dec. 27, 1851	Jan. 27, 1889
HOGUE, Sebastian...	..............., 1797	July 11, 1833
Mrs. Sebastian (Mary Magdalen ——).................	..............., 1804	July 29, 1840
Mrs. Joseph (Elizabeth Buck)...............................	..............., 1835	Sept. 22, 1893
Cecilia..	Oct. 29, 1858	July 21, 1883
Matilda Jane...	Jan. 14, 1875	Mar. 19, 1896
HORN, Mrs. Rose..	..............., 1815	Apr. 1, 1891
HOWELL, Thomas, Sr...	..............., ...	Mar. 7, 1855
Mrs. Thos. (Ann Crosby)..	..............., ...	Oct. 9, 1854
Hugh...	..............., 1802	..............., 1861
Mrs. Hugh (Mary Murphy)......................................	..............., ...	..............., 1876
Mordecai..	Jan. 15, 1806	Oct. 8, 1873
Mrs. Mord. (Ann Topper).......................................	Mar. 26, 1813	Aug. 30, 1872
Thomas, Jr..	Sept. 15, 1829	Jan. 26, 1853
HUFFARD, Christian..	Dec. 22, 1803	Nov. 18, 1865
Mrs. Christian (Christina Bostick)......................	Oct. 16, 1806	May 16, 1886

NAME.	Born.	Died.
(Huffard) Jacob	1853	May 26, 1882
Miss ——		Feb. 6, 1867
HUMPHREYS, John M.		Feb. 27, 1898
Mrs. John M. (Margaret M. Riffle)	1826	Jan. 19, 1859
INLOW, Mrs. James (Susanna Criste)	June 23, 1822	July 18, 1894
ITEL, John Sr	1795	Oct. 25, 1881
Mrs. John, Sr. (Mary Ann Seubert)	Sept. 25, 1801	Sept. 15, 1879
Joseph		May 15, 1897
George Philip (of Francis)	Jan. 3, 1860	Mar. 12, 1872
Mrs. Henry (Gertrude Sanker)	Nov. 15, 1854	Aug. 22, 1899
IVORY, Matthew	1797	June 2, 1856
Mrs. Matthew (Mary McGuire)	July 24, 1799	Oct. 1, 1881
William	July 7, 1820	Sept. 30, 1896
Mrs. William (Susan Kelly)	Apr. 3, 1826	June 4, 1899
Thomas M.	Dec. 14, 1843	Jan. 15, 1865
John	1802	Apr. 24, 1860
Frances		July 28, 1868
Mary Ellen	Aug. 2, 1837	Oct. 9, 1893
Mrs. Wm. A. (Eliz. J. Little)	Feb. 5, 1872	May 29, 1895
Patrick	1800	Feb. 1, 1858
Mrs. P. (Ellen Conley)	1798	Mar. 8, 1858
Matthew	1820	Nov. 28, 1898
John C.	1827	Nov. 14, 1862
Francis	1830	Apr. 22, 1899
JAMISON, William, M. D.	1840	Dec. 26, 1873
JOHNSON, Thomas	1782	Oct. 15, 1830
Mary	1786	Sept. 10, 1833
KANE, KEAN, CAIN.		
John (of Henry)	Mar. 30, 1817	Mar. 4, 1836
James		Aug. 7, 1865
Andrew	1795	Aug. 6, 1865
Mrs. Andrew (Sarah ——)	1795	Apr. 6, 1877
Col. James, Jr	1795	Sept. ..., 1827
Mrs. James (Milburg McGuire)	1797	Dec. 8, 1878
Mary Ann	Sept. 4, 1821	May 25, 1855
Mrs. James (Eliz. Amelia Kittell)	July 11, 1823	Feb. 11, 1818
John	May 16, 1830	Mar. 17, 1896
Mrs. Richard (Margaret Kane)		July 17, 1899
Mrs. George (Mary J. Kane)	Nov. 9, 1837	Feb. 25, 1899
KAYLOR, Peter	Nov. 12, 1753	Sept. 19, 1810
Mrs. Peter (Elizabeth Adams)	Oct. ..., 1757	Feb. 2, 1843
Mary		Nov. 2, 1887
Peter	1787	Nov. 11, 1874
Mrs. Peter (Agnes Leavy)	1795	May 27, 1874
Thomas	Nov. 11, 1818	June 8, 1868
Peter	Nov. 14, 1826	Dec. 5, 1863

NAME.	Born.	Died.
(Kaylor) Mrs. Peter (Mary Phalen)	Feb. 11, 1823	Apr. 16, 1898
Richard	Nov. 10, 1832	Apr. 26, 1863
Jacob	............, 1790	Apr. 7, 1860
Mrs. Jacob (Cath. McConnell)	............, 1796	Apr. 1, 1861
James J.	Feb. 11, 1826	July 26, 1894
Mark	Aug. 27, 1858	Mar. 10, 1891
William	Oct. 18, 1830	Jan. 10, 1873
Henrietta A	Oct. 1, 1840	Sept. 21, 1850
Mrs. John G. (Mary McCoy)	Nov. 1, 1835	May 1, 1858
Mrs. Zach (Ellen Parrish)	............, 1854	Oct. 10, 1898
Mary E.	Sept. 30, 1875	Aug. 11, 1898
Mrs. Peter B. (Veronica Itel)	............, ...	Feb. 1, 1892
Robert (of Jacob)	Aug. 22, 1858	............, 1863
Michael (of Peter)	Oct. 5, 1824	Feb. 28, 1892
Augustine (of Peter)	Oct. 21, 1830	Dec. 22, 1860
KEARNS, Mrs. John (Sarah Campbell)	Oct. 18, 1807	............, 1889
KEEFERS, Louisa	Mar. 29, 1812	July 7, 1893
KEENAN, Anastasia	............, 1817	Aug. 20, 1834
KELLER, John	............, 1725	Dec. 8, 1814
KELLY, Patrick	............, 1775	Apr. 24, 1857
Mrs. Patrick (Mary ———)	............, 1775	Jan. 26, 1854
Thomas	............, 1789	Mar. 27, 1857
Mrs. Thomas (Mary McMullen)	Mar. 23, 1801	Apr. 7, 1888
Hugh	Jan. 15, 1829	Feb. 22, 1859
Daniel	............, 1797	June 8, 1847
James	............, 1832	Feb. 17, 1849
Thomas	............, 1802	Oct. 18, 1856
Mrs. Thomas (———)	............, 1812	Mar. 18, 1854
Martin	............, 1804	Sept. 20, 1877
Ann	Feb. 21, 1842	Aug. 21, 1859
James	............, 1810	Feb. 26, 1888
KENNEDY, Mrs. John (Ann Howell)	May 2, 1826	............, 1858
Charles	............, ...	June 4, 1857
Mrs. James (Mary Connery)	............, 1779	............, 1853
KEPPLER, Jacob, Sr.,	............, 1775	............, 1845
Mrs. Jacob, Sr., (Sarah Fisher)	............, 1782	Jan. 24, 1874
Jacob, Jr.,	............, 1823	............, 1846
Andrew	............, 1826	July ...., 1850
John, Jr.	............, 1828	Dec. 18, 1891
KERNAN, Owen	............, 1800	Nov. 30, 1880
KERNEY, Bartholomew	............, ...	............, 1855
Mrs. Bartholomew (Ann ———)	............, ...	............, 1862
Ellen	............, ...	............, 1852
KERNS, Martin	............, 1790	Nov. 16, 1862
KERR, Annie	............, 1862	July 7, 1881

NAME.	Born.	Died.
KERRIGAN, Peter	............, 1755	Sept. 22, 1839
Mrs. Peter (—— ——)	............, 1760	Nov. 28, 1815
Michael, Jr.,	Mar. 24, 1824	Jan. 2, 1865
Peter	............, 1772	Dec. 11, 1872
KITTELL, Samuel	............, 1788	July 12, 1875
Mrs. Samuel (Barbara Cook)	Apr. ..., 1782	Oct. 3, 1845
Mrs. Samuel (Margaret Coons)	Apr. 28, 1817	Feb. 6, 1894
KRISE, Henry	............, ...	May 12, 1867
John A	............, ...	Oct. 24, 1890
KRUG, Valentine	............, ...	Nov. 11, 1838
LACY, Mrs. Christiana	............, 1814	Dec. 30, 1892
Elizabeth	............, 1841	Apr. 15, 1894
John	............, ...	Sept. 25, 1877
LAKE, William	............, 1792	Dec. 26, 1877
Mrs. William (Ann McCloskey)	............, 1806	July 25, 1859
John G.	Feb. 20, 1840	Aug. 24, 1880
LANTZY, Mrs. Joseph (Ursula Bitters)	............, ...	June 6, 1874
LATTERNER, Michael	Nov. ...., 1812	Sept. 26, 1885
Mrs. Michael (Cath. Sharbaugh)	Oct. 14, 1819	Oct. 9, 1882
LEAVY, James	............, ...	Aug. 16, 1808
Mrs. James (Catherine Byrne)	............, ...	Mar. 30, 1798
Michael	Mar. 30, 1795	Aug. 19, 1868
Mrs. Michael (Mary Ann Little)	July 7, 1796	Apr. 20, 1856
James	Mar. 24, 1824	Mar. 21, 1850
Bernard	July 19, 1825	Aug. 22, 1849
John F.	Apr. 11, 1828	Apr. 15, 1853
Henry A	Mar. 21, 1831	Feb. 1, 1854
Michael P.	Jan. 23, 1834	June 24, 1853
William A	Dec. 14, 1836	Aug. 17, 1865
Matilda J	Aug. 1, 1839	Feb. 13, 1852
Francis A	May 28, 1835	Nov. ...., 1863
William A., Jr.	Feb. 15, 1862	Sept. 22, 1887
LEMKE, Rev. H. P.	............, ...	Nov. 28, 1882
LENZ, Joseph	Mar. ..., 1783	Jan. 24, 1873
Mrs. Joseph (Catherine Heim)	............, 1786	June 6, 1874
Mrs. George (Eliz. Ann Bortman)	Nov. 11, 1837	Feb. 12, 1897
Charles Aug	Jan. 13, 1875	July 18, 1889
LETT, George	............, 1805	Dec. 13, 1871
LILLY, Joseph	Mar. 21, 1763	Sept. 2, 1823
Mrs. Joseph (Charity ——)	Jan. 30, 1763	Aug. 26, 1829
Isidore	Apr. 4, 1809	Aug. 17, 1845
Mrs. Thomas (Cath. Myers)	............, 1790	May 12, 1854
Mrs. Samuel (Cath. Troxell)	Oct. 30, 1805	Nov. 29, 1865

NAME.	Born.	Died.
LITTLE, Bernard	May 16, 1762	Mar. 13, 1839
Peter J	July 15, 1880	Apr. 13, 1883
Loretta (of W. A. B.)	Oct. 22, 1883	Nov. 26, 1888
John	Apr. 11, 1794	Dec. 29, 1846
Mrs. John (Elizabeth Bradley)	May 23, 1797	Sept. 22, 1849
Henry (of John)	Aug. 6, 1824	July 27, 1890
Patience (of Henry)	Sept. 23, 1858	Mar. 23, 1877
Sylvester (of John)	May 26, 1827	Jan. 28, 1876
Mrs. Edward J. (Mary J. Litzinger)	Jan. 12, 1845	Mar. 13, 1890
George		Aug. 5, 1879
Thomas (of George)	May 29, 1843	Jan. 3, 1870
Mrs. Philip	1810	Sept. 20, 1896
LITZINGER, Anthony	1781	Sept. 26, 1856
Mrs. Anthony (Mary **Susan** Durley)	1785	Mar. 4, 1857
Ann	1795	Apr. 2, 1832
Charles	Aug. 7, 1857	May 27, 1853
Mrs. Charles (Mary Ann Rodgers)		July 13, 1865
David	1808	Mar. 9, 1870
Mrs. David	1813	Oct. 16, 1852
Susan (of Charles)	1839	Apr. 28, 1873
James (of Charles)	Dec. 2, 1844	Jan. 12, 1874
George	Oct. 10, 1807	Dec. 18, 1893
Susan (of George)	July 21, 1837	Nov. 1, 1888
Susan (of David)	Feb. 10, 1845	Dec. 12, 1865
William	Oct. 3, 1818	July 17, 1887
Mrs. William (Monica McGuire)	May 4, 1817	Oct. 19, 1893
Serenus (of William)	Feb. 23, 1853	Mar. 22, 1854
Mrs. Eugene (Mary M. Bertram)	June 4, 1849	Feb. 5, 1882
Thomas	Apr. 22, 1814	July 22, 1838
John R	June 20, 1828	Apr. 19, 1848
Jane		July 15, 1831
John M		Apr. 1, 1885
John R		July 12, 1889
Mrs. James (Elizabeth McDermitt)		Oct. 1, 1877
Caroline (of James)	Jan. 7, 1845	June 21, 1870
George (of James)		Apr. 5, 1878
Mrs. Wm. E. (Eliz. Phalen)	Sept. 13, 1864	Sept. 27, 1898
Daniel		Mar. 28, 1864
Jennie (of Daniel)		Apr. 22, 1866
LOGAN, Sarah	1744	Jan. 1, 1813
Michael	1763	Aug. 22, 1822
John	1784	Feb. 9, 1867
LONG, Mrs. Anthony (Mary A. Coons)	Sept. 8, 1810	Jan. 25, 1876
LOWE, Mrs. John (Matilda Behe)	Feb. 17, 1855	Mar. 2, 1890
LUCKETT, Ellen	1775	Mar. 27, 1863
Thomas H	Dec. 13, 1748	Sept. 6, 1822
Thomas	July 9, 1826	Feb. 8, 1847
LUTHER, Christopher	1776	Mar. 20, 1820

NAME.	Born.	Died.
(Luther) Levi	Feb. 27, 1822	Jan. 2, 1890
Sarah Ann	Feb. 5, 1827	Dec. 19, 1898
Jacob	Oct. 11, 1817	Jan. 7, 1892
Mrs. Jacob (Sarah Bearer)	Mar. 17, 1819	July 11, 1864
MAGEEHAN, James	Feb. 10, 1778	Oct. 12, 1852
Mrs. James (Apollonia McGuire)	Feb. 10, 1779	May 21, 1861
Michael Dan	July 14, 1805	Feb. 6, 1864
Mrs. Michael D. (Mary Glass)	Oct. 31, 1802	May 17, 1890
Rachel	Oct. 18, 1806	Oct. 19, 1876
Anna Maria	Nov. 27, 1816	June 1, 1857
MALLOY, Mrs. ——		Jan. 27, 1864
James	1796	Dec. 3, 1881
Mrs. James (Susan Kelly)	1801	May 21, 1889
Mrs. Michael (Ann Bradley)	Sept. 2, 1841	Feb. 27, 1893
Mary	Jan. 14, 1872	Apr. 7, 1893
MALONE, Mrs. Patrick (Eliz. Sheehan)	1830	Jan. 27, 1895
MANSFIELD, Henry	July 21, 1825	July 21, 1897
Mrs. Henry (Abigail McCullough)	1824	Mar. 13, 1879
John		Oct. 31, 1887
Mary A	Oct. 18, 1858	June 10, 1885
Elizabeth	Sept. 25, 1861	Apr. 19, 1882
MARASCA, Agostino	1851	Oct. 9, 1894
MATTHEWS, John	Feb. 22, 1856	Aug. 6, 1897
MAUSE, Jacob	1817	Oct. 25, 1891
Mrs. Jacob, Jr., (Annette Daughenbaugh)		Aug. 10, 1890
M'ATEER, Patrick	1761	Dec. 29, 1842
Mrs. Patrick (Catherine ——)	1772	June 1, 1848
William	Mar. 26, 1790	Oct. 19, 1864
James	Apr. 8, 1810	Nov. 6, 1882
Mrs. James (Mary Ann Elder)	Sept. 26, 1819	Mar. 3, 1897
William W	Oct. 11, 1830	Dec. 24, 1894
Mrs. W. W. (Cecelia Adelsberger)	Mar. 5, 1842	Apr. 7, 1884
Augustine	May 20, 1843	Feb. 9, 1863
John Joseph	July 20, 1817	June 9, 1877
Mrs. John Joseph (Mary Jane Branniff)		Aug 18, 1880
Andrew	1857	July 27, 1875
Henry P	June 1, 1841	July 20, 1893
Francis	May 22, 1852	Mar. 11, 1890
M'CLAIN, Mrs. John	1780	Oct. 31, 1828
M'CLOSKEY, Mrs. Wm., Sr., (Ann McCloskie)	1783	Mar. 23, 1847
William	Dec. 21, 1813	Nov. 17, 1883
Mrs. Wm. (Louisa Giles)	Mar. 11, 1813	Feb. 26, 1839
Mrs. Wm. (Mary E. Webster)	Oct. 25, 1824	May 25, 1899
M'COMBIE, Mrs. Wm., (Mary Ann Weakland)	Dec. 15, 1822	Dec. 7, 1894

NAME.	Born.	Died.
M'CONNELL, John S..	.........., 1791	Mar. 25, 1854
Mrs. John S (Margaret Tierney)...................	.........., 1792	June 10, 1879
Francis A..	June 7, 1810	May 25, 1831
Arthur J. (of John H.)......................................	Mar. 3, 1816	Mar. 21, 1897
M'COY, Mrs. Hugh (Mary ——)..............................	.........., 1751	Oct. 22, 1827
John...	Aug. 10, 1771	Apr. 9, 1843
Peter...	.........., 1801	Aug. 1, 1880
Mrs. Peter (Margaret Durbin)............................	May 17, 1811	May 8, 1893
Anthony..	.........., 1806	Mar. 25, 1890
Mrs. Anthony (Mary McShane)...................	.........., 1804	May 1, 1877
Anthony Jr...	Nov. 18, 1837	May 28, 1890
John (of John and Susan)..................................	Apr. 29, 1814	Feb. 22, 1888
Mrs. John (Elizabeth Kaylor)...........................	.........., 1820	Sept. 8, 1899
Thomas (of Charles and Ann)............................	Nov. 1, 1834	Mar. 25, 1854
Catherine (of Charles and Ann).........................	Oct. 15, 1836	May 8, 1866
John T. (of Charles and Ann)............................	Feb. 5, 1843	Apr. 12, 1871
Mrs. ——...	.........., ...	Apr. 30, 1877
Kate...	.........., ...	May 16, 1865
M'CULLOUGH, John...	.........., ...	Jan. 12, 1871
Mrs. John (Bridget McAllister)........................	.........., 1801	Oct. 1, 1883
Roddy...	.........., ...	June 21, 1861
Mrs. Roddy (Ann Bradley)...............................	.........., 1778	Mar. 29, 1858
Michael...	.........., 1830	.........., 1850
Mrs. Francis (Elizabeth Mullen)........................	Nov. 30, 1830	May 13, 1893
John...	.........., 1832	Apr. 12, 1888
Mrs. Patrick (Ann Campbell)...........................	.........., 1818	Aug. 23, 1873
M'CUNE, Mrs. William (Mary Ann Dougherty)...........	Apr. 4, 1817	Jan. 14, 1849
M'DERMITT, John..	.........., 1783	July 9, 1836
James (of John and Mary)................................	Oct. 4, 1811	Feb. 17, 1859
Mrs. James (Lydia Ann Doneughe)....................	Mar. 31, 1817	Oct. 21, 1860
Eveline Mary..	Aug. 18, 1852	Dec. 21, 1872
Henry...	.........., ...	July 17, 1866
James C..	Aug. 9, 1813	May 1, 1882
Mrs. James C. (Mary Kittell)............................	Oct. 26, 1815	Oct. 25, 1844
Mrs. William..	.........., ...	June 28, 1885
Mrs. Jas. F. (Unietta ——)................................	.........., 1830	Apr. 19, 1853
James...	.........., 1854	Aug. 31, 1886
Michael D. (of Samuel)....................................	Jan. 8, 1824	Apr. 15, 1833
Catherine A. (of Samuel).................................	Jan. 13, 1826	Apr. 23, 1833
Arthur..	.........., ...	Mar. 15, 1850
James J...	.........., ...	Jan. 13, 1876
James...	.........., ...	Mar. 18, 1854
M'DONALD, Cornelius..	.........., 1767	Aug. 4, 1842
Mrs. Cornelius (Rachael A. White).....................	June ...., 1782	June 24, 1859
Alice S..	Feb. 8, 1815	Mar. 8, 1830
Philip...	Feb. 27, 1818	Oct. 11, 1857
Owen..	.........., 1780	Aug. 20, 1842
Mrs. Owen (Eliza Parsons)..............................	Jan. 16, 1792	Sept. 26, 1881
Alice S..	Feb. 6, 1820	Aug. 12, 1842

NAME.	Born.	Died.
(McDonald) Margaret	May 26, 1823	Jan. 21, 1832
Rose P.	Aug. 21, 1825	May 7, 1855
M'DUNN, James	July 16, 1837	Dec. 15, 1897
M'ELHENY, James J.	1815	Apr. 17, 1875
Martin Kelly	May 23, 1850	Feb. 6, 1890
Mary	June 26, 1852	Oct. 21, 1886
James, Jr.	Jan. 19, 1855	June 1, 1873
M'EVOY, Michael	1810	June 12, 1861
Mrs. Michael (Margaret Shields)	1809	Dec. 10, 1853
M'FEELY, Bernard, Sr.		Feb. 23, 1876
Mrs. Bernard		Feb. 1, 1873
M'GAUGHEY, William	1802	May 23, 1882
Mrs. Wm. (Catherine Bradley)		Aug. 20, 1870
Mary Ann	May 23, 1848	Feb. 10, 1872
Matthew	1810	Mar. 29, 1891
Mrs. Matthew (Martha Daly)	1814	Feb. 4, 1882
John	Oct. 14, 1839	Sept. 27, 1893
William	Oct. 26, 1847	May 30, 1875
M'GILLEN, Michael		Mar. 10, 1895
Mary	1867	Sept. 23, 1887
Joseph	Oct. 11, 1877	Aug. 6, 1892
M'GINN, Mary	1788	Feb. 11, 1888
M'GIRR, Rev. Terence		Aug. 12, 1851
M'GLADE, Michael	1793	Feb. 23, 1871
Mrs. Michael (Margaret ——)	1804	Aug. 9, 1872
Mary	1819	Feb. 14, 1875
M'GONIGLE, Mrs. Charles (Ann Dever)	1782	Apr. 8, 1876
Charles	1787	Apr. 1, 1832
Jeremiah	Feb. 1, 1825	Mar. 26, 1871
Ann	Aug. 24, 1831	May 22, 1890
M'GOUGH, Mrs. Arthur, Sr. (Susan ——)	1765	Feb. 13, 1845
James	Aug. 1, 1796	Nov. 1, 1870
Mrs. James (Margaret Glass)	June 17, 1801	July 11, 1871
George	Oct. 10, 1825	Apr. 15, 1868
Mrs. George (Mary F. Adelsberger)	Jan. 22, 1834	Mar. 16, 1861
Charles	June 23, 1830	June ...., 1896
Ann	June 26, 1832	Aug. 13, 1897
Andrew T.	June 13, 1838	Jan. 17, 1891
Demetrius A.	May 14, 1840	Aug. 23, 1897
William (of John and Sarah)	Jun. 1, 1819	Mar. 23, 1898
Peter (of John and Sarah)	Dec. 31, 1827	Jan. 5, 1899
Mrs. Peter (Mary Fitzgibbons)	Mar. 16, 1830	Dec. 12, 1897
William A.	Mar. 8, 1852	Sept. 25, 1899
M'GOWAN, Ellen	Dec. 4, 1797	Apr. 9, 1831

NAME.	Born.	Died.
M'GRANAHAN, Mary	Feb. 21, 1820	Jan. 9, 1899
M'GUIRE, Captain Michael	1717	Nov. 17, 1793
Cornelius	1750	Mar. 10, 1830
Peter	1763	Jan. 30, 1850
Mrs. Peter (Charity Shirley)	1773	Sept. 13, 1844
Peter	1814	Nov. 7, 1845
Mary	May 10, 1766	Nov. 21, 1829
Luke	Oct. 2, 1768	Apr. 17, 1831
Mrs. Luke (Margaret O'Hara)	1774	Jan. 19, 1833
Elizabeth	Sept. 3, 1801	June 27, 1870
Augustine	Sept. 3, 1801	Jan. 31, 1828
Margaret	Mar. 27, 1807	Sept. 1, 1878
Michael L.	Aug. 28, 1811	Dec. 21, 1832
Captain Richard	Dec. 12, 1775	Jan. 13, 1855
Mrs. Richard (Eleanor Byrne)	1782	Aug. 5, 1855
Susan	1791	Aug. 23, 1863
Henry J	Nov. 16, 1794	Oct. 8, 1843
Michael	Feb. 18, 1794	July 24, 1873
Mrs. Michael (Margaret Bostick)	1798	Jan. 6, 1891
Martha	1796	Apr. 8, 1876
Luke	Apr. 1796	Jan. 9, 1881
Mrs. Luke (Martha Cooper)		Apr. 10, 1876
Luke (of Michael and Patience)	May 9, 1800	May 19, 1836
John (of Michael and Patience)	June 25, 1805	June 1, 1877
Mrs. John (Susan Storm)	Apr. 29, 1806	Aug. 23, 1863
John		Apr. 27, 1878
Mrs. John		Mar. 2, 1878
Mary (of Michael and Sarah)	Sept. 1803	June 12, 1872
Patrick		Apr. 2, 1883
Mrs. Patrick (Mary Dougherty)		June 10, 1872
Mark (of Luke and Martha)	Oct. 23, 1837	Dec. 28, 1871
Rebecca (of Mark)	1871	Sept. 17, 1882
Mrs. James		Jan. 27, 1899
Andrew (of James and Aline)		May 14, 1872
John Gibson (of Heyden)	July 20, 1880	Apr. 2, 1897
John		Apr. 28, 1877
Mrs. John (Susan Storm)	Apr. 29, 1806	Mar. 3, 1877
John C.		Jan. 2, 1861
M'HUGH, John	1763	Sept. 6, 1833
Mrs. John (Elsie ———)	1769	Jan. 3, 1827
John	Apr. 3, 1805	Aug. 18, 1878
Matthew	1791	Aug. 31, 1874
Mrs. Matthew (Mary Ann McGuire)	Sept. 1801	Apr. 21, 1874
Matthew	May 26, 1831	Dec. 10, 1897
Catherine Cecelia	Aug. 6, 1842	May 27, 1851
John	Feb. 3, 1833	Feb. 2, 1873
John, Jr.	Oct. 21, 1862	July 4, 1880
Michael R.	1826	Jan. 17, 1856
M'KEEVER, Henry	1814	Mar. 2, 1869
Mrs. Henry (Isabella McCloskey)	1820	Mar. 19, 1882
Margaret	Aug. 21, 1840	Aug. 18, 1883

NAME.	Born.	Died.
(McKeever) Mary	Apr. 2, 1846	May 31, 1880
Elizabeth	May 2, 1848	Sept. 13, 1885
Henry Manasses	Nov. 21, 1853	Dec. 12, 1880
Daniel Alexander	Oct. 15, 1856	June 27, 1880
Lucy	Nov. 15, 1859	July 30, 1887
M'KIM, Mary		Feb. 9, 1888
Mrs. William (Rosanna ——)	1788	Aug. 4, 1868
Jane	Sept. 8, 1822	Mar. 17, 1849
M'KINZIE, Sarah	1803	Apr. ...., 1838
Mrs. John (Esther Hudson)	1805	Nov. 16, 1870
Henry	1855	June 1, 1876
Mrs. Andrew		Feb. 10, 1885
M'LAUGHLIN, John	1785	Oct. 25, 1855
Mrs. John (Eliz. McClain)	1811	June 20, 1876
Mrs. Mark, Sr.		Feb. 27, 1864
Mark		Sept. 12, 1870
Mrs. Mark (Bridget ——)	June 28, 1833	Aug. 10, 1863
M'MANAMY, Charles	1811	Oct. 20, 1888
Mrs. Charles (Elizabeth Glass)	Mar. 11, 1808	June 23, 1884
M'MULLEN, Samuel	1759	Jan. 14, 1853
Mrs. Samuel (Susan Logan)	1769	Mar. 16, 1851
Hugh (of Samuel)	1804	Jan. 21, 1887
John (of Samuel)	Dec. 15, 1808	Apr. 25, 1882
Alexander (of Samuel)	Mar. 2, 1806	Feb. 23, 1888
Mrs. Alexander (Catherine McGuire)	Mar. 20, 1808	Oct. 9, 1872
Samuel F.	Nov. 24, 1851	Feb. 8, 1869
Mrs. James (Ann Donoughe)	Nov. 24, 1777	May 16, 1840
Margaret	May 14, 1794	Aug. 6, 1880
James	Jan. 18, 1799	Nov. 26, 1847
Mrs. James (Rebecca McDermitt)	Sept. 13, 1802	Sept. 10, 1887
John A	Feb. 4, 1824	Oct. 29, 1890
Henry	Nov. 17, 1828	Nov. 27, 1898
James Chrysostom	May 22, 1841	June 10, 1874
Mary (of Henry and Elizabeth)	Mar. 23, 1818	Aug. 20, 1870
John Edwin (of James and Susan)	Aug. 10, 1838	Dec. 23, 1897
Susan	Dec. 13, 1841	Feb. 15, 1861
Mrs. Matthew (Adeline Ann Weakland)	May 23, 1818	Apr. 29, 1879
Hugh	1804	Jan. 26, 1864
Mrs. Hugh		Aug. 19, 1870
Mrs. John (Jane Wharton)	Aug. 7, 1819	Dec. 24, 1898
Mrs. Enos (Mary Ellen Wharton)	May 19, 1826	June 1, 1869
Bridget		Jan. 17, 1874
Martha		Apr. 16, 1864
Harriet		May 11, 1865
Alexander	June 17, 1826	Sept. 18, 1862
William H	Mar. 16, 1852	May 2, 1863
M'VEY, Patrick	1772	Apr. 20, 1872
Mary	Nov. 30, 1809	May 13, 1895

NAME.	Born.	Died.
(McVey) Michael	............, 1815	Aug. 9, 1896
Sarah	............, 1811	Apr. 30, 1885
James	Feb. ..., 1813	Jan. 15, 1875
Michael T. (of James)	May 18, 1850	Aug. 9, 1873
Susan (of James)	Apr. 23, 1852	Oct. 18, 1873
Patrick (of James)	Oct. 18, 1854	Nov. 3, 1873
Catherine (of James)	Dec. 19, 1859	Mar. 23, 1885
James (of James)	June 23, 1864	Aug. 18, 1873
MEALLY, Mrs. Bridget	............, 1807	Jan. 17, 1873
MELHORN, Emma	May 13, 1857	Mar. 7, 1895
Sylvester	July 11, 1863	Mar. 2, 1884
MELOY, William	............, ...	............, 1821
Mrs. William (Bridget McGuire)	............, ...	Aug. 17, 1814
John	Apr. 15, 1794	Jan. 8, 1872
Mrs. John (Sarah Gardner)	Apr. 17, 1795	Aug. 23, 1893
Mrs. James (Margaret McMullen)	............, ...	Jan. 27, 1864
MILLER, Daniel	............, 1792	Oct. 18, 1872
Mrs. Daniel (Elizabeth ———)	............, 1825	Oct. 22, 1875
MILLS, Mrs John (Linnie Keppler)	............, ...	Jan. 13, 1878
MITCHELL, Rev. Michael J.	............, 1820	Jan. 11, 1881
MOLEO, Francis	............, 1868	Jan. 2, 1892
MORAN, Francis	............, 1819	Aug. 13, 1899
Mrs. Francis (Bridget Bradley)	............, 1823	June 12, 1897
John E. (of Francis)	Jan. 13, 1847	Jan. 27, 1876
Ellen (of Patrick)	July 7, 1864	May 15, 1887
Clara (of Patrick)	Aug. 14, 1867	Aug. 5, 1887
Austin (of Peter)	July 22, 1884	Jan. 2, 1897
MORELAND, William Felician	June 9, 1842	Aug. 17, 1896
MORGAN, Rev. Pollard McCormick	............, 1831	Apr. 14, 1872
MULLEN, Mary	............, 1756	Oct. 17, 1829
Patrick	............, 1763	Oct. 28, 1843
Michael	............, 1793	June 6, 1853
Mrs. Michael (Eliz. Kerrigan)	............, 1794	Dec. 29, 1864
Michael	Dec. 29, 1822	Aug. 20, 1855
Robert	May 24, 1826	Dec. 29, 1853
Edward	............, 1800	Aug. 22, 1850
Mrs. Edward (Margaret Fagan)	Feb. 19, 1801	Oct. 19, 1871
Peter J.	Mar. 26, 1835	Mar. 1, 1878
Mrs. P. J. (Juliana Grove)	............, 1843	Dec. 17, 1875
Edward James	Feb. 11, 1840	May 15, 1897
Simon	Oct. 17, 1832	Mar. 23, 1843
John	Jan. 3, 1868	Dec. 12, 1897
Regina (of Peter J.)	June 18, 1868	Aug. 21, 1892
Julia (of John)	Aug. 16, 1877	May 16, 1898

NAME.	Born.	Died.
MURPHY, Michael...	............, 1748	Jan. 1, 1815
Mrs. Michael (Hannah ——).........................	............, 1763	Sept. 10, 1846
James...	............, 1784	Dec. 1, 1864
Mrs. James (Jane ——).................................	............, 1791	Mar. 4, 1867
Lawrence..	............, 1803	Aug. 16, 1838
MURRAY, Michael..	............, 1796	Dec. 30, 1860
Mrs. Michael (Mary Glacken)...........................	May 10, 1806	Jan. 1, 1878
James...	Nov. 28, 1794	Nov. 4, 1863
John...	............, 1794	Aug. 31, 1844
Mrs. John..	............, 1804	Dec. 21, 1881
James..	Jan. 28, 1798	Aug. 13, 1887
Mrs. James (Eliz. Scanlan)............................	............, 1806	June 18, 1879
James P..	............, ...	Oct. 8, 1878
Mrs. James P. (Mary McConnell)..................	............, 1805	May 11, 1887
MUTSKO, Andrew...	............, 1856	Dec. 18, 1885
MYERS, John, Sr...	............, 1753	July 24, 1834
Mrs. Nemuck..	Feb. 26, 1768	Apr. 12, 1832
John B..	Nov. 7, 1792	Feb. 13, 1875
Mrs. John B..	Feb. 9, 1808	Nov. 1, 1884
John...	............, 1792	May 19, 1858
Mrs. John (Catherine ——)..........................	Dec. 23, 1794	June 19, 1854
Henry J...	May 21, 1829	May 17, 1880
Mrs. H. J. (Ann Adelsberger)........................	Apr. 18, 1831	Sept. 24, 1879
Frances...	Aug. 16, 1856	Mar. 3, 1880
Harriet..	May 6, 1860	Apr. 14, 1878
Raymond Edward...	Oct. 18, 1867	Aug. 26, 1886
Ida Elizabeth..	Oct. 10, 1869	Aug. 19, 1886
Mrs. Joseph..	............, ...	Jan. 11, 1872
Mrs. Celestine..	............, 1868	Nov. 11, 1892
John...	Aug. 9, 1791	Aug. 19, 1858
Mrs. John (Ann Glass)...................................	Oct. 26, 1790	Oct. 24, 1875
James...	Feb. 20, 1818	July 10, 1893
Matilda...	Oct. 29, 1821	Sept. 25, 1871
Joseph..	Dec. 7, 1842	Aug. 7, 1875
NAGLE, John, Sr..	............, 1785	Mar. 6, 1871
Mrs. John, Sr., (Cath. Coons).......................	Feb. 18, 1798	Dec. 21, 1891
Mrs. Susan...	............, 1800	Dec. 25, 1891
Mrs. George (Sarah Dougherty)....................	June 22, 1860	July 12, 1897
Mrs. John...	............, ...	June 14, 1881
John (of John and Catherine)........................	May 1, 1823	Feb. 28, 1897
Mrs. John (Cath. Little).................................	Aug. 31, 1822	June 22, 1800
Michael (of John and Catherine)....................	Jan. 12, 1820	Aug. 18, 1895
Mrs. Michael (Mary Bradley).........................	Aug. 1, 1825	Apr. 1, 1873
Jacob Z. (of John and Catherine)..................	Oct. 3, 1825	June 15, 1880
Silas A. (of Jacob Z.)....................................	Oct. 28, 1863	July 11, 1893
Nicholas...	............, ...	Nov. 16, 1887
Mrs. Michael (Mary Keppler).........................	............, 1825	Oct. 27, 1854
NEASON, James..	............, 1769	Mar. 29, 1852
Mrs. James (Mary Crilly)..............................	............, 1771	Nov. 20, 1851

NAME.	Born.	Died.
(Neason) John		May 18, 1873
Mrs. John (Maria Donoughe)	1806	Sept. 1, 1883
Elizabeth	1803	June 1, 1880
Hannah	1807	Aug. 1, 1874
Mary	Oct. 1, 1893	Aug. 2, 1881
NEWMAN, Mrs. Jos. (Josephine McAteer)	July 15, 1846	Aug. 4, 1892
NOEL, Nicholas	1758	June 13, 1858
Joseph	1759	Nov. 3, 1887
Joseph	1790	Mar. 3, 1865
Joseph	1810	June 27, 1885
Mrs. Joseph (Catherine Stolz)	1818	Apr. 23, 1888
Philip J.	June 26, 1843	Feb. 4, 1870
Adam	Sept. 1, 1845	Jan. 23, 1887
Dorothy A.	July 26, 1847	Dec. 21, 1864
William	Oct. 26, 1849	Mar. 11, 1871
Abraham	1788	May 23, 1876
Josue	Nov. 8, 1807	June 12, 1828
Peter		Sept. 28, 1838
Mrs. Peter (Sarah Coons)	Nov. 24, 1819	Sept. 1, 1893
Joachim	Jan. 11, 1812	July 17, 1888
Mrs. Joachim (Mary A. Criste)	Feb. 14, 1814	Dec. 12, 1889
Philip	1821	Aug. 31, 1895
Mrs. Philip (Margaret Itel)	June 14, 1820	Jan. 15, 1877
Mary Angeline	Apr. 3, 1803	June 12, 1825
Philip		Feb. 3, 1870
Nicholas		Feb. 19, 1861
John (of John and Mary)	Apr. 1, 1828	Aug. 29, 1885
Margaret (of Isaac)	Sept. 13, 1839	Jan. 15, 1877
Charles Joseph	June 12, 1863	Nov. 29, 1897
NOLL, George	1790	Apr. 20, 1875
Mrs. George (Elizabeth ———)	1806	Jan. 21, 1889
Henry	1827	Oct. 11, 1872
NOON, Dominic		Feb. 9, 1859
Mrs. Dennis (Bridget O'Donnell)	1784	Mar. 16, 1879
Mary Ann	July 11, 1817	Dec. 31, 1888
James	July 18, 1824	Sept. 28, 1892
Margaret	June 8, 1829	Mar. 26, 1830
Michael		Aug. 26, 1868
Bridget	1800	May 30, 1870
Mrs. Philip (Ellen Luckett)		Nov. 29, 1834
Philip, Jr.		Mar. 7, 1836
NOONAN, Jeremiah	1808	Mar. 18, 1873
Mrs. Jeremiah (Eliza Ann Kaylor)	Apr. 5, 1817	Oct. 18, 1891
Elizabeth	Jan. 16, 1845	Oct. 23, 1876
NOWLIN, Thomas	1809	Oct. 12, 1879
NULL, Mrs. Joseph (Sarah Moore)	Sept. ..., 1814	Aug. 15, 1852
Mrs. Joseph (Susan Weakland)	Mar. 4, 1811	Apr. 23, 1877
NUZZO, Domenico	1837	July 6, 1891

NAME.	Born.	Died.
O'BRIEN, Joseph, Sr.	1869	Sept. 7, 1872
Mary	Sept. 22, 1854	Mar. 3, 1869
Thomas		Aug. 11, 1867
Mrs. James (Martha Myers)	Mar. 20, 1853	Apr. 1, 1893
O'CONNOR, Mary	1754	Mar. 8, 1819
Michael	1798	Feb. 22, 1883
Francis	1800	June 23, 1870
James	1817	Feb. 13, 1841
O'DEAY, Mrs. Michael (Ellen Biter)	May 13, 1861	May. 4, 1890
O'DONNELL, Mrs. Hugh (Esther Fagan)	Jan. 13, 1809	Nov. 14, 1894
Mrs. James (Ellen Kelly)	1819	Apr. 20, 1885
William	May 14, 1847	Apr. 21, 1858
Catherine	Dec. 21, 1850	Oct. 23, 1891
Dennis		Jan. 1890
James	Apr. 21, 1863	Sept. 13, 1889
O'FRIEL, Francis	May 30, 1811	Jan. 21, 1896
Mary	July 4, 1852	Oct. 13, 1863
O'HARA, Daniel	Feb. 9, 1761	Feb. 9, 1809
Mrs. Daniel (Rachel Friddle)	1770	1853
David	Mar. 6, 1796	Jan. 21, 1864
Mrs. David (Elizabeth Parrish)	Sept. 5, 1806	Apr. 29, 1887
Joshua	May 1, 1832	Dec. 30, 1878
Charles	Dec. 23, 1838	Feb. 20, 1867
Henry	1800	Feb. 18, 1898
Mrs. Henry (Patience McGuire)	May 1805	Sept. 23, 1884
Peter T.	July 1, 1838	Mar. 5, 1874
Frances M	Nov. 15, 1844	Dec. 2, 1876
David		Jan. 21, 1834
Mrs. Wm. (Catherine Itel)	July 4, 1828	Dec. 22, 1898
Sarah Catherine	May 14, 1854	June 2, 1892
Julia Ann	June 13, 1859	Jan. 3, 1887
O'NEILL, Henry	1769	Oct. 27, 1861
Mrs. Henry (Catherine ——)	1780	Aug. 4, 1845
Daniel	1772	Aug. 10, 1838
Mrs. Daniel (Isabella ——)	1782	Dec. 23, 1849
Isabella	1831	Dec. 31, 1876
Matthew	1782	Apr. 11, 1845
Mary	1816	Apr. 2, 1896
Peter	Aug. 4, 1814	Dec. 17, 1898
Simon Peter	Oct. 17, 1856	Nov. 21, 1881
Eugene	May 25, 1862	Mar. 4, 1893
Felix	1821	Nov. 1, 1896
James	Jan. 20, 1850	Jan. 17, 1898
Vincent Thomas	Dec. 1, 1866	Mar. 23, 1882
OWENS Mrs. Simon (Ann Connery)	Aug. 21, 1820	Apr. 12, 1863
PARRISH, Joshua	Nov. 20, 1770	Oct. 6, 1810
Mrs. Joshua (Barbara Thimble)	Feb. 27, 1770	Sept. 19, 1853

THE ORIGINAL NOTICE AND BOARD ARE STILL PRESERVED.

NAME.	Born.	Died.
(Parrish) Mrs. John (Mary McKinzie)		Sept. 23, 1839
George	July 28, 1795	Aug. 25, 1837
Mrs. George (Cath. Storm)	Sept. 28, 1799	Nov. 20, 1837
George Michael	Oct. 5, 1831	Nov. 9, 1895
James	......, 1797	Jan. 23, 1868
Mrs. James (Ann McCann)		......, 1843
Mary Ann (of James)	Sept. 17, 1826	......, 1843
Peter Benedict	June 30, 1814	Feb. 25, 1877
Mrs. Peter B. (Eliz. O'Connell)	June 16, 1819	Nov. 20, 1898
William (of Peter)	June 8, 1842	Mar. 20, 1878
Thomas C. (of Peter)	Apr. 16, 1843	Sept. 28, 1865
Cecilia (of Peter)	July 24, 1850	July 25, 1887
Catherine Mary (of Peter)	Apr. 9, 1854	Nov. 4, 1871
Joanna Caroline (of Peter)	Jan. 18, 1861	Sept. 5, 1898
Thomas	Feb. 20, 1804	Sept. 11, 1876
Mrs. Thomas (Mary Storm)	Sept. 14, 1802	Dec. 22, 1870
Anna Maria (of Thos.)	Nov. 18, 1830	Sept. 24, 1870
Sylvester Aug. (of Thomas)	Sept. 7, 1835	Oct. 6, 1894
Joseph	May 4, 1800	Oct. 28, 1845
Mrs. Joseph (Cath. McKinzie)	July 1, 1800	May 22, 1873
Lydia Ann (of Jos.)	Jan. 13, 1825	Nov. 8, 1870
Catherine Ann (of Jos.)	Oct. 26, 1829	Jan. 28, 1836
Ann M. (of Jos.)	Sept. 25, 1836	Nov. 21, 1858
Ellen (of Jos.)	May 14, 1839	May 16, 1886
Silas (of Jos.)	July 18, 1823	Sept. 27, 1874
Mrs. Silas (Eliz. McManamy)	Oct. 14, 1820	Dec. 2, 1884
PEACH, Mrs. Hugh (Mary Ann Davis)	Apr. 10, 1815	Dec. 15, 1837
PFIESTER, Joseph	......, 1804	May 31, 1874
Mrs. Joseph (Afra ———)	......, 1803	Jan. 17, 1887
Pelagius	......, 1843	May 15, 1891
Mrs. Pelagius (Cath. Hartman)	Mar. 19, 1841	Mar. 2, 1898
PFOFF, Frederick Joseph	......, 1780	Mar. 5, 1855
Joseph A.	July 22, 1836	July 19, 1862
Elizabeth	May 1, 1842	Jan. 11, 1863
Frederick	Sept. 9, 1829	June 15, 1865
Joseph	Mar. 16, 1853	June 15, 1865
PHALEN, Philip	......, 1800	Nov. 1, 1864
James	......, 1825	Jan. 29, 1875
Rose	Apr. 16, 1867	Oct. 31, 1876
PLUMMER, Thomas (of Isaac)	Feb. 24, 1829	Jan. 18, 1897
Samuel (of Isaac)	Sept. 3, 1837	Feb. 21, 1897
POLLARD, Rev. William		Sept. 23, 1888
POMPEO, Michael Angelo	......, 1857	Apr. 23, 1892
PORTER, Mrs. David (Ann Coons)	Mar. 19, 1856	Dec. 9, 1882
QUARTZ, Michael Aug.	Aug. 16, 1811	Sept. 22, 1899
REILLY, Peter B.	......, 1848	May 2, 1892

NAME.	Born.	Died.
REININGER, Mrs. Fred B. (Matilda J. Buck)	Oct. 16, 1844	July 25, 1894
Mary	Aug. 15, 1868	Dec. 19, 1888
REYNOLDS, Rev. Terence S.	............, ...	Feb. 24, 1881
RHEY, James	............, 1743	Nov. 25, 1818
George W.	Jan. 26, 1819	Mar. 7, 1898
RHINE, Mary	............, ...	Feb. 27, 1894
RHODES, John	............, ...	Sept. 2, 1880
RIFFLE, John	July 9, 1784	July 10, 1852
Mrs. John	............, ...	Apr. 19, 1864
James M.	Aug. 9, 1822	Oct. 7, 1871
Mrs. Jno. E. (Lucy A. Christy)	Jan. 3, 1823	Apr. 5, 1898
RIGGLE, Christian	............, 1797	July 26, 1857
Mrs. Christian (Mary A. ———)	Sept. ..., 1800	Jan. 6, 1881
Lazarus A.	Dec. ...., 1829	May 10, 1880
Christian	Dec. 12, 1842	May 19, 1869
John	Sept. 1, 1845	Aug. 17, 1862
RODGERS, Owen	............, 1777	May 7, 1876
Mrs. Luke (Catherine Dever)	June 10, 1824	June 18, 1890
Mrs. Thomas (Christina Coons)	Mar. 9, 1840	May 10, 1878
ROESSLEIN, George	Dec. 2, 1816	Feb. 9, 1897
Mrs. George (Cath. Thiemann)	............, 1815	July 13, 1882
Barbara	Mar. 4, 1850	June 15, 1866
ROSENSTEEL, Emma J.	July 18, 1857	Oct. 23, 1867
Ada Regina	Mar. 15, 1864	Mar. 16, 1892
RUDOLPH, Mrs. Christopher (Mary J. Stephens)	Aug. 28, 1862	Oct. 5, 1884
Caroline	Mar. 23, 1866	Nov. 24, 1880
RYAN, William, Sr.	............, 1786	Aug 11, 1869
Mrs. William, Sr.	............, ...	Apr. 9, 1865
David	Aug. 20, 1815	Apr. 10, 1897
SANDERS, Peter	Mar. 26, 1796	Jan. 23, 1869
Mrs. Peter (Ann Margaret Noel)	Mar. 21, 1796	Nov. 10, 1862
Joseph (of Peter)	Oct. 17, 1834	Sept. 5, 1870
Mrs. Jos. (Catherine Noel)	Jan. 9, 1839	Mar. 2, 1898
John (of Peter)	............, ...	Dec. 1, 1888
Frances Jane (of John)	June 24, 1854	Aug. 15, 1861
James (of John)	May 9, 1861	Feb. 22, 1875
William (of John)	............, ...	Aug. 4, 1893
SANKER, John, Sr.	June 3, 1790	July 12, 1868
Mrs. John (Ann Felix)	Apr. 25, 1802	Nov. 8, 1885
Aloysius	............, ...	Jan. 25, 1863
Susanna C.	Jan. 17, 1840	Jan. 15, 1865
Mrs. Anthony (Susanna Parrish)	Jan. 12, 1827	Feb. 2, 1875
Andrew J. (of John)	May 8, 1857	Jan. 22, 1863
Ella Irene (of John)	Nov. 30, 1871	July 4, 1895
Thomas (of Ambrose)	............, 1874	Jan. 29, 1899

NAME.	Born.	Died.
SARGEANT, James...	............, 1798	Oct. 5, 1853
Mrs. James (Bridget Connery)........................	............, 1802	Oct. 26, 1866
Rosanna..	Apr. 13, 1835	June 13, 1852
James...	Jan. 14, 1837	Nov. 2, 1858
Mary Jane...	May 4, 1847	Mar. 21, 1866
SCANLAN, John. Sr..	Aug. 13, 1776	Nov. 17, 1851
Mrs. John, Sr. (Theresa Kaylor).....................	Mar. 31, 1780	Oct. 24, 1853
Theresa...	May 17, 1808	June 10, 1885
Richard..	Jan. 5, 1810	June 9, 1857
Mrs. Richard (Cath. McGuire).........................	Apr. 22, 1814	Sept. 8, 1890
John, Jr..	July 19, 1811	June 18, 1839
John E..	Apr. 15, 1839	May 1, 1886
Peter...	Feb. 11, 1816	Aug. 5, 1854
Henry...	Apr. 14, 1818	Mar. 14, 1895
Mrs. Henry (Ellen Leavy).................................	Apr. 17, 1823	Dec. 29, 1881
James...	May 6, 1823	Sept. 21, 1844
SCHMITT, Mrs. Louis (Cath. Strohmaier)..........	Nov. 6, 1817	July 19, 1898
SCHNABEL, John...	July 31, 1813	July 1, 1892
Mrs. John (Christina Myers)............................	Sept. 1, 1815	Apr. 6, 1883
Mrs. Joseph H. (Clara Jane Topper).............	............, 1858	Mar. 13, 1889
SCHWAB, Charles...	Dec. 18, 1809	May 8, 1886
Mrs. Charles (Eleanor Myers).........................	Aug. 9, 1817	Feb. 2, 1860
SEYMOUR, Mrs. Peter (Mary E. Nagle).............	............, 1811	Mar. 20, 1879
Mrs. George (Philumena Hott)........................	Mar. ...., 1818	Feb. 17, 1896
SHAFFER, Jacob...	Mar. 8, 1812	July 18, 1889
James A..	Sept. 24, 1851	Aug. 27, 1885
SHARBAUGH, Mrs. John W. (Mary Sherry)........	Aug. 15, 1848	May 5, 1875
SHARP, George...	Oct. 22, 1810	Dec. 11, 1893
Mrs. George (Mary Denny)...............................	............, 1820	Aug. 14, 1898
George H...	............, 1850	Aug. 23, 1895
Mrs. Richard (Charity T. Carland).................	June 24, 1825	Feb. 17, 1892
SHEEHAN, Margaret..	Aug. 11, 1857	June 16, 1875
SHENK, Mathias, Sr...	............, 1810	Aug. ...., 1851
Mrs. Mathias (Theresa Walters).....................	............, 1819	Sept. 23, 1863
Nicholas...	Apr. 8, 1837	Apr. 7, 1863
Nicholas, Sr..	............, 1816	Jan. 6, 1884
Mrs. Nich. (Mary Eve Callies).........................	............, 1819	Oct. 31, 1898
Elizabeth...	June 4, 1849	May 22, 1871
Ellen...	June 17, 1863	May 4, 1899
John...	............, ...	Feb. 12, 1885
Francis...	............, ...	June 11, 1872
Mathias (of Francis)...	Mar. 21, 1850	Apr. 26, 1897
Catherine (of John)..	............, 1886	May 23, 1897
SHERRY, John, Sr..	............, ...	July 24, 1885

NAME.	Born.	Died.
SHIBER, Anthony	Dec. 7, 1829	Apr. 30, 1894
Mary Josephine	Aug. 25, 1850	Dec. 4, 1879
SHIELDS, Patrick H.	Mar. 6, 1807	Mar. 10, 1876
Mrs. P. H. (Anastasia McGuire)	Aug. 28, 1809	Apr. 30, 1875
Henry L.	Mar. 15, 1848	June 8, 1861
Mary A.	July 4, 1809	May 29, 1893
SHINAFELT, Mrs. Harry (Lottie Davis)	........, 1868	Sept. 3, 1892
SHOEMAKER, Edward	........, 1797	Apr. 22, 1867
Mrs. Edward (Jane Falls)	........, 1799	Sept. 2, 1829
Mrs. Edward (Mary Hanson)	Mar. 1, 1812	May 26, 1898
SHOFFNER, Casper	........, 1804	June 26, 1860
Mrs. Casper (Barbara Miller)	Dec. 16, 1803	June 1, 1873
SHORT, Catherine A.	........, 1832	Sept. 25, 1857
SILL, William	........, ...	Nov. 29, 1885
Mrs. Wm. (Agnes Haid)	Dec. 20, 1814	Feb. 20, 1863
Mrs. Wm. (Genevieve Shremp)	........, 1812	Dec. 31, 1882
Mrs. Anthony J. (Sarah McCoy)	May 10, 1847	May 16, 1872
Francis W.	Apr. 17, 1875	Mar. 8, 1891
SISK, Robert	........, 1805	Mar. 13, 1877
Mrs. Robert (Margaret Kearns)	........, 1798	May 17, 1876
SKELLY, Michael	........, 1745	Nov. 27, 1831
Philip	........, 1759	July 2, 1835
Michael	........, 1786	Jan. 18, 1817
Patrick	........, 1792	July 6, 1834
Rachel	May 16, 1800	June 26, 1832
Philip	Dec. 2, 1800	May 5, 1834
Mrs. Philip (Ann ———)	........, 1785	Oct. 2, 1825
Mrs. Daniel (Susan Noel)	........, ...	May 25, 1898
Philip	Apr. 8, 1836	Feb. 27, 1897
Felix	Dec. 16, 1759	July 2, 1835
Mrs. Philip (Margaret McAfee)	June 12, 1771	Jan. 11, 1851
Daniel	Apr. 19, 1798	Dec. 7, 1870
Ellen	June 4, 1804	Jan. 18, 1876
Catherine	Feb. 17, 1807	Apr. 17, 1879
Mary Ann	June 19, 1809	Mar. 19, 1886
Nicholas	Feb. 16, 1832	Sept. 22, 1861
Margaret	Apr. 17, 1834	Jan. 22, 1894
Luke	Mar. 14, 1845	May 29, 1859
Susan	Nov. 29, 1849	June 15, 1897
SMAY, Mrs. Christopher (Ann Burke)	........, ...	Mar. 14, 1895
SMELTZER, Peter	........, ...	Dec. 23, 1887
Mrs. Peter (Eliz. Kampfersach)	........, 1808	Jan. 2, 1889
Augustine	........, 1846	June 1, 1891
Mrs. Augustine (Louisa Vaught)	........, 1846	Apr. 15, 1876
Mrs. Joseph (Susan Malloy)	Feb. 12, 1862	Dec. 31, 1891

NAME.	Born.	Died.
SMITH, Thomas.................................	....	Mar. 20, 1857
Catherine................................	Mar. 15, 1817	May 23, 1833
Patrick....................................	....	Dec. 14, 1886
Mrs. Patrick (Cath. O'Connor)........	....	Feb. 16, 1884
SPIEGELHALTER, Conrad...............	............, 1829	Oct. 17, 1882
Mrs. Conrad (Veronica Schlember).......	............, 1833	July 5, 1894
SPIGELMIRE, Mary Eva.................	May 25, 1878	Jan. 21, 1894
SPRINGER, Mrs. Wm. (Mary Bishop)....	Sept. 15, 1843	May 24, 1882
SPROUL, Rose Ann.........................	Jan. 1, 1823	Oct. 17, 1862
STARK, Mrs. James D. (Sophia Elder).....	Aug. 6, 1809	Jan. 10, 1862
William D., M. D...........................	............, 1832	July 7, 1858
STEVENS, John.............................	............, 1799	Jan. 6, 1894
Mrs. John (Mary Eckenrode)...........	............, 1809	Mar. 24, 1892
Margaret..................................	July 27, 1854	Feb. 13, 1863
Julia.......................................	Sept. ..., 1844	Aug. 23, 1868
Jacob......................................	July 25, 1844	Aug. 14, 1849
John A. (of Jacob and Mary)..........	Dec. 21, 1840	July 1, 1860
Mrs. Jacob (Mary Ann Coons).........	Aug. 8, 1833	Aug. 16, 1872
Mrs. Jacob (Lucy Coons)...............	May 16, 1842	Sept. 14, 1899
Charles (of Michael)....................	June 9, 1859	Sept. 11, 1885
Robert (of Michael).....................	Mar. 25, 1870	Nov. 14, 1889
STOCK, Seraphim Lawrence.............	............, 1881	Mar. 3, 1892
STORM, John................................	May 3, 1756	Feb. 14, 1816
Mrs. John (Susan Wysong).............	July 25, 1777	Nov. 11, 1857
John.......................................	Feb. 23, 1797	Sept. 27, 1847
Mrs. John (Rosanna McCoy)..........	............, 1781	Jan. 11, 1859
Hugh F....................................	June 9, 1821	Oct. 19, 1865
David.....................................	Feb. 9, 1826	Mar. 6, 1865
Mrs. Arthur (Mary E. Criste).........	Aug. 17, 1821	Sept. 7, 1857
David Thomas............................	....	May 26, 1840
Peter......................................	May 17, 1798	Jan. 17, 1849
Mrs. Peter (Ann McConnell)..........	Oct. ..., 1801	Aug. 10, 1853
Susan.....................................	Jan. 27, 1826	Oct. 22, 1868
John T....................................	Dec. 21, 1835	June 27, 1891
Mrs. John T. (Matilda Parrish).......	July 30, 1838	Feb. 7, 1872
Joseph.....................................	June 28, 1811	June 3, 1826
Mrs. Francis Aug. (Sarah Buck).......	Sept. 22, 1827	May 25, 1875
Mary Ann Elizabeth......................	Oct. 1, 1852	May 6, 1866
Mary Regina...............................	June 27, 1854	Apr. 11, 1866
Mrs. Francis Aug. (Ellen Margaret Knighton).......	....	Apr. 26, 1893
Patrick....................................	Feb. 21, 1804	Nov. 7, 1885
Mrs. Patrick (Mary Parrish)..........	May 18, 1810	Mar. 10, 1883
James B...................................	June 5, 1831	Mar. 17, 1899
Michael...................................	May 8, 1849	Mar. 5, 1894
Louis......................................	June 12, 1869	May 2, 1892
Mrs. Louis (Margaret Pfoff)..........	Aug. 23, 1815	Sept. 14, 1898

NAME.	Born.	Died.
STOY, Samuel	Dec. 10, 1818	May 14, 1875
Mrs. Samuel (Ann Jane Douglas)	Apr. 7, 1821	Mar. 29, 1898
Henrietta (of Albert)	Jan. 24, 1873	May 3, 1880
Eveline (of P. U.)	Jan. 27, 1874	Dec. 13, 1887
STROHMAIER, Mathias	Aug. 15, 1815	Apr. 12, 1883
STRITTMATTER, Andrew	......., 1793	May 11, 1865
Mrs. Andrew (Francisca Myers)	......., 1790	Sept. 10, 1877
SUTTON, Mrs. John (Ellen Cath. Noonan)	Feb. 26, 1856	Mar. 7, 1895
SWEENY, Ellen	......., 1800	Nov. 13, 1880
Peter	......., 1814	Oct. 17, 1897
Mrs. Peter (Mary McBride)	......., 1825	Aug. 12, 1899
Bridget	Apr. 6, 1849	Dec. 22, 1870
John Baptist	Aug. 12, 1851	Sept. 22, 1883
Philip Francis	Nov. 27, 1853	May 1, 1893
Louis Terence (of J. B.)	......., 1881	June 19, 1891
Mildred (of J. B.)	May 18, 1883	Sept. 3, 1897
SYBERT, Sebastian P.	Jan. 20, 1825	June 21, 1898
Mrs. Sebastian P. (Martha Bradley)	Mar. 3, 1829	Mar. 16, 1895
THOMAS, Michael	......., 1751	......., 1835
John	......., 1792	Sept. 24, 1887
Mrs. John (Mary Ann Campbell)	Nov. 7, 1813	Sept. 24, 1870
Cecilia	Apr. 14, 1853	June 20, 1899
Mrs. Michael P. (Margaret Jos. Freidhoff)	......., 1851	Dec. 25, 1899
TODD, David	Oct. 6, 1799	Sept. 10, 1849
Mrs. David (Jane McConnell)	......., 1799	Apr. 28, 1863
William	Oct. 7, 1797	Aug. 17, 1844
Mrs. Wm. (Eleanor Wharton)	......., 1799	Sept. 3, 1844
Andrew	Apr. 16, 1820	Jan. 14, 1851
James	Jan. 12, 1827	Apr. 17, 1879
Mrs. James (Sarah Ann Ryan)	Apr. 4, 1829	Mar. 2, 1890
Joseph A.	Aug. 28, 1831	Sept. 24, 1856
TOMLINSON, Jacob	......., 1799	Feb. 1, 1852
Mrs. Jacob (Margaret Burkle)	......., 1804	Jan. 30, 1859
Rachel	......., 1831	Mar. 6, 1880
Catherine	Jan. 12, 1839	Sept. 30, 1889
Joseph	......., ...	Oct. 5, 1892
Mrs. Joseph (Catherine Noel)	Dec. 4, 1830	Sept. 3, 1893
Matilda Jane	Nov. 30, 1865	Mar. 11, 1889
Clara	Mar. 8, 1868	Jan. 23, 1891
Mrs. Francis (Mary Matilda Driskel)	Nov. 28, 1850	Aug. 4, 1886
Eliza (of Charles)	Feb. 28, 1878	June 5, 1897
TOPPER, William H.	Sept. 17, 1804	Mar. 15, 1884
Mrs. George (Elizabeth ———)	......., 1791	May 14, 1861
Martha	......., 1822	Sept. 1, 1882
Andrew	......., ...	Aug. 30, 1882
Andrew J.	Oct. 13, 1828	July 6, 1890
Mrs. A. J. (Martha Eliz. Dodson)	Dec. 23, 1822	Oct. 30, 1882

NAME.	Born.	Died.
(Topper) Elizabeth	1866	Aug. 20, 1888
George	1861	Jan. 15, 1882
Jeremiah	1831	Mar. 26, 1887
Mrs. Jeremiah (Henrietta Bertram)	1840	Apr. 29, 1893
Mary	May 13, 1860	Apr. 22, 1875
Andrew S.	Apr. 9, 1866	July 6, 1890
Mary Agnes	Sept. 3, 1879	Mar. 11, 1899
Mary Elizabeth (of Zachary)	May 11, 1863	May 17, 1881
Stella	Jan. 17, 1867	Mar. 22, 1889
Lavina		Mar. 17, 1882
Mrs. James (Ellen M. Behe)	Dec. 3, 1861	Sept. 18, 1895
Mrs. Jacob (Mary Howell)	May 3, 1804	Aug. ..., 1882
TREBUS, Bartholomew	1801	Mar. 26, 1856
TREESTER, Margaret	Mar. 30, 1806	Nov. 21, 1833
TREXLER, Peter	Apr. 15, 1808	Nov. 25, 1885
Joseph	Feb. 15, 1816	Jan. 10, 1892
Mrs. James	Nov. 15, 1822	..., 1848
TROXELL, Jacob	1779	May 24, 1833
Mrs. Jacob (Susan ——)	Apr. 10, 1780	Mar. 3, 1850
Sarah	June 10, 1807	Oct. 25, 1850
Abraham	Jan. 10, 1810	July 24, 1852
William	Dec. 17, 1811	Oct. 2, 1847
Henry	July 19, 1815	Nov. 17, 1883
Mrs. Henry (Hannah McElmee)	1827	Apr. 11, 1886
Mrs. John J. (Mary J. Gallagher)	Jan. 26, 1832	Jan. 18, 1887
TURNER, Jacob	1783	Apr. 3, 1866
Joseph	Mar. 5, 1817	Mar. 27, 1839
URBAN, Francis Joseph	Feb. 28, 1780	Dec. 12, 1836
Mrs. F. J. (Elizabeth Coons)	Sept. 6, 1799	Dec. 6, 1843
Clement	May 22, 1821	Apr. 15, 1845
John	Nov. 29, 1822	Dec. 17, 1843
Caspar Nicholas	Jan. 6, 1826	July 26, 1837
Joseph	June 17, 1835	Mar. 3, 1871
William Francis	Oct. 16, 1861	July 17, 1874
Harriet	1867	Aug. 7, 1874
VAUGHT, Mrs. John (Victoria Fechter)		July 3, 1866
Henry	Aug. 13, 1850	Oct. 17, 1875
Rachel	Oct. 3, 1856	May 9, 1897
Mrs. Daniel (Mary C. Tomlinson)	Mar. 5, 1863	Sept. 6, 1889
WAGNER, John	Dec. 20, 1827	Feb. 12, 1895
Mrs. John		Oct. 23, 1877
Mrs. Francis (Agnes Gill)		Aug. 3, 1886
WALTERS, Englebert	May 2, 1765	May 12, 1838

NAME.	Born.	Died.
(Walters) Mrs. Englebert (Susan Behe)	............, 1780	Oct. 20, 1850
Daniel	Mar. 6, 1802	Mar. 8, 1872
Mrs. Daniel (Susan Little)	July 19, 1806	Aug. 1, 1848
John	Sept. 7, 1805	July 11, 1840
Mary Elizabeth (of John)	Aug. 12, 1833	Apr. 17, 1853
Joseph	............, 1818	Nov. 20, 1886
Mary	............, 1800	Dec. 15, 1885
Augustine	Nov. 15, 1820	Mar. 19, 1894
WARDE, Sylvester A.	June 10, 1864	Aug. 23, 1893
WARNER, Mrs. John (Mary Ann Noel)	............, 1818	Dec. 2, 1898
Mrs Jacob (Eliz. Keppler)	Apr. 19, 1826	Jan. 2, 1878
WATT, Mrs Wm. (Elizabeth Downey)	....	Oct. 31, 1897
WEAKLAND, William	............, 1770	Aug. 13, 1864
Mrs. Wm. (Mary Barbara Ruffner)	............, 1773	Jan. 20, 1857
Simon	Jan. 11, 1807	Mar. 3, 1873
Mrs. Simon (Magdalen Little)	Mar. 26, 1802	Sept. 23, 1882
Bridget	............, 1800	Nov. 4, 1828
WEISE, Mrs. George (Margaret Himmel)	....	Sept. 4, 1876
Joseph	............, 1851	Nov. 30, 1871
WHARTON, Ann	............, 1759	Mar. 14, 1857
Theresa	............, 1788	July 18, 1864
Catherine	............, 1790	May 17, 1854
Stanislaus	....	Jan. 26, 1873
Mrs. Stanislaus (Mary McConnell)	....	May 10, 1870
WHERRY, Mrs. James (Margaret ———)	Sept. 2, 1831	Dec. 24, 1869
WHITE, Mrs. Patience (McGuire)	............, 1751	July 27, 1823
WILKINSON, Mrs. James (Agnes T. Adelsberger)	Nov. 16, 1844	Oct. 8, 1865
WILLEBRAND, Henry	June 30, 1809	Nov. 20, 1887
Mrs. Henry (Mary M. Myers)	Aug. 15, 1812	July 26, 1880
Mary J.	Sept. 12, 1841	May 25, 1866
Mrs. Florence (Rebecca Burkey)	Jan. 22, 1840	May 1, 1882
David Bennet	Dec. 17, 1863	Feb. 3, 1899
WILLS, John	............, 1781	Aug. 18, 1863
Joseph	............, 1790	Aug. 14, 1883
Anthony, Sr.	....	Apr. 5, 1865
Henry	Apr. 16, 1826	Sept. 20, 1883
Augustine	Apr. 8, 1828	Dec. 15, 1874
Mrs. Samuel (Mary Ann Burns)	May 5, 1829	Aug. 30, 1898
Mrs. Thomas (Mary Magd. Myers)	July 22, 1807	May 3, 1848
Anastasia	Oct. 16, 1812	Feb. 11, 1861
Mrs. Thomas (Elizabeth Fagan)	Mar. 9, 1804	Sept. 11, 1850
Mrs. Thomas (Mary Fox)	Mar. 16, 1820	Jan. 5, 1892

NAME.	Born.	Died.
(Wills) Anthony J..	............., ...	Jan. 20, 1891
Mrs. Thomas (Petronilla Dougherty)........................	May ...., 1844	Apr. 15, 1896
WILMORE, Godfrey...	 1751	Apr. 2, 1815
Mrs. Godrey (Mary ———)......................................	............., 1717	Aug. 28, 1822
Elizabeth..	............., 1796	Nov. 11, 1832
WILT, John..	............., ...	Sept. 30, 1869
WIRTNER, John...	............., 1795	June 24, 1848
Mrs. John (Mary Ruting Hertzog)............................	............., 1813	Nov. 5, 1846
WYSONG, Ludwig..	Feb. 1743	Jan. 23, 1808
Mrs. Ludwig (Ann Cath. ———)...............................	May 19, 1741	Nov. 5, 1802
YINGER, George..	............., 1806	Oct. 28, 1875
Albert (of A. P.)...	May 23, 1860	Oct. 11, 1873
ZIMMERMAN, Mrs. (Amanda McMullen).................	Apr. 8, 1817	Feb. 21, 1887

SOME INSCRIPTIONS COPIED FROM HEADSTONES IN ST. MICHAEL'S CEMETERY, LORETTO.

PETER FLANAGAN. Born in County Derry, Ireland, 1759. Died March 15, 1861. Aged 102 years, 7 months.
One of the first settlers of Cambria County.

ANN, wife of Peter Flanagan. Born in County Derry, Ireland. Died May 4, 1854. Aged 81 years.

Here lies the body of BRIDGET MELOY, amiable consort of William Meloy. Departed this life August the 17, A. D. 1814. Aged 65 years. (Born 1749.)

In memory of JOHN McCOY, a native of Ireland. Born in the County of Derry, August the 10th, 1771.
Migrated to the United States in A. D. 1801. Settled in this county in A. D. 1803. Departed this life April 9th, A. D. 1843.

In memory of PETER KEHLER (Kaylor). Born November 12, A. D. 1753. Came to this country A. D. 1774. Died September 19, A. D. 1840. May he rest in peace. Amen.

JAMES MURRAY, a native of Moynend, County Derry, Ireland. Died November 4, 1863. Aged 68 years, 11 mos. and 7 days. May he rest in peace.

WILLIAM WEAKLAND. Died August 13, 1864, in the 94th year of his age.

MRS. WILLIAM WEAKLAND. (Mary Barbara Ruffner.) Died Jan. 20, 1857, in the 84th year of her age.

LUDWIG WYSONG. Born Febr. —, 1743. Died Jan. 28, 1808.

ANN CATHERINE, wife of Ludwig Wysong. Born May 19, 1741. Died Nov. 5, 1802.

SUSAN WYSONG, wife of John Storm. Born July 25, 1777. Died Nov. 11, 1837.

JOHN STORM. Born May 3, 1756. Died Feb. 14, 1816.

Here lieth the body of COL. JAMES KEAN, Junior. Died Sept. —, 1827. Aged 32 years.

PETER CARIGAN. (Kerrigan.) Died Sept. 22, 1839. In the 84th year of his age.

PETER KERRIGAN. Died Dec. 11, 1872, in the 100th year of his age.

DANIEL O'HARA. Born Feb. 9, 1761. Died Febr. 9, 1809.

JOHN JACOB BENDER. Born Jan. 31, 1740. Died Dec. 6, 1828, in the 89th year of his age.

JOHN CRISTE. Died Dec. 14, 1868, in the 86th year of his age.

In memory of JAMES MAGEEHAN. Born in York Co., Pa., Febr. 10, 1778. Died Oct. 12, 1852.

JACOB GLASS. Born July 25, 1741. Died Jan. 18, 1821.
GEORGE GLASS. Born Apr. 1, 1770. Died Nov. 9, 1847.

ENGLEBERT WALTERS. Born May 2, 1765. Died May 12, 1838.

JAS. W. CONNERY. A member of Co. D, 125th Regt. P. V. Died in a hospital at Harper's Ferry, Jan. 21, 1863, in the 28th year of his age.

PHILIP L. CRAMER. Died in Loudon Camp, Ga., Oct. 29, 1864. In his 22d year.

JOHN SCANLAN, Sr. Born Aug. 13, 1776. Died Nov. 17, 1851.
THERESA KAYLOR, wife of John Scanlan, Sr. Born March 31, 1780. Died Oct. 24, 1853.

MICHAEL MURRAY. Born in the Townland of Ballynascreen, Co. Derry, Ireland. Emigrated to the United States in 1817. Died Dec. 30, 1869. Aged 73 years.

CHARLES BRADLEY. Born March 26, 1750. Died Apr. 9, 1826. Aged 76 years, 14 days.
MARY BRADLEY. Born Oct. 14, 1757. Died May 1, 1817.

THOMAS H. LUCKETT. Born Dec. 13, 1748. Died Sept. 6, 1822. Aged 74 yrs.
ELEANORA LUCKETT. Born 1735. Died Mar. 27, 1803. Aged 68 years.

ANN DIGGS. Born Sept. 13, 1749. Died Apr. 13, 1818. Aged 68 years, 7 mos.

JAMES GALLAGHER. Born July 10, 1761. Died Apr. 5, 1837. Aged 76 years.

Peter McGuire. Born 1763. Died Jan. 30, 1850. Aged 87 years.

Mrs. Peter (Charity) McGuire. Born 1773. Died Sept. 13, 1844. Aged 71 years.

Patrick McAteer. Born 1761. Died Dec. 29, 1842.

Samuel McMullen. Born 1769. Died Jan. 14, 1853. Aged 84 years.

Capt. Michael McGuire. Born 1717. Died Nov. 17, 1793. Aged 76 years.

Michael McGuire. Born 1742. Died May 1, 1818. Aged 76 years.

In memory of Capt. Richard McGuire. Died Jan. 13, 1855. Aged 83 years, 1 mo. and 1 day. The first of European extraction to settle in Cambria County.

Also Eleanor, his wife. Died Aug. 5, 1855. Aged 73 years.

Patience White. Born 1751. Died July 27, 1823. Aged 72 years.

Mary Durbin. Born Sept. 2, 1767. Died Dec. 17, 1835. Aged 68 years.

Barnabas Little. Born May 16, 1763. Died Mar. 19, 1839. Aged 76 years.

John Storm. Born Febr. 23, 1797. Died in Mexico Sept. 27, 1847.

In memory of John R., son of G. and Jane Litzinger. Died at San Angel, in the Republic of Mexico, Apr. 19, A. D. 1848. Aged 19 years, 9 mos., 19 days.

John Keller. Born 1728. Died Dec. 8, 1814. Aged 86 years.

James Burk, Sr. Born 1758. Died June 5, 1817. Aged 59 years.

Walter Elder. Born 1774. Died Febr. 23, 1842. Aged 68 years.

Mrs. Eleanora Myers. Born 1768. Died April 12, 1832. Aged 64 years.

John McHugh. Born 1768. Died Sept. 6, 1839. Aged 71 years.

Philip O'Skalley. Born 1759. Died July 2, 1835. Aged 76 years.

Ann Wharton. Born 1759. Died Mar. 14, 1857. Aged 98 years.

Michael Skalley. Born 1745. Died Nov. 27, 1831. Aged 86 years.

Godfrey Wilmore. Born 1751. Died Apr. 2, 1815. Aged 64 years.

John Brookbank. Born 1752. Died Jan. 22, 1820. Aged 68 years.

James Rhey. Born in the city of Dublin, St. Mary's Lane, 1743. Died Nov. 26, 1818. Aged 75 years.

Charles Bradley. Born in Co. Derry, Ireland, 1790. Died Dec. 23, 1882. Aged 92 years.

Mrs. Jonathan Douglas. (Monica Delozier.) Born 1786. Died July 9, 1881. Aged 95 years.

TWO INTERESTING DOCUMENTS.

(From the Cambria Tribune, October 20, 1899.)

E. R. Dunegan, Esq., of St. Augustine, has in his possession two receipts which, aside from the fact that they are more than one hundred years old, possess a peculiar interest at this time, inasmuch as they prove that Father Gallitzin was not the first priest to visit the Allegheny mountains, although he was the first resident pastor. At the time these receipts were given, Cambria County was yet a part of Bedford, one of the original five counties in the State. Mr. Dunegan has also a leaf from a memorandum book containing the list of subscriptions for the maintenance of the priest, in which the amounts are set down in pounds and shillings, showing that it must have been of still earlier date. It is so worn with age, however, that the date and a considerable number of the names are now illegible. The receipts referred to were obtained by Mr. Dunegan from Rev. Edmund Burns, the second pastor at St. Augustine, and he probably obtained them from Richard McGuire. They are as follows:

I received from Mrs. Rachel McGuire a dollar for her part of the sum that ought to be spent in buying a horse for the priest serving the parishes of Huntingdon, Sinking Valley, Allegheny, Path Valley, etc.

Allegheny, December 15, 1794.

LEWIS SIBOURD,
Priest.

I have received from the inhabitants over Allegheny, the sum of sixteen dollars for my maintenance for six months.

Allegheny, June 6, 1795.

LEWIS SIBOURD,
Priest.

PASCHAL COMMUNIONS. PASCHAL CONFESSIONS. CONFIRMATION.

NOTE.—In an old memorandum book, which the writer found among the personal effects of his deceased father, Father Gallitzin had written down the names of those who fulfilled the precept of Paschal Communion in 1810, and of Paschal Confession in 1811 and 1813, as also the names of those who were confirmed by Bishop Egan in 1811. These names are here copied in alphabetical order, except those on the Confession list of 1813 which is in great measure a reduplication of the list of 1811. In his Confirmation list Father Gallitzin gives the ages of the persons, especially of the children, confirmed; but the writer has thought it better to add the dates of birth, where such dates could be found among the early entries in the Register of Baptisms. It was the first time that Confirmation was administered in Western Pennsylvania, and it is to be noted that on that occasion children of very tender years, even infants a few months old, were presented for Confirmation. Thus, of the children confirmed, six were born in 1806, seven in 1807, eleven in 1808, seven in 1809, eleven in 1810, and four in 1811—the year Confirmation was administered.

PASCHAL COMMUNIONS.
1810.

ADAMS Eve.
    Elizabeth.
BARNICLE Sarah.
BAXTER George.
BLATT (Platt) John.
    Catherine.
    Joseph.
    Catherine.
    Mary.

BECHER Elizabeth.
BEHE Conrad.
    Emanuel.
BENDER Emerick.
    Ann Mary Elizabeth.
    Mary Ann.
    Martha.
BRADDOCK Nicholas.
    Eleanor.

BRADLEY Charles.
    Mary.
    Alice.
    Mary.
BRAWLEY Catherine.
BROWN Michael.
BURGOON Robert.
    Catherine.
    John.
    Temperance.
    Mary.
    Honora.
BURKE Prudence. (Widow.)
    Nicholas.
    Mary.
    Eleanor.
BYRNE John.
    Sarah.
    Agnes.
CANTWELL James.
    Margaret.
CARNEY Catherine.
CASSIDY Francis.
    Elizabeth.
CHERRY Mary.
CHRISTY Archibald.
    Mary.
    Francis.
COMMISKEY Bridget.
CONNOLLY James.
    Ann.
    Catherine.
CONWAY Patrick.
    Ann.
COONS (Kuhns) John.
    Catherine.
    Catherine.
    Christina.

COOPER Sarah.
COSTELLO James.
    Elizabeth.
CRISTE John.
    Sarah.
CURRAN John.
    Mrs. John.
DAWSON Mary.
DELOZIER Daniel, Sr.
    Providence.
    Ann.
    Monica.
    Anastasia.
    Belinda.
    Charity.
    Elizabeth.
DIARMITT Arthur.
DICKERHOFF John.
DIGGS Dudley.
    Ann.
DIMOND Daniel, Sr.
    Margaret.
    Ann.
    Mary.
DONECKER Joseph.
DOWLAN Richard.
DURBIN Mary.
    Honora.
    Theresa.
    Mary.
DWYER John.
FAGAN Bridget.
GALLAGHER James.
    Joseph.
    Mary.
    Mary.
GERSTENWEILER Andrew.
GLASS George, Sr.

(Glass) Ann.
    Susan.
    Ann.
    Jacob, Jr.
    Ann.
GORMAN William.
    Catherine.
HALEY Bridget.
HOLDER Elizabeth.
HORN Mary.
HURLEY Jeremiah.
INLOW (Inloes) John.
    Elizabeth.
JORDAN Eleanor.
    Margaret.
KAYLOR Peter.
    Elizabeth.
    Elizabeth.
KIMMAN Henry.
    Sarah.
LEAVY Agnes.
LILLY Joseph.
    Charity.
    Thomas.
    John.
LITTLE Bernard.
    John.
    Mary Ann.
    Anna Mary.
    Elizabeth.
LITZINGER Sarah.
LOGAN Elizabeth.
    Mary.
LOSHETT Henry.
    Anna Clara.
LUTHER Mary.
MAGEEHAN Ann. (Widow.)
    James.

(Murphy) Apollonia.
MALONE Joanna.
MARSHALL Christina. (Widow.)
McATEER Jonathan.
McCALLEY John.
    Mary.
McCONNELL John, Sr.
    Margaret.
    Margaret.
    Daniel.
    Mary.
    Catherine.
    Daniel.
    Sarah.
    Susan.
    Mary.
McCOY Ann.
McGONIGLE John.
McGOUGH Sarah.
    Esther.
McGRAW William.
    Henry.
    Mary.
McGUIRE Rachel. (Widow.)
    Richard.
    Eleanor.
    Luke, Sr
    Margaret.
    Luke, Jr.
    Michael.
    Henry.
    Milburg.
    Peter.
    Charity.
McINTOSH John.
McKEEVER Margaret.
McKESSAN ———.
McKINZIE Elizabeth.

210　SOUVENIR

(McKinzie) Mrs. ———.
McMULLEN Samuel.
　Susan.
　Lawrence.
　Robert.
　Mary.
MURRAY Mary.
MUSSELMAN Sarah.
NOEL Christopher.
O'HARA Catherine.
O'KEEFE William.
PARRISH Joshua.
PLUNKETT Patrick.
　Apollonia.
　Mary.
SCANLAN Theresa.
SKELLY Michael, Sr.
　Mary.
　Mrs. ———.
STEWART Mary.
STORM John, Sr.
　Susan.
　John, Jr.
　Joachim.

SULLIVAN Owen.
　Rose.
WALTERS Englebert.
WEAKLAND Barbara.
　Sarah.
WELSH John, Jr.
　Ann.
WHARTON Mrs. Ann. (Widow.)
　Ann.
　Catherine.
　Mary.
　Theresa.
WHITE Rachel A.
WILL Rachel.
　Mary Ann.
　Michael.
　Michael.
　Samuel.
　Mary.
WYSONG Ludwig.
YINGLING Elizabeth.
YOST Jacob.
　Margaret.
　Abigail.

Number of Males, 82; Females, 136. Total, 218.

PASCHAL CONFESSIONS.
1811.

ADAMS Richard.
　Thomas.
　Ann.
　Elizabeth.
　Eve.
　Mary.
　Theresa.
BAKER John.
　Mary.
BARNICLE William.

(Barnicle) Sarah.
BAXTER George.
BECHER Elizabeth.
BEHE Anthony.
　Conrad.
　Matthew.
　Mary Ann.
BENDER Jacob.
　Emerick.
　Elizabeth.

(Bender) Martha.
    Mary Ann.
*Blackburn Hetty.
Blatt (Platt) John.
    Joseph.
    Catherine.
    Catherine.
    Mary.
    Mary.
    Sarah.
Braddock Nicholas.
    Ann.
    John.
    Eleanor.
Bradley Charles.
    Charles.
    Edward.
    William.
    Dorothy.
    Elizabeth.
    Elizabeth.
    Martha.
    Mary.
    Mary.
Branniff Thomas.
    James.
    Margaret.
Brawley Dennis.
    Catherine.
Brown Michael.
Burgoon Robert.
    Catherine.
    John.
    Honora.
    Mary.
    Mary.
    Milburg.
    Susan.

(Burgoon) Temperance.
Burke James.
    Nicholas.
    Patrick.
    Apollonia.
    Eleanor.
    Elizabeth.
    Elizabeth (of James.)
    Margaret.
    Margaret (of Nicholas.)
    Mary.
    Prudence.
    Sophia.
Byrne John.
    Sarah.
    John.
    Agnes.
Cantwell James.
    Thomas.
    Margaret.
    Susan.
Carney Catherine.
Cassidy Elizabeth.
Christy Archibald.
    Mary (of Arch.)
    Francis.
    Mary.
    Mary.
    Sarah.
Commiskey John.
    Bridget.
Connery Patrick.
    Ann.
Connolly Hugh.
    Ann.
    Catherine.
Connor Mary.
    Margaret.

Coons (Kuhns) John.
    Catherine.
    Christina.
    Elizabeth.
Cooper Sarah.
    Ann.
    Elizabeth.
Costello Elizabeth.
Cramer Margaret.
Criste Elizabeth. (Widow.)
Crum Catherine.
Curran John.
    Ann.
    Elizabeth.
Decker Margaret.
Delozier Daniel, Sr.
    Providence.
    Anastasia.
    Ann.
    Belinda.
    Charity.
    Elizabeth.
    Monica.
Dempsey Patrick.
Diarment John.
    Michael.
    Samuel.
    Eleanor.
Diarmitt Mary.
Dickerhoff Joanna.
Diggs Dudley.
    Ann.
Dimond Daniel, Sr.
    Daniel, Jr.
    Ann.
Dodson Andrew.
Donecker Joseph.
    Mary.

Dougherty Edward.
    Margaret.
Driskel Ann.
Durbin Mary.
    Theresa.
    Honora.
    Mary.
Dwyer John.
Elder Priscilla.
Fagan Bridget.
Farrell Margaret.
Feltz Mary.
Flanigan Peter.
    Ann.
Flower Jacob.
    Mary Magdalen.
    Jacob, Jr.
    Elizabeth.
Gallagher James.
    Mary.
    Joseph.
    Mary.
Gerstenweiler Andrew.
    Catherine.
Glass George.
    Ann.
    George.
    Susan.
    Jacob.
    Jacob, Jr.
    John.
    Ann.
    Esther.
    Rufina.
Gorman William.
    Ruth.
    Sarah.
Grove Eleanor.

HALEY Patrick.
    Bridget.
HIGGINS John.
    Mary.
HORN Mary.
HURLEY Jeremiah.
    Mary.
INLOW (Inloes) John.
    Elizabeth.
JOANNA. (A negress.)
JORDAN Eleanor.
KAYLOR (Kehler) Peter.
    Elizabeth.
    Peter, Jr.
    Jacob.
    Catherine.
    Elizabeth.
KELLER John.
KERRIGAN Peter.
    Patrick.
    Elizabeth.
    Margaret.
    Elizabeth.
KIMMAN Henry.
    Sarah.
KOCH George.
    Eleanor.
LACY Mary.
LEAVY Agnes.
LILLY Joseph.
    Charity.
    Thomas.
    Richard.
    Joseph, Jr.
    Samuel.
    Ann.
LITTLE Bernard.
    John.

(Little) Mary.
    Elizabeth.
    Mary Ann.
LITZINGER Elizabeth.
    Mary Ann.
    Sarah.
LOGAN Dennis.
    Mary.
LOSHETT Henry.
    Anna Clara.
LUTHER Elizabeth.
    Mary.
MAGEEHAN Mrs. Ann. (widow.)
    Daniel.
    James.
    Apollonia.
MALONE John.
    Joanna.
MARKS Catherine.
    Sarah.
MARSHALL Catherine.
McATEER William.
McCABE Ross.
    Catherine.
McCALLEY John, Sr.
    Daniel.
    Mary.
    Ann.
    Mary.
McCARTY John.
    Elizabeth.
    Rose.
McCLOSKEY Patrick.
    James.
    Ann.
    Margaret.
    Mary.
McCONNELL Daniel.

(McConnell)·Mary (of Dan.)
    Arthur.
    John (of Arthur.)
    Margaret (of Henry.)
    Margaret.
    Margaret.
    Joanna. (Widow.)
    Joanna.
    John.
    Sarah.
    Susan.
    Susan.
    Catherine.
    Mary.
McCoy Alexander.
    John.
    Patrick.
    John.
    Ann.
    Rose.
    Susan.
McGough James.
    John.
    Thomas.
    Esther.
    Esther.
    Sarah.
McGraw Peter.
    Catherine.
    John.
    Sarah.
McGuire Luke, Sr.
    Margaret (of Luke.)
    Luke, Jr.
    Richard.
    Eleanor.
    Peter.
    Henry.

(McGuire) Michael.
    Ross.
    Agatha.
    Catherine.
    Charity.
    Margaret.
    Mary.
    Milburg.
    Patience.
    Susan.
    Michael (Irishman.)
McHugh Matthew.
    Margaret.
    Elizabeth.
    Mary.
    Elizabeth.
McIntosh John.
    Mary.
McIntire Peter.
    Elizabeth.
McKessan John.
McKinzie John.
    Elizabeth.
    Elizabeth.
McLaughlin Margaret.
McMullen Samuel.
    Henry.
    John.
    Elizabeth.
    Joanna.
    Margaret.
    Susan.
McVey Susan.
Meloy William.
    Hugh.
    John.
    Edward.
    Bridget.

(Meloy) Elizabeth.
    Susan.
MILLER John.
    Catherine.
MOONEY Margaret.
MULHOLLAN John.
MULLEN Hugh.
    Mary.
    Joanna.
MURPHY Eleanor.
    Elizabeth.
MURRAY Mary.
MUSSELMAN Sarah.
MYERS Catherine.
NAGLE Margaret.
    Honora.
NEASON Mary.
NOEL Nicholas.
    Joseph.
    John.
    Elizabeth.
    Mary.
    Magdalen.
NOON Philip.
O'CONNOR Henry.
    Mary.
O'HARA Francis.
    Elizabeth.
    Ann.
O'KEAN Henry.
    James.
PARRISH Joshua.
    John.
PLUNKETT Patrick.
    Apollonia.
REILLY Thomas.
RHEY James, Sr.
    James, Jr.

RHODES Mary.
ROSSITER Peter.
    Catherine.
RYAN Mrs. ———. (Widow.)
    Mrs. Patrick.
    Ann.
SCANLAN John.
    Theresa.
SHERRY Honora.
SHORT Peter.
    Catherine.
SKELLY Michael, Sr.
    Mary (of Michael)
    John, Jr.
    Catherine.
    Mary.
STEWART Mary.
STORM John
    Susan.
    Peter
    John.
    Catherine.
SULLIVAN Owen.
    Rose.
THOMPSON Mary. (Widow.)
    John.
    Elizabeth.
TREXLER Peter.
    Elizabeth.
TROXELL Jacob.
    Susan.
    Margaret.
WALTERS Englebert.
    Susan.
WEAKLAND Susan. (Widow.)
    William.
    Barbara.
    John.

(Weakland) Peter.
   William.
   James.
   Sarah.
   Susan.
   John.
   Mary (of John.)
WELSH Thomas.
   James.
WHARTON Ann.
   Catherine.
   Mary.
   Theresa.
WHITE Rachel A.

WILL Michael.
   Samuel.
   James.
   Mary Ann.
   Mary.
   Rachel.
WILMORE Mary.
   Elizabeth.
WIRE James.
WYSONG Ludwig.
YOST Jacob.
   Abigail.
   Margaret.

Number of Males, 170; Females, 257. Total, 427.

CONFIRMATION.

Names of those who were confirmed in the old log church, Loretto, by Rt. Rev. Michael Egan, first Bishop of Philadelphia, in September or October, 1811:

NAME.	Born.	NAME.	Born.
BARNICLE Mrs. Thaddeus		(Brown) William	1806
William		James	Dec. 27, 1807
James		BURKE John	
Philip		BURGOON Mrs. Robert	
Bartholomew	1798	John	1800
Michael	1800	Benedict	1803
Mary Ann	June 23, 1802	Catherine	Oct. 16, 1805
Bridget	Nov. 14, 1803	Mary Ann	Feb. 14, 1808
Catherine	Mar. 22, 1805	Mary Magdalen	1810
BAXTER George	1793	CANTWELL James	
BECHER Henry	1801	Mrs. James	
John	1804	COONS Catherine	1797
Mary	1806	Elizabeth	1799
Catherine	Nov. 21, 1808	Christina	1802
Elizabeth	May 2, 1811	John	1805
BROWN Mrs. John		Apollonia	Apr. 26, 1808
Michael	Jan. , 1797	Mary Ann	Sept. 8, 1810
Moses	1799	COOPER Henry	
John	Feb. 26, 1802	Augustine	1793
Sarah	Nov. 24, 1803		

NAME.	Born.	NAME.	Born.
(Cooper) Ann	1795	(Kimman) Henry	1802
Martha	1797	Joseph	1804
Leonard	1799	Mary Ann	1806
Francis	1801	Elizabeth	Mar. 22, 1808
Raphael	1803	Catherine	Mar. 29, 1810
Elizabeth	1805	LEAVY Michael	Mar. 30, 1793
Joseph	Feb. 19, 1807	Agnes	1795
Mary	Feb. 19, 1807	MAGEEHAN Mrs. Apollonia	
CRISTE Mrs. John (Sarah O'Hara)	1797	Michael Dan	July 14, 1803
Daniel	May 23, 1809	Rachel	Oct. 18, 1806
Robert Aloysius	Oct. 13, 1810	Joseph	Mar. 27, 1808
		James	1810
DRISKEL James	1795	McCALLEY Mrs. John	
William	1797	Ann	1777
Charles	1799	Henry	1785
Ann	1802	Mary	1786
Mary Ann	Nov. 2, 1805	Daniel	1788
Michael	Aug. 18, 1807	Elizabeth	1801
FELTZ Jacob	1799	Mary	1809
Catherine	1802	McGRAW Mrs. Sarah	
Anna Mary	1804	Peter	
Rachel	1806	Mrs. P. (Cath. McAfee)	
Mary Theresa	Nov. 14, 1808	Edward	June 2, 1808
Margaret	Sept. 21, 1810	Mary	1810
GLASS George	1770	John	
Mrs. Geo. (Susan Dougherty)	1780	William	
Ann	1795	McGUIRE Mrs. Richard	1782
Margaret	June 17, 1801	Henry (of Luke)	Nov. 16, 1793
Mary	Oct. 31, 1802	Luke	Apr. , 1796
Susan	Dec. 21, 1804	Milburg	1797
Jacob	Sept. 14, 1806	Mary	1799
Elizabeth	Mar. 11, 1808	Elizabeth	Sept. 3, 1801
George	Apr. 9, 1810	Augustine	Sept. 3, 1804
Jacob		Margaret	Mar. 27, 1807
Mrs. Rufina		Anastasia	Aug. 24, 1809
Daniel	May 16, 1809	Rachel Bridget (of Richard)	Sept. 9, 1803
Belinda Ann	Apr. 14, 1811	Catherine	May 9, 1807
GORMAN Mrs. Ruth	1780	Julia Ann	June 21, 1809
Mary Ann	1809	Mary Ann	1793
IVORY Matthew		McLAUGHLIN Margaret	
Mrs. Matthew		MELOY Mrs. Hugh	
Mary	1788	William	Feb. 28, 1810
Joanna	1793	Bridget	June 11, 1811
Jeremiah	1795	MUSSELMAN Mrs. David	1777
Matthew, Jr	1797	David R	1797
Patrick	1799	William	1800
John	1803	Henry	1802
KIMMAN Jacob	1799	Mary A. Magd	1805

NAME.	Born.	NAME.	Born.
(Musselman) Amelia Rachel.	Sept. 16, 1807	(Sherry) Jacob	1800
Daniel	May 11, 1810	George	Oct. 22, 1803
NAGLE Mrs. Richard		SHORT Samuel	1796
John	1779	Elizabeth	1797
Jacob	1781	Daniel	1799
Margaret	1785	Mary	1801
Richard	1787	TREXLER Peter	
George	1790	Mrs. Peter	
Honora	1793	WALTERS Mary	1800
O'CONNOR Francis (of Henry)	1797	Daniel	Mar. 6, 1802
Mary	1801	John	Sept. 7, 1805
O'HARA Mrs. Rachel		Susan	Mar. 3, 1808
Ann	1791	Catherine	Mar. 10, 1810
Francis	1795	WEAKLAND William	
Elizabeth	1797	Mrs. William	
Mary	1799	Catherine	Oct. 20, 1804
Henry	1801	Simon	Jan. 11, 1807
John	Apr. 27, 1803	John	Mar. 23, 1809
Esther	May 4, 1805	Susan	Mar. 4, 1811
Thomas	May, 1808	WILL Jacob (of Peter)	1790
RYAN Patrick	1786	Michael	1793
Mrs. Patrick	1788	Simon	1795
Ann	1808	Anthony	1799
James	1776	Joseph	Dec. 12, 1802
James	1804	WILMORE Mrs. Godfrey	1753
William	1808	Mary	1788
RHODES Mary		Elizabeth	1792
SHERRY Louis		John	1797
Mrs. Louis		Males........ 94	
John		Females....... 99	
Louis		Total......... 193	

NOTES ON FATHER GALLITZIN.

(From the Johnstown Tribune. October 13, 1899.)

Father Gallitzin having settled at Loretto in 1799, set about building a church; and his own hands, it is said, did much of the work. The building was of logs 25 by 44 feet. In this church, which was called St. Michael's by its founder, on Christmas Day, 1799, mass was first said, and, the building soon becoming too small, it was enlarged in 1809, and in 1817 was torn down and a frame structure, 40 by 80 feet, was erected on the same site. In 1854 the present commodious brick church was dedicated. It is now a matter of regret to many of the people of the congregation that the old church was allowed to fall to ruin, so much so that it had to be torn down in 1891.

Father Gallitzin not only administered spiritually to the wants of the people, but became in fact the founder of a colony, using for that purpose the large income which he received from his father's estates, expending in all $150,000, until the Russian Government saw fit, in 1808, to disinherit him because he was not a member of the Orthodox Greek Catholic Church, the established religion of Russia. It is said that his sister sent him pecuniary aid as long as she lived; nevertheless, he became financially involved by reason of his great outlays in assisting emigrants, building a grist mill near Loretto on a small branch of Clearfield Creek and a saw-mill on a larger branch near Cresson, the dam of which is still in existence and has long impounded the water for the mill of the late B. P. Anderson. When he found that his inheritance was swept away, he who had previously been a giver, and not a receiver, was compelled, by reason of a sense of duty, to appeal to the generosity and charity of Christian people to assist him to pay part of his debt, as shown by the accompanying appeal in his own handwriting, the heading having been recently appended by Father Kittell, the present pastor of St. Michael's congregation.

The following was written by Rev. D. A. Gallitzin himself.

Demetrius A. Gallitzin Son of Prince Demetrius of Gallitzin came to the United States in 1792 & having renounced all the flattering prospects of this world, consecrated himself in 1795 to the Missions of this Country from that to the present day. his time, property & faculties of Soul & body have been employ'd in improving the country, the place he selected for his abode (formerly a perfect wilderness, but now a flourishing settlem't) & in establishing & propagating Religion. Being the only Son of a wealthy father he did not spare expences in order to get the above ends accomplished, but still upon far below his supposed ability. Lately unexpectedly, & without having had it in his power to foresee or even to suspect such an event, he finds himself, by a Decree of his former Government, deprived of the whole of his Parents Estates, & with debts amounting to more than $5000 he Now very reluctantly, but from a sense of duty, calls upon the Charity of his fellow-Christians for assistance, to enable him to pay part of his debts, as his own exertions would prove insufficient for the whole.

APPEAL OF FATHER GALLITZIN FOR FINANCIAL ASSISTANCE, WRITTEN BY HIS OWN HAND.

The system of capitalization and division into sentences used is in singular contrast to that of the present day, common as well as proper nouns generally commencing with a capital letter, while the beginning of a sentence with a small letter may also be noted, as likewise the difference in orthography in the word "expences." The appeal was originally written on both sides of the first leaf of a notebook, but all that was written on the second page and a few words on the lower line following the character &, have been subsequently so completely crossed out by the pen, doubtless by the hand of Father Gallitzin himself, as to be entirely undecipherable to the naked eye.

On the second page are the five contributions, beginning with that of Charles Carroll, of Carrollton, the last of the

SUBSCRIPTIONS OF CHARLES CARROLL AND OTHERS IN RESPONSE TO THE APPEAL OF FATHER GALLITZIN.

signers of the Declaration of Independence, the phrase "of Carrollton" being first used when signing the immortal Declaration, which act, had the Revolutionary War proven a failure, would have cost the signers their lives. Some one remarked, "There go many," the meaning whereof was that there being many Charles Carrolls, the indentity of the signer would not be known; whereupon Carroll instantly added, "of Carrollton," which he ever afterward retained. Carroll's handwriting in this subscription and also in an indorsement of the worthy motives of the appeal on the third page, shows the tremor of age so much, compared with his autograph to the Declaration of Independence, that it is hardly recognizable as the same.

Of all the remarkable traits in the life of Father Gallitzin, none is more remarkable than the fact that his handwriting never showed the nervousness of age so common to other men, his last entries in the baptismal and marriage registers of the church in March 1840, when he was seventy years of age, being in as clear and legible a hand as his first records in January, 1800.

The person whose name is second on the accompanying list of subscriptions lived in Baltimore, was a member of the well-known Oliver family, and attorney for Father Gallitzin. Baron de Maltitz was Russian Minister to the United States, Jose Silvestre Rebello filled a similar position for Portugal, and Cardinal Capellari afterward became Pope Gregory XVI. Matthew Carey was an American publisher and author, the father of Henry C. Carey, the noted political economist. The next entry, "Cash $20," and the last "Collected along, the Canal below Blairsville, say $370," as may be seen by comparison, are in Father Gallitzin's handwriting.

In addition to the above, there were many collections, aggregating several thousand dollars, made along the Alleghany Portage Railroad, in which lists appear the names of many of the old Irish settlers.

It is somewhat singular that the list of contributors is remarkable for the absence of the names of those for whom Father Gallitzin had incurred the debt he was heroically endeavoring to pay—the pioneers of Allegheny Township. It may be that they contributed their mite in another way, perhaps by collections in the church, which were not entered in this little book, or perhaps they were paying for the land on which they had settled.

Doubtless, in the life of Father Gallitzin, there was nothing so humiliating as to be compelled to appeal to the generosity of Christian people, for of all men there is none whose name is farther removed from a suspicion of cupidity than his.

About the unselfishness of his motives in becoming an ecclesiastic there cannot be the slightest doubt, for in the history of the world there is perhaps not another instance of such self-sacrificing devotion of a person in high position

> I hereby earnestly recommend to all charitable persons to subscribe such sum as their inclination & ability will permit to second the views detailed in the opposite page by the Reverend Demetrius Gallitzin.
> Ch. Carroll of Carrollton
> 13th Nov. 1827

INDORSEMENT OF FATHER GALLITZIN'S APPEAL BY ONE OF THE SIGNERS OF THE DECLARATION OF INDEPENDENCE.

to what he believed to be his duty; certainly none to surpass that of the apostle of the Alleghenies.

Kings, tired of the cares of State, some doubtless through remorse, but nearly all of them disgusted with perplexities, have laid down the scepter and entered monasteries: but it is doubtful if there is another instance of a man on the threshold of life surrendering such flattering prospects of the world to follow the dictates of his conscience, and immune himself for a lifetime in the solitudes of an almost inaccessible wilderness. His appeal to those who knew him did not need the indorsement of the first citizen and last signer of the Declaration of Independence, which was given.

It may not be generally known that Captain Michael McGuire, the founder of the McGuire Settlement, had been dead six years before Father Gallitzin settled at Loretto.

Although Father Gallitzin at an early day had an assistant in the person of Rev. Terence McGirr, the Baptismal Register and the Record of Marriages were kept by himself. The first baptism recorded is in April, 1800, the child having been Joseph, son of Charles and Mary Bradley. This entry, which is in Latin, is signed Demetrius Augustinus de Gallitzin, *alias* Augustinus Smith, Parochus.

Father Gallitzin's entries of baptisms differed from those of the present day in that the surname given both parents was that of the father, except in cases where the parents were not married: so one can tell by looking at the baptismal register kept by Father Gallitzin whether or not a person whose name is recorded therein was born in lawful wedlock. Now the maiden surname of the mother is given in all cases.

It is probable that there never existed in Western Pennsylvania another community of equal size in which there were fewer illegitimate births than in the Loretto congregation during the time of Father Gallitzin's pastorate.

Of the entries immediately following this some are signed Demetrius Augustinus Smith, Parochus, some Dem. Aug. Smith, Parochus, others, Dem. Aug. Smith, Parochus, and still others Demetrius Augustinus Gallitzin, Princeps, Parochus,—Princeps having been with the exception of a single

THE OLD DEVER HOMESTEAD.   ERECTED 1817.

IMMERGRÜN.   SUMMER RESIDENCE OF C. M. SCHWAB, LORETTO.
VIEW FROM RUDOLPH'S WOODS.

instance crossed out with the pen, undoubtedly by Gallitzin himself. Later on the name Smith is no longer used. The registry of the last baptism recorded by Father Gallitzin reads as follows:

"Die 16° Aprilis baptisatus est Henricus filius Henrici et Mariae Annae Freithoff conjugum natus die 18 Martii."

"Patrinus, Henricus Henkel.

"Matrina, Maria Anna Beuter."

The first marriage recorded is in June, 1803, and is that of Nicholas Cherry, son of Andrew and Catharine Cherry, and Elizabeth Burgoon, and the last, in 1840, is that of Daniel Noel and Veronica Burke.

The life of Father Gallitzin was simple and austere in the extreme. He was strong in his convictions and unfaltering in his devotion to principle. He was charitable beyond measure, but uncompromising in his exactions of his parishioners in the performance of their duties as he was exact and punctilious in the performance of his own, even in the most minute particular. Although he was assisted by other priests, he never allowed any of them to dwell with him for more than a few days at a time. Father McGirr, who assisted him the greater part of the time, lived on a farm of his own, a couple of miles southwest of Ebensburg, on what was afterward the Old Plank Road. Indeed, one of his ecclesiastical superiors once said that no priest could live with this "singular old saint;" not so much that they would not overlook his eccentricities as that he would not have them dwell with him, as Father Lemke soon learned.

Notwithstanding this aversion to the society of his confreres, he often had spells of lonesomeness or melancholy, and on these occasions would play the violin, of the music of which he was particularly fond, and sometimes would have one of his numerous household play for him. Mrs. McConnell, mother of Englebert McConnell, of near Chest Springs, who often played the violin for him, is still living at an advanced age. Augustine Hott, who lives not far from Carrolltown, is the sole survivor of the male help Gallitzin employed on his farm. The number of orphans he raised was something remarkable, his house sometimes sheltering as many as seven or eight of these unfortunates. Although having the services of assistant priests, he often visited the most remote parts of his charge, which extended over what are now the dioceses of Pittsburg, Erie, and parts of Harrisburg and Scranton. Being incapacitated by a fall from his horse from riding in his carriage over the rough country roads, he had a light sled made, in which he rode winter and summer. On one of these visits to the home of Joshua Parrish, who lived near Munster, in 1834, he first met Father Lemke. Although the generally accepted account credits Augustine Hott with being the driver of the team on that memorable occasion, one of the descendants of Mr. Parrish says that such was not the case, the driver having been a Mr. McConnell.

After Loretto, Ebensburg was the first place to be erected into a congregation, next Hart's Sleeping Place (St. Joseph's), then Johnstown, and about simultaneously St. Aloysius', Summit, and St. Bartholomew's, Jefferson.

Prior to the time churches were built in Jefferson and Johnstown Father Gallitzin often visited these places and said mass and administered the sacraments. At Jefferson, now Wilmore, he used to stop at the home of Godfrey Wilmore, and afterward at James Young's, a son-in-law of Mr. Wilmore; but when the Irish laborers were at work on the Portage Railroad, there were so many to attend mass that no building then in existence about the place could accommodate them, and in summer time mass was often said under an apple tree in Mr. Young's orchard.

Mr. William Cover, of Johnstown, relates that on one occasion mass was being said on the park in Johnstown, near where the pavilion now stands, on a Sunday morning, as he was passing down Main street. He stopped out of curiosity and got mixed with the crowd. The celebrant, a tall, stately priest, seeing him with his hat on, ordered him to uncover his head. Not wishing to appear to participate in the worship of a religion to which he did not belong, Mr. Cover instantly but decorously walked on down street. That priest was undoubtedly Father Gallitzin.

As a theologian and a controversial disputant Father Gallitzin had few superiors. Among his writings were "A Defense of Catholic Principles, in Answer to Letters of a Protestant Minister" and "Touchstone of the New Religion."

The first of these works was published by Canan & Scott, Ebensburg, about the year 1834. "Sixty Objections of Protestants Answered by Quotations from Their Own Bible," published by the Catholics of the Pittsburg Diocese was probably his work.

While exact and uncompromising in things pertaining to religion, socially Father Gallitzin was a very affable gentleman, and lived on friendly terms with his Protestant neighbors; and it is the testimony of a trustworthy Ebensburg gentleman that he often visited Rev. Rhees Lloyd at the home of the latter in Ebensburg.

In his private dealings no one was more scrupulously honest than Father Gallitzin, and, notwithstanding his multifarious duties, he kept his accounts himself. The accompanying account with Joseph Itel, father of Mr. John Itel, of Portage Township, and grandfather of T. J. Itell, Esq., of Johnstown, will serve at once as an illustration of this exactness and also give an idea of the rates of postage at that time.

What the personal compensation to Mr. Itel outside of postage was for, the writer has not ascertained. It may have been for carrying letters to and from the postoffice at Munster, through which town the Pittsburg Pike ran. Munster, founded by Irish settlers in 1806 as a rival to Loretto, was so named in honor of the province of Munster in Ireland.

Although in a manner isolated from the civilized world, Gallitzin kept as well posted on current events as it was possible for him to do by his correspondence, and by reading the best papers of the day, the irregularity of mail service being on one occasion the subject of serious complaint in one of his letters; and he exercised the privilege of citizenship and took a lively interest in politics. He was an admirer and friend of Thomas Jefferson, and in his later years of Henry Clay, and was an ardent Whig. It was related by the late 'Squire Miller, of Wilmore, who lived with him at the time of his death, that upon one occasion after an election Father Gallitzin in a petulant humor entered a room where John Miller, a school teacher in his employ and father of the 'Squire, was seated

ACCOUNT OF FATHER GALLITZIN WITH JOSEPH ITEL, KEPT BY THE PRIEST HIMSELF.

and exclaimed, "Miller, I do believe that if the Evil One with Damnation written across his forehead were to run on the Democratic ticket some people would vote for him," and immediately left the room.

It is a matter of history that Father Gallitzin early established a school for the education of the children of the congregation. Archibald Christy is believed to have been its first teacher.

As an observer of the phenomena of nature no one was more intelligent than the pastor of Loretto. The late Francis Christy was working for him on his farm during the war of 1812. One day the priest said to him that undoubtedly a battle was being fought somewhere—he could tell by the condition of the atmosphere. In due course of time came the news of Perry's victory on Lake Erie, fought on the day on which Gallitzin had noted the meteorological phenomenon to which he had called attention.

One writer says that Gallitzin desired to have Loretto made the county seat on the formation of Cambria County, and another that he did not; that he did not wish lawyers to mingle with his people. The latter is probably correct. Gallitzin hated the pomp and vanity of the world, and in his own sphere sought nothing higher than the humble, arduous life of a missionary priest. All priests in this country were then, and until within the last quarter of a century, missionary priests. Now, what were congregations are parishes, and their pastors, rectors, or parish priests. With him there was no intriguing to be advanced to ecclesiastical dignity; he even declined such preferment; and in this lies his great merit, for which the impartial historian accords him a place second to none in the history of the Catholic Church in this country.

While kind and charitable in social life, as before stated, in his clerical capacity he exacted the most implicit obedience from those under his charge. His presence was commanding, his will inflexible, and his voice stentorian. 'Squire Miller used to relate that once upon a time some harvest hands employed upon Gallitzin's farm and those on adjoining lands, having imbibed too much liquor, which was at that time considered a necessity in all harvest fields, two of them got into a quarrel when one grasped a pitchfork and chased his opponent, who, to avoid serious injury or perhaps death, jumped across the mill race leading to Gallitzin's flouring mill, within sight of the priest's residence. Just then the aged priest happened to be walking about the field near his house, and, catching a glance of the combatants and fully realizing the seriousness of the case, thundered forth: "You, ——!" naming the one in pursuit. The effect was electrical. The angry man instantly dropped his pitchfork and forgot his resentment.

No fire was allowed in the church during Father Gallitzin's pastorate, and to this fact may possibly be attributed his death; for having said early mass (Father McGirr said the late mass), heard confessions, and preached on the Resurrection at the late mass on Easter Sunday, 1840, which was a chilly day, he suffered a congestive chill, his illness continued to increase, and his death occurred on the 6th of May following. His remains were interred in a common grave: but seven years afterward a tomb, surmounted by a plain monument, was erected in the enclosure in front of the present church, and with much pomp and ceremony the remains were transferred to this tomb, which is now surmounted by a more pretentious work of art. But the most enduring monument to the memory of the prince-priest and Apostle of the Alleghenies is the record of his heroic self-sacrice and abnegation, his simplicity of life, his unbounded charity and philanthropy, and his zeal for the spiritual welfare of those committed to his care, which will endure in the memories of the descendants of those who were his proteges and spiritual children and in the history of the truly great and noble, when the bronze monolith dedicated to his memory will have become disintegrated by the climate of the Alleghenies which undermined the physical constitution of the matchless hero whose memory it is designed to commemorate.

COPY OF AN OLD DEED OF CONVEYANCE IN FATHER GALLITZIN'S HANDWRITING.

Know all men by these presents that I, Rev'd Demetrius Augustine (Smith,) Prince of Gallitzin, of Allegheny Township, Cambria County and State of Pennsylvania, am held and firmly bound unto John Kuhns, of the same Township and County, State aforesaid, in the penal sum of four hundred and eighty Dollars, specie, to be paid unto the aforesaid John Kuhns, his certain Attorney, heirs Executors administrators or Assigns, for the which payment well and truly to be made I bind me, my heirs Executors Administrators, them and every of them firmly by these presents sealed with my Seal and dated the thirty first day of October, Anno Domini One thousand eight hundred and Six, 1806.

The condition of the above obligation is such that if the above bounden Demetrius Augustine (Smith) Prince of Gallitzin, he himself, his heirs Executors Administrators, him them or any of them do make over and convey by a good Deed of Conveyance to the aforesaid John Kuhns a certain piece or parcel of land containing forty acres, being a part of a tract of land in the name of Richard Brownson, which part the aforesaid John Kuhns is living on, and that as soon as possible after the above Demetrius Augustine (Smith) Prince of Gallitzin shall have obtained a Deed for the whole tract from Brownson's heirs, that if then conveyed as aforesaid without fraud or further delay, then the above obligation is to be void and of no effect; otherwise to be and remain in full force power and virtue. DEMETRIUS AUGUSTINE (SMITH.)
TESTES: Prince of Gallitzin.
    JAS. MAGEEHAN,
    JOHN HOLLANDS.

Oct. 31, 1806. Received of John Kuhns two hundred and forty Dollars, being the whole purchase money for the above piece of land.   DEMETRIUS AUGUSTINE (SMITH),
                                              Prince of Gallitzin.

NOTICE.

I. Scrape the dirt off your shoes on the iron scrapers provided for that purpose.

II. Do not spit on the floor of the chapel.

III. Do not put your hats and caps on the chapel windows.

IV. Do not rub against the papered walls of the chapel.

V. Do not put your heels on the washboards.

VI. After coming in at the passage door shut the door after you.
DEMETRIUS AUGUSTINE GALLITZIN,
Parish Priest of Loretto.

The following curious advertisement was published in the "Cambria County Gazette," 1825.

NOTICE.

A certain number of Protestants having manifested a great desire of becoming members of the Roman Catholic Church, I hereby acquaint the said Protestants and the public in general, that I have appointed the Second Sunday after Easter (April 17), for admitting them into the Church, according to the Rites and Ceremonies of the Roman Ritual.

DEMETRIUS A. GALLITZIN,
Loretto, March 22, 1825.   Parish Priest.

A large group was received into the Church at the time specified and many more during the summer.

APPEAL OF FATHER GALLITZIN FOR PECUNIARY ASSISTANCE—1827.

(Copied from his own hand-writing.)

Demetrius A. Gallitzin, Son of Prince Demetrius, of Gallitzin, came to the United States in 1792, and having renounced all the flattering prospects of this world, consecrated himself in 1795 to the Missions of this Country. From that to the present day his time, property and faculties of soul and body have been employed in improving the country, the place he selected for his abode (formerly a perfect wilderness, but now a flourishing settlement) and in establishing and propagating religion. Being the only son of a wealthy father he did not spare expense in order to get the above ends accomplished, but still spent far below his supposed ability. Lately, unexpectedly and without having had it in his power to forsee, or even to suspect such an event, he finds himself, by a Decree of his former Government, deprived of the whole of his Parents' Estates, and with debts amounting to more than $5,000. He now very reluctantly, but from a sense of Duty, calls upon the Charity of his fellow Christians for assistance to enable him to pay part of his debts, as his own exertions would prove insufficient for the whole . . . (The rest of the appeal is so crossed and re-crossed with the pen as to be altogether undecipherable).

I hereby recommend to all charitable persons to subscribe such sums as their inclination and ability will permit to second the views detailed on the opposite page by the Reverend Demetritus A. Gallitzin.

CH. CARROLL of Carrollton.
13th Nov. 1827.

Ch. Carroll of Carrollton	$100 pd.	William Ryan	10 00
Robert Oliver	100 pd.	John Mealy	10 00
Baron de Maltitz	100 pd.	Michael McGragh	10 00
Je. Silvestre Rebello	100 pd.	—— Savage	10 00
Cardinal Capellari (afterwards Pope Gregory XVI)	200 pd.	John McGuigan	10 00
		Thos. Stewardson	10 00
		Mrs. McDonough	10 00
		Rev. Michael Hurley	10 00
Matthew Carey	20 pd.	Rev. Wm. O'Donnell	5 00
Cash	20 00	—— Fisher	5 00
Jer. Reily	10 00	Felix McGirr	5 00
Collected along the canal below Blairsville, say	370 00	Philip Riley	5 00
		Eugene Cummiskey	5 00
		John Durney	5 00
Josep Dugan	20 00	B. Quinn	5 00
Simon Lonergan & Co.	18 00	P. Smith	5 00
Mr. Gilmartin	35 00	M. Keating	5 00
N. N. Canal men	17 50	Peter Mulvihill	5 00
John J. Hughes	19 00	John Ashley	5 00
J. J. Donaghue	10 00		

Then follow in the note book, from which these items are taken, the names of the Irish laborers on the canal near Blairsville, who responded to the appeal, generally in sums of one dollar. The more notable contributions were as follows:

Moore & McGrath	85 00	Moses Brown	2 00
Edmund Burke	5 00	Michael Conway	2 00
James Fenlon	5 00	Harry Heffron	2 00
Burke & Powers	10 00	John Meloy	2 00
John Bracken	6 00	Francis McGrath	2 00

The following account, copied from Father Gallitzin's own hand-writing, is interesting as showing how postage was calculated in those early times:

D. A. G., IN ACCOUNT WITH JOS. ITEL.

1833.	Jan.	—.	One letter to Robt. Oliver	12½
			Postage	18¾
	Jan.	25.	R. Oliver's answer	18¾
	Jan.	26.	Wrote a letter to D. Stanard	12½
			Postage on said letter	10
	Jan.	29.	D. Stanard's answer	10
	Febr.	17.	Double letter to R. Oliver, Balto.	37½
			Wrote power of attorney and letter to R. Oliver	1 00
	Nov.	1.	Letter from Baltimore	56¼
	Nov.	20.	Writing a letter to Baltimore, and postage 75 cts.	1 00
1834.	Jan.	22.	Letter to Rob. Oliver	31¼
	Febr.	16.	Triple letter from Baltimore	75
			Wrote 2 letters to Paris and Carspach	25

THE MURDER OF BETSY HOLDER.

June 22, 1807, after three proclamations of the banns, I united in marriage *John Holder* and *Elizabeth Yost*.

DEMETRIUS A. GALLITZIN.

Witnesses.   JOHN MCCARTY.
   MARTHY YOST.

(The above is copied from the Loretto Matrimonial Register. The following remarks on the murder of Mrs. Holder are taken from "Reminiscences of the Bench and Bar of Cambria County," by R. L. Johnston, Esq., at the dedication of the new Court House, May 25, 1882.)

On the 3d of July, 1841 (I well remember it, for there was a mid-summer frost), I was called upon, as a Justice of the Peace, upon the information of John Wherry, to issue a warrant against two good citizens of our county for the murder of Betsy Holder, an old lady whose cottage stood close by the turnpike, one mile east of Ebensburg. The murder was committed, but those then charged with it were wholly innocent. A reward was offered, pursuit made, and Patrick and Bernard Flanagan were arrested a few days afterward. They were strangers to the county; their object, plunder.

At October term, 1842, they were tried and convicted, and a motion for a new trial overruled by Judge White, and sentence pronounced. No death warrant was signed, but the following winter an act was passed authorizing Judge White to hear a motion for a new trial, and in case of his refusal, to notify the nearest president judge to hear the motion. Judge White promptly refused the motion, and notified Judge Woodward. He also refused, and pronounced the act unconstitutional.

The year 1843 then passed, and in 1844 an act was passed for the hearing of the motion for a new trial before a judge of the Supreme Court. Accordingly, Judge Molton C. Rogers on the 4th of July, 1844, heard the arguments and refused the motion.

The night before the election in 1844 the death warrant was received by the Sheriff. On the same evening the Flanagans escaped from prison. They owed their escape from prison to the heroic devotion of a sister.

PREFACE TO FATHER GIBSON'S REGISTER.

"Register of Baptisms, Marriages, etc., etc., of the Mission which comprises Ebensburg, Summit, Jefferson (now Wilmore), Munster, Johnstown, Reservoir (South Fork Dam), from the 1st of October, 1841, when I, Matthew William Gibson, received jurisdiction from the Rt. Rev. Francis Patrick Kenrick, Bishop of Philadelphia.

"To which are also added some Baptisms and Marriages performed by me in the congregation of St. Michael, Loretto."

BAPTISMAL REGISTER.

The first entry made by Father Gallitzin in the Baptismal Register of St. Michael's Church is dated simply "Month of April, 1800," and records the birth, on March 1st, preceding, of Joseph, son of Charles and Mary Bradley. It is signed: "Demetrius Augustinus de Gallitzin, alias Augustinus Smith, Parochus." Thereafter until December of that year he signed his name and title: "Demetrius Aug. Princeps de Gallitzin, Parochus." Then: "Dem. Aug. Smith," and in 1805 he dropped the "Smith" and resumed his real name, which he ever afterwards used without his title of "Prince." His last entry was dated "April 16, 1840," just twenty days before his death, and in it he records the birth, on the 18th of the preceding month, of Henry, son of Henry and Mary Ann Freidhoff.

The first entry made by Rev. Peter H. Lemke was dated June 14, 1840; the last, October 12, 1844.

The first entry made by Rev. Matthew William Gibson was dated October 2, 1841; the last, February 21, 1844.

The first entry made by Rev. Andrew P. Gibbs was dated March 6, 1844.

The first entry made by Rev. Thos. B. O'Flaherty was dated March 24, 1844.

Fathers Gibbs and O'Flaherty were stationed at Loretto as assistants to Father Lemke, who was then residing at Carrolltown, and attended Ebensburg, Johnstown, Jefferson (Wilmore), and Summit, from which outlying Missions the most of their baptisms are recorded. The last entry of Father Gibbs is dated July 27, 1845; of Father O'Flaherty, May 4, 1845.

The first entry made by Rev. Hugh P. Gallagher, as Pastor, was dated October —, 1844; his last, as Pastor, July 11, 1852.

The first entry made by Rev. Joseph A. Gallagher, as assistant, was dated June 30, 1847; his first, as Pastor, July 11, 1852; his last, October 8, 1855.

The first entry made by Rev. William Pollard was dated August 27, 1855; the last, November 5, 1859.

The first entry made by Rev. Terence S. Reynolds was dated December 12, 1859; the last, October 11, 1868.

The first entry made by Rev. M. J. Mitchell was dated December 27, 1868; the last, February 12, 1870.

The first entry made by Rev. E. A. Bush, as Pastor, was dated April 17, 1870; the last, April 6, 1890.

The first entry made by Rev. Martin Ryan was dated May 4, 1890; the last, February 22, 1891.

The first entry made by Rev. Ferdinand Kittell, the present Pastor, was dated April 12, 1891.

OFFICIATING PRIESTS

Whose names are found in the Baptismal and Matrimonial Registers of St. Michael's Church, Loretto, Pa.

PASTORS AND RESIDENT ASSISTANTS.

Dem. Aug. Gallitzin, Pastor	1799-1840
Terence McGirr	1824-45
Peter H. Lemke	1834-40

Peter H. Lemke, Pastor	1840-44
Matthew William Gibson	1841-44
Andrew P. Gibbs	1844-45
Thos. B. O'Flaherty	1844-45
Hugh P. Gallagher, Pastor	1844-52
N. Haeres	1846-48
Joseph A. Gallagher	1847-52
Joseph A. Gallagher, Pastor	1852-55
Albinus Magno, C. P.	1853-54
William Pollard, Pastor	1855-59
John Ford	1856-64
Francis J. O'Shea	1859-69
Terence S. Reynolds, Pastor	1859-68
Pollard McC. Morgan	1864-66
Edward A. Bush	1866-68
Andrew J. Brown	1868-69
Henry McHugh	1868
Michael J. Mitchell, Pastor	1868-69
Andrew A. Lambing, LL. D.	1869
H. Seymour Bowen	1869-85
Edward A. Bush, Pastor	1870-90
Daniel Devlin	1873-77
P. May	1877
Michael F. Foley	1887-88
Martin Ryan, Pastor	1890-91
Ferdinand Kittell, Pastor	1891-99
Patrick J. Hawe	1896

BENEDICTINE FATHERS, of St. Benedict's Priory, Carrolltown, who attended regularly to the spiritual welfare of the Germans of St. Michael's parish.

P. Thaddeus Brunner, O. S. B.	1849-50
P. Benedict Haindl, O. S. B.	1849
P. Lechner, O. S. B.	1850
P. Celestine Englebrecht, O. S. B.	1850-59
P. Odilo van der Green, O. S. B.	1852

LORETTO CENTENARY.   239

P. Ildefonse Boeld, O. S. B.   -   -   1853-55
P. Valentine Felder, O. S. B.   -   -   1856
P. Oswald Moosmueller, O. S. B. -   1857
P. Gerard Pilz, O. S. B.   -   -   1859
P. Utho Huber, O. S. B.   -   -   1859-60
P. Otto Kopf, O. S. B.   -   -   1860-63
P. Placidus Pilz, O. S. B. -   -   1860-61
P. Giles Christoph, O. S. B.   -   1863
P. Edmund Langenfelder, O. S. B.   -   1864
P. Constantine Leber, O. S. B. -   1888
P. Benedict Meyer, O. S. B. -   -   1890

TRANSIENT ASSISTANTS.

Patrick Rafferty,   -   -   -   1828
John C. Brady,   -   -   -   1846
J. F. Deane,   -   -   -   1847
P. Duffy,   -   -   -   1847
Ignatius Ginter,   -   -   -   1848
Nicholas Stauber,   -   -   -   1848
Edward F. Garland, -   -   -   1849
J. Berbigir,   -   -   -   1851
Rt. Rev. Jas. O'Connor, D. D., -   -   1851
Thomas Heyden,   -   -   -   1851
Gerald Murtagh,   -   -   -   1852
A. L. Roche,   -   -   -   1852
Richard Browne,   -   -   -   1852
Francis Grimmer,   -   -   -   1853
K. O'Branigan,   -   -   -   1854
P. J. Madden,   -   -   -   1854
James McGoun,   -   -   -   1855
Richard C. Christy, -   -   -   1855
John B. O'Connor,   -   -   -   1855
John Burns,   -   -   -   1856
Thomas McCullagh,   -   -   -   1856-57
J. Carroll,   -   -   -   1856
John Walsh,   -   -   -   1857
Thomas Quinn,   -   -   -   1859
John Hackett,   -   -   -   1861

Rt. Rev. M. Domence, D. D.,	1862
James Canevin,	1863
Edward J. Burns,	1863
James P. Pahaney,	1863
Angelo Lugero, C. P.,	1866
S. Guilbaud,	1866
William Power, C. S. Sp.	1882
George W. Kaylor,	1888-89
Boniface Sotter, C. P.	1891
James J. Deasy,	1892
H. P. Connery,	1892
Thos. W. Rosensteel,	1892-97
Thomas McEnrue,	1893
Athanasius Swingler, C. P.,	1893
Francis J. Coyle,	1895
Felix Ward, C. P.,	1895
Raphael V. O'Connell, S. J.,	1895
P. A. McDermott, C. S. Sp.,	1896

THE OLDEST HOUSE IN LORETTO. RESIDENCE OF MRS. SARAH McGUIRE.

THE HITCHING GROUNDS. AFTER MASS ON SUNDAY.

MARRIAGES AND BAPTISMS AT LORETTO.

Number of Marriages and Baptisms recorded in St. Michael's Parish, Loretto, Pa., from its foundation to August 15, 1899.

Year.	Marriages.	Baptisms.	Year.	Marriages.	Baptisms.	Year.	Marriages.	Baptisms.
1800		17	1834	24	133	1868	23	74
1801		9	1835	36	104	1869	8	56
1802		22	1836	12	114	1870	14	68
1803	1	18	1837	16	124	1871	12	66
1804		31	1838	23	117	1872	16	53
1805		32	1839	18	100	1873	9	58
1806		32	1840	17	68	1874	12	51
1807	3	48	1841	31	124	1875	10	60
1808	2	51	1842	48	220	1876	4	57
1809		45	1843	23	247	1877	12	52
1810		63	1844	34	244	1878	12	49
1811	1	53	1845	24	123	1879	11	54
1812	6	42	1846	16	58	1880	16	59
1813	8	47	1847	30	119	1881	16	48
1814	4	65	1848	23	102	1882	9	48
1815	9	70	1849	21	54	1883	11	57
1816	15	57	1850	14	58	1884	8	46
1817	13	76	1851	20	66	1885	13	51
1818	6	58	1852	16	68	1886	11	39
1819	22	76	1853	16	63	1887	17	48
1820	11	84	1854	15	61	1888	14	38
1821	9	103	1855	23	57	1889	12	40
1822	16	82	1856	18	74	1890	10	35
1823	11	101	1857	16	58	1891	6	33
1824	17	111	1858	8	72	1892	9	22
1825	19	111	1859	10	71	1893	8	38
1826	23	120	1860	11	65	1894	7	25
1827	16	124	1861	9	61	1895	7	37
1828	19	99	1862	5	69	1896	8	29
1829	19	116	1863	9	61	1897	12	31
1830	19	114	1864	10	53	1898	12	33
1831	14	90	1865	11	59	1899	10	30
1832	19	116	1866	20	61			
1833	38	124	1867	17	51	1343	7072	

MINUTES OF CHURCH MANAGERS.

At a meeting of the managers of St. Michael's Church held at the pastoral residence on the 17th of September, 1844, it was resolved that the Rev. A. Gibbs should receive for seven months salary from said Church One Hundred Dollars for which we have agreed to; and that the Rev. Peter H. Lemke should receive Eighty-Three Dollars, and leave all the proceeds of said farm, which was agreed to.

Managers Present.
- Rev. PETER H. LEMKE, Pastor.
- Rev. A. GIBBS.
- PETER URBAN.
- R. SCANLAN.

(Rev. H. P. Gallagher took charge as Pastor on Friday, September 27th, 1844.)

LORETTO, October 1st, 1844.

Rev. H. P. Gallagher as Pastor to receive Five Hundred Dollars per year salary.

LORETTO, September 19th, 1847.

Meeting of the managers of St. Michael's Church, Loretto. It was agreed upon that Rev. H. P. Gallagher should receive Three Dollars per week for boarding, etc. of Rev. Mr. Haeres, to commence on the first of June last.

Also it was agreed upon that Eliza Jane Little should receive Fifty Cents per week for playing the organ, to commence on the first of July past.

R. SCANLAN,
Treasurer of St. Michael's Church.

MAY 27, 1848.

Managers met for the purpose of arranging the pew-rent for the ensuing year, and to make out report for the year ending on the last of May; report to be concluded on first of

June. They also agree that the Church pay the rent half-yearly for the Convent of the Sisters of Mercy, amounting to 40 Dollars per year.

R. Scanlan, Treasurer.

March 7, 1849.

The Rev. Jos. A. Gallagher is to receive One Hundred and Fifty Dollars for attendance at Hart's Sleeping Place, in lieu of securing the service of a German clergyman for Loretto congregation.

June 4, 1849.

The managers of the temporal affairs of St. Michael's Church, Loretto, agreed to a reduction of ten per cent. on all pews on sale of 1847.

R. Scanlan, Treasurer.

(The only reference to the cost of the monument that can be found is the following, copied from the accounts of Rev. H. P. Gallagher.)

July 29, 1852. Paid borrowed money to pay Peter McDade balance on contract for monument of Rev. D. A. Gallitzin, deceased.

Principal.................................	$ 112 36	
Interest of same, four years from July 29, 1848.........................	26 96	$ 139 32

LIST OF SUBSCRIBERS TO THE MONUMENT.

The following list of subscriptions to the monument of Father Gallitzin is without date, but was evidently made up in 1847, the year the monument was erected. It is evident also that it does not furnish the names of *all* the contributors, but it is the only document of the kind that can be found. Without doubt there were other such lists which must have been lost. For easier reference the names are placed in alphabetical order.

Becher Nicholas	$1 00	Little Henry	2 00
Behe Conrad	1 00	Luckett Thomas	1 00
Behe Mathias	1 00	McConnell John	1 00
Bradley Charles	2 00	McCoy Anthony	1 00
Buck Joseph	2 00	McCoy John	1 00
Christ John	1 00	McGonegal Jeremiah	2 00
Christy John D	1 00	McGough James	1 00
Connery Edward	1 00	McGuire Michael	1 00
Conrad Jos. A	1 00	McMullen Alexander	1 00
Cooper Francis	2 00	McMullen J	1 00
Cooper Joseph	1 00	Miller Daniel	1 00
Delaney George	1 00	Moyer John	1 00
Dever Cornelius	1 00	Mullen Edward	1 00
Dever Neal	1 00	Mullen Robert	1 00
Donoughe Cornelius	1 00	Myers George	1 00
Donoughe Paul	1 00	Myers John B	1 00
Doyle James	1 00	Noon Dennis	1 00
Driskel Michael	2 00	O'Neill Felix	1 00
Dumm George	1 00	Parrish Peter	1 00
Eberly Francis	1 00	Parrish Thomas	1 00
Eckenrode Daniel	1 00	Phalen James	1 00
Fagan Simon	1 00	Richter Joseph	1 00
Flanagan Joseph	2 00	Sanders Peter	1 00
Flick Peter	1 00	Sanker John	1 00
Fury John	1 00	Scanlan Peter	1 00
Glass Henry	3 00	Schroth Martin	1 00
Glass William	2 00	Shoemaker Edward	1 00
Hertzog Philip	1 00	Storm Peter	1 00
Ivory Matthew	1 00	Waggoner Jacob	1 00
Keller (Kaylor) Jacob	1 00	Walters Aug	1 00
Kelley James	1 00	Weakland Simon	1 00
Kelley Patrick	1 00	Weakland William	1 00
Kerrigan Peter	1 00	Will Anthony	2 00
Leavy Michael	3 00	Will Thomas	2 00

$ 82 00

ERECTION OF BRICK CHURCH.—1847.

(The following bears no date, but the meeting was evidently held early in the year 1847.)

At a meeting held in the St. Michael's Church it was agreed that there should be twelve of a Building Committee, with the privilege of said twelve to add three others, if found necessary.

On motion of R. Scanlan, Henry Glass was chosen one of the committee.

On motion, Peter Scanlan was (chosen) one of the building committee.

On motion, John B. Moyer (Myers) was chosen one of the building committee on part of the Germans.

On motion, Charles Swaub (Schwab) was chosen on part of the Germans.

On motion, George Delaney was chosen one of the committee.

On motion, Patrick Shiels was chosen one of the committee.

On motion, Peter Sherry on part of the German committee.

On motion, Augustin Farabauch on part of the German committee.

On motion, Edward Glass was chosen on part of the English.

On motion, Joseph Buck was chosen on part of the committee.

On motion, Peter Forrester was chosen on part of the committee.

On motion, George Bruce was unanimously chosen one of committee.

On motion, Henry Glass and Patrick Shiels were appointed solicitors for Ebensburg and vicinity.

On motion, R. Scanlan and Peter Forrester for Summit.

On motion, Aug. Little and Peter Christy for Jefferson (Wilmore.)

On motion, Lewis Storm and Matthew Ivory for Ashland Furnace (Ashville.)

On motion, Philip Hartsock and Jos. Reighter and John N. Conrad for Hart's Sleeping Place.

On motion, Dennis Noon and John Kaylor for Munster.

ERECTION OF THE BRICK CHURCH.

(The following is copied from the original subscription list, but the names for easier reference, are placed in alphabetical order.)

We, the subscribers, promise to pay to the Building Committee, or a treasurer who may be appointed by said committee, the respective sums set opposite our names, in six equal annual instalments,— the first instalment to become due on the first day of April, A. D., 1848, and the last on the first day of April, A. D., 1853, for the erection of a Catholic Church near Loretto.

LORETTO, Cambria Co., Pa., February 17th, 1847.

Atkinson Hannah	$10 00	Bradley John (of Chas.)	$6 00
Baker John	20 00	Bradley Thomas	2 00
Barnett James	15 00	Branniff Patrick	18 00
Becher Nicholas	18 00	Brown James A.	25 00
Behe Jacob	40 00	Buck Joseph	120 00
Behe Conrad	25 00	Buck Christopher	25 00
Behe Mathias	20 00	Buck John	24 00
Beiter Caspar	25 00	Buck Henry	12 00
Bertram Francis	10 00	Buck Joseph (of Chris.)	3 00
Biller Joseph	18 00	Burke Elizabeth	10 00
Boley (Bohli) Sebastian	15 00	Byrne Henry	1 50
Bortman Peter	6 00	Campion Patrick	5 00
Bradley Charles	30 00	Carney Patrick	3 00
Bradley Roger	30 00	Christy Francis	100 00
Bradley Daniel	12 00	Christy Peter	100 00
Bradley Daniel Jr.	24 00	Christy Augustine	25 00
Bradley Dennis	12 00	Christy Samuel	5 00
Bradley William	12 00	Conrad Paul	36 00
Bradley John	12 00	Conrad John	20 00

Conrad John X	$12 00
Conrad James	18 00
Conrad Joseph	6 00
Coons John Jr	20 00
Cooper Francis	30 00
Cooper Joseph	20 00
Creaton Joseph	2 00
Criste John	30 00
Criste Robert	18 00
Criste Francis	12 00
Dawson Jerome	30 00
Delaney William	50 00
Delozier Francis	3 00
Dever Neal	18 00
Dever Cornelius	12 00
Dever William T	6 00
Donoughe Patrick	12 00
Donoughe Paul	12 00
Donoughe Cornelius	5 00
Dougherty William	1 00
Driskel Michael	60 00
Eberly Francis	9 00
Eckenrode Peter	24 00
Eckenrode Martin	15 00
Elder John	5 00
Fagan Simon	18 00
Ferenbach Aug.	30 00
Farren John	3 00
Fischer John George	35 00
Flanagan Peter, Sr	2 00
Flanagan Peter, Jr	12 00
Flanagan Joseph	25 00
Flick Charles	30 00
Flick George	12 00
Forrester Peter	50 00
Freidhoff Nicholas	12 00
Freidhoff Henry Jos.	10 00
Fry Sebastian	25 00
Gallagher Rev. Hugh P.	500 00
Gallagher Thomas	30 00
Glacken Michael	6 00
Glass Henry	100 00
Glass Edward	30 00
Grey John	24 00
Griffin John	25 00
Grimes Michael	$12 00
Hagan Thomas	15 00
Hagan John	5 00
Haid Sylvester	16 00
Hertzog Philip	40 00
Hertzog Dominic	25 00
Himmel Bruno	10 00
Hoffman John B.	18 00
Hogue Joseph	10 00
Hogue Andrew	2 00
Hoover Louis	50 00
Hoover Francis	50 00
Hott Augustine	20 00
Illig John	6 00
Ivory Patrick	50 00
Ivory Matthew	20 00
Kallis Wenceslaus	15 00
Kämpfersach Elizabeth	6 00
Kaylor Jacob	60 00
Kaylor John G	100 00
Kean Col. John	25 00
Kelly Patrick	30 00
Kelley James	10 00
Latterner Michael	20 00
Leavy Michael	100 00
Leavy James	30 00
Leavy Bernard	15 00
Leavy John T,	12 00
Lewis George	5 00
Lewis ——	5 00
Little Augustine	36 00
Little Henry	30 00
Little Catherine	18 00
Luckett John	30 00
Malloy James	12 00
Mansfield John	6 00
Mansel John	30 00
McAteer James	10 00
McAvoy Patrick	10 00
McCaffrey Dr	40 00
McCloskey James	10 00
McConnell John	12 00
McConnell Hugh	18 00
McCoy Anthony	15 00
McCoy Charles	20 00

Name	Amount	Name	Amount
McCullough John	$12 00	Sanker Anthony	$12 00
McDermitt Michael	5 00	Sanker John	12 00
McDermitt James	15 00	Sargeant James	18 00
McFeely John	3 00	Scanlan Teresa	36 00
McGlade Michael	30 00	Scanlan Richard	600 00
McGuire Mary	40 00	Scanlan John	100 00
McGuire Michael L	20 00	Scanlan Peter	30 00
McGuire Luke	12 00	Scanlan Henry	60 00
McHugh James	30 00	Schwab Charles	20 00
McHugh Matthew	15 00	Sell William	5 00
McKeever Henry	40 00	Sherry Peter	25 00
McMullen Enos C	24 00	Shields Patrick H	150 00
McMullen Samuel	25 00	Sisk John	30 00
McMullen James	50 00	Smith John	3 00
McNally P	5 00	Spain William	12 00
Melhorn Daniel	50 00	Stevens John	12 00
Meloney James	6 00	Storm Patrick	20 00
Meloy John	15 00	Storm Louis	60 00
Miller Daniel	10 00	Storm Peter	18 00
Mullen Edward	30 00	Storm David	6 00
Mullen Patrick	30 00	Storm Francis	6 00
Murphy James	12 00	Strittmatter Francis	5 00
Myers John B	40 00	Sweeny Peter	12 00
Nagle Michael	5 00	Thomas John	20 00
Neis Gabriel	1 00	Tierney Joseph	10 00
Noon Dennis	60 00	Todd James	15 00
Noon Michael	6 00	Todd Joseph A	10 00
Noon Philip Esq	25 00	Tomlinson Joseph	12 00
O'Donnell Hugh	12 00	Tomlinson William	6 00
O'Hara Thomas	20 00	Wagner John	3 00
O'Neill Henry	10 00	Walters Augustine	30 00
Parrish Peter	20 00	Watt Joseph	3 00
Parrish James	20 00	Weakland John, Sr	6 00
Parrish Thomas	50 00	Weakland John, Jr	5 00
Parrish John	6 00	Weakland Samuel	5 00
Parrish Catharine	6 00	Weakland William	25 00
Parrish John P	6 00	Weakland Simon	50 00
Pfoff Dr. Joseph	50 00	Weakland William, Jr	10 00
Phalen James	25 00	Weakland Peter	6 00
Richter Joseph	30 00	Weakland Henry	1 00
Riffell James M	20 00	Weakland Ellen	1 00
Riffell John	6 00	Wharton Catherine	20 00
Rosslein George	10 00	Whelan Philip	20 00
Sanders Peter	25 00	Will Anthony	20 00
Sanker John	20 00	Will Augustine	6 00

Will Basil	$ 5 00	Yinger James	$12 00
Will James	3 00	Zern Martin	12 00
Will John	6 00		
Will Samuel	25 00		$5,933 50

(NOTE.—The next page after the above list of subscriptions was torn from the book, and this leads to the supposition that the list as above is not complete.)

FOR THE COMPLETION OF THE CHURCH.
1853.

We, the subscribers, promise to pay to the Building Committee, or a treasurer who may be appointed by said Committee, the respective sums set opposite our names for the completion of the new Catholic Church now erected in the Borough of Loretto.

April 4th, 1853.

Adams Joseph	$ 1 00	Malloy James	5 00
Becher Samuel	5 00	Masterson Peter	5 00
Behe John	10 00	Matthews Lawrence	2 00
Behe Henry	5 00	McCoy Anthony	5 00
Buck Joseph	15 00	McHugh Matthew	5 00
Buck Wm. J	8 00	McManamy Charles	10 00
Christy Augustine	5 00	McMullen Hugh	5 00
Connery Patrick	5 00	Meloney William A	5 00
Cooper Francis	5 00	Mullen Thomas	10 00
Cramer Joseph	10 00	Murray James	5 00
Daily Joseph	20 00	Myers John	5 00
Dever Cornelius	10 00	Noon Dominic	10 00
Dever Cornelius, Jr	5 00	Noon Michael, Jr	5 00
Dever James	5 00	O'Friel Francis	10 00
Dodson William, Jr	5 00	Parrish James	10 00
Donoughe Patrick	5 00	Parrish Thomas	10 00
Eberly Francis	5 00	Sanders Peter	10 00
Elder George	10 00	Sanders Martin	1 00
Fagan Jane	5 00	Sanker Anthony	5 00
Farren Dennis	5 00	Sanker Samuel	5 00
Freidhoff John	2 00	Scanlan Richard	50 00
Fury Edward	5 00	Sherry Peter	2 00
Gallagher Daniel	6 00	Shields Patrick	10 00
Gallagher Thomas	5 00	Storm Marianne	2 00
Glass Jacob	20 00	Topper James	1 00
Glass Edward	5 00	Volk Hubert	5 00
Glass William	5 00	Walters Joseph	3 00
Gwinn William	40 00	Whelan Philip	12 00
Hogue Joseph	5 00	Yinger George	10 00
Kaylor James J	3 00		
Kelly James	20 00		$483 00

EXPENSES OF BUILDING BRICK CHURCH.

FROM OCTOBER, 1849, TO APRIL, 1854.

(Taken from the Account Book of Richard Scanlan, Contractor.)

Adams Joseph, carpenter work, etc.................................$	328 75
Adelsberger Michael, bricklaying	749 23
Behe Jacob, lath and boards...	90 00
Biller Sebastian and Anthony, labor	178 00
Bishop Valentine, mason work in full............................	4 37
Blackiston C. R., plaster and carriage (freight)................	80 17
Boards, pine, 3,500 feet..	43 75
Boley Sebastian, Oliver and Henry...............................	124 87
Bradley John C., carpenter work	8 50
Brick, making 636,000...	2,400 98
Bruce George, lumber...	327 00
Buck John, 4 men shingling	29 50
Buck Joseph, 280 feet plank for ceiling.........................	2 10
Byrne Aug., hauling brick	30 00
Carr John, lime	5 75
Carroll John, making mortar..	82 25
Christy Daniel..	10 00
Christy Peter, smith work..	79 18
Conrad John, quarrying for cut stone............................	9 00
Conrad John X., shingling...	7 50
Conrad Stephen, laborer at tower.................................	16 00
Coons John..	223 75
Coons Joseph...	17 61
Coons William..	84 00
Cramer Joseph, plastering lath.....................................	64 00
Criste John, 5,000 feet joists and hauling.....................	34 00
Crosby Michael...	58 75
Dawson Jerome, 100 bushels lime................................	22 00
Elder Richard, sawing lumber......................................	25 00
Farabaugh Andrew, mason work..................................	30 00
Fry Sebastian, glazing and turning................................	16 50
Funk James, 491 bushels of lime..................................	50 00
Gallagher Hugh, 50 bushels hair...................................	6 50
Gallagher James, lumber...	25 00
Gills Frank, 4,000 feet pine boards...............................	20 00
Glasser Francis, shingles...	150 00
Glasser George, shingles...	150 00
Goodfellow D., cast steel...	6 60
Grading grounds, in part...	8 50
Grove James, 6 wheelbarrows.....................................	16 00
Hammond Harvey, sash springs...................................	4 50
Hauling stone, lumber, lime, sand, etc..........................	816 67
Hertzog Thomas, chopping wood.................................	103 19
Hughes Ezechiel, 43 pounds nails.................................	3 87
Kane Matthew, labor..	171 43
Kelly Michael, hauling sand and plaster........................	11 55
Kelly James, smith work..	11 66
Kerrigan Michael, 5000 feet joists and hauling...............	37 50

Kittell Samuel, 1 wheelbarrow..................................$	4 50
Lime, 1,580 bushel and hauling..................................	316 00
Linseed oil, 6 gallons...	5 85
Little Sylvester, carpenter work.................................	658 72
Little Edward J., carpenter work................................	54 25
Litzinger Wm., lumber, hauling and mdse..................	81 92
Locks, 3 heavy...	9 00
Maloney James, cutting glass......................................	5 00
Masons and tenders...	227 68
McCoy Anthony, quarrying for cut stone.....................	102 18
McCullough John, quarrying for cut stone...................	36 75
McDevitt John & Co., spades and shovels...................	12 25
McGough Peter, 3,500 feet lumber and hauling..........	36 75
McGuire Michael, sawing lumber.................................	35 00
McGuire Michael L., hauling..	156 26
McKee S. & Co., 12 boxes of glass and carriage..........	51 00
McMullen Matthew, 1,000 feet lumber.........................	10 00
Melhorn Peter..	91 81
Meloy John, stone privilege..	10 00
Moore Johnston, lumber and hauling..........................	33 00
Moyer Martin, paint and painting................................	349 65
Moyer Michael, 325 bushels lime and hauling.............	70 00
Nagle Jacob, hauling sand and boards........................	55 75
Nails, 3 kegs and carriage...	13 50
Null Joseph, architect and carpentering.....................	695 75
Onslow John, carpentering...	20 75
Quarrying rubble stone...	181 02
Rhey, Matthews & Co., nails and carriage..................	128 01
Roberts Edward, nails, screws, etc..............................	54 19
Royer & McNeal, 6 kegs nails.......................................	27 00
Rudolph Adam, laborer at tower..................................	28 00
Scanlan H., gears..	13 00
Sell William, mason work in full..................................	5 00
Shaffner Caspar, carrying tools to be sharpened........	15 00
Shiels Patrick, lumber, etc...	66 58
Singer William, spouting and repairing......................	72 12
Smeltzer Peter, quarrying for cut stone............$90 81	
" " hauling lime, sand, etc.......... 49 50	
	140 31
Smith Haden..	2 00
Smith George, sharpening tools...................................	9 56
Stoy Samuel, 7,540 feet lumber....................................	64 09
Thompson John, stained glass and carriage...............	9 25
Toole James, laying brick..	25 00
Trebus Bartholomew, stone cutting................$835 13	
" " boarding men at quarry.......... 26 18	
	861 31
Urban Peter, block and tackle.....................................	18 00
Walters Aug., smith work...	162 48
Water barrels...	3 50
Will Samuel, Jr., sawing lumber, etc...........................	64 22
Young & Morris, plastering..	1,120 71
Sundry small bills...	34 95
	$13,024 10

ITEMS FROM THE CHURCH ACCOUNT BOOKS.

DECEMBER 11, 1848.

Received from Mr. Henry Glass, treasurer of the new Catholic Church at Loretto, the sum of Seventy-Three Dollars, being the amount of Order No. 1 from Building Committee for services as architect. $ 73 00

HADEN SMITH.

Receipts and expenditures of St. Mary's (St. Michael's) Church at Loretto. From commencement (of subscription) up to February 28th, 1857, inclusive.

Henry Glass, treasurer. Peter Scanlan, Augustine Little, Henry Glass and others, collectors for same.

(Totals only are given here.)

Total expenditures $ 13,495 56
Total receipts 13,412 50

By balance at settlement $ 83 06

We, the undersigned, do certify that the above statement is correct to the best of our knowledge.

Witness our hands. F. O'FRIEL, } Auditors.
February 28th, 1857. JOSEPH HOGUE, }

(Among the items on the *Dr.* side is the following:—)

To total amount paid on subscription $ 6,720 08.

(The following is not signed, but is copied from the handwriting of Rev. Jos. A. Gallagher, the then pastor.)

LORETTO, September 20th, 1854.

A settlement was this day made between Richard Scanlan and the Building Committee of the new Catholic Church, in which it appears that said Building Committee owe said

Richard Scanlan, contractor for said church, at this date the sum of Three Thousand and Twenty-Eight Dollars.

$ 3,028

Up to that date R. Scanlan had given receipts on his contract for 10,080 22

Making the cost of the building $ 13,108 22

January 23, 1856.

Received of Henry Glass, treasurer of new church at Loretto, in part of contract, One Thousand and Ten Dollars, Thirty-three Cents.

$ 1,010 33. R. Scanlan.

(On same date, Father Pollard notes: "Bal. now due. $ 2,017 67.")

January 23, 1856.

Received of Henry Glass, Tr., of new church, One Hundred Eighty-two Dollars Thirty-one Cents, in full of interest on balance due me on the settlement with the Building Committee, dated September 20, 1854.

$182 31. R. Scanlan.

(This was his last receipt recorded in the committee's book. He died June 9, 1857.)

January 4, 1863.

Balance due estate of Richard Scanlan, deceased, as ascertained by statement furnished by Mrs. C. Scanlan per her attorney, W. Kittell, Esq. $ 681 57.

November 30, 1868.

On this day Mrs. C. E. Scanlan, the above named party, told me that she was paid in full.

F. O'Friel.

The Finance Committee in the year 1862 was composed of the following:

> Rev. T. S. Reynolds, President.
> Jerome Dawson, Treasurer.
> Philip Hertzog.
> Thomas Gallagher.
> John Bradley, Secretary.

Rev. Father (P. McC.) Morgan commenced as Assistant Pastor of St. Mary's Church, 15th October, 1864, at salary of $300 per annum.

(Note.—The brick church was dedicated to the Blessed Virgin under the title of "St. Mary;" the original title, that of "St. Michael," patron of the parish from its foundation, was subsequently restored.)

1867. May 19. Indebtedness of St. Mary's Church, $1,100 00
1869. Jan. 7.   "   "   "   "   "   832 05

ITEMS FROM THE ACCOUNT BOOK OF RICHARD SCANLAN, CONTRACTOR AND BUILDER OF THE BRICK CHURCH.

1853. May 20. P. Shiels got the postoffice. Paid him the postage—52 cts. in advance—on two papers from Pittsburg—"The Catholic," and "The Iron City."

EXPENSES OF SINKING A WELL AT NEW CHURCH—1851.

Joseph Tomlinson and Peter Flick	$6 00
Boarding same	3 50
James Miller and Peter Melhorn	8 00
" " " " " for boarding	6 00
" " " " " walling well	2 00
John and Richard Griffith	21 00
" " " " for boarding	4 00
" " " " for powder	8 00

Peter Christy & Co., pump irons, 50 lbs.	$ 6 33
Pine timber for pump	3 00
Cost R. Scanlan	$67 83
Amount received towards well (see below)	22 14½
	$45 68½
Had to pay Joseph Idel since	7 00
Cost R. Scanlan	$52 68½

COLLECTION FOR WELL.

Adams Jos.	$ .50	Melhorn Peter	$ .25
Adelsberger Michael	.25	McGough James	.25
Bradley Matthew	.25	McGuire Michael L.	.50
Buck Joseph	.50	McMullen Enos C.	.50
Christy Peter	.50	Miller James	.50
Conrad Paul	.25	Moyer Jno B.	.25
Coons John	.50	O'Donnell James	.25
Coons William	.25	Parrish George	.50
Crain Robert	.25	Pfoff Dr. Joseph	1.00
Delany George	.25	Sanker John, Sr.	.25
Elder Richard	.25	Scanlan John	1.00
Flick Peter	.25	Scanlan Mrs. Teresa	.50
Flick Francis	.10	Scanlan Henry	.50
Gallagher Rev. H. P.	5.00	Scanlan Peter	.50
Gallagher Rev. Jos. A.	1.00	Scanlan Miss Teresa	.50
Gallagher Daniel	.50	Shiels Patrick	.50
Glass John	.50	Stehle Adam	.25
Kelly James	.50	Walters Augustine	.92
Little Augustine	1.00	Yahner Michael	.25
Little Sylvester	.12½		
Little Edward J.	.25		$22.14½

LORETTO, June 1850.

Memorandum of men who worked at the digging of foundation, and of inspectors who came to examine the foundation and work.

Amongst the most famous was Francis Christy who said in presence of Valentine Bishop, William Sell and ———— it was the solidest foundation he ever saw.

Peter Christy, A. Little also examined. Peter Forrester, John C. Bradley, John Baker, John ————, Michael Yoner, Al. Sanker, Joseph Adams (were) all day at the foundation.

Masons, Peter Sherry, Augustine Farabaugh, Valentine Bishop and William Sell, who did the work in the months of June and July (1850.)

David Trexler saw and examined the foundation. It was so solid that a man could not sink a heavy, sharpened pick more than one inch.

Joseph Tomlinson, Michael Yoner, Peter Flick, Jr., and Al. Sanker dug out the tower foundation. Augustine Christy said in their presence that it was the solidest foundation he ever saw. He tried it with a heavy crowbar and could not sink it one inch.

1850, September 11th. Had the brick inspected by Michael Adelsberger, John Carr and James Tool, who pronounced them good.

1851, May 13th. Commenced laying brick. The bricklayers were Michael Adelsberger and son Matthew, James Tool, John McMullen, Peter Shiels, George Lewis and Michael Shiels, who pronounced the brick to be of good size and quality.

1851, May 20th. Rev. H. P. Gallagher had Jerome Dawson to examine the brick and work. He proved all good, and said that he could break a wagon load of the Summit Church brick with one brick of the fourth course down from top of kiln.

1852, March 3rd. Haden Smith, Esq., examined brick and work of new Catholic Church, and pronounced brick to be good and well laid. To A. Little, D. Melhorn and M. Adelsberger he said the tower was put up too fast.

1852, July 3rd. Building Committee and Rev. H. P. Gallagher had the architect from Pittsburg, Mr. Bargeburger (Bartberger) who examined all the work and pronounced it good. Said the tower could be rebuilt without taking down any brick.

(During the progress of the work the Building Committee changed some parts of the plans, in consequence of which Richard Scanlan makes out a bill for extras not set forth in the specifications, amounting to $1,250.92.)

THE LORETTO JAIL. DILAPIDATED FOR WANT OF USE. REMOVED FROM PUBLIC VIEW A FEW DAYS BEFORE THE CENTENARY.

Loretto, January, 1856.

The coldest weather on record. Thermometer 20 degrees below zero frequently; from 10 to 12 commonly. About eight feet of snow fell at different times; drifted so as to close all the roads; no thawing from Christmas to April 1st, making some four months of continual freezing. April commenced beautiful overhead, with about 16 inches of snow where it had not drifted. Drifts about 15 feet high. People crossed stake-and-rider fences (on the snow) on 10th of April.

April 13th. The greatest storm on record, unroofing almost every other barn and tearing some down to the foundation. It tore part of the roof off both churches, and tore down the Missionary Cross planted 1851, which was 15x12 inches at the ground.

May 30th. Snowed in the afternoon; wind, cold weather. Very hard frost on following morning.

CARROLLTOWN AND VICINITY.

CONTRIBUTED BY A BENEDICTINE FATHER.

About one-half mile south of the present St. Benedict's Church, Carrolltown, on the northern slope of the "old Loretto Road" were seen until recent years the ruins of buildings erected at the beginning of this century by a colony of Trappist monks. Towards the end of the last century they were driven from their home in Europe by the storms of the revolution then raging; and first fled to Switzerland, from which country, threatened by the French, they went to Russia, thence to Prussia; and at last a small band of them under the guidance of Rev. Urban Guillet came to the place above described. It seems though that our severe winter climate did not agree with them; so in June, 1805, they abandoned their settlement and went to Kentucky.

Under the direction of Father Gallitzin a church dedicated to St. Joseph was erected about 1830, or somewhat earlier, at a spot three miles north of Carrolltown called Hart's Sleeping Place. Father Gallitzin visited this church at stated times until the care of his own congregation at Loretto compelled him in 1834 to give it in charge to his new assistant, Rev. P. H. Lemke. It was the earnest wish of Father Gallitzin to have in this place a second Loretto, an entirely Catholic settlement. Accordingly in 1836 Father Lemke bought a tract of 400 acres three miles south of St. Joseph's, and built thereon a small log house,—the lower story being cellar and spring-house, the upper a dwelling room and kitchen. About twenty paces to the east he erected a small chapel, where the inhabitants of the incipient Carrolltown heard mass on week days. On Sundays, however, mass was said in St. Joseph's until the summer of 1850.

On September 30th, 1846, Father Boniface Wimmer on the invitation of Father Lemke, came to Carrolltown, which was originally intended as the site of the first monastery of the Benedictine Order in the United States. But Rt. Rev. M. O'Connor, Bishop of Pittsburg, persuaded Father Wimmer to give up this plan, and to locate at "Sportman's Hall," the site of the present St. Vincent Abbey, forty miles east of Pittsburg.

In the summer of 1848 the Benedictines bought from Father Lemke his tract of land, the latter going to Reading, Pa., and the charge of the congregation at Carrolltown was transferred to them, and has been held by them ever since. The corner-stone of the new church was laid on the Sunday within the Octave of Corpus Christe, 1849, by Bishop O'Conner. About the same time a little church was erected in Glen Connell (St. Lawrence's). The church in Carrolltown was dedicated by Rev. Father Celestine, O. S. B., on Christmas Day, 1850, just fifty-one years after the dedication of the first church at Loretto, nine miles distant.

Subsequently, other churches were erected in the vicinity, viz.: St. Boniface's at St. Boniface, St. Nicholas' at Nicktown, St. Bernard's at Hastings, Holy Cross at Spangler and St. Mary's at Patton: all of which are in charge of Benedictine pastors.

ST. FRANCIS' COLLEGE, LORETTO, PA.

SAINT FRANCIS' COLLEGE, LORETTO, PA.

CONTRIBUTED BY A FRANCISCAN BROTHER.

This institution, situated on an elevation some distance west of Loretto, and almost hidden by a stately growth of pines, was founded by the first Bishop of the diocese, Rt. Rev. Michael O'Connor, of holy memory, in the year of our Lord, 1847. It has been conducted by the Brothers of the Regular Third Order of Saint Francis since its very humble foundation.

The first little band, six in number, who responded to the earnest solicitation of the illustrious Bishop, came from the country whose children are scattered all over the world— poor, persecuted Ireland—in order to carry on the pious works they were engaged in, especially that of imparting a Christian education to youth.

By a Rescript dated November 12, 1848, Our Holy Father, Pius IX, granted to Bishop O'Connor all the faculties necessary to establish a community of the Regular Third Order at Loretto, and to ensure its religious and canonical character, ordaining that it should be subject to the ordinary of the diocese, *pro tempore*.

The Brothers had much to contend with from the beginning. The means at their disposal were very limited; they were practically unacquainted with the nature of the soil, mode of tillage, and customs of their adopted country; and they had no inducements to offer any one who wished to join the Order but hard labor, scanty fare, and a promise of something better in the distant future.

Having before them the example of humble fishermen, who formed the first religious community, the Brothers never dreamed of failure in what they had undertaken for the glory of God; and, no matter what trials might be in store for them, they were determined to hew their way through ebon darkness to light. They had been taught that God often makes use of the most lowly to accomplish great things, despite the wagging of wise heads and the suggestions of worldly prudence.

The tract of land assigned the Brothers had been farmed out for years, so that whatever fertility might have been in it had long since been taken out of it; and not a little labor would be required to make it even moderately productive. Nothing in the shape of buildings fit for man or beast had ever been erected, and the Brothers were obliged to take up their abode in a log house kindly offered them in the village. The oldest brother was chosen Superior, and regular observance, as far as practicable, was at once established.

A piece of ground joining the land already given on which a frame building had been erected, was purchased by the Brothers soon after they came to the settlement; the house was deemed suitable for a temporary habitation, though it had done service as a brewery, and six months after their arrival they were able to date their letters from Saint Francis' Monastery, at Loretto. The old brewery was infested with rats; indeed, these rodents, considering the place their own private property, resented the intrusion of the monks and could not be induced by any manner of flattery or coercion to leave.

I may write of the little community the exact words Archbishop Spalding used in speaking of the Trappists who were beginning their now famous Abbey of Gethsemani in Kentucky the same year under more favorable auspices, and having fewer difficulties to contend with.

"Their penitential austerities seem almost incredible to this age of boasted progress and enlightenment, as well as of boundless self-indulgence. Their vigorous lives astonish the worldling, who can appreciate nothing which does not contribute to material progress and enjoyment; they are a matter of admiration for all true Christians, who, enlightened by Christian faith, are able to estimate the awful malice of sin and the absolute necessity of penance. He who himself led a poor and hard life, and who said to his disciples, 'If any one will come after me, let him deny himself, take up his cross, and follow me,' must look down with a smile of complacency on those pious recluses, who, to expiate their own and others' sins, devote themselves for love of Him to a life of such severe privations.

"Yet in the midst of their hard labor and penitential austerities these good monks are remarkably cheerful and happy. The peace of God, surpassing all understanding, beams constantly from their countenances and they enjoy more peace of mind and more heartfelt happiness than many who, reposing in the midst of luxury, deride their lives as mere folly and fanaticism."

The Brothers immediately began preparations for the erection of the College. All set to work with alacrity; the Superior encouraging the others by his own example not to lose one precious moment, but to labor whilst it was yet day, for the night cometh when no man can work. Young and old, noble and plebeian, learned and unlearned, took pleasure in giving a helping hand to rear a structure wherein the youth of the future might obtain a Christian education.

In a short time space was cleared, the dimensions staked off, and the earth excavated for the foundation. Stones fit for the basement wall were procured without much trouble, and clay suitable for making bricks was to be found quite convenient. The corner-stone was laid by Bishop O'Connor, the firm, life-long friend of the Brothers, on August 23, 1849, in the presence of an immense throng of people, who had come from the village in solemn procession headed by the reverend clergy.

Very few men understood the fundamental principles and purposes of education better than our first illustrious Bishop; hence the discourse he delivered on that memorable day was a masterpiece of its kind, and it made a lasting impression on the minds of those who had the good fortune to be present. He showed the good results which might be expected from the efforts of men who had severed all earthly ties to devote themselves to the special service of the young. The value of education is incalculable, but it must be understood in its completest sense as the full and harmonious development of all those faculties that are distinctive to man. It is not, therefore, mere instruction or the communication of knowledge. In fact, the acquisition of knowledge, though it necessarily accompanies any right system of education, is a secondary result of education. Learning is an instrument of education, not its end. The end is culture and mental and moral development.

The good, simple Superior did not give much attention to plans and specifications. He had a model made of the kind of building he would like to have erected, and when the artisans came to work on the superstructure he pointed to the model and told them to follow that. Not very definite instructions, surely. The Brothers performed much of the work which did not require skilled labor. They quarried the stone, collected the sand along the public roads, and hauled all the material, sometimes from a distance of fourteen miles. The employment of many hired hands was out of the question; hence the Brothers were obliged to put all the joists and heavy timbers in place, and in some instances to relieve a hod-carrier who might become exhausted from the excessive heat. Their assiduity and constant cheerfulness was a revelation to those who had heard so many stories about the idle, selfish monks.

The work was pushed on with such vigor that a good, substantial brick building was ready for the community early in the summer of the following year; and the 2d of August, a day which is always remembered by every true Franciscan, was appointed for the celebration of the first holy mass in the modest little chapel. Bishop O'Connor preached on the occasion, and expressed the satisfaction he felt at seeing the Brothers prepared to carry on the object he had most at heart—the education of Catholic boys.

The good Pastor of St. Michael's Church in Loretto, Rev. Hugh P. Gallagher, had announced the coming event from the altar on the previous Sunday, inviting all to go over to St. Francis', where they might gain the indulgence of Portiuncula, provided all the conditions prescribed were fulfilled. As this indulgence can be gained more than once on the same day, the small chapel was not often without devout worshipers during the whole day.

The part of the house set apart for school purposes was fitted up for the reception of students, and the classes were started in September. It was an easy matter to accommodate the few who applied for admission at first; but in a short time, owing to the increase of students and the number of candidates for the order, a new building, forty by seventy, two stories high, had to be erected. Addition followed addition, and improvements were made year after year, even to the present time, when the College with the outbuildings covers more than an acre of ground.

In the process of time the waste spot on which the Brothers had settled underwent a complete transformation: a little world populous with busy life sprang up in its midst, and far and near in its vicinity the briars and bushes were grubbed up, and the barren soil coaxed back to its original fertility. Arbor Day had not yet been inaugurated and the monks did not wait for the Governor's proclamation to begin planting trees: for one would think they bound themselves by rule to plant two trees every time they cut one down; and to this cheap and charming act of benevolence we are indebted for the cluster of pines which rear their heads higher than the cross on the main building, and shut out noise and bustle from the monastery.

In 1856 the Brothers felt themselves strong enough to petition the Legislature for a charter. They were prepared for a severe test of their literary abilities or a scorching exam, as the boys would express it; but they never dreamed that their religious belief would be used as a pretext for withholding the privilege of conferring degrees, especially since the petitioners asked for no exclusive favors, for no patronage, for no unusual power, for nothing incompatible with the policy of our legislation, but simply for what the Legislature was in the habit of granting every day. When the bill came up in the House it met with much opposition; but the friends of the College, particularly Mr. Foster who had reported it, by generous and staunch support gained the day by a majority of one. The commotion that was raised about entrapping the blue-eyed youth of Cambria and the neighboring counties under pretense of giving a classical and scientific education, caused the Brothers to have the petition withdrawn; but the charter was obtained two years later without any trouble at all.

It would be truly a labor of love, as suggested by the present Rector of Saint Michael's Church, Reverend Ferdinand Kittell, to give biographical sketches of the first Brothers who labored so long and faithfully at Saint Francis; but these good simple-minded men have taken care to do away with anything which might be used for that purpose. They had indeed renounced kith and kin when joining the Order, which was to be for them henceforth all the world most prizes, wealth, name and fame.

The College has been blessed with excellent resident priests from its foundation. They have always shown themselves the true guides, philosophers and friends of the religious and students; and though they had to endure many inconveniences at times, they never failed in the faithful discharge of their duties.

The alumni of Saint Francis' College are to be found in every State of the Union, and many of them have attained eminence in Church and State. The College, like a fond mother, watches with jealous eye the career of all her children, and she is amply rewarded for all her care when it can be said of each cherished son:

> "He moved, a man among his fellow-men,
> And they beheld a man whose eyes and brow
> Looked up and onward, as tho' there and then
> He made his faith, and to his faith did vow
> Full concord and submission, modest worth
> And noble aspiration, gentle heart,
> Where Charity seemed constant in its birth
> And blessed all near."

Dear old St. Francis' has passed the half century mark of its existence but it shows no decrease of youth or vigor; doomed to death it has been, time and again, though fated not to die. At times the raging tempest threatened to engulf the frail bark, and a few faint-hearted ones, unmindful of the Master's "Why are you fearful, O ye of little faith," having grown weary of battling with the waves, gave up the fight; but, He arising, rebuked the wind and the raging of the water, and it ceased, and there came a great calm.

THE CHILDREN'S HOME, FORMERLY ST. ALOYSIUS' ACADEMY, LORETTO, PA.
CONDUCTED BY SISTERS OF MERCY.

A SKETCH OF THE ORDER OF MERCY IN LORETTO.

CONTRIBUTED BY A SISTER OF MERCY.

More than a golden cycle of years has woven its myriad changes into the world's history since first the black-robed figure of the Sister of Mercy appeared in "Our Lady's Village" on the mountain-top. When the sainted prince-priest saw the result of his heroic self-sacrifice,—thousands of sturdy, upright Christians living brave and earnest lives of faith and industry,—transforming the well-nigh inaccessible mountain wilderness into a dwelling-place of peace and pleasure,—then it was his zealous heart longed for religious to instruct the little ones of his flock; and so perpetuate his work. But the iron horse and the more potent electric power had not as yet almost annihilated space. Methods of travel and communication with friends at a distance were matters of primitive simplicity and slowness. This and other reasons delayed the advent of the Sisters; and so it happened that, when, on that cool May evening in 1840, the noble soul of Gallitzin quitted the scene of his earthly labors, his earnest desire was yet unfulfilled,—there were no religious among the devoted flock who mourned the loss of Father and friend. Yet the time of their coming was not far distant. Three years later, Bishop Michael O'Conner, when conducting the pioneer Sisters of Mercy from Philadelphia to Pittsburg promised a branch at Loretto. And in fulfillment of this promise he sent out from Pittsburg a devoted little band of four Sisters in May, 1848.

Sister M. Catherine Wynne was named first local superior. This estimable lady was of Irish parentage. She entered St. Mary's Convent, Pittsburg, on February 4th, 1845, and was professed March 22nd, 1847. She remained at Loretto for more than a year. The last six years of her life were spent in Baltimore, where she died September 28th, 1861.

Her first companions in Loretto were Sisters M. Augusta Goold, M. Rose Hosteller and M. Lucy McGivern.

The journey from Pittsburg, then of necessity by stage, occupied a day and a night. Reaching Ebensburg the party of four was hospitably received at the home of Mrs. Shoemaker. After a short rest they proceeded down the old road to Loretto. It was Father Hugh Gallagher who received them in their bleak mountain home. The first unpretentious abode of the Sisters (as tradition has painted it) was, in its humble appointments, not unlike that other Loreto of sacred memory in the far sunny east. For two or three years a small frame dwelling in the village sufficed to shelter them. Tradition is rich in anecdotes of the hardships of the first winter on the mountain-top, when food and fuel were not always at hand, and the sturdy mountaineers, while ever grateful for the tender, self-sacrificing ministrations of the Sisters, often forgot that their quiet, unobtrusive lives needed other support than prayer and teaching. But they were unflagging in their zeal and earnestness; and all the while the tiny "mustard-seed" was taking root,—deep and firm enough to resist all mountain tempests,—and to send forth noble branches,—high and wide enough to shelter not the "birds of the air" but the precious human flowers that were to blossom 'neath its protecting shadow.

Mother M. Gertrude Blake was the second superior; Mother M. Stanislaus the third; Mother M. Regis the fourth, and Sister M. Christina Newman the fifth. It was during her administration that the Sisters moved from their frame dwelling into the present convent, and called it St. Aloysius'.

Towards the close of the last century Captain McGuire, "the first white man that settled in what is now Cambria County," gave to Bishop Carroll, for church purposes a tract of land of four hundred acres. On part of this the present Convent is built. It is a substantial brick structure, surrounded by a spacious and well-kept grounds. On all sides the noble pines keep sentinel-like guard, and whisper secrets with the softest summer zephyr, and moan in sympathy with winter blasts. Out beyond the pine-trees there are on both sides mementos of Loretto's noble founder; to the north the brick church and his monument; to the south the cemetery and the old stone chapel.

The convent attained its present proportions not all at once: but additions were made from time to time, as the needs of the boarding school increased. In 1875, on account of its distance from Pittsburg, the Bishop of the diocese erected the Loretto community into an independent Motherhouse. The Academy had now grown to important proportions: the Sisters had charge also of the village public schools. At the present time they have in various parts of the diocese seven branch houses engaged in active work.

Meantime the requirements of the boarding school at Loretto were constantly increasing. Most gratifying was the educational success which attended the institution. In order to give the students every advantage and convenience afforded by modern architectural improvements, a piece of land of thirty-five acres, on an eminence opposite the Mountain House at Cresson Springs, was purchased in 1891. Later, plans were devised for a building which would in every feature suit the requirements of an Academy. The result is most satisfactory. The attention of the visitor to Cresson is at once attracted by the picturesque symmetrical building, simple in outline, massive and graceful in form, and refined in detail. The entire length of the front is two hundred and twenty feet, with a wing of one hundred and eighty feet. Entering the building through the main center entrance, a spacious vestibule, with an Italian mosaic floor opens on both sides to the arched cloister or loggia, and gives admittance to the main hall. This is panelled in oak, and the ceiling is heavily beamed in the same wood. The spacious corridor crossing the entrance hall intersects with corridors extending down the center of the wings. The building throughout is finished in natural woods and hard wood floors. It is warmed by steam, and at night made brilliant by electricity.

THE CHILDREN'S HOME, FORMERLY ST. ALOYSIUS' ACADEMY, LORETTO.

On the fifteenth of June, 1897, the Sisters took possession of this most complete of modern schools, the new Mount Aloysius. The success and blessing which have ever rested on the efforts of the Loretto Sisters, seem to be with them here: and each year finds numbers of young women, happy inmates of the Academy, enjoying its many advantages, and under the wise, firm training of the Sisters, forming mind and heart and character to fill their respective places in the world as noble Christian women.

Since the boarding school has been transferred to Cresson, the spacious Loretto Convent grounds serve the double purpose of a Novitiate and a home for children. There are at present about thirty little ones who are here being taught and cared for.

The number of Sisters now in the community including novices, is eighty-five.

In taking this rapid glance over the history of the Order of Mercy in Loretto, one cannot but note its almost phenomenal growth; and although there have been hours and moments of sadness and trial (for what human life was ever exempt from these?) yet through all is manifest the special protection of Divine Providence over those who nobly work for God on the spot consecrated by the labors of the sainted Father Gallitzin.

REMINISCENCES OF FATHER LEMKE.

CONTRIBUTED BY HON. JAS. J. THOMAS.

Rev. Peter Henry Lemke, the immediate successor of the illustrious Father Gallitzin in the pastorate of St. Michael's Church, Loretto, was born in the town of Mecklenburg-Rhena, Germany, July 27, 1796. All the members of his family were Lutherans, and they seem to have been distinguished in the middle class of German citizens for their wealth and superior educational attainments. His father filled the position of village magistrate—an honorable one in that country. His mother was the daughter of a schoolmaster; hence it may be inferred that she was an educated woman. It seems from his autobiography that his early religious training had been very much neglected. His father's time being mostly taken up with official duties, and his mother being sickly and apparently indifferent or careless as to the future of her son, it is not to be wondered at that in his youth he knew little, and cared less, about religion. Fortunately his grandfather and an old physician who boarded with the family, took some pains to imbue his mind with some little knowledge of the eternal truths. He early developed extraordinary talents; and being studious, he, with the assistance of his grandfather and the old physician, acquired even in his early youth a considerable amount of knowledge.

Much as religion was neglected in his own family it was even more so in those evil days in the great world around him, so that his associations and environment were not calculated to imbue his mind with religious principles. But these adverse conditions could not suppress the innate religious instincts of his nature, or, rather, could not alter the destiny of one fore-ordained to carry the saving and consoling truths of Faith to his wandering and neglected fellow countrymen and others on the mountains and amid the primeval forests of faraway North America.

Reverses in his father's business affairs made it impossible for him to acquire an education at home, so he resolved to run away and search for it elsewhere. He went to Schweren where there was a good school, applied for admission, and, after a successful examination, was admitted as a student, supporting himself by giving lessons in music. This was in 1810.

While at Schweren he became acquainted with a Catholic family who persuaded him to attend church with them. This was his first opportunity of becoming acquainted with Catholics or their religion. By listening to the sermons and observing the pious and moral conduct of his Catholic acquaintances he soon became so deeply impressed that he could often be seen during services kneeling and praying with devotion.

He continued in this school until 1813, when war broke out between France and Germany. Although only 18 years of age, Lemke, with many other students, responded to the call to arms to repel the French invaders under Napoleon, and he remained in the service of his country until the close of the war. He belonged to the cavalry, and his training in the army made him a wonderfully expert and fearless horseman. It was his delight, during his career as a missionary, to give to the admiring settlers exhibitions of his skill in riding and subduing wild and untrained colts.

The writer had once the privilege of witnessing one of these exhibitions in the little town of Munster. Father Lemke was on his way to Jefferson (now Wilmore), and stopped for dinner at the tavern kept by Peter Collins. When the time came for him to resume his journey, the horse, a spirited young sorrel, was brought out in front of the tavern in readiness for the priest to mount. From the

MUNSTER. FOUNDED AS A RIVAL TO LORETTO IN 1806.

actions and appearance of the animal the bystanders judged that this would be no easy matter; yet Father Lemke, taking the reins from the hostler and refusing all proffered assistance, jumped like a flash into the saddle. Then commenced the display of horsemanship. The animal had apparently

REAR VIEW OF ST. MICHAEL'S PASTORAL RESIDENCE, CHURCH AND PAROCHIAL HALL, LORETTO, PA. — 1899.

made up his mind that he would throw Father Lemke, and that he would not go to Jefferson that day; yet during the whole scene of rearing, plunging and kicking the priest maintained his seat in the saddle as if he were glued to it, all the time refusing to permit any of the spectators, who feared for his safety, to interfere. Despite the determination of the horse to have his own way he was compelled to yield to the stronger will and superior skill of his master; and eventually both he and his rider disappeared in a cloud of dust on the road to Jefferson.

After receiving his discharge from the army young Lemke entered the University of Rastock in order to prepare himself for the Lutheran ministry. Of his life in this school he writes: "But I did not study much, and I thank God that I did not, for the teaching of theology was of that sort that all sentiments of Christianity must have been extinguished in my soul then and there. We had professors of theology who would not blush to ridicule before an audience of beardless youths the most sacred mysteries of religion." As for the life of the students it was nothing but continuous rioting, gambling, dueling and drinking. Lemke was like the other students he describes, but for a short time only. Fortunately he became acquainted with a Catholic student named Adler, older than himself, who had also been a soldier. They became intimate friends, and Lemke placed himself under his tuition. Adler prescribed for his young friend a course of reading which, with the close intimacy that grew up between them, resulted, later on, in the latter's conversion to the Catholic faith.

In 1819 he finished his studies, passed his examination and was admitted to the ministry of the Lutheran Church. He went to his native village of Rhena to preach his first sermon, which, despite the trepidation that overcame him in the beginning, is said to have been a very eloquent one.

While he was assistant he found in the library of his superior some old writings of Luther, and asked permission, which was readily granted, to take them to his rooms. With all the ardor of a religious student wearied of unsettled beliefs, he pored over these works. When he had finished reading the last volume he had nothing but contempt, as he says, for the reformer: in fact, he was no longer a Lutheran. True to his conception of conscientious duty he resigned his position, although by this action he was left without any means of a livelihood.

What was now to be done? He might enter the professions, any one of which by his talents and education he was fitted to adorn, or embark in commercial life and succeed, but to none of these did he turn for his vocation. He must first satisfy his determined purpose to find truth, if it was to be found, in religion, and afterwards subscribe to its practices.

He thought of his Catholic friend of the University—Adler, but before seeking him began again with stubborn patience a thorough research through the Prostestant field of doctrine. But the further he went, and the more he investigated the teachings and practices of the various sects, the more he was convinced that for conviction and peace he must look elsewhere. He renounced forever all adherence to Protestant belief and set out to seek Adler.

He found him at Ratisbon, was graciously received, and the same evening was introduced to Diepenbrock. Diepenbrock, like Lemke, had been in the army, and was in his youth somewhat careless in religion, but from reading Bishop Sailer's works he saw the error of his ways, and from that time had become a most zealous religious teacher.

Being of the same age and their previous lives having been in many ways similar, they naturally became warm friends. After months of association with Adler and Diepenbrock, who meanwhile had become a priest, Lemke found himself in belief a Catholic, and applied to Bishop Sailer for instruction and admission into the Church. The Bishop sent him to the Seminary to receive the necessary instructions under its saintly rector, Father Wittman. On the 21st of April, 1824, he was received into the Church and confirmed by Bishop Sailer, his friend, Father Diepenbrock, being his godfather. Bishop Sailer, fully understanding the religious character of young Lemke, sent him to one of his old priests in the country to take a course in theology. He made such progress that on the 11th of April, 1826, he was ordained to the priesthood, less than two years after his reception into the Church. After his ordination Father Lemke served for three years under his old preceptor, Father Buchner, as assistant.

In 1829 his friend, now Cardinal Diepenbrock, called him to Ratisbon, where he was made Vicar and intrusted with the duties of preaching to the garrison of the city and giving religious instruction to the students of the high schools. In 1831 Father Lemke was, on the recommendation of his Bishop, appointed chaplain to one of the great old churches on the estate of a rich nobleman.

This was a very desirable position, with large salary and little to do, but in no way satisfactory to the missionary spirit of Lemke, for, as he says himself, the duties entailed the care of the agricultural interests of the estate more than of the souls of men. However, these agricultural experiences of Neuberg did much to make him the successful farmer he afterwards proved, and stood him in good stead in developing the lands of his various settlements in America.

During the fall of 1833, while engaged in superintending the work in a vineyard on the estate, he received a visit from his friends Diepenbrock, Clement Bretano and Dr. Raes. During the conversation Dr. Raes read a letter from Bishop Kenrick, in which he deplored the lack of German priests in his diocese.

"This would be something for you, Lemke," said Bretano, sarcastically: "a young man endowed, soul and body, with all required for a laborer in the vineyard of the Lord, and here you are like an article of luxury growing fat and lusty whilst our poor Catholics in America starve for want of spiritual food." This remark gave to America one of her most zealous and successful missionaries. On the spot all his impulsive nature was aroused and he resolved to go to America.

In the spring of 1834, after completing all his arrangements, armed with his passport, a letter from Dr. Raes to

Bishop Kenrick, and his Bishop's Exeat, he started for the United States.

Sending his baggage ahead he started on foot with a knapsack on his back for Paris, expecting to find there means of transport to Havre, the port he meant to depart from. When he arrived at Havre he found a packet ready to sail for New York, but to his discomfiture his baggage had not yet arrived, which delayed him for a considerable time. What must have been his feelings, when, arrived at New York, he learned that the packet he had missed, with all on board, had been lost at sea. He reached New York August 20, 1834, and a few days after took a steamer for Philadelphia.

On reaching the city he went to the house of Rev. Mr. Guth, who, the same evening took him to the house of the Bishop. Bishop Kenrick was delighted at his coming and forthwith appointed him assistant at Holy Trinity Church. He soon found it necessary to acquire a knowledge of the English language. Fortunately for him Bishop Kenrick and his brother were engaged in the study of the German language. Father Lemke went daily to the Bishop's house and exchanging service with his illustrious pupils, gave lessons in German, receiving from them in return instruction in English.

An incident happened while he was assistant that caused him to leave Philadelphia. He used to enjoy telling the story which was as follows: A special celebration was being held by the Lutherans commemorative of Luther, and as Father Lemke had been a Lutheran, and posted about the reformer, he took occasion on the following Sunday to preach a sermon on the life of Luther from his point of view. After his return to the pastoral residence he was waited upon by a committee of the trustees that was ushered into his room where he was eating his dinner. The spokesman commenced by saying:

"That was a fine sermon you preached to-day, but as we wish to live in peace with our Protestant neighbors we come to tell you you must not preach any more such sermons in our church."

Springing to his feet and seizing the poker he thundered: "You blacksmiths, you carpenters, you tailors! How dare you come here and tell me how to preach! Get out of here;" and they did get out.

On the following day he related the occurrence to the Bishop and asked to be relieved. The Bishop then gave him permission to engage in missionary work in other parts of the diocese. Father Lemke took his course to the mountains, visiting and ministering to the scattered Catholics on his way. His main object was to visit Prince Gallitzin at Loretto. He reached Munster in the month of September, 1834. The records show that he took the first steps necessary to being naturalized as an American citizen by filing his first papers January 2, 1835. On October 7, 1840, he took out his naturalization papers, Michael Dan Mageehan and John Murray swearing to his residence.

The story of his arrival in Munster and of his meeting with Gallitzin is best told by himself, and reads as follows:

"I arrived at last in safety at Munster, a little village laid out by Irish people on a tableland of the Allegheny mountains, only four miles from Gallitzin's residence. The stage stopped at the house of a certain Peter Collins, a genuine Irishman, who kept the postoffice and hotel. The next morning, for it was evening when I arrived, and they would not on any account let me go on, a horse was saddled for me, and Thomas, one of the numerous Collins children, now a man of influence and reputation, stood ready with a stick in his hand to show me the way, and to bring back the horse. We had gone about a mile or two in the woods when I saw a sled coming along drawn by two strong horses. N. B.—In September, in the most beautiful summer weather.

"In the sled half sat and half reclined a venerable looking man, in an old, much worn overcoat, wearing a peasant's hat which no one, it is likely, would have cared to pick up in the street, and carrying a book in his hand. Seeing him brought along in this way I thought there must have been an accident, that perhaps the old gentleman had dislocated a limb in the woods, but Thomas, who had been on ahead, came run-

FIRST MEETING OF FATHER LEMKE AND FATHER GALLITZIN. SEPTEMBER, 1834.

ning back and said: 'There comes the priest,' pointing to the man in the sled. I rode up and asked: 'Are you really the pastor at Loretto?' 'Yes, I am he.' 'Prince Gallitzin?' 'At your service, sir, I am that very exalted personage,' saying this, he laughed heartily. 'You may perhaps wonder,' he continued, when I had presented to him a letter from the Bishop of Philadelphia, 'at my singular retinue. But how can it be helped? We have not as yet, as you see, roads fit for wagons; we should be either fast or upset every moment. I cannot any longer ride horseback, having injured myself by a fall, and it is also coming hard for me to walk; besides I have all the requirements for mass to take with me. I am now on my way to a place where I have had for some years a station. You can now go on quietly to Loretto, and make yourself comfortable there, I shall be at home this evening; or, if you like better, you can come with me, perhaps it may interest you.' I chose to accompany him, and after riding some miles through the woods we reached a genuine Pennsylvania farm house.

THE OLD PARRISH HOMESTEAD, WHERE FATHER GALLITZIN USED TO HOLD "STATIONS."

"Here lived Joshua Parrish, one of the first settlers of that country, and the ancestor of a numerous posterity. The Catholics of the neighborhood, men, women and children, were already assembled in great numbers around the house, in which an altar was put up, its principal materials having been taken from the sled; Gallitzin then sat down in one corner of the house to hear confessions, and I, in another corner, attended to a few Germans. The whole affair appeared very strange to me, but it was extremely touching to see the simple peasant home, with all its house furniture, and the great fireplace, in which there was roasting and boiling going on at the same time, changed into a church; while the people, with their prayer books and their reverential manners, stood or knelt under the low projecting roof or under the trees, going in or out, just as their turn came for confession. After mass, at which Father Gallitzin preached, and when a few children had been baptized, the altar was taken away, and the dinner table set in its place. . . . In a word, all was so pleasant and friendly that involuntarily the love-feasts of the first Christians came to my mind. In the afternoon we went slowly on our way, Gallitzin in his sled and I on horseback, arriving at nightfall at Loretto."

After this visit to Loretto it appears that Father Lemke went back to Philadelphia, but his stay there was brief, for on his return to Loretto he was immediately conducted by the venerable Father Gallitzin, to Ebensburg, and on December 23, 1834, installed there as pastor. This appointment surprised Father Lemke, for he had expected to reside with Father Gallitzin, and so he told him. "Oh, no," replied the latter, "these people (in Ebensburg) have built a church and want a resident priest, and besides I have no room in my house for you. And what is more," he continued, "the winters are so severe on these mountains that it would be impossible for you to get here from Loretto. You will come to me once a month to care for my Germans, and for that I shall contribute something to your support." And so he left him.

Father Lemke thus describes his first experience in his new charge:

"I am now, since the 23d of December, here in Ebensburg, which is the principal town in Cambria County. But lest you get a wrong impression of what is meant by 'the principal town,' I must at once tell you that there is nothing to be seen here resembling a town except one large walled up building with a tower, the court-house of the county or circuit, and very few houses which resemble the dwellings of Europeans; but mostly log and clap-board houses. As to paved streets and such like it is not to be thought of here; but instead one is compelled evenings to feel his way with a stick in order not to break his neck falling over stumps.

"Prior to twenty years ago all this country round about was woods, and if one will now go one thousand steps away he will find himself again in the primitive forest. For these reasons the place looks more like a bivouac than a town, as for example such things as kitchens, cellars and other rooms and conveniences, which, according to our ideas of human comforts, are necessary, are not much to be thought of here; and I am willing to bet that in this entire principal town there are not five doors to be found which can be locked.

"My host is one of the first magistrates, that is, the collector and accountant of public revenues of the entire district covering a territory of about four hundred square miles, and, besides, he carries on the carpenter trade and farming business without an apprentice; for apprentices and maid servants are unknown here. The 'squire, also called the district judge, met me yesterday with a load of wood, which he himself had cut down and loaded.

"When I return from my horseback trip through the woods I lead my horse to the stable, unsaddle him and give him the attention which he needs; then I hang up my boots and coat, which are covered with several pounds of clay, to the fire, and seat myself before it while the children climb up on my knee and the housewife busies herself getting me something to eat. On the following morning the dried coat is rubbed out; the boots and harness are cleaned and so on. That I do these things does not strike any one as strange; but, on the contrary, I would be looked upon as singular if I did not do them. In the place itself there are but few Catholic families and not one German soul. I can, therefore, not get a drink of water without asking for it in English, and I am thus compelled to learn what the different things are used for. It is this very necessity which is of the greatest importance to me. In Philadelphia, or any other place among German surroundings, I might have remained for years and days without learning English; but here it comes without effort: methinks, indeed, the very winds blow here in English. I would wish that every missionary would find himself so situated as I am here. With a dictionary, grammar, and English Classics, one may torment himself dreadfully, and yet when he gets among these people he understands as much about their English as if he had never seen a letter of it.

"I already hear confessions and administer the other sacraments in English, and on last Sunday I even read the Gospel and gave a short exhortation in English before the German sermon. I have here a wooden church just like a large Bavarian barn. In a circuit round about live a great many Germans, most of whom are Catholics. and, as is generally the case, the Germans, according to long-established custom, prefer to settle in the woods, while the Irish, French and other emigrants locate with the Americans in the cities, on the highways, and along the canals, and carry on trade and hotel business.

"These Germans come diligently and gladly to church, although they often have to leave home at night in order to get here. On one Sunday of the month I go to Loretto, six miles from here; and on a second Sunday I go to the new settlement, twelve miles, "Hart's Sleeping Place," where there are fifty-four German Catholic families, mostly Alsatians and Rhenish Bavarians who have thrown their resources together and built a church.

"During Easter time I will have to make a trip to Erie. I am already anticipating the pleasure of it, for I expect to make a detour to see the Falls of Niagara. Now you will probably want to know what resources I have here. I have none but what the people give me, and as the people have very little I likewise have very little; and I can really say that I have never in my life been so poor and at the same time so rich. For here I feel satisfied and happy and have everything in abundance that is necessary for the maintenance and support of life; and for what purpose should I want money? My health becomes better with every hardship. In Philadelphia I was sick a good deal and thought several times I was going to fall a victim to cholera. In regard to food and drink it certainly fares badly with me: and since I came to America I cannot think so hard of the children of Israel for having, in their journey to the promised land, frequently become dejected and discouraged when thinking of the flesh pots of Egypt."

From Ebensburg Father Lemke visited "Hart's Sleeping Place," so-called from its being the camp or stopping place of Hart, the trader, situated on the old Indian trail from the East to Kittanning, on the Allegheny River. It is about three miles north of Carrolltown, and at the time we write of, was the centre of a small settlement of Catholics who worshiped in a little church built and dedicated by Father Gallitzin a short time before Father Lemke's arrival. During his stay in Ebensburg, until the year 1837, his time was spent in visiting and ministering to the scattered Catholics throughout the county. At that time he and Father Gallitzin were the only resident priests within its limits. Much of his time, also, was given to the pastor of Loretto, who had now become old and feeble.

It was about this period that Lemke's active mind devised the project of a settlement and home in the northern part of the county. The influx of German emigration, he foresaw, would, if a church were erected, make the place the center of a large Catholic population. Accordingly he purchased lands at Hart's Sleeping Place and moved there some time in 1837. Then with a pious old widow as housekeeper, and her children as helpers, he began confidently to apply his knowledge of agriculture, acquired at Neuburg, to the cultivation of his farm in the wilds of Cambria County. It was not long until he saw that Hart's Sleeping Place was not the best location for the church he contemplated building, so in 1840 he sold his farm and purchased a tract of land about three miles south of the old church upon which now stands Carrolltown with its large church, convent and schools.

With all the energy and enthusiasm of his nature Lemke applied himself to the founding of his projected settlement. He encouraged settlers in buying land, clearing the forests, making roads, being to them all for the time, lawyer, doctor and priest in one. His unfailing cheerfulness and hope did much to encourage and sustain the many homeless emigrants who soon began to flock to Carrolltown, the name suggested by Father Gallitzin for the new settlement. Having laid out part of his land in town lots he proceeded to make a home for himself. With the assistance of his parishoners he erected a house and barn and small chapel, all of which are still standing. Under his care and by his industry cultivated fields began soon to emerge from the wilderness.

His people gave him time and labor in place of money, and along with them he wielded the axe and maul as effectively as the best. His life-long friend and counsellor, the late Judge Johnson, told the writer that, visiting him once on business, and not finding him at the house he proceeded to the "clearing." There he found the great man rolling logs and as black from smoke and dirt as any African. Along about this time, by Gallitzin's advice, he founded the missions of St. Augustine, St. Lawrence and St. Boniface—all of them now large Catholic congregations.

During the month of April, 1840, Father Gallitzin was taken ill and Lemke was sent for, but he could not take the journey because of a wound in the foot inflicted by a slip of the axe in chopping. Gallitzin's illness becoming serious, he sent his sled for Lemke who rose from his own bed of sickness and hurried to the side of his friend. He remained with him until the end on that sad May 6th. After Father Gallitzin's death Bishop Kenrick ordered Father Lemke to take his place at Loretto. He objected to this as he was loath to leave his people in the north, but the Bishop insisting, he could do nothing but submit. He was now the only resident priest in the county, this fact necessitating an amount of labor on his part hard at the present to appreciate. In 1843 the Pittsburg Diocese was established and Bishop O'Connor sent Fathers Gibbs and O'Flaherty to Cambria, thus relieving Father Lemke of much of his responsibility.

He turned his attention once more to Carrolltown. It is easy to trace his ambition and hope to build up the place and make it, as a Catholic community, a rival of Loretto. Therefore he secured the permission of the Bishop to visit Europe to collect funds for the building of a church. In September, 1844, he was succeeded in the pastorate of Loretto by Rev. Hugh P. Gallagher, and just before Christmas that same year he took leave of his parishoners and started on his mission.

We may certainly presume that he was cordially received by his old friends in Germany, Dr. Raes, Sailer and Diepenbrock, who was now Cardinal Bishop of Breslau. The Cardinal Bishop tried to induce him to remain with him, but in vain. His heart was with his people in Carrolltown who were anxiously awaiting his return, fearing all the time lest they would be deprived of their father and friend. He was quite successful in raising money. Schlosser, his patron, gave him 500, the King of Munich, 3,000 florins. These sums would be sufficient to meet the greater part of the cost of his new church, and he was no doubt elated at the near realization of his cherished ambition.

From the time of his advent to America he had been impressed with the belief that this country offered a grand field for the operations of the Benedictine Order, famous as it is for expert farming and reclaiming of land.

Meeting in Munich some Benedictine Fathers he explained to them the advantages and inducements America held out, and urged them to consider the matter. Soon after this one of the fathers, Rev. Boniface Wimmer, informed Lemke of his readiness to consent to his proposal and come on to America. Father Lemke gave every encouragement, offering his lands at Carrolltown as a site for the community, and to him is due the coming of the Benedictines to our country, for Father Wimmer followed his impulse and the results are known.

After nine months stay in Europe Father Lemke returned to Carrolltown, rich in money, books and vestments bestowed by his friends for the use of his beloved missions. Here he began in earnest the building of his church which he completed by Christmas, 1850. In the meanwhile, in anticipation of the arrival of the Benedictines, he had purchased several hundred acres of land in the vicinity of his tract in Carrolltown, hoping to insure by these important and still larger possession of good farming lands, the location of the Monastery in his fast growing town. In the fall of 1846 he received word that Father Wimmer and nineteen others were on their way. He immediately repaired to New York to meet them. The party, which landed on September 15, 1846, consisted of Father Wimmer, four students and fifteen lay brothers. He brought them to Carrolltown and domiciled them in his own small house until other provision could be made for them.

But a cruel disappointment awaited the zealous priest. Father Wimmer made a visit to Pittsburg to consult with Bishop O'Connor, who advised him to locate in Westmoreland county, instead of Carrolltown, which Father Wimmer agreed to do, the Bishop offering as an inducement Sportsman's Hall, a tract of land belonging to his diocese, now the seat of St. Vincent's Abbey.

By this arrangement Father Lemke saw for the time being the postponement of his hopes to have the Benedictines established on his lands and himself a member of the community.

Father Wimmer and his subjects left Carrolltown on the 15th of October, 1846.

This disappointment and many other vexing complications weighed heavily on the mind of Father Lemke. He became discouraged, and resolved to leave the diocese. Having disposed of his lands to the Benedictines he returned to his old friend, Bishop Kenrick, who cordially received him and assigned him once again to missionary work among his churches. In 1849 he paid a visit to his friends, the Benedictines in Carrolltown. He found a flourishing condition of affairs, lands had been cleared, buildings erected and all things on a successful and prosperous footing. During this visit with the brothers he resolved to take the step he had long contemplated, which was to become a Benedictine, and to retire from the world. With the approval of the Bishop of Philadelphia he was, on the 2nd of February, 1852, invested with the habit of the Order. At Carrolltown he assumed the duties of a Benedictine Father, gladly welcomed by his faithful parishioners. Not long afterwards complicated business relations and certain misunderstandings impelled him to again leave Carrolltown. He went to Kansas where Bishop Miege kindly received him and quickly affected an amicable adjustment of the differences between him and his Abbot. His observations of Kansas convinced him of the great possibilities of that agricultural state for the workings of his Order, and while there he urged the Abbot to send out a branch settlement. The Abbot heard him favorably and sent several Fathers, who, under Father Lemke's direction, located a house of the Order at Atchison, now the great Abbot of that name. Thus we see that whithersoever Lemke went or adversities sent him, Catholic communities, churches, schools and monasteries sprang up, increased and flourished.

Father Lemke returned to St. Vincent's Abbey in the latter part of 1858, or early in 1859, for in the last named year he made a trip to Europe to collect money for the monastery and to attend to some matters of his own. He spent a year in Germany, sojourning principally in Vienna, from which place he wrote that "he had collected six thousand dollars and had written a 'Life of Dr. Gallitzin,' " of which Life but few copies are now extant.

He returned to America in 1860, was assigned to the Diocese of Newark, N. J., and given charge of a congregation at Elizabeth. "Here," his biographer, Dr. Flick, writes, "he settled down to parochial work in his old age and lived a life of peace and content." In 1864 he undertook a visit to Cambria, the scene of his early labors, but being injured by an accident on the railroad was obliged to give up the journey. About this time he made a will leaving all the property still in his name to the Bishop in whose diocese he resided. In April, 1876, he celebrated his Golden Jubilee as a priest in his church at Elizabeth, N. J. In his settlement of his affairs with the Abbot there was a condition that he should always have a home at St. Vincent's or Carrolltown. He chose the latter, and at the age of eighty-two came to Carrolltown, never more to leave it.

His last days were full of calm. He enjoyed the peace of his retreat, surrounded by his brethren of the monastery, who did all in their power for his happiness, ministering to his every want as though he were a child. His old parishioners, to whom in the days long gone by he had been benefactor and friend, delighted to visit him whom they still revered and loved as a father.

It was a common thing in those last years of his life to see groups of those old patriarchs, men whom he had ministered to, and with whom he had labored half a century before, wending their way to the monastery to meet and talk again with their good old priest.

He was always glad to see them; and many and interesting were the reminiscences recalled at those meetings of the old times with their hardships and vicissitudes they had passed through. Nor were these visitors all Catholics. Protestants as well were among those old friends of Father Lemke. The few in the early settlement who were not Catholics shared alike in his friendship and benevolence. While he was still in New Jersey, a Protestant friend of the writer in Carrolltown, called out on his death bed, "Oh, if I could only see Father Lemke once more!"

The writer's father had been among his earliest friends at Loretto, and in later years used to make an annual visit to Carrolltown to visit him and to recall old times and incidents. The last visit was in 1881. The aged priest met his venerable friend and the writer at the door of his room, and seizing the former in his arms, went waltzing with him around the room, then exultingly exclaimed: "I am an older man than you Mr.

GROUP OF THOSE WHO CLEANED AND DECORATED THE CHURCH FOR THE CENTENARY.

Thomas, and I can yet shake the life out of you." "Pardon me, sir," replied the other, "but wait until you are as old as I am and then boast of what you can do." "Why, in what year were you born?" asked Father Lemke, amazed, leading him to a chair. "In 1792." "And I in 1796. True, true, my old friend, you are my senior by four years, but neither of us will see four years more of life." This prophecy was but partially fulfilled; Father Lemke died the following year, and his venerable friend nearly five years later.

During the last four years of his life he seldom left the monastery, but spent his time in reading, writing and entertaining his many visitors. During this time he wrote an interesting history of his life, the first half of which was published as a serial in "The Carrolltown News," and the remainder was sent by him to a friend in Germany. Until almost the end his health was comparatively good; but the weight of years and his increasing infirmities gradually undermined his iron constitution, and for the last seven months of his life compelled him to keep to his room.

HON. JAMES J. THOMAS.

He is buried in the cemetery at Carrolltown, surrounded by the graves of the pioneers to whom he had been father, friend and benefactor, and who in return had loved and revered him so much. A beautiful monument in the lot set aside for the graves of the Benedictine Fathers marks the last resting place of this great friend, faithful companion and worthy successor of the illustrious Demetrius Augustine Gallitzin.

PART THIRD.

BY REV. FERDINAND KITTELL.

CENSUS OF ST. MICHAEL'S PARISH, LORETTO, PA.

TAKEN AUGUST 15, 1899.

BOROUGH OF LORETTO.

BANNAN Hugh J.
    Mrs. Mary Louisa (McCloskey).
    Mary Cecilia.
    Louisa Victoria.
    Julia Agnes.
    Regina Maria.
    Joseph Augustine.
    Elizabeth Mary Liguori.
    Beatrice Adele.
BENGELE Mrs. Francis (Haid).
    Mary.
    Sophia.
BENGELE Englebert M.
    Mrs. Carlotta (Tomlinson).
BITER Otho.
    James D.
BITER William F.
    Mrs. Anna M. (Krumenacher).
COMERFORD Arthur.
    Mrs. Elizabeth (Hein).
CONRAD Linnie.
CONRAD Ambrose.
    Mrs. Caroline (Stevens).
    Edna Catherine.
CROUSE Herman J.
    Rose D.
DAWSON Mary.
ELLWOOD Leo Anthony.
FARABAUGH Michael J.
    Mrs. Mary (Gonsman).
    Paul Leroy.
FISHER Simon.
FLICK Charles.
    Mrs. Theresa (Hertzog).
FURY Mary.
GLASS Annie E.
HERMAN Camilla A.
HERTZOG Joseph D.
    Mrs. Theresa (Lenz).
    Rufina.
    Catherine C.
HOGUE Mary M.
    George.

Illig Augustine.
  Mrs. Ann Elizabeth (Crouse).
  Rose Martina.
  Anicetus John.
  Leo Philip.
  Cyril Augustine.
Kittell Andrew J.
  Mrs. Margaret Ann (Murray).
  Francis Joseph.
  Henry Michael.
  Mary Elizabeth.
Kittell Samuel H.
  Mrs. Matilda (Hertzog).
  James Thomas.
  Rose Margaret.
  Louis Joseph.
  Marie Gertrude.
  Leo Raymond.
  Charles Francis.
  Margaret Mary.
Lacy Mary.
  Pierce A.
  Pierce B.
Leavy Mrs. Mary Josephine (McDermitt).
Little Edward J.
  Mrs. Rebecca (Cooper).
  Joseph B.
  Madeline G.
Little Mrs. Susan.
Little W. A. B.
  Mrs. Susan Catherine (Storm).
  Susan E.
  Bernard W.
  Leo Thomas.
  Andrew Vincent.
  Michael Constantine.
  Tibertus Aloysius.
Little Louis M.
  Mrs. Ellen (Hobart).
  William Hobart.
Litzinger Eugene.

(Litzinger) William Peter.
  Bertram Leo.
Litzinger Bernard W.
  Mrs. Annie E. (Pfoff).
  Walter Frederick.
Malloy Michael.
  Caroline E.
  Joseph M.
  Frances A.
  Oswald D.
  Vincent E.
  Harry.
  Martina.
McAteer Mrs. Della (McElheny).
  Bertha.
  James.
McCoy Theresa.
McCullough Thomas J.
  Mrs. Margaret (Little).
McDonald Morgan F.
  Mrs. Elmira B. (Pfoff).
McElheny Mrs. Margaret (Kilgore).
  Joan A.
McGillen Mrs. Catherine (Linn).
  Martin.
  Catherine Loretta.
McGuire Veronica.
McGuire Mrs. Sarah (Glass).
Miller Charles.
  Mrs. Mary (Null).
Moran Patrick.
  Mrs. Elizabeth (Maher).
  John.
  Mary.
  Catharine.
  Edward.
Moran Charles W.
  Mrs. Mary (Hite).
  Helen Elizabeth.
  Gallitzin Bowen.
  William Leroy.
Murphy John, M. D.

(Murphy) Mrs. Anna (Selvitz).
    Nellie.
    Marie.
    Margaret.
MYERS Robert.
    Mrs. Sarah (Troxell).
    Leo.
    Myrtle.
    Gordon.
    Olive.
    Roy.
    Ross.
NAGLE Mrs. Elizabeth (Neason).
NAGLE Catherine.
NAGLE Mrs. Ella (Fisher).
    Myrtle.
NULL Joseph.
O'DONNELL Charles F.
    Mrs. Ella (Lacy).
O'FRIEL H. Thomas.
O'HARA Rachel.
PARRISH Alexander.
    John.
PFOFF, Michael J.
RIGGLE Eliza.
RUDOLPH Adam.
    Mrs. Louisa (Heineman).
    Michael.
RUDOLPH Christopher.
    Mrs. Helen (Topper).
    Joseph Faber.
    Walter Francis.
    Edward Gallitzin.
RUDOLPH Henry.
    Mrs. Matilda (McAteer).
    Coletta.
SANKER Mrs. Sarah (Meloy).
SCHWAB John A.
    Mrs. Pauline (Farabaugh).
    Gertrude.
    Edward.
SCHWAB William C.
    Mrs. Mary Elizabeth (Ivory).

(Schwab) Kathleen E.
SEYMOUR Delia.
SHIELDS John E.
    Mrs. Mary Henrietta (Luther).
    Edward. J.
    Eleanor.
    Mildred.
SMELTZER Joseph.
    Mrs. Ida (Nagle).
    Oswald L.
SPADE William.
STEVENS Andrew.
    Mrs. Jane Frances (Seymour).
    Lawrence Joseph.
    Henry Herman.
    Louis Isidore.
    Joseph Englebert.
    Emma Catherine.
STEVENS Clement.
    Mrs. Margaret (Conrad).
    Bertha Catherine.
    Pauline Cecilia.
WEAKLAND Austin P.
    Mrs. Margaret Emma (Hileman).
    Mary Elvira.
    Russell Bernard.
    Regis Francis.
    Charles Faber.
WILLS Augustine.
    Mrs. Ellen (Settlemire).
    George Howard.
    Augustine Edward.
    Lawrence.
    Ferdinand Hugh.
    Catherine Elmira.
    John Elmer.
WILLS John F.
    Mrs. Henrietta M. (Fagan).
    Bernard W.

OUTSIDE THE BOROUGH LIMITS.

ANDERSON Mrs. Mary Josephine (Bruce).
    Alice M.
    George Bruce.
    John William.
    Ruth D.
    Mary A.
ANSMAN Albert M.
    Mrs. Helen Ann (Eckenrode).
    James William.
    Mary Agnes.
    Albert.
    Ann Helen.
    Walter Emanuel.
    Bertha Emma.
ANSMAN Valentine.
    Mrs. Apollonia (Wisman).
ANSTEAD Ida.
BAKER William.
    Mrs. Cath. Elizabeth (Bishop).
    Philumena Matilda.
    Mary Loretta.
BAKER William Valentine.
    Mrs. Margaret T. (Weakland).
BANNAN John.
    Mrs. Mary Ellen (Bradley).
    Joseph Charles.
    Mary Ann.
    John Edward.
    William Francis.
    Susan Elizabeth.
    Matilda Gertrude.
    Edward Hubert.
BANNAN Julia.
BARD Henry.
    Mrs. Unity (Hanlon).
    John P.
    Annie.
BAVER William A.

(Baver) Mrs. Wilhelmina (Rosensteel).
    Mary Emma.
    Blanche Genevieve.
    Bertha Cecilia.
    Eleanora Anastasia.
    Francis William Thomas.
    Arthur Joseph.
BECHER Linus.
BEHE Henry.
    Mrs. Catherine (McConnell).
BEHE Elias.
    Mrs. Elizabeth Jane (Eckenrode).
    Sarah Jane.
    Michael Joseph.
    Andrew Chrysostom.
    Raymond Francis.
BEITER John.
    Annie Gertrude.
    Joseph P.
    Henrietta Loretta.
BEITER Ignatius.
    Rose.
    Annie M.
BEITER John Chrysostom.
    Mrs. Annie (Litzinger).
BEITER William.
    Elmer William.
BENDER Mrs. Catherine (Boley.)
BERTRAM John F.
    Mrs. Catherine (Volk.)
    Louis Vincent.
    Herman William.
    Lawrence Benedict.
    Jane Elizabeth.
    Mary Rose.
BILLER Joseph J.
    Mrs. Mary C. (Shenk).
    Mary Adeline.
    Francis Nicholas.

(Biller) Mary Susan.
    Helen Elizabeth.
    Mary Ellen.
    Leo Joseph.
    Emma Regina.
    Silas Jerome.
    Alice Victoria.
    Edward Louis.
BILLER Mrs. Clara (Nagle).
    Albert A.
BISHOP Valentine, Sr.
    Mrs. Cordelia (Haid).
BISHOP Thomas.
    Mrs. Matilda J. (Flick).
    Edward Charles.
    Rosalia Catherine.
    Gilbert William.
    Helena Margaret.
    Philumena Elizabeth.
    Esther Mary.
    Hilda Irene.
BISHOP Valentine, Jr.
    Mrs. Dorothy (Strittmatter).
    Grace Mary.
    Andrew Valentine.
    Frances Cordelia.
    Mary Josephine.
    Ruth Lucy.
    Agatho Ferdinand.
BISHOP Valentine Sylvester.
    Mrs. Rose (Hite).
    Clarence.
BITER Henry Celestine.
    Mrs. Sarah (Itel).
    Albert.
    Leo.
    Sherman.
    Thomas.
    Margaret Ellen.
    Esther Gertrude.
    Clara Bertha.
    Mary Martina.
BOES John.
    Mrs. Catherine (McCullough).

(Boes) Edward.
    John.
    William Benjamin.
    Mary.
    Michael Albert.
    James Francis.
BOLAN Peter.
    Mrs. Rebecca (Hupfer).
    Thomas.
    Philip.
    Annie.
    Martha.
BOLEY Mrs. Ann (Delozier).
    Edward V.
    Raymond Cornelius.
    Morgan Sebastian.
    Edith Agatha.
    Alma Eleanor.
BOLEY Joseph.
    Mrs. Cecilia (Hertzog).
    Charles Chrysostom.
    Elizabeth Bernetta.
    Ann Lucy.
    Alphonsus Ignatius.
    Theresa Magdalen.
    Francis de Sales.
    Elsie Matilda.
    Edna Louisa.
    Nelson Modestus.
BOLEY Joseph L.
    Mrs. Agnes (Buck).
    Catherine Ruth.
BOVIN Michael.
    Mrs. Rose (Bannan).
BRADLEY Anselm J.
    Mrs. Catherine (Driskel).
    Mary Matilda.
    Mary Jane.
    Louis.
BRADLEY James Michael.
    Mrs. Caroline C. (Sanker).
    Wilfred Joseph.
    Zita Mary.
    Mildred Catherine.
BRADLEY Alexander.
    Mrs. Theresa (Flick).

Bradley Edward.
   Joseph Morgan.
   John Leonard.
   Mary Eliza.
   Thomas Austin.
Brady Robert J.
   Mrs. Matilda (Glass).
   Mary Cora.
   Mary Augusta.
   Mary Bernardine.
   Harriet.
Bruce George Bernard.
   Mrs. Flora (Sanker).
   Margaret Agnes.
   Alice Marie.
   Zita Ann.
   Ellen Flora.
   Benedict Russell.
Buck William J.
   Mrs. Mary (Glass).
   Andrew Michael.
   Emma M.
   Ida Jane.
   Albert.
   Edward James.
Buck Demetius A.
   Mrs. Elizabeth (Comerford).
   Maurice William.
   Caroline Marie.
Buck James M.
   Mrs. Sarah (O'Neill-Glass).
   Cyrus.
   Maurice.
Burgoon Margaret.
Callan Thomas.
   Mrs. Regina M. (McGuire).
   Regina Mary.
   Josephine R.
   Mary E.
   Margaret M.
   William A.
   Frances J.
   Anna.

(Callan) Henry Joseph.
   Edward Albert.
   Gertrude.
Carney Mrs. Rose (Boland).
   Daniel Jerome.
   Margaret.
   John.
   Augusta.
Cassidy Alice M.
   Amanda P.
Christy William.
   Mrs. Catherine (Lenahin).
Christy Mary M.
Connolly Mrs. Susan (Bannan).
Conrad Mrs. Ellen A. (Bradley).
   Catherine.
   Matilda.
   Englebert.
   Robert S.
   Cecilia.
Conrad Eugene.
   Mrs. Eliza (Moore).
   Mary.
Conrad J. Harvey.
Coons Joseph Ambrose.
   Mrs. Caroline (Shenk).
   Walter.
   Vincent.
   Mathias.
   Louis.
   Flora.
   Charles.
   Caroline.
Coons Thomas Augustine.
   Mrs. Mary A. (Bender).
   Nannie Clara.
   Genevieve Catherine.
   Bertha Theresa.
   Zita Frances.
   Rose Loretta.
   Irvin Thomas.
   Grover Marcellus.
   Jennings J.
Coons Joseph.

COONS Francis Joseph.
    Edward Lewis.
    James Emmet.
    Chester Lawrence.
    Mary Christina.
    Robert Bernard.
COOPER Mrs. Catherine (Walters).
    Susan M.
    Henry Joseph.
    James Englebert.
COOPER Michael J.
    Mrs. Jane (Rudolph).
    Mary L.
    Annie M.
    Della S.
    Francis W.
    Marie.
    Morgan.
    Raymond.
    Irene.
    Bertha.
    Shell Augustine.
CRAMER Pius.
    Mrs. Ann (Dodson).
    Mary Regina.
    Mary Blanche.
    Mary Agnes.
    Anna Mary.
    Mary Margaret.
    Joseph Philip.
    Eleanor Catherine.
    Theresa Alma.
    Veronica Gertrude.
CRILLEY Mrs. Ann Jane (Mullen).
    John.
    Edward.
    Thomas.
    Patrick.
    James.
CRISTE Charles Augustine.
    Mrs. Margaret (Donahoe).
    Bertha Mary.
    Hildebert James.
    (Criste) Beatrice Elizabeth.
    Matilda Agnes.
    Leo Augustine.
CULLY Mrs. Bridget (Keyes).
    Mary Elizabeth.
DAILY Mrs. Margaret (Gibbons).
    James W.
DAVIS Mrs. Agnes (Eckenrode).
DAVIS Howard.
    Harry.
DECORTE Joseph P.
    Caroline M.
DELANEY Mrs. Ann (Grove).
DEMPSEY Mary E.
    Winifred.
    Januarius.
    Genevieve.
DENNY Richard J.
    Mrs. Charlotte (Parrish).
    Oscar T.
    Victor Richard.
    Mary Angela.
DEVER Philip.
    John.
    James.
DONAHOE Harriet.
    George H.
DONOUGHE Silas H.
    Mrs. Margaret (Mullen).
    Mary Margaret.
    Charles Edward.
    Ella.
    William Henry.
    Peter Andrew.
DONOUGHE Mark E.
    Mrs. Angeline (Storm).
    John.
    Raymond.
    Joseph Alexander.
    Edmund Claver.
DONOUGHE Jane.
DOUGHERTY Hugh C.
    Mrs. Elizabeth (Gray).
    Dennis J.

(Dougherty) Clara A.
    Mary T.
    Elizabeth E.
    Grace C.
    Laura Cecilia.
DOUGHERTY John W.
    Mrs. Ann (Fogle).
    Margaret Ellen.
    James Mortimer.
    Louis.
    Otho Thomas.
DOUGLAS Margaret.
DRISKEL James.
    Mrs. Mary J. (McCloskey).
    Matilda.
    Rose.
    Alice.
    John.
DRISKEL Hugh.
    Mrs. Matilda (Rudolph).
    Mary Matilda.
    Philumena.
    Anna Regina.
    Frances Catherine.
    Michael James.
    Bertha.
    Irene.
DRISKEL George.
    Mrs. Bernetta (Latterner)
    Mary Dorothy.
DURBIN Mrs. Eliza J. (Glass).
    Herman
    Leo.
    Zita.
DURBIN James.
    Mrs. Ellen M. (Douglas).
    Blair.
    Francis Roy.
    Olive.
    James Ray.
EBERLY Henry Joseph.
    Mrs. Emma (Glass).
    Caroline.
    Paul.
    Germaine.

EBERLY Joanna.
    William Augustine.
EBIG Francis W.
    Mrs. Mary (Boley).
    Stella Genevieve.
    Mary Myrtle.
    Elmer Louis.
    Oscar Charles.
ECKENRODE Mrs. Susan (Meloy).
ECKENRODE Peter Augustine.
ECKENRODE Mrs. Mary (Douglas).
    John.
ECKENRODE Joseph W.
    Francis D.
    Tibertus.
ECKENRODE Charles Chrysostom.
    Charles Henry.
    Oscar Francis.
    Martin Raymond.
    Mary Edith.
    Simon Walter.
    Susan Myrtle.
    Ida Jane.
ECKENRODE Mrs. Monica A. (Stoy).
    Harriet M.
    Bernadette.
    Olive M.
    Nellie M.
ECKENRODE Mrs. Margaret (Eckenrode).
    Anna Mary.
    George Howard.
    James Romanus.
    Joseph Walter.
    Augustine Faber.
    Ferdinand.
ECKENRODE Sylvester.
    Mrs. Mary (Trenkley).
    Eliza Jane.
    Catherine May.
    Hugh Raymond.
ECKENRODE Jerome B.

(Eckenrode) Josephine.
    Maude.
ECKENRODE Albinus.
    Mrs. Elizabeth (Lintz).
    Catherine Bertha.
    Clement.
    Elmer Joseph.
    Martin Ellsworth.
EVERLY George.
    Mrs. Elizabeth (Coons).
    John.
    May.
    Englebert.
FARABAUGH Mathias.
    Ida.
    Minnie.
    George.
    Edward.
FARABAUGH Augustine E.
    Mrs. Bridget (Gooderham).
    Henrietta.
    Erhart Augustine.
    William Thomas.
    Rupert Henry.
    Maurice Sylvester.
FARREN Mrs. Genevieve (Bertram).
    Mary.
    Gallitzin.
    James.
    Agnes.
    Jane.
    Margaret.
FARREN Daniel.
    Mrs. Martha (Hannah).
FISHER Joseph F.
    Mrs. Bertha (Quinn).
    Simon John.
    Gertrude.
    Edna Mary.
    Francis Joseph.
    Bertha Agnes.
    Alice Elizabeth.
    Mary Theresa.
FLICK Mrs. Josephine (Hertzog).
    Eliza Jane.
FLICK Martin.
    Ella.
FLICK Peter.
    Mrs. Cath. (McIntosh-Pfoff).
    Alice.
    Emma.
FLICK Philip Lawrence.
    Mrs. Mary Frances (Shenk).
    Herman Henry.
    Mary Theresa.
    Rose Mary.
    Emanuel P.
    Albert Thomas.
    Frances Augusta.
    Ida Gertrude.
    Philumena Blanche.
FLICK Jerome.
    Mrs. Mary (Sharp).
    Joseph.
    Anicetus.
    Mary.
    Jerome.
    Rosie.
    Andrew.
    Alma.
FREIDHOFF Mrs. Veronica (Beiter).
FREIDHOFF Nicholas R.
    Louis Francis.
FREIDHOFF John C.
    Mrs. Mary Albertina (Eger).
    Henry Joseph.
    Mary Elizabeth.
    John Celestine.
    Vincent Sylvester.
FRY Edward D.
    Mrs. Juda (Callahan).
    Mary Adeline.
    Magdalene.

(Fry) John Joseph.
   Mary Leo.
   Edith Hedwig.
   Francis.
GALLAHER Mrs. Emily (Elder).
GALLAHER John Edward.
   Mrs. Alice C. (Eckenrode).
   Matilda.
   Harriet.
   Hugh.
   Thomas.
   Benjamin.
   Suibert.
   Francis.
   Michael.
GARRETT Mrs. James (Cath. Farabaugh).
   Marian Catherine.
GLASS Demetrius A.
   Mrs. Martha (Durbin).
   Gorman.
   Mary Fidelis.
   Clair.
   Oliver.
   Adeline.
   Demetrius.
   Raymond.
GLASS Winfield S.
   Mrs. Laura (O'Hara).
   Leonard.
   William J.
GLASS James Sherman.
   Mrs. Ella (Little).
   Anna Helen.
   Sylvester.
   William Edgar.
   James Reardon.
GLASS William Edgar.
GLASS Mary Josephine.
GLASS Eugene.
GRIFFIN Joseph W.
   Mrs. Margaret Eliz. (Parrish).
GRIFFIN Francis Patrick.
GRIFFIN Marie.

GROVE John.
   Mrs. Martha Ann (Mause).
   Martha Jane.
GROVE Sarah.
HAID George.
   Agnes.
HALL Mrs. Angelina (Donoughe).
   Charity.
   William.
HAMMOND Mrs. Adam (Annie Fisher).
   Peter.
   Cecilia.
   Albert.
   Edward.
   Rose.
   William.
HAMMOND George.
   Mrs. Jennie (O'Brien).
   Edna Elizabeth.
HATCH Cora.
   Francis.
   Lorene.
HAUPT Mrs. Wm. (Mary McHugh-Decorte).
   Sarah Jane.
   Frances Matilda.
   Theresa Elverna.
   Gertrude.
   William Leonard.
   Elsie Marie.
   Arthur Gilbert.
HERTZOG John P.
   Mrs. Agnes (Buck).
   William.
   Bernetta.
   Joseph.
   Edward.
   Rosemary.
   Hildebert.
   Loretta.
   Thomas Jesse.
HERTZOG James.
   Mrs. Alice (Seymour).

HOFFMAN Michael.
   Anthony.
   Mary E.
HOGUE Joseph.
   Regina.
   Agnes.
HOGUE William J.
   Mrs. Francis (Ivory).
   Leo Walter.
ITEL Joseph B.
   Mrs. Christina (Hahn).
ITEL Francis.
   Mrs. Elizabeth (Gerst).
   Charles Albert.
   Augustine P.
ITEL Francis Henry.
   Mrs. Gertrude (Sanker).
   Mary E.
   Albert William.
   Gertrude Irene.
IVORY Henry Joseph.
   Mrs. Mary Catherine (Watt).
   Margaret.
   Edward.
   Harry.
JONES Clarinda.
   Alice.
KANE Sarah.
KAYLOR Mrs. Cecilia E. (Burke).
   Rose C.
   Irene.
   Louis E.
   Mary C.
KAYLOR John G.
KAYLOR Zach.
   Flora.
   Ettie.
   Rose.
   Dora.
   Annie.
KERRIGAN Mrs. Mary Ann (Helsel-Moreland).
KITTELL Rev. Ferdinand.

LATTERNER John.
   Mrs. Mary Ellen (Luther).
   John Michael.
   William Frederick.
   Charles Henry.
   Theresa.
LENZ George.
   Mrs. Mary Ann (Lantzy-Eckenrode.)
LENZ Tiburtus.
   Mrs. Mary Eliz. (Hertzog).
LENZ Edward.
   Mrs. Susan (Baker).
   Ira Anthony.
LINZ Joseph.
LITTLE Francis L.
   Mrs. Catherine (McAnulty).
   John Henry.
   William Joseph.
   Ida M.
   Rose Sarah.
   Dora M.
LITTLE Joseph Venantius.
   Mrs. Eleanora Susan.
   Clarence Veritas.
   Daniel Meredith.
   Martin Glenna.
   Joseph Aloysius.
LITZINGER Jesse F.
LOWE Mary Matilda.
   Howard.
MAUSE Mrs. Mary (Daughenbaugh).
   Anna Irene.
McATEER Gertrude.
McCOY Rachel.
   Jane.
   Agnes.
McCOY Edward.
McDERMITT Mary J.
McDERMITT Francis A.
McDERMITT Alonzo.
McDUNN Josephine L.
McGOUGH Mrs. Jane (Null).

(McGough) Francis Joseph.
  John E.
  Herman J.
  Laura.
  Margaret.
  Sarah.
  Louis.
  Mildred.
McGuire John Heyden.
  Mrs. Mary J. (Coons).
  Michael Luke.
  Catharine Magdalen.
  George Albert.
  Alice Sarah.
  Susan Jane.
  Mark Abbot.
  Bernard William.
McGuire George Luke.
  Mrs. Matilda (Luther).
  Edward Augustine.
  William Albert.
  Ann Elizabeth.
  Rose Mary.
  Zita Matilda.
  Charles Herman.
  Sarah Elizabeth.
  Viola Margaret.
McGuire Mary.
McHugh Matthew.
McHugh Mrs. Matilda (Sanders).
  Michael Henry.
  Frances Amelia.
McHugh Venantius M.
  Mrs. Annie L. (Brown).
  Margaret E.
  Mabel M.
  Catharine G.
  Eugene V.
  Harry J.
  Veronica E.
McLaughlin James.
  Mary.
McMullen Annie C.
  Mary R.

McMullen Joseph A.
  Mrs. Ann Cath. (Sanker).
  Martha Mary.
  Samuel F.
  Edna Susan.
  George Edward.
  Walter Anthony.
McQueeny Margaret.
McVey Daniel.
McVey Mrs. Sarah (Eckenrode).
Melhorn Peter A.
  Mrs. Ellen (Douglas).
  Charles.
Melhorn Jonathan W.
  Mrs. Lydia E. (Eckenrode).
  Peter Augustine.
  Bertha Mary.
  Sylvester John.
  Chester Edward.
  Warren William.
  Caroline.
  Raymond Roy.
Meloy John C.
Miller Mary.
Moran Peter.
  Mrs. Frances (Nagle).
  Walter.
  Alexander P.
  Honora Elizabeth.
  Francis Elmer.
  Mary Eulalia.
  Louis Ferdinand.
Moran John E.
  Mrs. Catherine (Sproat).
Moyer Mrs. Ann (McConnell).
Mullen John.
  Mrs. Mary Ann (Delaney).
  Margaret Ann.
  Mary Elizabeth.
  Mary Josephine.
  Cleophas.

(Mullen) Regina.
  Aloysius Clair.
MULLEN Mrs. Anna Jane (Ingard)
  Blanche.
  Harvey.
  Simon.
  Charles.
  Thomas.
  Alexander.
  Joanna.
MULLEN Catherine.
  Vincent.
MULLEN Mollie L.
MURPHY Mrs. Michael (Barbara Itel).
MYERS ANTHOY.
  Mrs. Mary (McGuire).
  Catherine.
  Henry Augustine.
MYERS Henry Chester.
NAGLE John M.
  Mrs. Della (Gallagher).
  William.
  Richard.
  Vincent Arthur.
  Priscilla.
  Mary.
  Raymond.
  Michael John.
NAGLE Clarence.
NASE Francis.
NOEL Samuel.
  Mrs. Rose (Kane).
  Joseph.
  James S.
NOEL Albert J.
  Mrs. Mary A. (Sybert).
  Laura.
  Francis.
  John.
  Charles.
  Mary Ruth.
  Catherine.

NOLL Mrs. Christina (Willebrand).
  John A.
NOLL Louis.
  Mrs. Elizabeth (Biter).
  Henry Otho.
NOON Michael.
  Mrs. Eleanor (Noon).
  James P.
  Joseph.
  Dennis.
  Jane.
  Dominic
  Chrysostom.
  Philip S.
  Margaret.
NOON Philip.
  Mrs. Mary (Hanlon).
O'BRIEN Howard.
  Stella.
  Bertha.
O'HARA William.
  Mary Ann.
  Henry J.
O'HARA Francis C.
  Mrs. Theresa (Fisher).
  Mary Frances.
  Simon Peter.
  Andrew Joseph.
  Maude Ellen.
  Morgan Francis.
  Robert Michael.
  Leo Paschal.
O'NEILL Mrs. Catherine (Sanders).
O'NEILL Joseph F.
  Mrs. Ella J. (Brawley).
  Simon Homer.
  Esther Marie.
  Cora Eulalia.
  Arline Agatha.
  Arthur Joseph.
  Morgan Ferdinand.
  Leo Robert.
O'NEILL Herman C.

(O'Neill) Mrs. Ida (McCarthy).
    Francis H.
    Louisetta A.
    Eugene Victor.
    Lawrence Earl.
    Mildred de Sales.
PARRISH Thomas L.
    Mrs. Ann (Kennedy).
    Andrew G.
    Walter A.
    Raymond A.
    Leo P.
PARRISH Alexius.
    Mrs. Catherine (Rhyne).
    Edward.
    Alexius F.
    Mary.
    Helen.
    Robert.
PARRISH Rose.
PARRISH Amelia.
PFIESTER Mary Elizabeth.
    Peter Joseph.
PHALEN Mrs. Mary Ann (Behe).
    James Sylvester.
PLATT Celestine C.
    Mrs. Mary (Rudolph).
    Mary Caroline.
    James Gordon.
    Mary Matilda.
    Henry Raymond.
    Rachel Esther.
PRINGLE John W.
    Mrs. Annie E. (McCloskey).
    Thomas Webster.
PRUNER Mrs. W. H. (Mary Little).
    Mary Bertha.
    Henrietta.
    Emma Caroline.
    Loretta.
    William Henry.
    Camilla Marie.

(Pruner) Edward Raymond.
    John Walter.
RAYMOND Emma.
REILLY Mrs. P. (Rose Ellen Noel).
RIGGLE Urbanus.
    Joseph.
RODGERS Peter.
    Sarah Genevieve.
RUDOLPH Mary Matilda.
RUDOLPH William
    Mrs. Caroline (Biter).
    Louisa Mildred.
    Stella Catherine
SANDERS Philip J.
    Mrs. Catherine (Eberly).
    Joey.
    Morgan.
    Eva.
SANKER Anthony.
    Emanuel.
    Mary R.
    Clara.
    William.
    Zita.
SANKER John.
    Mrs. Elizabeth (Storm).
    Luke T.
    Angela.
SANKER Ambrose.
    Mrs. Elizabeth (Rudolph).
    Emma.
SANKER Linus J.
    Mrs. Margaret (Smeltzer).
SARGEANT Thomas.
    Mrs. Agnes (Kaylor).
    William H.
    James T.
    Mary J.
    Emma.
    Loretta.
    Rose.
SCANLAN James Cornelius.

LORETTO ROAD STATION, CAMBRIA & CLEARFIELD DIVISION, P. R. R. FROM THE BRIDGE OVER THE "BIG CUT." THE GROUND TO THE RIGHT (2 1-5 acres) DONATED TO THE P. R. R. CO. BY REV. FERDINAND KITTELL.

(Scanlan) Mrs. Philumena
    (Strittmatter).
  George Louis.
  Herman Augustine.
  Stella Cordelia.
  Bernadette Margaret.
  Mary Eveline.
  Leo Joseph.
  Mary Theresa.
SCANLAN Joseph Augustine.
  Mrs. Harriet (Conrad).
SCHNABEL John A.
  Mary.
SCHNABEL Joseph H.
  Rosalia.
SEYMOUR Martin.
  Mrs. Rosanna (Buck).
  Sylvester.
  Henrietta.
  Anna Mary.
  Englebert Joseph.
SEYMOUR George.
  William.
  Tibertus.
  Leonard.
  Blanche.
  Edgar.
SEYMOUR Isidore.
  Mrs. Theresa Cordelia
    (Bishop.)
  Regis Thomas.
  Mary Matilda.
SHARP John C.
SHARP Joseph.
  Mrs. Elizabeth (Fogle).
  Ellen Theresa.
  John Francis.
  Mary Walburg.
  Henry Ralph.
  Olive Ann.
  Loretta Cecilia.
  Catharine Thecla.
SHEEHAN Timothy.
  Mrs. Rebecca (Burgoon).
  Mary Ann.

(Sheehan) Edward A.
SHERRY Jacob.
  Mrs. Regina (Flick).
  Amelia.
  Francis Xavier.
  Vincent Damian.
  William Jerome.
  Rosalia Regina.
  Gervaise Anicetus.
  Almira Bertha.
  Henrietta Luella.
SHERRY John C.
  Mrs. Mary Helen (Rosensteel).
  John Edwin.
  Peter Albert.
  Purcell Pius.
  Mary Elizabeth.
  Anna Philumena.
  Raymond Albert.
  Libertus Andrew.
  Romanus Titus.
  Genevieve Regina.
SHIBER Mrs. Susan (Beiter).
  Ella.
  Aloysius.
SILL Anthony J.
  Mrs. Elizabeth (Cooper).
  Austin Anthony.
SMELTZER Mrs. Anastasia
    (Kerrigan.)
  Wilfred P
  Leila Gertrude.
  Prudence Blanche.
  Michael Joseph.
  George Augustine.
  Mary Esther.
SMITH Emory L.
  Mrs. Mary E. (Dougherty.)
  Clara Mary.
  William Howard.
  Walter Leonard.
  Eliza Rebecca.
SMITH Charles Alan.

(Smith) Mary Eleanor.
STEBERGER Jacob.
   Mrs. Walburg (Behringer).
   Joseph.
   Elizabeth.
   Alexander.
   Henry.
   Francis.
STEVENS Jacob.
   Mrs. Lucy (Coons).
   Raymond.
   Englebert.
STEVENS Michael.
   Mrs. Mary J. (Gardner).
   Matilda.
STEVENS Harry.
   Mrs. Elizabeth (Hammond).
   Laura.
   John.
   Marie.
   George.
   Bertha.
   Leonard.
STEVENS William F.
STOCK George.
   Mrs. Mary (Simindinger).
   Michael.
   Mary.
   George.
   Harry.
   Patience.
   Bertha.
   Irene.
STORM Francis Augustine.
STORM Gilbert Andrew.
   Mrs. Elizabeth (O'Hanlon).
   Gilbert Eligius.
   Alfred Joseph.
   Mary Edna.
STOY Andrew.
   Jennie.
   Sophia.
(Stoy) Edward.
STOY William.
   Mrs. Ida (Bradley).
   Mary Irene.
SYBERT Catherine.
   John.
   Jennie.
SYBERT Pius Alphonsus.
   Mrs. Annie M. (Haid.)
   William Joseph.
   Ralph John.
   Charles Adrian.
   George Bradley.
THOMAS Ann U.
   Margaret R.
   Bridget A.
   Susan M.
THOMAS Michael P.
   Eleanor V. J.
   James J.
   Mary G.
TIERNEY John J.
   Mrs. Susanna (Bradley).
   Mary V.
   James F.
   Sarah Jane.
   John A.
   Joseph.
   Margaret J.
TOMLINSON Charles.
   Mrs. Ellen Cath. (Shaffer).
   Caroline.
   Michael.
   Laura.
   Howard.
TOMLINSON John E.
   Mrs. Lucy (Strittmatter).
   Stella Margaret.
   Clement Joseph.
   Walter Augustine.
TOMLINSON Simon P.
TOMLINSON Cecilia.
VAUGHT Simon.
   Mrs. Mary Magd. (Hertzog).

(Vaught) Mary Emma.
    Charles Augustine.
    Henry Vincent.
    Clement Clifford.
    Mary Dorothy.
    Ida Rosalia.
    May Myrtle.
    Ethel Lorene.

VOLK Henry
WILLEBRAND Peter J.
WILLIAMS James.
    Mrs. Matilda C. (Hammond).
    Henry Augustine.
WILT Thomas.

SUMMARY.

		LORETTO BOR.	OUTSIDE THE BOR.	TOTAL.	
Under 5 years of age	Males	16	65	81	
	Females	7	51	58	
		23	116		139
Between 5 and 15	Males	20	127	147	
	Females	15	134	149	
		35	261		296
Between 15 and 21	Males	12	77	89	
	Females	10	95	105	
		22	172		194
Over 21 years of age	Males	58	283	341	
	Females	71	285	356	
		129	568		697
Total		269	1117		1326

Males over 21, married	41	158	199
" " " unmarried	17	125	142
	58	283	341
Females over 21, married	45	174	219
" " " unmarried	26	111	137
	71	285	356
Total	129	568	697

Males under 21	48	269	317
Females under 21	32	280	312
	80	549	629
Total	209	1117	1326
Families	45	185	230

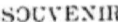

THE CENTENARY.

On April 1, 1891, Rev. Ferdinand Kittell assumed charge of St. Michael's Church, Loretto. Having from his early youth entertained a feeling of deepest reverence for the saintly Father Gallitzin, he determined while in his new position to do all in his power to make more widely known the name and the memory of the illustrious apostle of the Alleghenies. With this view he sought first of all to restore, where possible, and to preserve from further decay, the buildings erected by Father Gallitzin in the early part of the century. The old log barn, which stood near the "Plank Road," a little distance in front of the old pastoral residence, was for years appropriated by the tramping fraternity as a convenient nocturnal abode, and was found on examination to be not worth preserving. Consequently it was razed to the ground and the pine logs hauled to Himmelwright's sawmill and converted into boards, which, with the stone of the foundation, were used in the construction of the new Parochial Hall.

The frame church, erected by Father Gallitzin at his own expense in 1817, and which served as the parish church until 1854, was found to be in a greatly dilapidated condition. It was the earnest desire of the pastor to repair it, and to preserve it as a valuable historical landmark; and for this purpose he deputed all the carpenters of the congregation to carefully examine the structure, and to report on the possibility and cost of restoring it to its original condition. They reported unanimously that the building was too much damaged by the ravages of time and weather to justify any outlay for repairs, which at the best could not be of permanent character; and it was therefore decided to take down the building, and to lay out the ground on which it stood in burial lots. The sanctuary part was reserved for the interment of the parish clergy, and the area of the auditorium, 40x60 feet, was laid out in eight lots 15x18 feet, with a walk four feet wide dividing them, and sold at $50 each to the following named persons:

No. 1. Elizabeth Lacy.
No. 2. Rev. Geo. W. Kaylor.
No. 3. P. J. Sanders.
No. 4. Rev. F. C. Noel.
No. 5. Eug. and B. W. Litzinger.
No. 6. Francis R. Flick.
No. 7. B. W. Litzinger.
No. 8. Mrs. Susan Gallagher.

The entire area of the old building was enclosed by a neat railing to mark the spot where the first church was erected on the Alleghenies,—the first indeed at that time between Lancaster, Pa., and St. Louis; for the frame church, taken down in 1891, was erected on the site of the original log structure built a century ago.

To obtain the means wherewith to carry out his plan as to the other buildings, the pastor issued the following appeal to the public:

AN APPEAL FOR FUNDS

To Preserve from Ruin and Decay, the Chapel and Residence of Rev. Demetrius A. Gallitzin, and to Erect a Suitable Monument to His Memory.

"Died on the 6th of May, A. D. 1840, at his residence, Loretto, Cambria County, Penna., Rev. Demetrius Augustine Gallitzin, forty-one years pastor of the flock in the midst of whom he expired, beloved and lamented. He was a son of Prince Gallitzin, Minister Plenipotentiary of Russia at the Court of Holland, and was born at The Hague, on the 22nd of December, 1770. At the age of twenty-two he came to America to prepare himself, by traveling, for the high station he was to occupy in life; but he soon chose a different career, and entered the Seminary of Saint Mary, Baltimore, to prepare for the holy ministry. He received the holy order of Priesthood from the hands of Dr. Carroll, then only Bishop of Baltimore, on the feast of St. Joseph, March the 19th, in the year 1795, and was subsequently employed in the sacred ministry at Conewago, whence he visited the immense district (around Loretto) where he fixed his residence in 1799. In the midst of a few poor families he began his apostolic labors, and lived to see several large congregations gathered around him, whose spiritual wants, in the remote parts of the country, required the aid of several priests. His boundless charity has been experienced by thousands, who owe to him every temporal comfort, besides the blessing of Religion."

The above obituary, printed in the "Catholic Herald" soon after his demise, gives but a faint outline of the life and labors of the Pioneer Missionary of the Alleghenies. They can be appreciated only by those who consider the immense obstacles he had to overcome before he succeeded in firmly establishing a colony on the rugged mountains and in the inhospitable climate of Cambria County. He generously devoted forty-one years of his noble life, all his brilliant talents and a princely fortune to the great undertaking which brought such benefits to Religion and to the State. More than a half century has passed since his death, and, as yet, his merits have never been adequately recognized.

In this connection the Very Rev. Thomas Heyden, D. D., of Bedford, Pa., one of his biographers, wrote as follows:

"As the railroad cars of the Central Pennsylvania route pass westward through the great tunnel, and emerge thence over the cloud-capped peaks of the Allegheny chain of mountains, the listless, unsuspecting throng of passengers are suddenly awakened by the cry of the conductor, when he sounds forth the name given to this station, Gallitzin! And this, to use the words of a late reviewer, is all there is to remind them of the son of one of Russia's proudest, noblest families, who for nearly half a century toiled so disinterestedly for the spiritual and temporal welfare of his fellow men, on this same mountain.

"It is true, his inconsolable flock, not long after his decease, erected to his memory an humble monument, but not at all worthy of this great man, and it is to be hoped that a more suitable and superb one will soon mark the sacred spot where so much worth is interred, a spot worthy to be a place of pilgrimage, where all who want to have revived in them the spirit of faith and sacrifice and charity, will often resort, *locus pietatis* (the place of piety) as the tombs of the martyrs and confessors were called in the primitive church."

It is to realize this ardent hope that the undersigned issues this appeal. The old stone house in which for so many years the venerable Prince-Missionary made his home, and from which his well-tried soul ascended to heaven, and the humble chapel, likewise of stone, in which for so long a period he exercised the sacred ministry, have commenced to succumb to the ravages of time, and, unless they be repaired, will soon form but a shapeless mass of ruins. Erected in the early part of this century, they are valuable historical landmarks, and are worth preserving for the sake of the hallowed associations and memories with which they are connected.

The old frame church, built at Prince Gallitzin's expense in 1817, which at that time was considered a marvel of architecture, is thought to be too far decayed to merit the cost of repair. But the foundation wall will always remain to mark the spot where the sacred edifice was erected.

The "humble monument" of shapeless sculpture, erected by the congregation in 1847, is composed of blocks of rough mountain stone, which the frosts of our long and severe winters have forced apart, leaving large crevices, annually growing larger, through which the rain and the melting snow penetrate to the vault beneath, where the remains of the heroic missionary are preserved. These blocks will have to be re-set and securely clamped so as to maintain them permanently in position; and when this is accomplished, it is proposed to replace the unsightly (and now decayed) wooden cross and coffin which surmount the so-called monument, with a life-size and life-like statue of the venerable Gallitzin, for which the pile of massive blocks would serve admirably as a pedestal.

To accomplish all this is beyond the means of this congregation. At any rate, the name and fame of Gallitzin are not the exclusive property of the Loretto parish: they belong to the Church and to the country at large.

If, therefore, you who read this appeal, care to aid in perpetuating the memory of one who was great as a Prince, a Missionary, and an American citizen, kindly send a contribution, however small, to

REV. FERDINAND KITTELL, Pastor.

St. Michael's Church, Loretto, Cambria County, Pa.
June 15, 1891.

The appeal met with a hearty response on the part of the general public. From near and far contributions came flowing in, until the total amount reached the sum of $2,138.12. With this money the pastor was enabled to rebuild Father

CHAPEL AND RESIDENCE OF FATHER GALLITZIN.

Gallitzin's chapel, part of which had already fallen in, and the rest was in danger of falling; to repair Father Gallitzin's house, which until 1874 had been the pastoral residence, and to render it again useful as a domicile; to secure a metallic casket into which his venerated remains were transferred from the original, then greatly decayed, coffin, and to repair the ravages which time had made in the monument erected in 1847.

When all this had been accomplished there was nothing left towards completing the design of honoring the name of Father Gallitzin, and of perpetuating the record of his life's work, by erecting "a suitable monument to his memory." Years passed, and money was needed, and generously contributed by the parishioners, for other improvements. The time for celebrating the great Centenary was fast approaching, and it was seen that it would be impossible for the people of this agricultural parish, where very little money circulates, to raise the large sum required to procure a statue of the illustrious Gallitzin. It was under these circumstances that on the 19th of last April Father Kittell laid the case before Mr. C. M. Schwab, President of the Carnegie Steel Company, Limited, who was pleased with the suggestion, and at once most generously offered to defray the entire expense of the statue. The contract for its erection was given to Mr. O. E. Wilkinson, of the marble and granite firm of Jas. Wilkinson & Son, Ebensburg, Pa. It was at first intended to place the statue on top of the stone monument as it stood; and the credit for procuring the magnificent granite base which now supports the statue is due to Mr. Wilkinson, who represented to Mr. Schwab that the design would not be complete without it. It is needless to state that Mr. Schwab heartily approved of this suggestion, and cheerfully bore the extra, and quite considerable, expense.

O. E. WILKINSON.

In the meantime the most active preparations were being made for the worthy celebration of the Centenary, which was first fixed for September 29, the Feast of St. Michael, Patron of the parish, and afterwards changed to October 10. Committees were appointed to arrange for the various details, invitations were issued, and the celebration duly advertised in the public press. The citizens of Loretto vied with each other in their efforts to make the old town assume a gala-day appearance. A dozen arches spanned the main

THE MAIN STREET OF LORETTO, FROM CORNER NEAR THE CHURCH.

street of the borough at various points, and every house was decorated with evergreens, bunting and flags. The members of the Loretto Council Y. M. I. had charge of the decorations on the church grounds and down at the old house, and the three arches that they erected were much admired. The papal colors, yellow and white, displayed in honor of Monsignor Martinelli, the Apostolic Delegate, were everywhere in evidence, and mingling with our glorious red, white and blue, produced a pleasing and beautiful effect. The interior decorations of the church were very elaborate. A large picture of Father Gallitzin was suspended high above the sanctuary, and from it festoons of evergreen were looped to the five columns on either side of the nave, connecting with large pictures of his ten successors in the pastorate at St. Michael's, one on each column. Intermingled with the festoons of evergreen were festoons of yellow and white bunting; and from the organ gallery was suspended a national flag, 24x36 feet, kindly loaned for the occasion by the County Commissioners. On the Gospel side of the sanctuary was erected a throne for the Apostolic Delegate, and directly opposite, a similar one for the Rt. Rev. celebrant of the Pontifical Mass.

Great anxiety was manifested lest the statue, cast by Bureau Bros., sculptors, Philadelphia, should not be in readiness for the date announced for the unveiling. It was not

ARRIVAL OF THE BASE OF THE STATUE, OCTOBER 6.

until the evening of Friday, October 6, that the three immense blocks of polished granite, weighing fifteen tons, and destined for the base of the monument (see picture) arrived at the church. Yet it speaks well for the energy displayed by Mr. Wilkinson and his corps of workmen, that he finished his contract by the following Monday afternoon, and announced everything in readiness for the ceremony of the next day.

On Sunday, October 8, rain fell copiously, and though it did considerable damage to the bunting already in place, it did not dampen the spirits of the parishioners, for the novena which they were making for beautiful weather on the 10th was not yet concluded, and they felt sure that their prayers would be heard. And, as the event proved, their prayers were heard beyond their utmost expectations.

On Monday, the 9th, the weather was still of a threatening aspect, but in the afternoon the clouds rolled by, and all nature gave indications of a beautiful day on the morrow. A grand demonstration had been arranged in honor of the Apostolic Delegate, whose arrival was expected at about 5 o'clock in the evening. At the request of the pastor, nearly the entire congregation assembled in the church yard, where at the proper time the procession was formed. First went the cross-bearer and two acolytes bearing processional lanterns; then the flag-bearer carrying the Stars and Stripes, followed by the Loretto Cornet Band; then marched the children who on the morrow were to make their first Holy Communion and to be confirmed, each carrying a flag; these were followed by the students of St. Francis' College, and by the older members of the parish. The Rev. pastor, accompanied by Rev. Martin Ryan, of Gallitzin, and a number of acolytes, all vested in cassock and surplice, brought up the rear. Four papal flags were carried in the ranks.

The procession moved down the road to Cresson, and halted near the foot of the hill to await the arrival of the Most Rev. Delegate. In due time his carriage was seen descending the opposite hill, escorted by fifty young men of the parish on gaily decorated horses, marshaled by Mr. W. Edgar Glass, and followed by a long retinue of conveyances decked out with the papal and national colors. At the first sight of the Monsignor's carriage a mighty cheer was raised by the waiting ranks; handkerchiefs were waved, the band played a lively tune, and these demonstrations of welcome, as hearty as the one given in Loretto to the Papal Nunzio, Monsignor Bedini, in 1853, were frequently renewed as the procession slowly returned, and only ceased when the Delegate, alighting from his carriage, entered the church, and thence passed to the parlor of the pastoral residence. Monsignor Martinelli was accompanied on his trip by Rt. Rev. Bishop Curtis, of Baltimore, and by Very Rev. J. A. Zahm, D. D., Provincial of the Congregation of the Holy Cross, Notre Dame, Ind., whose mother was born and reared in this parish, and was baptized by Father Gallitzin.

The distinguished guests were soon joined by Mr. C. M. Schwab, and also by His Excellency, Governor Stone, who, coming on a later train from the east, had been welcomed at Cresson in the name of the pastor and people by Dr. John Murphy, and conducted thence to Loretto. After a brief interval of rest the entire party proceeded in carriages to Immergrün, the beautiful summer residence of Mr. Schwab, on the hill overlooking the town, where they were in time to welcome His Grace, Archbishop Ireland, of St. Paul, who, accompanied from Pittsburg by Rev. William Kittell, chancellor of the diocese, had just arrived from Loretto Road station. It was then learned that Rt. Rev. Bishop Phelan, who had made all preparations for the trip to Loretto, had been obliged by sudden illness to forego the anticipated pleasure, and it was arranged that Rt. Rev. Bishop Curtis would solemnly pontificate in his stead on the following morning.

Their guests were most hospitably entertained at dinner and afterwards by Mr. and Mrs. Schwab, and were serenaded by the Loretto Band. At a convenient hour the Apostolic Delegate and Bishop Curtis returned to the pastoral residence for the night, while Archbishop Ireland and Governor Stone remained the guests of Immergrün.

The morning of Tuesday, October 10, dawned fair and serene upon favored Loretto; the sun soon dispelled the light mist and shone with unusual brightness throughout the day; not a breath of air was stirring, and the rains of the previous

Sunday having laid the dust, the roads were dry and smooth, and never in better condition. The golden hues of the changing foliage, mingled with the red, the yellow, the white and the blue of the flags and bunting so lavishly displayed, formed a very kaleidoscope of color; and, as if nature itself had been waiting to do homage to the memory of Gallitzin, it was not until the next day, as was noticed by many, that the leaves commenced to drop from the branches. It was the universal verdict that a more beautiful day for such a celebration could not have been desired.

On that morning all roads in Cambria County led to Loretto. The number of vehicles of every description coming from all directions could only be estimated by the hundreds. The two fields in front of the church were dotted

VIEW AT MID-DAY, OCTOBER 10.

with conveyances and horses, yet the greater number was cared for in other parts of the town and on adjacent farms. An immense crowd came by railroad to Loretto Road station, whence they were brought to the town in special conveyances. So great was the interest everywhere manifested in the Loretto Centenary, that the public schools within a circuit of many miles were closed for the day, while the neighboring towns for the time being were almost depopulated.

One great feature of the celebration was the arrival at Loretto Road of the special train, arranged for by Mr. C. M. Schwab, which left Pittsburg at 6.15 a. m., and brought nearly a score of representatives of the city press, the entire Cathedral Choir (32 members), the celebrated Duquesne Band of 45 pieces, and, besides a large number of others, the Loretto Club of Homestead, an organization composed of one hundred young men, all former residents of this parish. With their tall hats, their beautiful badges and their manly bearing, they attracted general attention, and excited unstinted admiration, as they marched from the station to the inspiring music of the band.

Ample provision had been made by the parishioners to feed the vast crowd that was expected. Dinner and supper were served in the upper story of the Parochial Hall, while in the lower story and on the church grounds lunch and refreshment booths were erected and admirably managed. This is not the place to mention particular names; but the writer desires to place on record the fact that the glorious success of our Centenary celebration was due in no small measure to the ladies and gentlemen, who labored so long, so assiduously and so unselfishly in decorating the interior of the church and its surroundings; in serving the dinner, lunch and refreshments, and in managing the thousand details, of which the general public can form no idea. And in this connection the Cathedral Choir, which assisted our home talent in rendering the music for the occasion, both at the Pontifical mass and at the ceremonies of the unveiling of the statue, and the Duquesne Band, which enlivened the proceedings from its unequaled reportoire, will long be remembered by the parishioners of St. Michael's.

At 7 o'clock Archbishop Ireland, assisted by Rev. Thos. W. Rosensteel, of Tyrone, said mass in Father Gallitzin's Chapel, at the same altar at which that true priest of God

INTERIOR OF ST. MICHAEL'S CHURCH, LORETTO, DECORATED FOR THE CENTENARY.

offered up the mass on week days during the last eight years of his saintly life. On this occasion he wore the vestments, often worn by Father Gallitzin, which were made by the latter's mother from the material of her wedding gown, and which were kindly loaned for the occasion by the Sisters of St. Joseph, of Ebensburg.

At 7.30 Monsignor Martinelli celebrated mass in the parish church, which was crowded to the doors. He was assisted by Very Rev. J. Boyle, V. F., of Johnstown, and by Rev. William Kittell, chancellor, and brother of the Rev. pastor. During the mass he gave First Holy Communion to a number of children, and immediately after the mass he administered the Sacrament of Confirmation to a still larger number. Amongst these were a few adults; several students of the College, and some children from adjoining parishes. The reverend pastor collected the tickets and read out the names. The sponsor for the males was the venerable Mr. Arthur Comerford; for the females, Mrs. Sarah Sanker. The names of the favored children of the parish only are here given:

FIRST HOLY COMMUNION AND CONFIRMATION.

BOYS.

ANSMAN Albert.
BITER Leo.
    Sherman.
BOLEY Frank.
COONS Mathias.
    Louis.
DRISKEL Michael.
DURBIN Blair.
ELWOOD Leo.
FARABAUGH William.
GLASS Gorman.
KITTELL Louis.
LITTLE Veritas.
    Meredith.
    Glenna.
McGUIRE Charles.
McMULLEN George.
MELHORN Sylvester.
(Melhorn) Chester.
MULLEN Thomas.
    Alexander.
NAGLE William.
    Sanford.
O'BRIEN Howard.
O'HARA Robert.
PLATT Harry.
SCANLAN Herman.
SHARP Frank.
SMELTZER Ossie.
STEVENS John.
STOCK Harry.
WILLS Howard.

GIRLS.

BOLAN Martha.
BOLEY Alma.
    Theresa.
BISHOP Esther.

(Bishop) Fannie.
BRADY Harriet.
BRUCE Ettie.
COONS Rose.
COOPER Irene.
DOUGHERTY Laura.
EBERLY Caroline.
EBIG Stella.
ECKENRODE Ida.
FARREN Margaret.
FLICK Ida.
FRY Edith.
KITTELL Mary.
LITTLE Rose.
LOWE Mary.
McGOUGH Mildred.
NOEL Laura.
O'NEILL Esther.
PRUNER Emma.
SANDERS Eva.
SHARP Ella.
THOMAS Mary.
VAUGHT Ida.

(Gallagher) Thomas.
GLASS Eugene.
   Clair.
HALL William.
HAMMOND Bert.
HERTZOG Edward.
LITTLE Michael.
LITZINGER Jesse.
MALLOY Harry.
McGOUGH Louis.
NOEL Frank.
O'NEILL Homer.
SCANLAN Louis.
SHERRY Gervaise.
   Romanus.
SMITH William.
STEBERGER Frank.
STEVENS William.
STOCK George.
STOY Edward.
SYBERT William.
TOMLINSON Howard.

CONFIRMATION ONLY.

BOYS.

BANNAN Edward.
BILLER Louis.
BISHOP Andrew.
BITER Albert.
BRADLEY Thomas.
CALLAN Edward.
CONRAD J. Harvey.
COOPER Raymond.
DENNY Oscar.
DONOUGHE Harry.
   Peter.
EBERLY Paul.
ECKENRODE Romanus.
   Clement.
FARABAUGH Erhart.
FISHER Simon.
FREIDHOFF Louis.
FRY Leo.
GALLAGHER Hugh.

GIRLS.

ANSMAN Annie.
BANNAN Della.
BOLEY Theresa.
BISHOP Minnie.
BUCK Lorene.
CALLAN Gertrude.
COONS Flora.
CRAMER Mary.
DRISKEL Katie.
ECKENRODE Nellie.
   Myrtle.
FARABAUGH Henrietta.
FLICK Augusta.
HERTZOG Rose.
ITEL Mary.
JONES Clarinda.
KAYLOR Dora.
LITTLE Dora.
MALLOY Martina.
McDUNN Josephine.
McGUIRE Zita.

Moran Nora.
Murphy Nellie.
Parrish Amelia.
Pruner May.
    Hattie.
Schnable Rose.

Sherry Elmira.
Shields Millie.
Smeltzer Blanche.
Stock Mary.
Vaught Dora.

The Pontifical High Mass was celebrated by Rt. Rev. A. A. Curtis, Vicar General of the Archdiocese of Baltimore, and formerly Bishop of Wilmington, Del. The officers of the mass were as follows: Assistant Priest, Very Rev. E. A. Bush, V. G., for twenty years (1870-90) pastor of St. Michael's; Deacon, Rev. Henry McHugh, pastor of St. Agnes' Church, Pittsburg, who was baptized by Father Gallitzin: Sub-deacon, Rev. Thomas McEnrue, of Irwin; Master of Ceremonies, Rev. Regis Canevin, Rector of St. Paul's Cathedral, Pittsburg; Assistant Master of Ceremonies, Rev. Martin Ryan, formerly pastor of Loretto, now of Gallitzin; Cross-bearer, Rev. C. O. Rosensteel, of Forest Glen, Md.; Thurifer, Rev. Thos. W. Rosensteel, of Tyrone; Acolytes, Rev. Francis Hertzog, of St. Andrew's, Allegheny, and Rev. Joseph Burgoon, of St. Kieran's, Pittsburg.

On his throne at the Gospel side Monsignor Martinelli in Cappa Magna sat in a plain arm-chair, which Father Gallitzin used for years in his confessional. His attendants were Very Rev. Dr. Zahm, C. S. C., and Rev. Wm. Kittell. Archbishop Ireland in his episcopal robes sat in front of the altar, attended by Very Rev. J. Boyle, V. F., and Rev. Francis McCarthy, S. J., of New York, formerly a priest of this diocese. About sixty priests occupied the other seats in the sanctuary and the front pews in the auditorium. After the first Gospel Very Rev. Father Bush, V. G., ascended the pulpit and spoke as follows:

"*This is the victory which overcometh the world, our faith.*"
—St. John I.-v. 4.

To fully understand the value of the life of the Prince-priest, the centennial of whose work in founding this community we are assembled here to celebrate, we must look into it from the standpoint of the inspired writer whose words I have just quoted.

Two young men about the same time in the history of our country, left Europe to come to America. One was born amidst the romantic scenery of Switzerland, whose lofty mountains capped with eternal snow, and whose beautiful lakes nestling at their feet, attract the lovers of nature by their many charms; and whose every hamlet has its story of the undying love of liberty that gives to that favored land its strongest claim: the other first saw the light of day in the capital city of Holland, a land lying low, with artificial watercourses, whose sturdy inhabitants have for centuries resisted the encroachments of the mighty ocean, and have wrested from his grasp thousands of acres, which they have converted into fertile fields, by whose product they have added immensely to their wealth and importance. The former belonged to the middle class and was well educated in all that could help him to success in life; the other was of princely lineage, and all along the pages of his country's history he could find the record of one after another of his ancestors illustrious for wisdom in the councils of the sovereign and for prowess on the field of battle. In his youth he was trained in all that was deemed necessary to fit him for the brilliant future that was mapped out for him; and prophetic ability was not required to predict for him a career of glory that would equal at least, if it did not surpass, the career of any of his progenitors in all that the world most prizes.

Gallatin left his fatherland in order to cast his lot with the nation that had just exchanged the swaddling clothes of colonial life for the toga of Aurelius among the nations. Step by step he rose until he reached the highest point that could be attained by a citizen of foreign birth. He was a man of great usefulness to the American people, who conferred upon him all the honors at their disposal: and from the world's point of view his life was a grand and most successful one.

Demetrius Gallitzin came only with a view of finishing his education, and of learning all that he could about the social life of other peoples. This he could not do in Europe on account of the perturbed state of society, which, undermined by atheism, was about to become a prey to the horrors of revolution. The fashionable people in those days and the nobility were infected with atheistical doctrines. His mother also, having long associated with atheists in her younger days, became one of them. But when children came to her, her mother's heart desired for them something better, nobler, purer than all this mere learning could provide. Therefore, she investigated and studied, and as a result of her investigation she became a sincere Catholic, and then effected the conversion of her children.

So it was as a fervent Catholic, thoroughly disciplined in all educational matters, that Gallitzin came to America. Among the letters of introduction with which he had been supplied, was one to Bishop Carroll, of Baltimore, that grand old hero of the Church in America, who recognized in the young enthusiast the workings of the Holy Spirit of God. As a prudent man he tried to discourage him from taking upon himself the burthen and hardships of a missionary career; but he was soon convinced that the call to the new life, so widely different from the one to which his parents had destined him, and from the one to which the Swiss had devoted himself, came directly and irresistibly from on high.

With a fitting preparation he knelt at the altar of God to receive the holy order of God's priesthood; and in doing so he laid aside the princely crown and turned his back on the inviting allurements which the world held out to him; and, as the world would say, he cast himself away. Unlike those who find no difficulty in relinquishing attachment to things that they do not possess, but only hope for, he actually relinquished all that he had and was to own, and thus his sacrifice was complete.

From the steps of the altar he arises a priest of God. Being of a retiring disposition and of a studious turn of mind, he might have entered the sacred ministry in Europe, where by associating with learned men and by frequenting renowned educational institutions, he might have had all his natural longings gratified. All this he gave up to become a poor and humble missionary in a rough and sparsely settled country, where the harvest was great, but the harvesters few.

It was not long until he received another inspiration from God, like unto that which called him from the world to embrace the sacred ministry; and obedient to its impulse he left the cities where he might have achieved great eminence in his holy calling, and came to this region which was then little better than a wilderness. Away from all the grandeur of the world to which he had been accustomed; separated from home, family and friends; with no one near at hand intellectually his equal to associate with; with no prospects in the future but those of continued poverty, hardships, seclusion and never-ending labor,—surely his was a condition to try the faith of the strongest. But his faith was tried and it conquered; it was strong within him, and it made him victorious over the great enemies of man—the concupiscence of the flesh, the concupiscence of the eyes and the pride of life. Ambition he had surrendered: greed for wealth he had not: all that he received through the bounty of his friends abroad he spent not on himself but in helping the poor and in building up this community; and of him it may be truly said that he founded the first orphan asylum in Western Pennsylvania, and founded it in his own house, down there at the bend of the hill. Was there an orphan? He regarded that child as his by adoption from God. Was there one in distress? No ear, no heart was so open to the tale of misery as was his. He considered himself merely the steward of what he received or possessed, to manage it for the benefit of others; and he never stopped to inquire what were the antecedents of those who appealed to him, or whether their appeals were worthy of being heard; but he relieved instant distress as far as lay in his power, and then sought means to extend the relief. There were some of his flock who upbraided him for his indiscriminate charity in that respectful, loving way they had with him; but he would reply that he gave for the love of God, that he was not mistaken in the motive; and that, given the necessity of relief, it was not for him to judge of the worthiness or unworthiness of the recipients.

He laid aside his princely name. No doubt there were many reasons for this, some of them unknown to us. But it may be presumed that one of the strongest arose from the deep humility which, with charity and faith, seemed to be the cherished virtue of his soul. He must have felt the incongruity of a missionary known by that illustrious surname, traveling on such a horse as he could get through forests where there were but bridle paths; frequently passing the darkest hours of the night in the same forests when going to or returning from distant sick calls, and living in a small log cabin, scarcely, if at all, more comfortable than the rude habitations in the neighborhood, and by no means as commodious. In the lapse of time legal requirements compelled him to resume his family surname, but not his title: and when this happened the grand old soul could not stand up before his parishioners and tell them himself, but got a priest from a distance to come and to make the public announcement. The surprise with which the people heard that their humble, devoted pastor, who lived as poorly as the poorest among them, was no less a personage than a prince of one of the oldest and noblest families of Russia may be better imagined than described.

Now, he worked as a priest, he worked for his flock, and in his ministrations he covered a large extent of almost unbroken territory. He had to labor with all kinds of people of all kinds of dispositions, and to encounter hardships and overcome obstacles of which we, at this late day, can form no adequate idea. But they were matters of fact with him, and the trials that he underwent bore more heavily upon him, so gently nurtured, than they would have weighed on others reared amid rougher surroundings. And while he worked he prayed; for he was distinctively a man of prayer, a man of meditation. Amongst his books was one that was found some years ago, and that gave evident signs of being the one most used by him, and it was a book of meditations on the passion of our Lord Jesus Christ. What strength, what courage he must have drawn from those meditations! And he needed all that he could thus acquire, for being of a supremely sensitive character the reverses that happened to him, and the ingratitude that he met with, tried his patience and fortitude to the utmost, and would have disheartened many another less disciplined in the school of Christ. And if the story be not true, it might have been true, that God himself in a supernatural manner condescended to raise the courage that was drooping in that noble soul which had given up so much for love of Him.

Now, the ground work of that life, a life comparatively unknown, but oh! how rich in all that makes life valuable from the standpoint of God, was *Faith*,—the faith that overcometh the world. A scroll one day will be unrolled before the eyes of the whole human race, a scroll written in indelible characters, that will reveal and will preserve unto an eternity of eternities the character, the life, the workings, the sufferings, thoughts of every human being; and high up upon that list will be found the records of those who, for the love of God, gave up all and lived and died faithful to that engagement; and who as a reward for their fidelity are now in possession of the kingdom prepared for them.

Amongst these are apostles and martyrs and confessors, and thousands of others who do not rank so high, but whose degree of glory is proportionate to their merits acquired on earth. And we may well imagine that on this glorious day, while we are commemorating the one-hundreth anniversary of his coming hither to establish this Catholic community, the soul of the sainted Gallitzin, the apostle and confessor of the faith on these Alleghenies, is looking down benignly upon us from his high place in the heavenly kingdom, and is gladdened at the sight of the abundant harvest that has been gathered as a result of his forty-one years of unremitting toil.

Now you know I have always tried to be practical, and the practical part is this: Love that faith which Father Gallitzin planted and watered, and to which God in His goodness, during the hundred years now closing, has given such a wonderful increase; prize it, be true to it in all the circumstances and vicissitudes of life, so that you may demonstrate in the most unmistakable manner that you are worthy children of those who had the enviable fortune to receive his instructions and to be encouraged by his living example; and that you are determined to preserve intact, and to transmit to future generations the grand and noble heritage that you have received, than which none could be nobler or grander,—the heritage of Catholic faith, which alone overcometh the world.

The ceremonies in the church closed at noon. The more notable guests had been courteously invited by Mr. Schwab to dine at his residence, and among those who sat at his hos-

THE PROCESSION FROM IMMERGRÜN TO THE CHURCH.

pitable table were: Monsignor Martinelli, Archbishop Ireland, Bishop Curtis, Governor Stone; Hon. A. V. Barker, President Judge of the county; C. A. Wood, Very Rev. E. A. Bush, V. G.; Rev. F. McCarthy, S. J., of New York; Rev. E. J. Flynn, of Mount Vernon, N. Y.; Rev. Martin Ryan, of Gallitzin, and the pastor, Rev. Ferdinand Kittell.

Promptly at 2 o'clock a procession, headed by the Duquesne Band, and composed of the Loretto Club of Homestead, St. Patrick's L. & B. Society, and two Polish societies, of Gallitzin, St. Michael's T. A. Society, and others, arrived at Immergrün, where Mr. W. A. Kessler, President of the Loretto Club, in the name of the club presented to Mr. Schwab a large and beautiful silk flag. The procession, followed by the dignitaries in carriages, then marched down the main street of the town to the church yard.

THE STATUE VEILED.

It had been intended that the carriages conveying the distinguished guests should be driven up to the grand stand, but, owing to the immense throng that packed the church yard almost to suffocation, this was found to be impossible. The dignitaries therefore were compelled to alight at a considerable distance from the stand, and to make their way with no little trouble to the place prepared for them. When all had been seated Father Kittell, acting as chairman, advanced to the speaker's stand and opened the interesting proceedings by reading the following letters of regret:

CARDINAL'S RESIDENCE,
Baltimore, Md.

SEPTEMBER 7, 1899.

REV. DEAR FATHER KITTELL:

His Eminence, the Cardinal, is very sorry, indeed, that the celebration of your Centenary falls on October 10, as it will be impossible for him to be absent from home on that date. He says he must be on hand to receive the archbishops and to attend to other important duties which devolve upon him at that time.

He wishes your celebration every success and sends you his kindest regards.

J. T. O'BRIEN, Chancellor.

SEPTEMBER 15, 1899.

DEAR FATHER KITTELL:

In my enforced absence Rt. Rev. Bishop Curtis will represent the Archdiocese of Baltimore and myself at the approaching celebration. I hope it will be worthy of the man in whose memory it is undertaken. Faithfully yours in Xt.

J. CARD. GIBBONS.

ST. PETER'S CATHEDRAL,
Cincinnati, O.

OCTOBER 2, 1899.

REV. DEAR SIR:

The Most Rev. Archbishop is sorry to say that duties in Cincinnati will keep him from attending your celebration on the 10th inst. Yours sincerely in Xto.

REV. E. A. DAVIS, Secretary.

P. S.—It is a new obligation which has arisen since I accepted your kind invitation. I cannot leave before the 11th. Kindest regards.

W. H. ELDER.

ARCHBISHOP'S HOUSE,
   Philadelphia, Pa.

SEPTEMBER 10, 1899.

DEAR FATHER KITTELL:

I regret that it will not be possible for me to be with you for your celebration on the 10th of October. I have to leave that evening for Washington, to be present the next morning at the annual meeting of the Trustees of the Catholic University. I am sure that any of the clergy of this archdiocese whom you may invite will be happy to attend on so very interesting and historic an occasion.

Hoping that the celebration will prove worthy of such an occasion, I am, Dear Father Kittell,

Yours faithfully.
P. J. RYAN, Archbishop.

BISHOP'S RESIDENCE,
   Wheeling, W. Va.

SEPTEMBER 20, 1899.

REV. DEAR FATHER:

I beg to thank your reverence most cordially for the kind invitation conveyed in your favor of the 11th inst. I regret to say that my numerous engagements for the month of October will deprive me of the pleasure of being with you on the great occasion of the Centenary of the foundation of your parish. It would be a great delight to me to assist, but I have been away in Europe for five months, and I am consequently much crowded in my confirmation and other engagements. However, from the programme that you have laid out, and from the names of the distinguished guests, I feel that you are to have a glorious celebration. This is my wish for you and your parishioners. May the example, too, of the illustrious and saintly founder be an inspiration for us all. Yours devotedly in Xto.

     P. J. DONAHUE, Bishop of Wheeling.

 ST. MALACHY'S CHURCH,
  Philadelphia, Pa.
         SEPTEMBER 19, 1899.

DEAR FATHER KITTELL:

 I assure you that I will try to be with you on the 10th of October, but I cannot say positively at present that I will be free to do so. Yours truly in Dno.

 E. F. PRENDERGAST, Auxiliary Bishop of Philadelphia.

(At the last moment he was unavoidably detained.)

 BISHOP'S HOUSE,
  Erie, Pa.
         SEPTEMBER 9, 1899.

REV. DEAR FATHER:

 I regret very much that it will be impossible for me to attend the celebration of the Centenary of your parish on the 10th prox. I have made a series of appointments in the diocese for that week, and it would be impossible for me to break them without great inconvenience to those interested. Wishing you a happy occasion, I am,

         Yours in Xto.

  JOHN E. FITZMAURICE, Coadjutor Bishop.

 BISHOP'S HOUSE,
  Harrisburg, Pa.
         SEPTEMBER 7, 1899.

DEAR FATHER KITTELL:

 On Sunday, October 8, I begin work in the northern part of the diocese, and I cannot leave there for two weeks. Regretting that I shall not be able to attend your celebration, and thanking you for inviting me, I remain,

         Very sincerely.

   J. W. SHANAHAN, Bishop of Harrisburg.

BISHOP'S HOUSE,
   Scranton, Pa.

OCTOBER 5, 1899.

REV. DEAR SIR:

Since writing to you the other day (accepting the invitation) I have been reminded by the President of our Diocesan Temperance Union (one of my priests), that the Temperance Societies of the diocese will parade here next Tuesday, October 10, and, of course, they will expect me to be "in evidence."

I regret very much, therefore, that I shall not have the pleasure of being with you on Monday next, as I had expected.

Permit me to wish you the most complete success in your Centenary celebration, and to remain

      Faithfully yours in Xt.

         M. J. HOBAN, Bishop of Scranton.

ST. VINCENT'S ARCHABBEY,
   Beatty, Pa.

SEPTEMBER 27, 1899.

REV. AND DEAR FATHER:

Your kind invitation to attend the grand celebration of next month has been received. Accept my heartfelt thanks for the same. I am very sorry, however, to state that it will be impossible for me to be present, though I would very much appreciate attending the celebration. Our abbey will certainly be well represented by the attendance of the neighboring Benedictine pastors. With best wishes, I remain

      Yours sincerely in Dno.

        LEANDER, O. S. B., Archabbot.

COLLEGE OF ST. THOMAS AQUINAS,
   CATHOLIC UNIVERSITY,
     WASHINGTON, D. C.

OCTOBER 2, 1899.

MY DEAR FATHER KITTELL:

Your invitation to the Centenary of the foundation of your parish honors me. I only wish that I could do more than thank you for it. But the fact is that I must be in Indianapolis that very day giving the diocesan Retreat there.

God bless your new century. I am one of the very many who are to be present in good will, hearty congratulations, fervent prayers, although not bodily, among the vast concourse of people and the distinguished personages of your great celebration. Most faithfully yours in Xt.

WALTER ELLIOTT.

HOLLIDAYSBURG, September 26, 1899.

DEAR FATHER KITTELL:

I regret exceedingly that I cannot accept your kind invitation to attend the ceremonies in memory of the illustrious Gallitzin on the 10th of October next. Our court meets in Pittsburg on the 9th for a continual session of six weeks. It is my official duty to be present on the 10th.

Nothing would afford me more pleasure than to meet the illustrious prelates who will be present, and so many of my old Cambria County friends. No one reverences the Christian character of Father Gallitzin more than I; that character shines through all the early records of the county, deeds, wills and contracts. Much of his work passed under my eye as judge in that county. He was a Christian lawyer in this, that taking human nature as it existed, he sought to allay and prevent strife by wise, just and clear writings, as well as by Christian counsel. With kindest regards, I am

Very truly yours,
JOHN DEAN,
Justice of the Supreme Court of Pennsylvania.

OFFICE OF GENERAL SUPERINTENDENT P. R. R.
ALTOONA, Pa., September 20, 1899.

MY DEAR SIR:

I beg to acknowledge your letter of the 15th inst., and to thank you for your invitation to assist on Tuesday, October 10th, prox., at the celebration of the Centenary of the foundation of Loretto, and regret very much that on account of our annual track inspection beginning on that date it will be impossible for me to attend.

It will give me great pleasure, however, to delegate Mr. C. A. Wood as my representative, and I thank you very much for the suggestion.

Trusting that the weather and all other conditions may be most favorable, I remain

Very respectfully.
J. M. WALLIS, General Superintendent.

OFFICE OF C. & C. DIVISION P. R. R.
CRESSON, Pa., September 26, 1899.

DEAR FATHER:

Replying to your very kind note of the 18th inst., I regret very much to say I will be unable to attend the celebration of the Centenary of Loretto on the 10th of October, owing to the fact that our annual track inspection commences upon that day. I am very sorry to be compelled to miss so interesting an occasion, and trust you will be favored with pleasant weather and the greatest success in your efforts.

Very sincerely yours.
F. P. ABERCROMBIE, Superintendent.

Father Kittell then spoke as follows:

Your Excellences, Distinguished Guests, Friends:

Born almost within sound of the bell of this parish church, the very year the tomb of Father Gallitzin there before us was erected, I had always from my earliest remembrance a reverential regard for that saintly Apostle of the Alleghenies. In my boyhood days I frequently visited this quaint old town and gazed with rapt astonishment on the tomb and church which to my youthful vision appeared wonderful specimens of architecture. Little then did I imagine that I would live to see what I behold to-day. But Divine Providence so ordained that my first appointment in the sacred ministry 27 years ago should be to the position of President of the College on the opposite hill and Assistant Priest of this congregation; that my first confession should be heard in Father Gallitzin's old chapel, which I had the good fortune to rebuild and preserve, and that my first sermon should be preached in the church of which I am now the pastor. And no sooner did I become pastor than I resolved to revive and perpetuate, as far as it was in my power, the name and memory of the one in whose honor we are assembled to-day. How far I have succeeded with God's blessing and most generous co-operation you are about to witness.

In his life of Father Gallitzin, published 30 years ago, Father Heyden wrote: "It is true, his inconsolable flock, not long after his decease, erected to his memory an humble monument, but not at all worthy of this great man; and it is to be hoped that a more suitable and superb one will soon mark the sacred spot where so much worth is interred, a spot worthy to be a place of pilgrimage, where all who want to have revived in them the spirit of faith and sacrifice and charity will often resort."

Quoting these words in an appeal to the public issued in 1891, I stated: "It is proposed to replace the unsightly (and now decayed) wooden cross and coffin which surmount the so-called monument with a life-size and life-like statue of the venerable Gallitzin, for which the pile of massive blocks would serve admirably as a pedestal."

For nearly nine years it has been my prayer, my hope and my endeavor to see the tomb of the founder of this community surmounted by his statue; and it is with the deepest reverence and most lively gratitude that in this centennial year of the foundation of the parish I thank Almighty God that my prayer has been heard, my hope realized, my endeavor crowned with success.

For this happy consummation we of this community hereby make public acknowledgment of eternal indebtedness to one whose praise it is not necessary to proclaim; to one of whom we are and always will be proud; to an old Loretto boy, Mr. Charles M. Schwab, President of the great Carnegie Steel Company.

He then announced that he had a great surprise in store for all present, and especially for the members of the parish,

Loretto
Oct 10th 1899

My Dear Father Kittell,

Since our residence amongst the good people of Loretto and vicinity we have been so kindly received, and so considerately treated by all that Mrs Schwab and I would like to show our appreciation of their kindness by consummating on this great day a project which we have had in our minds for some time.

Therefore Dear Father Kittell with your permission and that of the Rt Rev Bishop we would like to present to this town and parish of my boyhood days a new church adapted to the requirements of your people — our friends —

Accept the same from us with our very best wishes.

We trust work may be started at once

Sincerely Yours
Mr & Mrs C. M. Schwab

and that it would be revealed in a letter handed to him a short time previously by Mr. C. M. Schwab, which he would proceed to read, as follows:

LORETTO, October 10th, 1899.

MY DEAR FATHER KITTELL:

Since our residence amongst the good people of Loretto and vicinity we have been so kindly received and so considerately treated by all that Mrs. Schwab and I would like to show our appreciation of their kindness by consummating, on this great day, a project which we have had in mind for some time.

Therefore, Dear Father Kittell, with your permission and that of the Rt. Rev. Bishop, we would like to present to this town and parish of my boyhood days, a new church (Here the vast audience raised a long and mighty cheer,) adapted to the requirements of your people—our friends.

Accept the same from us with our very best wishes. We trust work may be started at once. Sincerely yours,

MR. AND MRS. C. M. SCHWAB.

On concluding the reading of this letter the Rev. Chairman introduced Mr. Schwab, who was greeted with the most enthusiastic applause as he stepped forward in full view of the people. After thanking them most sincerely for their cordial greeting, he delivered the following address:

"He believed that he was not born for himself but for the whole universe."

Thus spoke Lucanus of old of one whose deeds of boundless benevolence live in immortal fame.

In vain the pages of history may be searched for another more deserving of this tribute, or one life that exemplified this unselfish belief more fully than that of the pioneer, priest and nobleman, noble by nature as by the title entailment of birth—who, one hundred years ago, founded this flourishing community, and whose life of heroic self-sacrifice for the spiritual and temporal welfare of our ancestors we of Cambria commemorate to-day upon the centennial anniversary of Loretto.

What inspiration for the pen of a poet the life of Gallitzin affords! A descendant of rulers of European empires; kin to many of Russia's greatest statesmen, diplomats and counselors of Peter the Great; of an ancestry distinguished on fields of battle where history was made. A prince of the Russian Imperial Court himself, trained to command hosts in the valorous profession of arms; a life of glory, pomp and power was this young man's prospect at the age of 22. But he was born to other and nobler things, and flinging ambition and his princely expectations to the winds, he voluntarily banished himself from the favor of his Czar, renounced wealth, lofty titles, estates and all the dazzling splendor of imperialism that were his by right of birth, and became an exile in a far away land. All this he abjured to fulfill his duty to his fellowman according to his own conception, which involved physical peril, the pangs of hunger, and a life of self-abnegation which ended here on this mountain fifty-nine years ago among those he served and loved and who loved him.

The younger Pliny said that the erection of a monument is superfluous, as the memory of us will last if we have deserved it in our lives.

The memory of Prince Gallitzin and his noble work has survived over half a century without such reminders, and will endure for all time. He erected a monument more lasting than metal or granite in the hearts of his devoted followers and their children, but we wish our posterity and the generations yet unborn to believe that we of the present were not unmindful of the claims upon our tribute that his life imposed, and on this centennial anniversary of the parish, founded by the pioneer and Apostle of the Alleghenies, we dedicate this testimonial as a slight token of grateful remembrance of the loving descendants of those who were succored through hardship and adversity by him who endured mental and bodily anguish that they might not suffer.

Addressing the pastor, Rev. Ferdinard Kittell, he concluded:

Reverend Father: Mrs. Schwab and myself are pleased beyond expression to present through you to my native

MOST REV. JOHN IRELAND, D. D. ARCHBISHOP OF ST. PAUL, MINN. THE ORATOR OF THE DAY.

and beloved Loretto and the parish of which it is the center, this figure in bronze of its founder and benefactor of mankind—Rev. Prince Demetrius Augustine de Gallitzin.

Mrs. Schwab then came to the front, and by simply pulling a string which ran over pulleys from the stand to the statue, thereby loosened the arms of the trolly-frame, invented by the pastor, which held the veil; and in an instant the arms opened and the frame slid down the inclined wire on which it was suspended, carrying with it the veil, and the statue of Father Gallitzin and its majestic polished granite base stood revealed in all their beauty. Then arose from the throats of the five thousand spectators such a cheer as never before echoed over the old Alleghenies, and many wept for very joy.

When the excitement had finally subsided, for it continued a considerable time, the Rev. Chairman introduced the Most Rev. John Ireland, D. D., the illustrious Archbishop of St. Paul, who had kindly consented to respond for the pastor and parishioners to the noble address of Mr. Schwab. He spoke as follows:

There are men whom the friends of humanity and of God would wish to see live forever—men whose life was an inspiring example to their fellows, whose passage over earth was as a visit of beings from a higher world. Let us strive at least, as best we may, to send down over the stream of time their memories and the influence of their power—erecting to them enduring monuments, writing their acts and words on the scroll of story, reproducing in our lives something of their lives.

Of such men Demetrius Augustine Gallitzin was a noble exemplar. Truly great was he; his name will not be forgotten by Loretto, by America, by the Catholic Church, by humanity itself. The truly great men are the few. Let us, if you will, forget the many who but come and go without being able to make themselves deserving of eternal fame; but when one passes over earth who is singularly worthy of admiration and love, let us guard well his memory and transmit it faithfully to future generations.

Men are great who are able to conceive a magnificent ideal through which they may confer precious benefits upon humanity, and are able during the years allotted to them to live worthy of that ideal. And thus Gallitzin was great.

A statue is erected to him in the village of Loretto, amid the Allegheny mountains of America. It might have been that his statue would grace to-day a public square of Berlin, or of St. Petersburg, and that the passers-by would point to it as the monument of a noted warrior or a noted statesman. In Loretto the monument tells of a priest of the Church of God, of a pioneer missionary through these mountain ranges; but as such Gallitzin is great, aye, greater than he could have been had he been the warrior or the statesman in the capital cities of European countries.

Demetrius Augustine Gallitzin was born of a most illustrious family; he was the heir to large estates in Russia; he was appointed an officer in the Austrian army; he was called by the sovereign of Russia to be a chieftain in the armies of that great empire. His education had been such as to fit him for a magnificent career, to put him side by side with the great warriors and statesmen of Europe. Yet in a moment of communion with Heaven he offered himself to the Almighty to be a priest, and for the sake of the Christian priesthood he set aside all earthly hopes, all earthly ambitions.

He had come to America to journey through the young republic and study its institutions, with the intention of returning soon to Europe and there taking the high position to which birth, wealth and talent entitled him. The thought of dedicating himself to God in the priesthood came to him while he was visiting the city of Baltimore.

A priest, with God's help, I will be, he said. He entered the seminary of Baltimore, and after a few years he was ordained a priest. How are we to explain this sudden change in the career of Gallitzin? His noble mind had lifted him up as in vision to the skies; he had seen that he could do more for God and for humanity by devoting himself to the ministry of Christ, than by following in the wake of kings and emperors. The priesthood of Christ is, indeed, the noblest, the grandest career that opens to a child of man.

When Christ Jesus, the Son of the Most High, walked upon earth, he was a priest, a being commissioned by the Eternal Father to reconcile humanity with Heaven, to invoke upon humanity the graces of Heaven, and to lift up humanity even to the throne of the Almighty. Christ instituted the priesthood to continue upon earth His own mission; and no work is so divine, because no work brings man so closely to God, as the priesthood. We must see things as God sees them; glorious as earthly crowns may be, worthy as they may be of human ambition, high above them in the eye of God is the eternal priesthood of His Incarnate Son.

And what work confers so great benefits upon humanity as the work of the priesthood worthily accomplished? The purpose of the priesthood is to save the souls of men, to put them into union with Christ, to open to them the gates of eternal glory. The work of the priesthood is to bring down the dew of Heaven upon souls of men, to strengthen them, console them, guard them against sin, to procure for humanity even upon earth a happiness sweeter than aught else could procure for it, and finally to crown the life upon earth with the glories of the life in Heaven.

Gallitzin, in the light of faith, understood the grandeur of the priesthood; it was to him no too arduous sacrifice to turn away from a brilliant worldly career; no sacrifice to bid farewell to rich estates. He abandoned earth for Heaven; he abandoned courts and armies for the Christian priesthood.

Oh, soul of Gallitzin, I can fancy thee soaring upwards towards the skies, and saying, Oh, for the sake of God, for the sake of God's people, I put aside ambitions of earth; I choose as my portion humility, poverty, sacrifice. Great is the soul capable of sacrifice, capable of grasping a high ideal, —and such the soul of Gallitzin.

Gallitzin vowed himself to the priesthood in America. Why in America? Here is a further proof of the grandeur of his soul, of his earnestness in the consecration of himself to the priesthood. He was told by his father and by his friends that if he wished to be a priest he should at least return to Europe where illustrious episcopal sees would fall to his lot. Had he hearkened to their prayers, he might one day have become a prince-bishop in Germany as his schoolmate Von Droste became the prince-bishop of Cologne. A play-fellow of his became King of Holland; he would have opened to him avenues to highest preferment in his kingdom. Gallitzin could have been a priest in Europe and there gathered around his priesthood whatever earth could give to decorate, in the eyes of men, the priesthood. But, he said: I will be a priest in America, because here in America I take to myself the priesthood for its own merits; if I become a priest where earthly glory awaits me, I shall perhaps be tempted to think much of the earthly glory and little of the priesthood of Christ. In America a hundred years ago to be a priest was to vow one's self to poverty, to constant sacrifice, to a life of ceaseless labor: naught but the beauty itself of the priesthood could there have won to it the youthful courtier and prince.

In America, too, there was more to be done for God and for humanity than in Europe. Here the harvest was abundant: the reapers, few. Only a few priests and one bishop were there in the United States: and Catholics were scattered from one end of the country to the other, receiving the administrations of religion once in a year, or, perhaps, once in two or three years. And in America Catholics were poor, and formed, both socially and politically, an unimportant and prestigeless element. The heart of Gallitzin went out to the Catholics of America. He said: Here I will stay, these I will serve. I will labor for my fellows who are most in need of me; I will be a priest for the sake of the priesthood alone. Oh, Gallitzin, truly was thy priesthood pure from all unholy alloy! Truly, was thy consecration of thyself to the Catholics of America disinterested and entire! Catholics of America to-day thank thee, and invoke thy intercession with the eternal God that thy spirit of sacrifice burn brightly in the bosoms of tens of thousands of men and women to-day in America.

Gallitzin became a priest in America,—a priest in Loretto. Why in Loretto? **Again** because of his greatness of soul. Placed at first in the missions of Eastern **Pennsylvania he was** one day called to visit a dying woman on the summit of the wild ranges of the Alleghenies. Hither he came a hundred years ago. The country was covered with dense forests; the wild beast and the Indian roamed through the wilderness. A few families were here already, Catholics, pioneers of the faith. Who to-day will not pronounce with deep emotion the name of the brave Capt. Michael McGuire? Having fought for his country in the Revolutionary War, he sought, when peace had come, to make for himself and his children a home on the distant frontier, where land was cheap, and independence of character was possible. His log hut once erected to shelter him from rain and storm, he remembered holy Church; he was a child of the race of martyrs and missionaries. He had secured a large tract of land; of this he marked out a portion as his gift to God, and sent word to the Bishop of Baltimore that four hundred acres were awaiting his good will. Loretto, thou wast, indeed, cradled in the faith; thou hadst as thy founders stern Christians, and thou hadst the noble Gallitzin as thy pioneer priest. Visiting the McGuire settlement Gallitzin felt that here more than elsewhere in America was there need of a priest; the place was so wild, so uninviting, that it was not to be hoped in the ordinary course of ecclesiastical appointment that a priest would come hither for years. Then, said he, I will come. I will labor where there is the greatest need; I will stand in the front of the battle where no one else is likely to be. He returned eastward, secured the permission of his bishop and again went his way to the Alleghenies. At the same time he gave yet further evidence of his grandeur of soul: he conceived a great ideal which would be carried out by his dwelling on the mountains. He was too great a man, too noble a priest, to be satisfied with common routine work. He could have lived on in Lancaster or in Conewago, doing quietly the work that came before him; but he said, let me do more. His soul soared into superior regions, and his heart carried him wherever his ideas led. Let me, he said, take with me the Catholic people, scattered homeless through the cities of the east, and bring them out upon the land where they will have their own homes, where they will grow into social independence, where they will no longer be the hewers of wood and drawers of water, slaves of others. Let me in free America bring them to free homes. By going on the mountains I will attract thither hundreds and hundreds, and to the mountains I will go.

Gallitzin was in America the pioneer in the work of Catholic colonization. From time to time during the century now past others, in one part or another of the country, did something for Catholic colonization, enough to show in the country at large, what Loretto was showing in the Alleghenies, that Gallitzin had grasped an idea, wondrous in its power for good, if duly put into effect, and that Gallitzin's example, if continuously followed out in America, would have led to richest results for the Catholic Church and for Catholics in America. At the close of a century of Catholic American history, we can say in all truth that if leading priests and laymen in the Church had worked systematically during this century to draw the people from the streets and slums of large cities and settle them out upon the land, advancing year after year further westward, the Catholic Church to-day in America would be a power so great that we do not dare contemplate the vision for the grief which would take possession of our souls at the thought that such vision had not become a reality.

Gallitzin said, too: In bringing the people where they will find homes, I am benefiting the country; I am making of them useful citizens. The thousands and tens of thousands of people homeless in large cities are of little use to Church or country, while on the rich farming lands of America they become independent, honored citizens, the strength of the country as well as of Church. He thought, too let me get them around me, away from the moral and religious perils of

ARCHBISHOP IRELAND ADDRESSING THE CROWD AT THE UNVEILING OF THE STATUE OF FATHER GALLITZIN.

cities, and I will, God helping, build up amid the mountains an ideal Catholic community, where Christian thought and Christian practice will dominate.

Sacrifices were to be made. Gallitzin was to cut himself off from the comforts of Eastern Pennsylvania, slight as they were, to live in districts yet overrun by savages, exposed to the bitter cold of the mountain winter, amid the poverty of frontier settlements. But the sacrifice itself made the task the more inviting to Gallitzin. This was one hundred years ago. And what do we see to-day? Thousands of men and women, happy and contented, enjoying beautiful homes, devoted, intelligent children of the Church, honored, influential citizens of the nation. A hundred years ago Gallitzin wandered slowly over an Indian trail into this wilderness. He found here a few Catholic families forming the "McGuire Settlement." He set to work on the hill hard by, and he, to whom the imperial palaces of St. Petersburg would have gladly opened their portals, built for himself a log hut fourteen by sixteen feet. Adjoining the hut he erected a little chapel, and on Christmas day of the year 1799 he sang out in the joyousness of his soul, "Gloria in Excelsis Deo—Glory to God in the Highest." He thought that he was now really doing something for God and for humanity; and there on that Christmas morning, with those few families surrounding him, Gallitzin was greater before Heaven than if he had commanded the triumphant armies of Russia or Austria,—greater than if he had sung that Christmas mass under the domes of the Cologne or Mayence Cathedrals. And he had courage to continue his life for forty years in full accordance with that high ideal. It is not so difficult, perhaps, for men and women to grasp in a moment of exultation a great ideal,—not so difficult to give one's self to that ideal for a few months or for a few years. But to devote to it forty-one years of one's life amidst all sorts of trials, persecutions, disappointments, never swayed by difficulties, never yielding to discouragement, always steadily working for God—there we discover greatness of mind, there we discover nobleness of purpose, there we behold the power of grace working in frail man.

You have learned the traditions of your mountains, and you can without effort picture to-day to yourselves Demetrius Augustine Gallitzin—always the noble man, dignified in manner and speech; always the scholar, fond of his books, and, as occasion afforded, displaying, in sermon or in writing, that power of mind which would have commanded armies on the battlefields or made illustrious the diplomacy of Europe; kind-hearted, gentle and patient; going from cabin to cabin, smoothing away the furrows and care-worn faces; coaxing the child to learn its catechism; counseling the aged in matters temporal and spiritual; journeying off through frosty fields fifty, sixty, seventy miles, at times in the darkness of night to visit the sick—always prompt to sacrifice himself for men and for God.

Some would say: But these are little things; what glory is there in teaching the catechism to children, in attending the dying, in encouraging the newly-come immigrant, in writing letters to the east to men searching information about the mountain wilderness? My friends, the nobleness of acting is not to be measured by the act itself; but by the purpose of soul in the act and by the greatness of the results that are intended to follow; and the smaller and the seemingly more indifferent the act is, the greater is the soul which for a great purpose can bend itself to small things. Gallitzin was so great that he saw in every little act of his ministry the priesthood of Christ Jesus; the work of saving souls through the blood of Calvary; the lifting up of his people to a standard of comfort and social happiness, which gave them influence for the good of country and the good of religion—and he never tired for forty-one whole years. Careful was he to instruct his people; the strong, intelligent faith deeply instilled by him into the minds of Loretto's early settlers lives in the minds of their children and their grandchildren. He put before his people the enduring principles of the Gospel, the life-giving dogmas of the Catholic Church. He built his people into strong Christians. He did not feed them, as is sometimes done, on mere incidentals of religon, which, unless clearly set forth in their merely relative importance are likely to draw the mind away from the essentials, and which, without the essentials, are as dreams and shadows. The books which he wrote, the memories of his sermons and of his catechism classes, tell what deep, thorough instruction he gave. Most anxious was he ever to bring people to the sacraments: how he waited for them during long hours in the cold church, never complaining, always finding his abundant reward if one soul came to be refreshed in the blood of Christ the Savior.

Trials came to him. We should not have known fully the grandeur of Gallitzin's soul if he had encountered no trials, if he had suffered no persecutions. Trials and persecutions came to him from his own people. God permitted such things that we to-day might know how truly great he was. He was proven in adversity, and in prosperity, more even in adversity than in prosperity. Settlers who had come under advice from him complained; they blamed Gallitzin if they did not become rich at once. They blamed him for the lonesomeness of their hearts, for their pains in felling the forest tree. As he had conferred favors upon them, spending over $150,000 of money he had received from Europe, building mills and roads, making loans never to be repaid, they blamed him all the more virulently. The man who is benefited, unless there is in him a noble soul, is always likely to hate the benefactor. So it was with Gallitzin. A few even there were who strove to drive him from Loretto, who so calumniated him that he had to go from Loretto and appeal in the name of justice and truth to fair minded non-Catholics of Greensburg. Some there were who threatened attacks upon him when he was entering the chapel to celebrate mass. His soul, however, rose above all trials: his courage and his consciousness of his righteousness affrighted all enemies; and after a few years opposition ceased—some leaving the settlement, others repenting of their ingratitude, and uniting with the faithful ones, who were always the greater number, in love and obedience towards him.

Gallitzin was ever ready, as a good pastor should be, to give counsel and aid in temporal matters. Many a poor struggling emigrant coming hither was put by Gallitzin in posession of a farm and told to pay for it in five, ten or twenty years— whenever he could. Many a plan Gallitzin framed to teach his people how to obtain the best market prices for their products. And while teaching them to be prosperous farmers and good Catholics, he taught them to be good citizens. Never did a foreigner come to America with a mind more capable of understanding the grandeur and beauty of American institutions and a heart more ready to love them than Demetrius Augustine Gallitzin.

He was quickly transformed into a loyal son of the republic. He wrote to friends that he loved America and loved its liberty. He did what he could to teach his people to love and serve their country, and when, in the year 1812, the armies of Great Britain were burning the Capitol at Washington, and a son of old Captain McGuire had raised in Loretto a company of volunteers, Gallitzin gathered the new soldiers around his altar and celebrated mass for them, and promised them his prayers while they would be fighting on the eastern coast in defence of the Star Spangled Banner. Two of Loretto's soldiers became homesick and wandered back to the mountains. One Sunday morning in front of the old chapel they stood amid a wondering crowd telling eloquently of battles which they had not fought, of great generals whom they had not seen. As Gallitzin advanced from his house, forward they went to make reverence to him. "No," said he, "I never shake hands with deserters." In this there was Americanism, there was patriotism; in this there was an example to priests and to laymen of then and now. Men of Loretto, be ever as Gallitzin and your forefathers were, noble Christians and noble Americans. These titles are yours for which you must ever thank the great God of Heaven. You are Catholics to save your souls; you are Americans to enjoy the freedom of the flag and all the social happiness which abounds wherever it is unfurled.

Such was Gallitzin, the prince-missionary of the Alleghenies. His native country, Russia, is proud of him. In Russia the name of Demetrius Gallitzin is mentioned more frequently, I am sorry to say, and more gratefully than it is in America outside, of course, of Loretto. Russia is proud that such a man was one of her sons. Members of the Gallitzin family are to-day ministers of state, eminent writers, commanders of armies; and they all know Loretto, where rests their great kinsman. Only three years ago your honored townsman, Mr. C. M. Schwab, visiting St. Petersburg, was invited to dinner by a minister of state, and in the course of the dinner the minister said: "Tell me, Mr. Schwab, do you know of a place in the United States called Loretto?" "I do," said Mr. Schwab with pride, "I was reared there." "Well," said the minister, "fifty years ago, no one knowing who I was or what I was doing, I rode on horseback from Philadelphia to Loretto to see there the grave of my great kinsman, Demetrius Augustine Gallitzin." America is proud of Gallitzin, proud that such a great man sought her shores and became one of her citizens,—proud that her institutions captivated his mind and heart. When a man, such as Gallitzin, loves fondly America and the liberty of America, there is there a lesson for us, that America deserves all the homage we can pay her.

The Catholic Church of America is proud of Gallitzin. I regret that the Catholics of America do not know, as they should, the full history of the parish of Loretto, do not know the full greatness of the man, whose statue is here to-day unveiled. Demetrius Augustine Gallitzin is an honor, an inspiration, to the whole priesthood of the Catholic Church. Oh, that we catch up something of the divine fire which coursed through his soul, and that we do for fellow-men and for God something of what he did!

And what an honor to Loretto! Daughters and sons of Loretto, be proud that the name of your village was first spoken by Gallitzin, that your first priest was Gallitzin; be proud of the traditions which have come down to you from his missionary labors among your fathers. Never forget his name, never forget the lessons of his pastorate. I rejoice to have to-day before me the evidences that you do not forget him. Your presence in thousands proves your gratitude to his memory. What has been done by two of Loretto's sons, Father Kittell and Mr. Schwab, proves that he is not to be forgotten by you. Father Kittell has made it the duty of his priesthood to gather together every souvenir of **Gallitzin**, and to reconstruct the old chapel in which Gallitzin prayed to his God. I shall never forget the **emotion of my soul this** morning as I said mass in that old chapel, **standing before** the altar at which Gallitzin so often stood, **and robed in the** vestments **worn by** Gallitzin, made in Europe **by the loving hands** of his **noble** mother out of the rich **silks in which she had been** gowned on **her wedding day.**

And what shall I say of the generosity, of the munificence of Mr. Schwab in erecting to the memory of Gallitzin this noble monument. What shall I say of the glorious gift which a few moments ago he promised to Loretto—the home of Gallitzin, a temple worthy of Loretto and worthy of Gallitzin? Mr. Schwab, Mrs. Schwab, I have no right to thank you in the name of the people: they will speak for themselves. In the name of the Catholic Church of America I thank you. In the name of the episcopate and the priesthood of America I thank you. In the name of Demetrius Gallitzin I thank you. You have done more than you may think. You have erected a statue to Gallitzin: you will build a temple in the memory of Gallitzin. All this is not to be for Loretto alone: the statue will speak to all America, to the whole priesthood, to the whole laity of America; the church which you will build will be a holy shrine whither will pilgrim those, who in America love greatness of soul, devotion to religion, true and sterling citizenship.

A century has gone by since first he planted the cross on your mountains. What a change in America from 1799 to 1899! In 1799 Gallitzin's log church was the only Catholic Church between Lancaster to the east and St. Louis to the west. To-day the continent teems with churches, convents and schools. There was then in America one bishop, there are now nearly a hundred; instead of a few priests there are nearly twelve thousand: the number of Catholics has grown from a few thousand to thirteen or fourteen millions, the whole population of America from three millions to seventy-five millions. What a change! In all his dreams, never could Gallitzin have imagined what was to come to America. But while America has grown to be so great, I put a question to give answer to which I leave to the angels of God—Have men become better men? What high ideals given to us a century ago by your Gallitzin in the clergy and your McGuire in the laity! Had we to-day a thousand, a half thousand Gallitzins, their souls filled with great ideals, their hearts burning with divine love, ready for sacrifices, absolutely unselfish; had we tens of thousands of laymen such as the pioneer McGuire, so loyal to religion, so generous in defence of its works, how glorious the church would quickly become!

One thing I must not forget which shows to me as much as anything else he may have done, Gallitzin's true grandeur of soul. In the early part of the century, over thirty years before Father Theobald Matthew was heard of, Gallitzin announced in Loretto that he was a total abstainer, that he never drank wine or liquor, drinking only milk and water. He had seen the evils of intemperance; he had wished to teach his people by example, and had promised to drink only milk and water. God reward Gallitzin for his noble example of total abstinence, so much needed in America. And God reward his present successor in Loretto, Father Kittell, for his stern devotion to the beverages which gave to Gallitzin health and strength—milk and water.

May I tell of the influence of another of Gallitzin's good works upon my own personal labors? Some twenty-five years ago I did a good deal of Catholic colonization work in Minnesota;—and the inspiration to my work in Minnesota came to me in great part from what I had known of Gallitzin's work in Western Pennsylvania. And as I read of Gallitzin's trials in the early days of Loretto, I easily understand them. Human nature is much the same to-day, or, was to me twenty years ago, as it was with Gallitzin a century ago. It looks to me as if the whole story of Gallitzin's colonization difficulties was reproduced in mine, even to the establishment by some colonists of a rival village. Only I did not have the patience that Gallitzin had—I usually ended the troubles much more quickly than he did. And I had an advantage which Gallitzin had not; I lived a hundred miles from my colonists, and when they were too obstreperous I simply kept away; while Gallitzin lived with his colonists and had to meet complaints and frowns each day, morning and evening. I am sure he must often have said to his, as I often said to mine: "I permit you to curse me, you will curse me whether I permit you or not; I merely announce to you that in five years you will bless me." When I now go among my colonists I sometimes ask: "Where are those who were willing to curse me?" And they are not to be found.

I bid farewell to Loretto. I speak no farewell to Gallitzin. His memory will ever live in my heart.

At different points in the Archbishop's address his remarks were greeted with lively applause, and the narration of his experience with his Minnesota colonists caused considerable merriment. When he concluded, the enthusiastic cheer that went up from the crowd showed that his address, an entirely extemporaneous one, had touched a tender cord in the hearts of his hearers, and would long be remembered.

Father Kittell then introduced Governor William A. Stone, a synopsis of whose remarks, taken from the Altoona Times of the following day, is here given:

He said: "I have been so deeply impressed this day with all that I have seen and heard that anything I said would be but a repetition. It does not become me to speak of the priestly character of Father Gallitzin after what Archbishop Ireland has said. I can only express my gratitude at being present at the honor paid to the man who made Loretto."

The Governor eulogized Mr. Schwab as "a young man going out, without name and without money, coming back to honor the town of his boyhood." He wished we had more such men. "We are long on politicians"—and here he was interrupted by laughter and applause—"but short on Schwabs.

"I am greatly impressed with the history of Father Galtzin. I know of no sacrifice like his made in this country.

HON. W. A. STONE, GOVERNOR OF PENNSYLVANIA.

There was no inducement for a young man, wealthy and educated, to come to these bleak hills, where no one lived. There must be some influence greater than man to produce such a miracle. There must be some higher power to lead a man to such sacrifice. He has left the mark of his character on Church and on this grand old State.

"No man in building up this great State has done greater wonders than Gallitzin. He Christianized and colonized the western part of Pennsylvania and did for it what Franklin and Gallatin did for the eastern part.

"He worked for the future, lived for the future. These hills would not be peopled by this loyal people were it not for Father Gallitzin. He came here to build a Church and State and he succeeded. To such men as Gallitzin we owe all our wealth and power to-day.

"This country has grown beyond the expectation of the pioneer. The late war with Spain has shown what we are as a nation. The countries of the world are beginning to realize our standing among the nations. We owe it to such men as Gallitzin. We are strong because we were planted right. In our infancy we were properly nurtured, and now no country can compete with this nation.

"We have no longer a bloody chasm between the North and the South. To-day we are united, a great nation to set the pace in morals and religion for the world. So we go on growing great and powerful while we are becoming more numerous.

"No one in this great State will shout with greater applause for Gallitzin than myself."

The address of our chief magistrate was well received and heartily applauded. It was the first time in its long history that Loretto had been honored by the presence of a Governor of the State, and his reception on this occasion left nothing to be desired.

Father Kittell then stated that several weeks previously he had addressed a petition to the Holy Father, requesting three favors. First, the apostolic blessing for himself, his parishioners and all who would assist at the ceremonies of the Centenary: second, a special blessing for Mr. and Mrs. C. M. Schwab for their generosity to the parish; and lastly, that the Most Rev. Apostolic Delegate be delegated to impart these blessings at the conclusion of the ceremonies of the day, in the name of the Holy Father himself. He then read the following letter which contained the announcement of the granting of the petition:

S. CONGREGATION DE PROPAGANDA FIDE.

ROME, September 15, 1899.

REVEREND SIR:

The information given me in your letter of recent date concerning the festivities with which the Centenary of the foundation of your parish will be celebrated on the 10th of next month affords me great pleasure. The Holy Father, graciously acceding to your request, has granted to Monsignor, the Delegate Apostolic, the faculty to impart on that occasion the papal blessing, and I have already written to him on the subject. Moreover, this Sacred Congregation bestows the tribute of special and well merited praise on Mr. and Mrs. C. M. Schwab, who, as you relate, are such generous benefactors of your parish.

M. CARD. LEDOCHOWSKI, Pref.

It was expected that Monsignor Martinelli, vested in full pontificals, would impart this blessing from the front door of the church, but it was judged impossible to pass through the dense crowd that occupied every foot of space between the stands and the sacred edifice, and that part of the programme had to be omitted. Consequently, when all at the request of the pastor had knelt down, the Apostolic Delegate amid intense silence intoned the Papal Benediction, and all arose comforted by the reflection that the Holy Father, by blessing those present, had worthily crowned the great Centenary of Loretto.

The Cathedral Choir then sang a grand *Te Deum*, the audience joining in the chorus: and with the last prolonged note the celebration came to an end. As the distinguished guests left the stand they were surrounded by throngs of ardent admirers who desired to do them honor and to show them reverence; and their passage to the pastoral residence was slow and difficult. The crowd lingeringly dispersed, as if loath to leave a spot forever consecrated by such hallowed memories; yet by nightfall the old town had relapsed into its customary state of quietude, undisturbed by the world-wide renown conferred upon it by the day's celebration. And although the crowd present was estimated at from five to eight thousand souls, it was noticed as a subject for congratulation that no sign of disorder was visible, not the slightest accident occurred, and every part of the programme was carried out without a hitch. It was truly a day long to be remembered, and Mr. and Mrs. C. M. Schwab, who made it so, have no need to be assured of the warm affection and lasting gratitude of the members of St. Michael's parish.

LORETTO NOTES.

(From the Altoona Times, October 11, 1899.)

Altoona was represented by nearly 200 persons at the celebration.

The Duquesne Band of forty pieces rendered excellent music.

Mayor Giles and Postmaster Wilson were among the participants.

W. A. Wills, formerly of Altoona, but now of Homestead, was with the Loretto Club.

Road Supervisor James Cullen, of Spruce Creek, and his family were among the participants.

Leman Bros.' Orchestra, of this city, was very much in evidence in the excellence of its music.

D. J. McCarthy, Commissioner of Allegheny County, was among the prominent visitors at Loretto.

Miss Mollie Dunphy and Mr. John H. Conrad, of the Sacred Heart Choir, were among the singers.

Miss Carter, organist at the Cathedral, Pittsburg, officiated in that capacity at Loretto yesterday.

The large attendance was admirably handled on the trains and other conveyances to and from Loretto.

It is estimated that there were about 900 conveyances, mainly buggies and carriages of all kinds, at Loretto.

P. H. McGuire, of Homestead, Grand Secretary of the Young Men's Institue, was with the Loretto Club yesterday.

W. Fitz Cullen, of Spruce Creek, was very highly complimented, as was also Herman Myers, of Ebensburg, on his singing.

A free day was given in several of the public as well as parochial schools in that vicinity, to afford the families an opportunity of being present.

Miss Lulu Fyan, of Bedford, and Miss Venie Hartzel, of Somerset, were the guests of Mr. and Mrs. A. J. Spigelmyer and family, of Braddock, at the celebration yesterday.

Mrs. Peter O'Neill, the only surviving member of the choir of Father Gallitzin, was an interested participant in the celebration yesterday. She is past 70 years, but is still very active.

Misses Alice Carter, Katharine McAllister and Katharine Ward and Messrs. Smith and Riketts, of the Cathedral Choir, contributed largely to the excellence of the music rendered at the pontifical mass.

Otto E. Reinhardt, Mr. Schwab's secretary, had charge of the details of the Loretto Club's excursion yesterday and like all his affairs it was most successfully conducted. Mr. Reinhardt is an obliging and very courteous gentleman.

W. A. Kessler, of Braddock, was presented with a gold-headed cane by the members of the Loretto Club for his active services in assisting in the arrangements. The presentation speech was made by Mr. P. H. McGuire en route to Loretto, to which the recipient feelingly responded.

The device by which the unveiling of the monument was instantly effected by the releasing of a cord by Mrs. C. M. Schwab on the honored guests' stand, was the invention of the Rev. Father Kittell, pastor at Loretto. It consisted of a trolley system, operated by wires and a dual cord, and discounts anything we have ever seen in that line in rapidity and accuracy.

The reverend and esteemed pastor at Loretto, Father Kittell, was the happiest man there yesterday, not only because of the successful consummation of the Centenary, but also because of the munificent additional gift yesterday offered by Mr. and Mrs. C. M. Schwab—a new church for Loretto, at which place he first officiated after his ordination to the priesthood twenty-seven years ago.

A conspicuous personage was Governor William A. Stone, who was the guest of Charles Schwab, at the pretty summer residence of the latter at his home on the outskirts of the town. He occupied a pew with the president of the Carnegie Steel Company at the pontifical mass in the morning and sat among the specially invited guests during the exercises of the afternoon.

Mingled in the assemblage were some, now burdened with the weight of years, who had seen the prince-priest as he trod over the same ground. There were thousands of the descendants of the men and women who had gathered around Father Gallitzin when he founded this mountain colony. It was a gathering from all the country around Loretto, and many had come from a long distance to witness this testimonial to the deeds of his life, which fifty-nine years since his death, are still cherished in the land which was the scene of his missionary labors.

The Altoona delegation of the Loretto Centenary and monument unveiling went up on Johnstown Accommodation and Pacific Express yesterday morning. A special train from Pittsburg, carrying several hundreds from western points, had arrived at the little town before the Mountain City people got there. On arriving at the Loretto Road Station, on the Cambria and Clearfield Railroad, a large variety of vehicles was waiting to receive them. Here were seen undoubted evidences of a gala day in the trappings of the horses and the decorations of the carriages and wagons. The national colors were conspicuous in the trimmings. When the town was reached it was observed that the place had indeed been prettily decorated. There were pretty arches, gay with bunting, contrasting with the evergreen of the mountain pine and hemlock. And there were noticeable throngs in the streets, although the crowd had not yet obtained the dimensions that it reached later in the day. All roads led to St. Michael's Church. The confirmation services, at which Monsignor Martinelli had officiated, had already passed and the time had not yet arrived for the pontifical mass, to which tickets of admission were issued.

But interesting sights were to be seen. The vault under the monument containing the venerated remains of Dr. Gallitzin was open for inspection, and there was to be seen all that is left of Gallitzin's body. By the light of a couple of matches, and afterwards of a candle, the Times representative was able to see distinctly, through the glass lid, the little that is left of the prince-priest's body. There is no semblance of a human form remaining. The skull is to be seen, but the rest of the body's substance has passed into ashes. The vault was thronged with people, many of whom had never gazed on the little that is left of Dr. Gallitzin's body. The chapel in which Father Gallitzin officiated and the house in which he lived and died are near by and contain many interesting relics. The repairs which were necessary to prevent these buildings becoming ruins have, however, removed much of the appearance that they had at the time of the missionary priest. But there can be seen the altar at which he officiated, a plain, little unpretentious affair. In the house are some of the articles of furniture that he used, conspicuous among them being his bed.

BIOGRAPHICAL SKETCHES.

MOST REV. SEBASTIAN MARTINELLI, O. S. A., D. D., ARCHBISHOP OF EPHESUS, AND DELEGATE APOSTOLIC TO THE UNITED STATES.

Monsignor Martinelli, the Apostolic Delegate, who was the guest of Rev. Father Kittell, pastor of St. Michael's, Loretto, on the occasion of the unveiling of the Gallitzin monument on October 10th, this year, has a charming personality. He has made an excellent impression in this country by his engaging manners, his thorough knowledge of things American, and the ease and fluency with which he speaks the English language. These qualifications combined with his great executive ability and deep knowledge of Church affairs, led to his selection to the important post of ambassador plenipotentiary of the Pope in this country. He had studied America, its customs and its people, and was familiar with its language and history long before he dreamed of representing the Church in any capacity in this country. To this knowledge he added much by a visit of three months to the United States in 1893, at which time he visited the establishments of the Augustinian Order, and then spent some time at the Augustinian Monastery at Bryn Mawr, Pa., working for the order.

Monsignor Martinelli is a charming talker. He is retiring and does not pretend to gifts of oratory. As a philosopher and theologian he stands high in the Church. He comes of a family which won distinction in the Church. The

MONSIGNOR MARTINELLI, THE APOSTOLIC DELEGATE.

late Cardinal, Thomas Martinelli, was his brother, and another brother occupies a high office in the Augustinian Order. He was born near Lucca, Italy, August 20, 1848, and at the age of fifteen entered the Order of the Hermits of St. Augustine. In a little more than a year he was made a monk. His ordination to the priesthood came six years later. During these years he was a teacher at the convent and college of the Irish Augustinians at their House of Santa Maria Posterula, on the banks of the Tiber at Rome. He was next chosen Assistant Secretary of the Holy Congregation of the Index, and was later made regent at the Irish House of the Augustinian Fathers, at Santa Maria Posterula. He became professor and master of theology, emeritus, and was recognized as one of the most learned of the order.

When Monsignor Martinelli was made Apostolic Delegate in 1896, he was prior general of the Augustinians, the highest position in the order. He had already held that office for six years, and had just been re-elected for another term of six years when the order of the Pope transferring him to this country came. As prior general he was head of the Augustinians throughout the world. His appointment was a surprise even to those who were supposed to be near the Pope, but the success of Monsignor Martinelli in guiding the Church in the United States during the last three years has confirmed the wisdom of Leo XIII. Early in the year it was rumored that he would receive further preferment at the hands of the Pope as Nunzio to Paris, but Monsignor Martinelli has always said that next to his native Italy he is most pleased with the United States.

RT. REV. RICHARD PHELAN, D. D., BISHOP OF PITTSBURG.

He was born in the townland of Sralee, near Ballyragget, County Kilkenny, Ireland, January 1, 1828. His parents, Michael Phelan and Mary Keoghan, were of respectable position and independent circumstances, and his ancestors, for generations before, had owned the homestead where he was born. He was the oldest of nine children, of whom four came to America. One entered the ranks of the clergy in Ireland, and is the Very Rev. Patrick Canon Phelan, P. P., in the Diocese of Ossory. Two of the daughters became nuns: one of the Order of St. Bridget, near her native place, and went on the mission in Australia; the other of the Order of Sisters of Mercy in Pittsburg.

He received his elementary education from private tutors in his father's house, and feeling himself destined for the sacred ministry, he entered St. Kieran's College, Kilkenny, to pursue the higher branches of study. His thoughts were early turned towards the rising missions of America, and when the learned and saintly prelate, Rt. Rev. Michael O'Connor, first Bishop of Pittsburg, applied to St. Kieran's for students, he cast his lot with the new diocese, then embracing the western half of Pennsylvania. In December, 1849, he came to the United States and resumed his studies in the old seminary of St. Michael, situated near the place where St. Michael's Church now stands in South Pittsburg.

In September, 1851, he entered St. Mary's Seminary, Baltimore, where he received minor orders and was ordained Subdeacon and Deacon by Archbishop Kenrick. When the Diocese of Erie was formed (April 29, 1853), Bishop O'Connor was transferred from Pittsburg to that See, and the subject of this sketch, while yet a Deacon, was chosen for the new diocese.

Leaving Baltimore in the beginning of 1854 he hastened to Erie; but owing to the strong opposition which the removal of Bishop O'Connor had aroused in Pittsburg, his ordination did not take place as soon as the Bishop intended it should, and on account of the delay some weeks of the spring of 1854 were passed in the seminary at Cleveland, Ohio. In the meantime Bishop O'Connor had been recalled to Pittsburg (February 20, 1854), where in the chapel of the Episcopal residence, on May 4th, of the same year, he was raised to the priesthood.

His first appointment was to the small mission of Cameron's Bottoms, in Indiana County. After a few months' service in this remote and lonely place he visited the city,

RT. REV. RICHARD PHELAN, D. D., BISHOP OF PITTSBURG.

where the people were in dismay, the priests overworked and too few for the great and sorrowful duty that was before them. The dread cholera was in their midst, and during the autumn of 1854, cast a gloom of sadness and fear over Pittsburg. Father Phelan unselfishly offered his services to administer to those suffering from the pestilence; and during the months that the plague claimed the greatest number of victims, he stood at his post to assist and console the stricken and dying. When the cholera abated he returned to Cameron's Bottoms, but only for a short time.

In February, 1855, he was called to St. Paul's Cathedral, where he labored for three years and a half, performing the varied round of duties of an assistant in a large city parish, besides occasionally looking after the spiritual welfare of several small congregations in the outlying country districts. He was then appointed to the charge of Freeport, Kittanning and the smaller missions of a territory which now contains a number of flourishing congregations with resident pastors. During his residence at Freeport he purchased a cemetery, paid for a house for the pastor, repaired and improved the church, and also secured the ground and began preparations for the church at Natrona, which was erected after his departure.

In 1868 Very Rev. Tobias Mullen was appointed Bishop of Erie, and on July 21st of that year Father Phelan was named to succeed him in the pastorate of St. Peter's Church, Allegheny City. Here, under his able management, several lots adjoining those already owned by the congregation on the corner of West Ohio Street and Sherman Avenue, were purchased, the new and stately church was erected, the handsome residence fronting on the park was built, and other improvements made. The corner-stone of the church was laid April 16, 1871. The building was completed in three years, and solemnly dedicated on Sunday, July 5, 1874.

Rt. Rev. M. Domenec, who succeeded Bishop O'Connor, and Rt. Rev. J. Tuigg, who succeeded Bishop Domenec, both in turn chose Father Phelan to administer the affairs of the diocese during their absence in Europe. After the return of

Bishop Tuigg from Rome in 1882, Father Phelan held the responsible position of Vicar General until his consecration, August 2, 1885, as titular Bishop of Cybara, and Coadjutor, with right of succession, to Rt. Rev Bishop Tuigg, who, on account of sickness could no longer perform the duties of his office.

Bishop Tuigg died in Altoona, December 7, 1889, and at his death Bishop Phelan became Bishop of Pittsburg. In June, 1891, he left the parish, in which twenty-three years of his life had been spent, to occupy the Episcopal Residence, Grant Street, Pittsburg.

Half a century has rolled away since first he came to Pittsburg, and in this half century there have been great changes in the conditions of the Church in the diocese, as well as in his own life. In 1850 the Diocese of Pittsburg had about 25 priests, 35 churches,—the greater part of them small and plain,—and a Catholic population that did not exceed 40,000. Catholics were not only few in number, but they were, as a rule, without wealth, position or influence. Since then he has beheld a flourishing organization formed around him. Priests have been ordained, churches built, asylums and hospitals erected, parochial schools founded in almost every parish, religious orders, male and female, multiplied, and the broad foundations laid by the first Bishop of Pittsburg, built up year by year. The fourth Bishop of the See finds the 35 houses for divine worship grown into 245, and the 25 clergymen into 222 diocesans, and about 150 regulars. Where fifty years ago were ten schools there are now 122, with some 30,000 children attending. The less than 40,000 Catholics have now become 300,000. When Father Phelan began his work in the sacred ministry religious prejudices ran high, and misguided men said and did things which it were better not to recall. Placed in the most trying positions, he always disarmed bigotry by his straightforward adherence to principles of justice and charity towards all men, and by his considerate treatment of those who in belief and worship were separated from him.

C. M. SCHWAB.

He is now at the threshold of his 72d year, and his rugged constitution bids fair to carry the burthens of many more years of a useful life.

RT. REV. ALFRED A. CURTIS, D. D., TITULAR BISHOP OF ECHINUS.

He was born in Somerset County, Maryland, July 4, 1831. Feeling an inclination for a religious life he studied for the ministry in the Protestant Episcopal Church, and was made minister in September, 1856. In April, 1872, he abjured Protestantism and was reconciled with the Church in Edgebaston, Birmingham, England. Returning to this country he was ordained to the priesthood in the Cathedral, Baltimore, on December 19, 1874. Was consecrated Bishop of Wilmington, Del., in November, 1886, and resigned his See in May, 1897. He is now Vicar General of the Archdiocese of Baltimore, and resides with the Cardinal Archbishop.

CHARLES M. SCHWAB.

One of the men universally recognized as pre-eminent among those who have built up the iron and steel industry of America to its present stage of development, where it leads the world and ranks commercially secondarily only to the agricultural and transportation interests of the country, is Charles M. Schwab, President of the Carnegie Steel Company, Limited, Pittsburg, Pa. The progress made in the United States in the branch of manufacturing with which Mr. Schwab is associated is unparalleled in the industrial history of the world, and few men have been more conspicuously identified with its advancement or could be accorded a modicum of credit greater for the result than this gentleman.

He is a native of Pennsylvania and was born February 18th, 1862, at Williamsburg, Blair County. His remote progenitors were Germans, but his parents are native Americans. His father was a woolen manufacturer in Williamsburg for many years. In 1872 the family located in Loretto, Cambria County, Pa., where young Schwab attended St. Francis' College, taking a scientific course under the tutelage of the Franciscan Friars. When but a small youth, before he became a student, his time was employed on the farm and in driving the coach which carried visiting relatives of the students from the railway station to the college, and there are many who still have a pleasant remembrance of the President of the Carnegie Steel Company as that smiling, chubby, courteous lad, who met them at the Loretto Station with the college carry-all twenty-five years ago.

In July, 1880, he graduated from college and immediately set out to earn his livelihood. During the same month he engaged to take a position in a grocery store at Braddock, Pa., and thus the executive head of the largest steel manufacturing enterprise in the world began his career. The grocery trade, however, did not impress the young man as promising limitless opportunities, and when after two months' experience behind the sugar counter, he found an opening more suited to his tastes and abilities, he relinquished his first position to enter the service of the Carnegie Steel Company, Limited, in the engineering department.

His ambition was to become an engineer, and the story of how he succeeded in that is part of the familiar history of the American steel industry for the last fifteen years during the period of its marvelous expansion. His beginning as an engineer was at the bottom. The first duty assigned to him was stake driving with the corps under P. F. Brendlinger at the Edgar Thomson Works, Bessemer. From the outstart it was evident to his superiors that the young man was capable of filling any position in the department, and the transition in his fortunes was consequently rapid. In six months he was appointed chief engineer, and while at the head of the engineering department supervised the construction of eight of the blast furnaces now comprising the Edgar Thomson plant, which is the most extensive one in operation.

Mr. Schwab also originated other engineering works of considerable magnitude at Bessemer, including an addition to the rail mill capacity which gave the works an output exceeding any mill in the world, and with improved blast furnace and steel conversion practice effected such large economies in manufacturing cost as to make competition possible in the markets of the world to the extent that the product of this mill is now to be found in every quarter of the globe where railroads are operated. He continued as chief engineer and assistant manager of the Edgar Thomson furnaces and rail mill from 1881 to 1887. The late Captain William R. Jones, whose enduring works must ever be associated with the early development of the American steel industry, was general manager of the plant at that time, and showed abiding faith in the genius and capacity of his assistant.

Mr. Schwab co-operated with Captain Jones in the development and practical demonstration of the invention known as the "metal mixer," which has made Captain Jones' name almost as famous in the steel industry throughout the world as those of Sir Henry Bessemer, Siemens and other renowned metallurgists, whose genius has made steel manufacture on the present day scale possible. By the metal mixing process molten iron instead of cold pig iron is used in steel making; the initial heat of the iron as it comes from the blast furnace being retained by running the molten metal into a large mixing reservoir, thus facilitating its conversion into steel, and saving the labor and expense of casting the iron into pigs in sand beds and remelting.

This method, before its successful demonstration by Captain Jones and Mr. Schwab, was considered impracticable by experts, as it was feared the molten metal would chill before it reached the steel converter, causing disastrous delays and losses, but with the daring characteristics of all their achievements Jones and Schwab discarded the iron making practice of nearly fifty years and persevered with untiring resolution until they triumphed.

The process is now followed in every large works in the United States and Europe, as it greatly reduced manufacturing cost and relieved blast furnace operatives of the most exhausting drudgery man ever performed.

In 1887 Mr. Schwab was appointed Superintendent of the Homestead works of the Carnegie Steel Company and reconstructed the entire establishment, making it the largest mill in the world producing steel blooms, billets, structural shapes, bridge steel, boiler, armor, ship and tank plate and steel castings.

Shortly after Mr. Schwab assumed the management of the Homestead works, the Carnegie Company undertook the manufacture of armor plate for the United States Navy at the request of the Navy Department, and the success attending this great enterprise from the first day of operation may be attributed to the engineer's clear perception of the mechanical and metallurgical difficulties involved, and the manner in which he overcame obstacles in the work seemingly insuperable. No branch of the steel industry presented in its inception such hazards to the engineer and steel maker as did the armor plate manufacture, and the work accomplished by Mr. Schwab was particularly creditable from the fact that he succeeded from the outstart while every previous attempt failed at the beginning, and armor was not produced successfully until after a long experimentative period.

Mr. Schwab remained at Homestead as Superintendent until October, 1889, when upon the death of Capt. William R. Jones, resulting from an accident at the Edgar Thomson Works, he was appointed General Superintendent of the Edgar Thomson works and furnaces.

In 1892 the Homestead works were again placed under Mr. Schwab's management for the second time and with headquarters at Homestead he directed the operation of both the Edgar Thomson and Homestead plants. He was elected a member of the Board of Managers in 1896, and in February, 1897, he succeeded John G. A. Leishman as President of the Carnegie Company.

This, in brief, is the record of Charles M. Schwab's career from the country boy on the driver's seat of the college coach to the president's chair of one of the largest commercial institutions of the world.

Among European engineers and metallurgists, Mr. Schwab is ranked with the foremost men of the profession throughout the world. His services to the iron and steel industries are highly valued abroad and have been amply rewarded, as many of the rolling mill devices and steel works equipments now used in Europe are the inventions of the Pittsburg engineer. He holds membership in various scientific and industrial organizations in America and Europe, including the American Iron and Steel Association, the American Institute of Mining Engineers and the British Iron and Steel Institute.

Mr. Schwab possesses a forceful character, keen judgment and a manner openly frank and unassuming, but the predominating trait of his nature is a gentle, affable and sympathetic temperament which prompts a feeling of admiration and has won the friendship of all who have met him.

Appreciating the necessity of training the youth of to-day that they may be self-dependent in after life, Mr. Schwab founded and equipped a free polytechnic school in Homestead in which instruction is given in mechanical drawing, rudimentary engineering and kindred practical studies. The school is conducted as a branch of the state schools, and has been such a gratifying success that the founder now contemplates building and equipping a training school for girls. His beneficence has been well applied in this undertaking as well as to numerous public charities which he liberally but quietly supports. He is a director of the Mercy Hospital of Pittsburg, which was organized by the late Thomas M. Carnegie and others.

Mr. Schwab is endeavoring to do as much to make Pittsburg the American home of art as he has done to make that city the work-shop of the world; contributing liberally to every enterprise promoted in furtherance of that object. He has given substantial encouragement to the many musical organizations in and about Pittsburg, and is defraying the expenses of an European education of more than one promising artist. He is a musician of no mean order himself and takes an enthusiastic interest in everything devoted to the æsthetic taste of the public. He is connected with a number of social organizations, including the Pittsburg and Duquesne Clubs of Pittsburg, and the Metropolitan Club of Washington. His sponsor in the latter organization was Admiral George Dewey, whom Mr. Schwab numbers among his close friends.

Mr. Schwab's domestic life is ideal. He was married in 1898 to Emma, daughter of R. E. Dinkey, of Weatherly, Carbon County, Pa., and resides in Braddock, a suburb of Pittsburg, and about a mile distant from the great Edgar Thomson Works, within view of the theatre of his early struggles and late triumphs.

VERY REV. E. A. BUSH, V. G.

He was born in Montreal, Canada, June 5, 1839, and at the death of his parents in the year 1851 came to the United States under the care and protection of Rev. W. Pollard, a near relative, and began his preparatory studies at St. Francis' College, Loretto. By the advice of the Bishop, Rt. Rev. Michael O'Connor, D. D., he was sent the following year to St. Vincent's College, Beatty, in order that he might there learn German. After some years he was sent, with other students, to St. Thomas' College, Bardstown, Ky. Later he was recalled to the newly restored St. Michael's Seminary, Pittsburg. Here he completed his theological studies, and on February 7, 1863 was ordained to the priesthood by Rt. Rev. M. Domenec, D. D.

He was immediately assigned to duty as professor at the seminary until he was appointed to the presidency of St. Francis' College, Loretto, which position he filled until recalled to the seminary in 1868. In 1870 he was appointed to the pastorate of St. Michael's Church, Loretto, where he continued as pastor for twenty years. Soon after his appointment he was chosen to be a member of the Bishop's Council, and has retained this position during the administrations of Bishop Domenec, Bishop Tuigg and Bishop Phelan.

In April, 1890, he was transferred to the pastorate of St. John's Church, Altoona, where he was soon appointed Vicar Forane of the eastern portion of the diocese. Here he remained until November, 1894, when he became Rector of St. Peter's Church, Allegheny City, and soon after was pro-

ST. PAUL'S CATHEDRAL CHOIR AT THE LORETTO CENTENARY.

moted to the Vicar Generalship of the diocese by Rt. Rev. Richard Phelan, D. D., the fourth of the eminent prelates who have governed the prosperous diocese of Pittsburg.

REV. MARTIN RYAN.

He was born near Nenagh, County Tipperary, Ireland, February 14, 1845. Coming to this country he entered St. Michael's Seminary, where he pursued his philosophical and theological course, and where he was, on June 7, 1873, ordained to the priesthood by Rt. Rev. Bishop Domenec.

Immediately thereafter he was assigned as Assistant to the late Rev. James Treacy, pastor of St. Bridget's Church, Pittsburg. In May, 1876, he was appointed pastor of St. Peter's Church, Brownsville, and of the outlying missions at Uniontown, Fayette County, and at Waynesburg, Green County. In October of the same year he was transferred to St. Paul's Cathedral, Pittsburg, where he remained until his appointment in November, 1877, to the pastorate of St. Stephen's Church, Hazlewood, in the 23rd ward of the city. In July, 1879, he was transferred to the pastorate of St. Augustine, Cambria County, where he remained for nearly eleven years, during which period he erected the new church at Chest Springs, and formed the congregations at Ashville and Frugality.

When in April, 1890, Very Rev. E. A. Bush, the present Vicar General of the Diocese of Pittsburg, was appointed Rector of St. John's Church, Altoona, Father Ryan succeeded to the pastorate of St. Michael's, Loretto.

In March, 1891, he was appointed pastor of St. Patrick's Church, Gallitzin, in succession to Very Rev. J. Boyle, V. F., transferred to Johnstown. Here, in Gallitzin, he has since remained, and on June 7th, last year he happily celebrated his Silver Jubilee,—the 25th anniversary of his ordination to the priesthood.

REV. FERDINAND KITTELL.

He was born at Ebensburg, Cambria County, April 20, 1847, the fourth of a family of nine children. His father, William Kittell, a lawyer well known in his day, was born in

Adams County, Pa., and his mother, Margaret McDonald, first saw the light near the town of Monaghan, Ireland, whence her family came to the United States over eighty years ago.

Having at an early age manifested an inclination to the ecclesiastical state, he was sent, soon after the breaking out of the Civil War in 1861, to St. Michael's Seminary, Pittsburg, where he continued the study of the classics, pursued for a couple of years previously under the tuition of Rev. M. J. Mitchell, then pastor of Ebensburg. On October 18, 1863, he entered the College of the Propaganda, Rome, to occupy a place procured for him by Rev. James Keogh, D. D., then vice president of the diocesan seminary. He witnessed the occupation of Rome by the Italian army on September 20, 1870, and, by permission of the rector, early on the morning of that eventful day, while the bombardment was at its height, placed over the college two American flags, which had safeguarded the institution during the revolution of 1848.

On June 3, 1871, in the third year of his theological course, he was raised to the priesthood in the Basilica of St. John Lateran, by Monsignor Castellacci, Vicegerent of the Cardinal Vicar. In June of the following year, 1872, having completed his studies, he left the College, and on his arrival home was appointed president of St. Francis' College, and assistant at St. Michael's Church, Loretto. In 1873 he was transferred to St. Michael's Seminary, where he taught his classes during the week, and on Sundays and holidays assisted Rev. A. P. Gibbs, pastor of St. Mary's Church, Lawrenceville, Pittsburg, who had baptized him.

In January, 1876, the Diocese of Pittsburg was divided, and owing to the financial troubles then existing, the Seminary was closed at Christmas that same year, and Father Kittell received the appointment of Secretary to Bishop Tuigg,—the new Bishop of Pittsburg. In January, 1877, he was sent by the Bishop to Rome in company with Rev. James Holland, then pastor of St. Agnes' Church, Pittsburg, and now for many years a member of the Society of Jesus, and quickly effected the reunion of the Dioceses of Pittsburg and Allegheny under the sole administration of Bishop Tuigg, and the restoration of St. Xavier's Academy to the Mother House in Pittsburg. In February, 1881, he was again sent to Rome by the Bishop on other matters connected with the diocese, and he remained abroad for eighteen months. During this trip he procured from the Holy See for all the churches and chapels of the Dioceses of Pittsburg and Allegheny the privilege of having two requiem masses each week celebrated on feasts of simple double rite.

On his arrival home in the fall of 1882 he resumed his duties as Diocesan Secretary, and also acted as chaplain to the Mercy Hospital. In the spring of the following year he accompanied Bishop Tuigg to Charleston, S. C., where the venerable prelate remained a couple of months in the hope of regaining his health, which had been greatly impaired. Two days after their return to the diocese, the Bishop was seized with a paralytic stroke, from which he lingered until his death, nearly six years later. It was about this time that Father Kittell invented and patented his adjustable candelabrum, which, under the control of Benziger Bros., New York, has been sold so extensively.

In August, 1883, he resigned the position of Diocesan Secretary, and on March 1, 1884, took charge of St. Patrick's Congregation, Newry, Blair County. On February 9, 1887, he was transferred to the pastorate of St. Mary's Church, Hollidaysburg, and on November 6, 1889, to the pastorate of St. Matthew's Church, Tyrone. In all of these places he made valuable improvements. In Tyrone he had commenced the erection of a new church, the plans being drawn, and the foundation excavated, when on April 1, 1891, he was sent to take charge of St. Michael's Church, Loretto, where he happily arranged, and has just successfully carried out, the now historical celebration of the Centenary of the parish.

At the Diocesan Synod held November 9, this year, he was raised to the grade of Irremovable Rector, and is the only native of the diocese upon whom this distinction has been conferred.

REV. WILLIAM KITTELL,

A younger brother of the pastor of Loretto, was born in Ebensburg, Cambria County, November 30, 1850, and likewise, at an early age, manifested a disposition to embrace the ecclesiastical state. Another brother, still younger, also entered on the ecclesiastical career, but in 1873, while about to finish his classical course as a student of St. Michael's Seminary, was taken from earth after a brief illness from typhoid pneumonia. The eldest of the family has for thirty-seven years been a member of the Order of the Sisters of Mercy, of Pittsburg, and is at present Mother Assistant of the Community.

REV. WILLIAM KITTELL.

Father William made his preparatory studies at St. Francis' College, Loretto, and at St. Michael's Seminary, Pittsburg. In the fall of 1867 he entered the College of the Propaganda, Rome, and after a successful course was, on March 28, 1875, raised to the priesthood in the Basilica of St. John Lateran by His Eminence, Cardinal Patrizi, the Vicar of the Holy Father. On his return he was appointed professor at the diocesan seminary, and in subsequent years labored on the missions at Alpsville, Connellsville, Johnstown, St. Augustine, Freeport, and at St. Mary's, and at St. John the Baptist's, Pittsburg. Several years ago he was appointed pastor at Uniontown, where he labored with great success until he was called by Rt. Rev. Bishop Phelan in 1893 to the onerous and responsible position of Diocesan Secretary and Chancellor, which he continues to fill to the satisfaction of all.

REV. RICHARD CALLIXTUS CHRISTY.

He was born in the town of Loretto, October 14, 1829, of Peter Christy and Catherine Shirley, who were among the early settlers of that entirely Catholic community, and was baptized by Father Gallitzin. At an early age he manifested an inclination to devote himself to the service of God in the holy priesthood, and was among the first students of St. Michael's Seminary, when that institution was located in Birmingham, now the South Side, Pittsburg. Thence he was sent to St. Mary's Seminary, Baltimore; and on the completion of his studies was ordained to the priesthood in St. Michael's Church, Loretto, by Rt. Rev. Bishop O'Connor.

REV. R. C. CHRISTY.

After his ordination he had charge for several years of the congregation at Clearfield, Butler County. At the outbreak of the Civil War in 1861 he was elected Chaplain of the regiment raised by Colonel Sirwell, of Kittanning, and accompanied his command through their long marches in the Southern States. He endeared himself to all, officers and soldiers, by his pleasantry in camp, his heroism on many a battle field, and by the ministrations of his sacerdotal

FATHER CHRISTY'S BIRTH-PLACE. FOR MANY YEARS THE VILLAGE POSTOFFICE.

functions. Gifted with a high sense of honor and duty, possessed of a commanding exterior, endowed with more than ordinary physical and moral courage, thoroughly imbued with the spirit of the Union cause, every inch a soldier-priest, it is no wonder that he received, and was ever afterwards known by the sobriquet of "The Fighting Chaplain of the Army of the Cumberland." At the expiration of his term of service he returned to the diocese, and was appointed pastor of the Church of the Holy Name, Ebensburg, where he remained for a number of years, and where he built a large and beautiful church, and introduced the Sisters of St. Joseph to assume control of Mt. Gallitzin Seminary, which he established for the education of small boys. Leaving this place he accepted a position in Columbus, Ohio, where after a long and painful illness he died on Wednesday, October 16, 1878. He was buried at Ebensburg on the following Friday.

REV. HENRY M'HUGH.

The subject of this sketch was born December 8, 1835, in Munster Township, Cambria County, Pa., and was baptized by the illustrious Father Gallitzin. His parents, Michael McHugh and Elizabeth McManus, emigrated from County Fermanagh, Ireland, in 1821, and in the following year settled on a farm about midway between Loretto and Wilmore, where he was born and reared.

He entered St. Francis' College, Loretto, as a student in 1856, and during the winter of 1858-59 taught the public school near Munster. He was enrolled among the students of St. Michael's Seminary, Pittsburg, February 22, 1859, and in the following September was, with several other students, sent to St. Vincent's College, Beatty, where he spent one term. In September, 1860, he was recalled to St. Michael's Seminary, where he continued his studies until he was ordained to the priesthood on June 6, 1868.

His first appointment was as assistant to Rev. Terence S. Reynolds, pastor of St. Michael's Church, Loretto, where he commenced his ministrations on July 12 following. On February 2, 1869, he was appointed pastor of the church at

HENRY M'HUGH, RECTOR ST. AGNES' CHURCH, PITTSBURG, PA.—BAPTIZED BY FATHER GALLITZIN.

the Sand Patch Tunnel, in Somerset County, which was then in course of construction. Soon afterwards he located at Myers' Mills, from which place he attended to the spiritual wants of the men who were working on the railroad. His mission then extended from Myers' Mills to Ohio Pyle Falls. Mass was celebrated in private houses, shanties and in the open.

In the fall of 1869 he was assigned to the Brownsville mission, which included Uniontown, Fayette County, and stations south to the Maryland line; also Waynesburg, Greene County, and Jefferson, Jacktown, Jollytown and points west and south to the boundary of West Virginia. The extreme length of this mission was about eighty miles. In 1870 he built the present church in Waynesburg, when there were not more than twenty Catholic families in all Greene County.

January 18, 1873, he was appointed pastor of St. Bartholomew's Church, Wilmore, Cambria County—the church to which his family had belonged ever since its erection. Here he passed more than twenty-three years of his priestly life. He made many needed and substantial improvements and repairs on the Wilmore church and church property, adding a commodious and beautiful pastoral residence of brick, all clear of debt. In 1882 he formed the congregation at Ehrenfeld and erected a substantial frame church; and after the debt was paid off he handed it over to the Rt. Rev. Bishop to be assigned to a resident pastor.

On March 28, 1896, he was promoted to the pastorate of St. Agnes' Church, Pittsburg, which position he still occupies. Besides reducing the debt on the church he has erected a beautiful and commodious pastoral residence of brick, something that was long and badly needed, and has made many other notable improvements.

REV. THOMAS M'ENRUE

Was born near the village of Wilmore (formerly Jefferson), Cambria County, on October 28, 1842, and was baptized by Rev. Matthew W. Gibson, then assistant pastor of St.

Michael's Church, Loretto. After obtaining a knowledge of the branches at that time taught in the public schools, he spent one year at St. Vincent's College, Beatty, and one at St. Francis' College, Loretto. In the fall of 1862 he entered St. Michael's Seminary, Pittsburg, where he pursued his philosophical and theological course, and on June 6, 1868, was ordained to the priesthood by Rt. Rev. Bishop Domenec. His first appointment was to what was known as "the Washington mission," comprising Washington and Greene Counties and a part of Allegheny. In January, 1873, he was made pastor of St. Augustine, Cambria County, which place, though small, contained more Catholics than the combined territory of his former mission. After five years of arduous labor he was transferred to the western end of the diocese, and is now pastor of Irwin, Pa.

REV. THOMAS McENRUE.

REV. HILDEBERT P CONNERY.

He was born August 12, 1844, on a farm near Munster in the parish of Loretto, and was the youngest of ten children. His parents, Patrick Connery and Margaret McCloskey, were among the early settlers of "the mountain," and were united in marriage by Father Gallitzin in the year 1819.

His early education was received at St. Francis' College, Loretto, whence he passed to St. Michael's Seminary, Pittsburg, to pursue his philosophical and theological studies. He was ordained to the priesthood by Rt. Rev. Bishop Domenec, then Bishop of Allegheny, at St. Vincent's College, Beatty, on December 5, 1876.

His first appointment was as assistant at St. John Gualbert's, Johnstown. After laboring for a brief time in that position, he was made pastor of Suterville, which was afterwards united with the parish of St. Patrick, Alpsville. He remained pastor of the united missions for one year, when he was transferred to Brownsville, where he continued for two years. He was then appointed to Murrinsville, from which place, after one year, he returned to Brownsville, where he remained for seven years. Once more he went to Alpsville, where he spent about nine years. On September 5, 1895, he assumed charge of St. Agnes' Church, Pittsburg, where he was actively engaged until his death, which was caused by appendicitis. Some ten days previous to his demise he, at his own request, was taken to the Mercy Hospital, where he peacefully surrendered his soul at 8.30 a. m. Monday, March 2, 1896.

REV. H. P. CONNERY.

During all his priestly career he was remarkable for his apostolic zeal. His life was holy, and his death precious in the sight of the Lord.

REV. CHARLES OSCAR ROSENSTEEL.

The subject of this sketch and his brother, Rev. Thomas Warren Rosensteel, are worthy representatives of an old and honored family of Baltimore. Their ancestors settled in Maryland long before the Revolutionary War. Their maternal great-great-grandfather, Capt. Joseph White (Blanc), was a Frenchman who carried on trade with the West Indies, being the owner of a line of merchant vessels, which sailed regularly between Baltimore and Cuba, San Domingo and other West India islands. Several of his vessels were captured by the British during the War of Independence. Their paternal great-grandfather, Capt. George Rosensteel, was also a sea-faring man. Their father, Thomas G. Rosensteel, was born at Taneytown, Md., and their mother, Mary S. Singer, near Emmitsburg, in the same state. Like many other Catholics of Maryland they were attracted by the fame of Father Gallitzin and of the community founded by him at Loretto, and came hither to establish a home in the year 1855.

REV. C. O. ROSENSTEEL.

Rev. C. O. Rosensteel was born near Emmitsburg. May 13, 1855, and was brought by his parents the same year to Loretto, where, as he advanced in age, he received his first religious instruction under Fathers Reynolds and Bush, the then pastors. He made his preparatory studies at St. Francis' College, Loretto; then entered Mt. St. Mary's College, Emmitsburg, where he studied the classics and philosophy; and after a creditable course of theology at St. Mary's Seminary, Baltimore, was ordained there on December 20, 1884, by His Eminence, James Cardinal Gibbons. He had the happiness of celebrating his first mass at Loretto in the presence of his family and of the friends of his youth.

His first appointment was to the position of assistant priest at St. Ann's Church, Baltimore, where he remained from January 1 to September 1, 1885. He was then promoted to the pastorate of St. Mary's Church, Newport.

Charles County; and on November 5, 1889, was transferred to the pastorate of St. Mary's, Rockville, and of St. John's, Forest Glen.

After a residence of nine years at Rockville, during which period he had labored hard and successfully to build up the two parishes, the latter were separated, and he was made pastor of Forest Glen, another priest being appointed to Rockville. At Forest Glen he was instrumental in building a brown-stone church, one of the finest church structures in the Archdiocese of Baltimore, which was dedicated to the honor of God and to the memory of Bishop Carroll, the first pastor, afterwards first Bishop, and first Archbishop of Baltimore.

Besides his work at Forest Glen he was given charge of two outlying missions with the duty of building a church in each. Through his exertions the corner-store of St. Peter's, at Olney, Md., was laid on November 13, 1898, and on Christmas Day following the first mass was said in it. He is now making efforts to begin work on a new church at Brightwood, D. C.

Having built a fine pastoral residence at Forest Glen he now, to crown his work there, contemplates erecting a monument to the memory of Archbishop Carroll's mother, whose remains lie at rest beneath the ancient shady oaks in the old graveyard, close to the spot where her illustrious son erected the first rude church for the few scattered families of Maryland and Virginia. Thus the little mustard seed, planted by Father Carroll in 1774 at Rock Creek, now known as Forest Glen, has grown into a great tree whose branches extend far and wide. It has been well said that "Forest Glen was the Bethlehem of the Church in the United States, and Baltimore the Jerusalem."

REV. THOMAS WARREN ROSENSTEEL

Was born near Loretto, August 20, 1859. He made his preparatory studies in St. Francis' College, Loretto; his classical studies in Mt. St. Mary's, Emmitsburg, and completed his course in philosophy and theology at the Grand

Seminary of Quebec, Canada, where on June 13, 1886, he was ordained to the priesthood by His Eminence, Cardinal Taschereau, Archbishop of Quebec.

His first appointment on his return to his native diocese was to the position of assistant priest at St. John Gualbert's Church, Johnstown. He labored here successfully for two years, and was then appointed assistant at St. Agnes' Church, Pittsburg, where he remained for 14 months, when he was made first resident pastor of Ashville, Cambria County, from which place he attended the adjacent missions of Frugality and Baker's Mines. Only those who have a knowledge of the country as it then appeared, can form an idea of the difficulties with which he had to contend; yet in spite of all he built commodious churches and pastoral residences in Ashville and Frugality, and did much to improve Baker's Mines. After six years of hard, constant and successful work in a rough, mountainous district with a far-scattered population, and paying off all debts, he was, in December 1894, promoted to the pastorate of St. Matthew's Church, Tyrone, Blair County, where he has since built a beautiful church, and where he still remains the honored pastor of a devoted flock.

REV. THOMAS W. ROSENSTEEL.

REV. JOHN C. M'ATEER.

He was born near Loretto March 27, 1858, of James McAteer and Mary A. Elder, who twenty years previously had been united in marriage by Father Gallitzin. Early developing a spirit of piety he resolved to devote himself to the sacred ministry, and to prepare himself for his high vocation he entered St. Vincent's College, Beatty, Pa., in September, 1875. In 1881, having been affiliated to the Diocese of La Crosse, he became a student of St. Francis' Seminary, Milwaukee, Wis., where he pursued his course of philosophical and theological studies. He was raised to the holy priesthood on the Feast of SS. Peter and Paul, June 29, 1885, in St. Joseph's Cathedral, La Crosse, by the Rt. Rev. Kilian C. Flasch, then Bishop of that See. He celebrated

REV. JOHN C. McATEER.

his first mass on July the 5th following, in the church attached to St. Vincent's Arch-Abbey, Beatty, Pa., in the presence of the members of his family, who some years previously had moved from Loretto to Westmoreland County.

His first appointment was as assistant to Very Rev. James Schwebach, V. G., now Bishop of La Crosse. In February, 1886, he was appointed pastor of St. Philip's Church, Crawford County, Wisconsin, where he remained until the following September, when he was transferred to the pastorate of St. Thomas' Church, Richland Centre. Here he labored until October 6, 1898, when he was promoted to the pastorate of St. Bridget's Church, Stanton, St. Croix County,—which position he continues worthily to fill.

REV. FRANCIS C. NOEL,

Present Rector of Corpus Christi Church, Chambersburg, Pa., and Dean of the Central and Southern Districts of the Diocese of Harrisburg, was born at Noel's Station on the

Ebensburg and Cresson Railroad, in the Loretto parish, February 2, 1859, of Joseph Noel and Catherine Stolz.

REV. FRANCIS C. NOEL.

Being eager for an education he, at an early age and by more than ordinary industry, fitted himself for the profession of teaching, and for three years was employed in teaching the public schools of the district. Then for the two following years he was engaged as professor in St. Francis' College, Loretto,—at the same time pursuing there the study of the classics. After one year's course at St. Vincent's College, Beatty, Pa., he entered the Grand Seminary, in Quebec, Canada, where he completed his philosophical and theological studies; and on April 11, 1888, he was ordained to the priesthood at the Pro-Cathedral, Harrisburg, by Rt. Rev. Bishop McGovern, then recently consecrated second Bishop of the diocese.

His first appointment was to the pastorate of the Sacred Heart Church, Lewistown, Pa., where he labored zealously for five years, completing the church structure and making it one of the prettiest little churches in the diocese. On May 6, 1893, he was transferred to his present position, where he has had charge also of the outlying missions of South Mountain and Doylesburg. In the former of these missions he has built a pastoral residence, and completed the Church of St. Ignatius; and he is now engaged in erecting at Chambersburg a new parish church of stone.

REV. GEORGE W. KAYLOR.

He was born near Loretto, May 21, 1863, his parents being William Kaylor and Margaret Connery-Scanlan. He entered St. Francis' College, Loretto, in 1876, and St. Vincent's College, Beatty, in 1880. In 1882 he was sent by Rt. Rev. Bishop Tuigg to the American College, Rome, where, in 1885, he received the degree of Ph. D. On account of failing health he returned home towards the end of 1886 and entered St. Mary's Seminary, Baltimore, where, on December 17, 1887, he was ordained to the priesthood for the Diocese of Pittsburg by His Eminence, Cardinal Gibbons. On the following Christmas morning he said his first mass in St. Michael's Church, Loretto. His first appointment was as assistant at St. Peter's Church, McKeesport, where he remained until October, 1889, when he was made pastor of Sewickley. He retained this position until August, 1892, when he was transferred to the pastorate of St. Canice's Church, S. S., Pittsburg. Owing to continued and increasing ill health he resigned the pastorate in June, 1896, and obtained a six month's leave of absence, which he spent in traveling in the South. On his return he attended temporarily to Perrysville and Meyersdale, and in October, 1897, was appointed pastor of Ellwood City. Here he remained until last spring, when his health completely failed and he has since been incapacitated from duty.

REV. GEORGE W. KAYLOR.

REV. FRANCIS HERTZOG.

He was born in the borough of Loretto on September 2, 1870. His parents, Joseph Dominic Hertzog and Theresa

Lenz, are old and faithful members of the parish. He made his preparatory studies under the Franciscan Brothers, Loretto, and his higher studies at St. Vincent's Seminary, Beatty. He was ordained to the priesthood July 2, 1898, by Rt. Rev. Bishop Phelan, and said his first mass in St. Michael's Church, Loretto, on the Sunday following. Soon afterward he was assigned to duty as assistant at St. Andrew's Church, Allegheny City, which position he continues to fill with great ability and zeal.

REV. FRANCIS HERTZOG.

REV. BROTHER LAWRENCE O'DONNELL.

He was born July 6, 1818, at Rathronan, parish of Lishronagh, County Tipperary, Ireland. He gave early evidence of sincere piety, and manifesting an inclination towards a religious life he became a member of the Community of Franciscan Brothers at Roundstone, County Galway, in 1844, and on July 16, 1846, was professed by the Most Rev. John McHale, the illustrious Archbishop of Tuam. In the following year he was sent to a house of the Order, called "Holy Trinity Monastery," at Market Weighton, Yorkshire, England, where he labored for three years. In 1850 with three other Brothers he was sent by his superiors to the newly established monastery at Loretto, the first foundation of the Order in the United States. Landing in New York the Brothers came by railroad as far as McVeytown, thence by canal to Hollidaysburg, thence on the "Old Portage" up the five inclined planes to the Summit, and thence on foot to Loretto.

It may be truly said that none of the Brothers of the Loretto Community is as well or as widely known as Brother Lawrence. For thirty years he was manager of the institution, and he erected all the buildings as they stand to-day. Under his administration St. Francis' College attained the zenith of its fame, and the seniors of the diocesan clergy recall with pleasure his genial humor and affable manners, and the warm-hearted, genuine, Irish hospitality which ever awaited (and still awaits) them at "The College."

BROTHER LAWRENCE O'DONNELL.

For several years he has taken no very active part in the administration of the institution, but he bears the burthen of his 81 winters nobly; and there are but few signs yet appearing to distinguish him from the Brother Lawrence of old.

ADAM RUDOLPH was born in Gieboldehausen, Hanover, August 15, 1824. In his youth he was apprenticed to a miller and thoroughly mastered the trade. In the year 1847 he married Louisa Heineman, and in the following year emigrated to the United States, and fixed his residence first in the city of Pittsburg. In 1851 he brought his family to Loretto, and has resided in this vicinity ever since. He proudly recalls the fact that almost his first wages here were earned as a helper to the brick-layers employed in building the present church. For many years he has been active in promoting the cause of Total Abstinence, and by industry and honest dealings has secured a competency. No one in this vicinity is better known than "Old Adam," as he is familiarly called; and assisted still by his faithful wife, and surrounded by his children and numerous grandchildren, the evening of his life is passing serenely.

ADAM RUDOLPH.   JOSEPH NULL.

JOSEPH NULL was born in a house near Emmitsburg, Md., on the line between that State and Pennsylvania, January 1, 1811, of John Null and Mary Koontz. He received his education at a subscription school in the neighborhood of his home, and at an Academy conducted in Emmitsburg by an Irishman named James Mullen. He can remember Mt. St. Mary's College when it consisted of two log houses, and has a distinct recollection of Archbishop Purcell's first sermon, and of the crowd that went out from Emmitsburg to the College for the occasion.

He served a regular apprenticeship at the carpenter trade, being legally indentured to James Storm, and worked three years without wages. For the next three years he worked as a journeyman in the towns along the northern border of Maryland, and settled in Cumberland in the spring of 1833, being then 22 years of age. At that time, he says, there was only one Catholic family (named Mattingly) in the town, and a priest was looked upon as a curiosity. About the year 1838 he built the first Catholic church in Cumberland, the first pastor being Rev. Henry Myers. He also built the German church there.

In 1848 he was called to Loretto to inspect and alter the plans for the new church, which had been designed and drawn by Haden Smith. Passing over to Brownsville on the National Pike he came down the Monongahela River to Pittsburg; then up the canal to Johnstown, and by the Old Portage to No. 4 (Lilly); thence by Munster to Loretto. Here he passed a week, changing the specifications and cutting down the estimates in the plans for the new church.

In 1851 he returned, at the earnest solicitation of the Building Committee, to take charge of the carpenter work of the new building at a salary of "two dollars a day and boarded." He assisted at the laying of the corner-stone. With his own hands he built the high altar of St. Michael's Church for $75. He contracted to build the altars in St. Aloysius' Church, Summit, for $100, but Father McCullagh was so well pleased with the work when finished that he gave him $20 extra. He also made and set in place the pews in St. Bartholomew's Church, Wilmore.

When he had the roof of the Loretto church nearly completed, the tower was built up to the square. He urged the contractor to stop work on it until the following spring, so that the brick might have time to settle, but the latter, having the brick-layers and material ready, concluded, since it was so late in the year, to go on with the work, with the result that the top of the tower, which was then 20 feet higher than it is now, fell and damaged the roof considerably.

In 1852 he took the contract for building the convent of the Sisters of Mercy at Loretto. He drew the plans for the Loretto Springs Hotel, and for the first union school house in Ebensburg.

In 1858 he went to farming on the farm of his father-in-law, William Weakland, on the outskirts of the town. In 1880 he sold the farm to Adam Rudolph, the present owner, and came to live in Loretto, where he still resides, reasonably hale and hearty, in the 89th year of his age. He has shaken hands with Presidents Andrew Jackson, William Henry Harrison and James K. Polk, and retains a vivid recollection of the most celebrated statesmen of early times.

MRS. CATHERINE COOPER.   MRS. ELIZABETH McCONNELL.

The two old ladies seen in the above picture are sisters, daughters of Englebert Walters and Susan Behe, who were among the pioneers of this district. Mrs. Cooper was born March 10, 1810, and Mrs. McConnell, February 21, 1812. They were both baptized by Father Gallitzin, and were married by him on the same day,—April 28, 1835,—the former to Joseph Cooper, the latter to Hugh McConnell, who was reared in the prince-priest's house, and whose wife also lived for a time with Father Gallitzin. They are residing on the same farms to which they were taken after their marriage,—the former near Loretto, the latter near Chest Springs. Despite their advanced age they are still remarkably active, and surrounded by their numerous descendants they are peacefully biding their time.

MRS. SUSAN GALLAGHER was the daughter of George Glass and Susan Dougherty, who settled on a farm near Loretto towards the close of the last century and were the progenitors of a numerous posterity. She was born December 24, 1804, and was baptized by Father Gallitzin. On May 14, 1848, she was married to Thomas Gallagher, who died February 4, 1863. Having no children of her own she lavished her affection on orphans, many of whom she reared to matur-

MRS. SUSAN GALLAGHER.

ity and gave them a fair start in the world. She was a woman of remarkable energy, which remained with her to the end of her long and holy life, and was gifted with wonderful powers of management. For many years she successfully conducted a summer resort at her home,—Pinegrove,—a mile and a half from Loretto. Charitable to the needy, exemplary in her life, strong in her faith and steadfast in the practice of it, "Aunt Susan," as everybody loved to call her, passed to her reward on July 8, 1898, in the 94th year of her age. She was buried in the enclosure which marks the site of the old log church in which she was baptized, and in which, in 1811, she was confirmed by Bishop Egan, being then in the sixth year of her age.

THOMAS WILLS, son of John Wills and Rachel Durbin, who were among the first settlers of this section, was born near Loretto, June 11, 1807, and was baptized by Father Gallitzin; and though now in his 93d year, and a widower for the third time, is remarkably active and healthy. He led the life of a farmer until the burthen of increasing years rendered him incapable of such hard and rough work. He now resides with his daughter, Mrs. Joseph Baker, near St. Augustine; and occasionally visits Loretto to talk over old times with the few surviving friends, not of his youth, but of his manhood; for he has outlived all his cotemporaries.

THOMAS WILLS.

ARTHUR COMERFORD was born in Castle Blaney, County Monaghan, Ireland, December 25, 1813. His family emigrated to this country in 1828 and settled in Philadelphia.

ARTHUR COMERFORD.

On September 27, 1837, he was married to Elizabeth Hein, and in May, 1843, moved to Pittsburg. In 1878 he came to Loretto, where with his estimable wife he has ever since resided.

MRS. VERONICA FREIDHOFF, daughter of Caspar Beiter and Mary Sill, was born in Wurtemberg, Germany, February 2, 1817. Her parents brought the family to this country in 1836, and settled on a farm about a mile south of Munster, which they bought from Jacob Hemm, and which is now owned and occupied by their son, Ignatius Beiter.

On November 20, 1838, she was married by Father Gallitzin to Nicholas Freidhoff, and has since resided on the farm adjoining the one on which her family settled. Her husband died December 28, 1881. Of her twelve children only two survive. Four of her daughters became nuns, and are all dead. Although bent with the weight of years her health continues reasonably good.

MRS. VERONICA FREIDHOFF.

Philip Dever, son of Cornelius Dever and Margaret Noon, was born on a farm near Munster, April 20, 1819. He followed farming until old age and failing health incapacitated him from active work. He and his brother John are the only survivors of a numerous family, and neither of them

APRIL AND DECEMBER. (PHILIP DEVER.)

ever married. The little child seen in the picture is Elmer, son of William and Annie Beiter, with whom Mr. Dever is at present residing.

Augustine Hott was born in Germany in the year 1820. He came to this country in 1834, at the age of 14, and entered the service of Father Gallitzin, remaining with him until his death. He then worked for James Rhey, of Ebensburg, and by industry, economy and perseverance laid by enough money to buy the farm in Carroll Township on which he has since resided.

AUGUSTINE HOTT.

A RARE AND PRECIOUS DOCUMENT.

From the Pittsburg Catholic November 22, 1899.

The Catholic had in its possesion this week a copy of the will of Father Gallitzin. It was taken at the time of the original document, and the handwriting is as fine as copy plate. This is the first time the will has been in print in the diocese. It reads as follows:

In the name of God, Amen, I, Demetrius Augustine Gallitzin, parish priest of St. Michael's Church, near Loretto, in the County of Cambria, in the Commonwealth of Pennsylvania, do make and publish this my last will and testament, hereby revoking and making void all former wills by me at any time heretofore made, and as to such worldly estate as it has pleased God to entrust me with I dispose of the same as follows: First, I direct that all my debts and funeral expenses shall be paid as soon after my decease as possible, and for the purpose of enabling my executors so to do I hereby authorize them to sell and convey by sufficient deed or deeds to the purchaser or purchasers thereof any part of my real estate except such parts as is hereinafter disposed of. I give and bequeath to the Right Reverend Francis Patrick Kenrick, Bishop of Arath and Coadjutor of the Bishop of Philadelphia, and to his successor, or to the Bishop that may be appointed for the eastern diocese of Pennsylvania and his successor (when such appointment shall be made) in trust forever for the support and use of the Roman Catholic clergy, duly appointed by said Bishop or Bishops or their successors, according to the rights of the Holy Roman Catholic Church, to officiate at St. Michael's Church, above mentioned, all the farm wherein said church is erected, together with the land and appurtenances thereunto belonging. I also give and bequeath to the Bishop or Bishops above mentioned, in trust forever for the purpose of erecting a church thereon, all the square of six lots in the town of Loretto, known and numbered in the plan of said town as number twenty-five, twenty-six, twenty-seven, twenty-eight, twenty-nine and thirty. I give and bequeath to Mary Wharton the sum of five hundred dollars, to be paid by my executors to her. I give and bequeath to Catherine Wharton the sum of two hundred and seventy-five dollars.*

And, whereas, there is money due me from Europe, the receipt of which is doubtful, I therefore direct my executors to exercise a sound discretion in distributing according to circumstances the residue of my estate as follows, viz.: One part or portion towards the relief of poor widows and orphans, one other portion for masses for the souls of the faithful departed, one other part for to aid in the erection of a Catholic church in the town of Loretto upon the lots above mentioned, and one other part to be paid to Susan Christy, Sarah Durbin, Elizabeth Durbin, Ann Storm, Frances McConnell and Hugh McConnell, all of whom were raised by me. And I do hereby constitute and appoint Michael Levy, William Todd and Henry J. McGuire executors of this my last will and testament. In witness whereof I have hereunto set my hand and seal, the 29th day of April, A. D. 1840.

DEMETRIUS AUGUSTINE GALLITZIN.

*The words "two hundred and seventy-five dollars" interlined before signing, signed, sealed, declared and delivered in presence of us who in the presence of the testator, and each other subscribed our names as witness.

PATRICK SHIELS,
PETER CHRISTY,
AUGUSTINE HOTT.

ANCIENT FAMILY RECORD.

MARRIAGES, BAPTISMS AND DEATHS AMONG THE STORMS.

(From the Johnstown Tribune.)

After the death of Rev. Father Davin, the beloved pastor of St. Columba's Church, Sixteenth Ward, his library was sold at auction. In a book obtained by Mr. Ed. F. Creed was found the leaf of an old church record containing memoranda of marriages, births, and deaths in the Storm family. The leaf is well-browned with age. It is presumed it came into Father Davin's possession while he was pastor at the Summit some years ago. The Storm family—as is well known—is one of the oldest in Cambria County history. Several branches of it still live on the mountain. The popular artist—George Storm—formerly resided at the Summit. The record dates back to 1796, when John Storm, the main stem of the family tree, was united in marriage to Susan Weissang. Following is a copy of the ancient document:

RECORD OF BAPTISMS AND DEATHS.

John Storm and Susan Weissang (Wysong) were united in marriage at Conewago Church March 6, 1796.

John Storm was born May 3, 1756, and died February 14, 1816.

Susan Storm was born July 25, 1773, and died November 11, 1837.

Their children are:

John, born February 23, 1797, baptized May 28, 1797; Peter, born May 18, 1798, baptized July 29, 1798, and were baptized by Rev. Patrick Lonergan.

Ann Catherine, born September 28, 1799, baptized October 3, 1799.

Elizabeth, born November 13, 1800, baptized December 8, 1800.

Mary, born September 14, 1802, baptized September 27, 1802.

James, born October 24, 1804, baptized November 4, 1804.
Susan, born April 29, 1806, baptized May 13, 1806.
Lewis, born June 12, 1809, baptized July 3, 1809.
Joseph, born June 28, 1811, baptized August 15, 1811.
Michael, born July 31, 1813, baptized August 15, 1813.
Henry, born February 20, 1815, baptized April 13, 1815.
All baptized by Rev. D A. Gallitzin.
James died 1806.
Joseph died 1826.
Henry J. Storm died September 13, 1847.
John Storm died September 27, 1847.
Peter Storm died ———.

AN OLD RESIDENT GONE. SOME REMINISCENCES.

(Carrolltown News.)

The demise of Mrs. Mary Elder, of this place (February 12, 1885), deserves more than the mere mention made in last week's issue. Her father, John Myers, grandfather of ex-Sheriff Myers, of Ebensburg, was one of the earliest settlers on the Allegheny mountains. He started in the wilderness on what is now the mountain road, east of Ashland Furnace, now in Gallitzin Township, where deceased was born. Deceased was married to John Elder, who shortly afterward located in the wilderness of what is now Elder Township, about the year 1825, and built a grist and saw-mill on the site now owned by Mr. Jacob Thomas. At that time only five settlers resided in the whole neighborhood, and when Mr. Elder first visited what was to be his future abode, he slept on a large rock during the night, which remains to-day in the orchard of Mr. Jacob Thomas. Besides operating his mills Mr. Elder carved out of the woods a fine farm, where he and his faithful partner resided until about ten or twelve years ago, when they removed to Carrolltown. Mr. Elder preceded his wife to the grave about six years, at the age of about 82 years. Of her family Mrs. Elder was the last survivor.

THE NEW CHURCH.

The following circular, which explains itself, was mailed on the date specified to 440 contributing members of the parish:

St. Michael's Church, Loretto, Pa., July 19, 1898.

Mr. ....

It has long been admitted that something should be done to improve the condition of our parish church. To know precisely what should be done the committee and myself recently called three parties, skilled in architecture and building, to examine and report on the structural condition of the edifice, and to make appropriate suggestions. These examinations were conducted separately and independently, one from another, and the reports embody the unbiased views of the examiners as follows:

The first report emphatically condemns the structure and recommends a new building on a smaller plan at the lowest estimated cost of $20,000.

The other two are practically identical. They condemn only the floor and the upper part of the tower and facade, and recommend repairs at the highest estimated cost of $5,000, which would guarantee the safety of the building for another fifty years.

In order to learn the sentiment of the congregation the committee desires to know:

I. Are you in favor of taking down the present church structure and rebuilding as suggested. Yes or no. ....

If yes, how much will you subscribe for the purpose? $........

II. Or, are you in favor of repairing the church as suggested? Yes or no. ....

If yes, how much will you subscribe for the purpose? $........

Sign your name here.................................

After having filled the blank spaces please enclose the sheet in accompanying addressed envelope and return to
FERDINAND KITTELL, Pastor.

When the returns came in it was found that only forty were in favor of replacing the old church with a new one, subscribing for this purpose less than one thousand dollars; and that the rest, with the exception of some who did not vote, were in favor of repairing the present edifice, and subscribed for the purpose $2,135.00, with the understanding that their subscriptions, if falling short of the amount needed, were to be increased.

While all would have been pleased to see a new church arising on the site of the old one, yet the vast majority of the parishioners understood that its erection would entail a very heavy burthen upon a community depending for its existence on agriculture, and struggling under the depressed condition of the farming interests. This burthen, if unavoidable, would have been patiently, if not cheerfully, borne; and each one would have contributed his utmost to the success of the undertaking, but it was judged more prudent to make the repairs needed at present to insure the safety of the structure for another generation; and in the meantime to accumulate a reserve fund, which, increasing year by year, would facilitate the erection of the new edifice at the proper time.

But before the repairs could be commenced, the pastor received an intimation of the project, which Mr. and Mrs. C. M. Schwab had been entertaining for some time, of a new church for the parish, and which they happily made public on the occasion of our glorious centenary. With this foreknowledge, and taking advantage of an ingenious pretext, he announced that the work of repairs would be delayed. And so it happened that, when at the unveiling of the statue of Father Gallitzin, Mr. Schwab, for himself and his estimable wife, formally donated the new church to the parish, the announcement came as a most welcome surprise, and was hailed with unbounded delight.

In compliance with the expressed wish of the generous donors, work on the new building has already commenced, and, under the superintendence of Mr. John A. Schwab, the father of Mr. C. M., will be pushed to speedy completion. The plans are being drawn by Mr. F. J. Osterling, a famous architect of Pittsburg, who kindly sends the following architectural description:

"The ground plan of the church will be in the form of a Latin cross, the extreme dimensions over the transepts will be 92 feet and the total length of the building 134 feet. The height from the ground to the ridge of the roof is 50 feet and 92 feet from the ground to the top of the cross on the tower. In addition to the church proper there will be a chapel for winter services adjoining the left transept of the main church.

"The buildings will be connected with the pastoral residence by means of a cloister or covered arcade about 50 feet in length. The total seating capacity of the ground floor of the church will be 900, including 80 seats contained in the winter chapel, which is arranged to communicate with and form part of the main auditorium if required. There is also additional seating room for 200 in the gallery at the rear in the church proper. The style of architecture used is that of the round arched Gothic period, made to conform to modern requirements. The superstructure will be plain and substantial of buff colored bricks, trimmed with light brown terra-cotta: the roof covering will be of red tile. The principal feature of the exterior will be a massive and generous tower at the center of the front, which marks the main entrance to the church and terminates in a belfry arcaded on four sides.

"In addition to the main center entrance there are two side entrances placed at the front corners of the church, which are also used as ingress to the gallery. The winter chapel has an independent outside entrance and all entrance ways are provided with double vestibules. The organ and choir are placed in the gallery at the rear of the church over the three entrances facing the high altar and the two side altars at either side. There will be three sacristies located at the sides of the sanctuary and directly back of the side altars all conveniently connected with the closed arcade communicating direct with the pastor's residence. There will be four confessionals, one back of each side altar and one at each side of the main entrance to the church. The interior of the auditorium will be consistent architecturally with the exterior of the building and will have vaulted and groined arched ceilings, relieved with stucco ornamentation and frescoing, and without posts or columns. The pews and interior woodwork will be of polished quartered oak. The church windows will be of ecclesiastic art glass, susceptible of memorials. The entire church will have a high and well lighted basement underneath. A Sunday School room will be placed in this basement having seating capacity of about 300 and provided with two direct outside entrance ways. The basement will also contain receiving vaults for the remains of such as may be worthy.

"The building will be heated by steam through warm air flues and ventilated by a large special ventilating stock at the rear of the building."

MEMBERSHIP OF BRANCH 111, CATHOLIC MUTUAL BENEFIT ASSOCIATION, LORETTO, PA. OCTOBER 10, 1899.

(ORGANIZED JANUARY 6, 1892.)

SPIRITUAL ADVISER, Rev. F. Kittell.
PRESIDENT, Bernard W. Litzinger, Esq.
FIRST VICE-PRESIDENT, Joseph A. Scanlan.
FINANCIAL SECRETARY, Bernard W. Wills.
RECORDING SECRETARY, William A. Sanker.
ASS'T. RECORDING SEC'Y, Louis E. Kaylor.
TREASURER, W. A. B. Little, Esq.
MARSHAL, A. Gibbs Parrish.
GUARD, J. Sherman Glass.

Rev. Philip Brady, George B. Anderson, Englebert Conrad, Joseph F. Fisher, Fletcher C. George, Demetrius A. Glass, Luke F. Ivory, J. Vincent Lilly, Peter J. Little, Esq., Walter F. Litzinger, Thomas L. Parrish, J. Edward Shields, Gilbert A. Storm, Edward Tomlinson, Oscar E. Wilkinson.

TRUSTEES, Rev. F. Kittell, Thos. L. Parrish, Jos. A. Scanlan, B. W. Wills.

THE ALTAR BOYS.
UPPER ROW: Michael Little, Leo Little, Harry Malloy, Joseph Rudolph, Leo Elwood.
LOWER ROW: Andrew Little, Edward Selwah, Harry Kittell, James Kittell.

ST. MICHAEL'S CHURCH CHOIR.
STANDING: Albert J. Noel, Lulu Bannan, John H. Little, Sophie Benzele.
SITTING: Zita Sanker, William A. Sanker, Mary Bannan, Organist.

MEMBERSHIP OF LORETTO COUNCIL, 450, YOUNG MEN'S INSTITUTE, AT PRESENT DATE, OCTOBER 10, 1899.

[ORGANIZED OCTOBER 25, 1896.]

PRESIDENT, **Wm. A. McGuire.**
FIRST VICE PRESIDENT, **Raymond A.** Parrish.
SECOND VICE-PRES., Edward **A.** McGuire.
COR. AND REC. SECRETARY, **Wm. J. Little.**
FINANCIAL SECRETARY, **John W. Anderson.**
TREASURER, **L. T. Sanker.**
INSIDE SENTINEL, **Jos.** Steberger.
OUTSIDE SENTINEL, **Martin** McGillen.
MARSHALL (AND JANITOR), Lewis M. **Little.**

EXECUTIVE COMMITTEE:
{ Philip S. Noon.
  Wm. J. Little.
  Jos. B. Little. }

Anderson, Geo. B.
Baver, W. **A.**
Bengele, Bert M.
Biller, **Francis.**
Bishop, **Edw. C.**
Boley, Jos. **L.**
Boley, Edw. **V.**
Boes, Edward.
Bradley, **Alex. J.**
Bradley, **Lewis.**
Boes, Albert.
Conrad, Ambrose.
Crilley, James.
Denny, Harry **J.**
Ebig, Francis.
Eckenrode, Harry.
Fisher, **Jos.** F.
Gallagher, Alvin.
Grove, John.
Hall, James.
Hall, Patrick **J.**
Hall, Albert **M.**
Hogue, William.

Itel, Charles.
Itel, Augustine.
Itel, Anthony.
Ivory, George H.
Ivory, Gilbert.
Kaylor, Lewis E.
Lentz, Anthony T.
Luther, J. Lawrence.
McGuire, Henry F.
Myers, Henry.
McGough, Francis.
McGough, **John E.**
Melhorn, Wm.
Melhorn, **Chas.**
Noon, **Austin.**
Parrish, **Edw. J.**
Randall, **William J.**
Sanker, **Linus J.**
Sanker, **Francis.**
Sanker, Michael.
Seymour, Thomas A.
Sherry, **Francis.**
Smeltzer, Jos.

MEMBERS OF ST. MICHAEL'S CHURCH COMMITTEE, 1899:
Messrs. Zach Kaylor.   P. A. Sybert.   W. A. B. Little.   B. W. Litzinger.   P. J. Sanders.

Stevens, Edward.
Stoy, William.
Stoy, Andrew J.
Sheehan, Edward.
Shiber, Aloysius E.

SUMMARY.

Married members,   15

Single members,   47
Married since becoming
  members,   5
Deaths of members,   0
Transferred to Cresson,   9
Transferred to Wilmore,   1
Dropped from rolls,   6

There were eighteen charters members. Since October 25, 1896, the date of organization, there have been seventy-eight different names on the membership roll. Of these sixteen have either been transferred to other Councils or have been otherwise dropped from the roll.

MEMBERS OF THE CHURCH COMMITTEE—1899.

REV. FERDINAND KITTELL, Pastor
W. A. B. LITTLE, ESQ., of Loretto.
BERNARD W. LITZINGER, ESQ., of Loretto.
PHILIP J. SANDERS, of Munster Twp.
ZACH KAYLOR, of Allegheny Twp.
P. ALPHONSUS SYBERT, of Gallitzin Twp.

SEXTON, Thomas J. McCullough.
ORGANIST, Mary C. Bannan.

COLLECTORS IN CHURCH.

Middle Aisle: { Adam Rudolph.
               { J. E. Shields.
North Aisle: Michael Malloy.
South Aisle: W. A. B. Little, Esq.

For several years past Mrs. Hugh J. Bannan and her daughters have unselfishly given their time and devoted their engeries to the care of the altars, sanctuary and sacristies.

THE NEW ST. MICHAEL

IURCH, LORETTO, PA.   F. J. OSTERLING, ARCHITECT, PITTSBURG, PA.

www.ingramcontent.com/pod-product-compliance
Lightning Source LLC
Chambersburg PA
CBHW051847300426
44117CB00006B/289